CW00825690

THE QUEST FOR SECURITY

The

QUEST FOR SECURITY

PROTECTION WITHOUT PROTECTIONISM AND ★ THE CHALLENGE OF ★ GLOBAL GOVERNANCE

EDITED BY

Joseph E. Stiglitz and Mary Kaldor

Columbia University Press
Publishers Since 1893
New York   Chichester, West Sussex
cup.columbia.edu
Copyright © 2013 Columbia University Press
All rights reserved

Library of Congress Cataloging-in-Publication Data

The quest for security : protection without protectionism and the challenge
of global governance / [edited by] Joseph E. Stiglitz and Mary Kaldor.
pages cm
Includes bibliographical references and index.
ISBN 978-0-231-15686-8 (cloth : alk. paper) — ISBN 978-0-231-52765-1 (ebook)
1. Social problems. 2. Crises. 3. Economic policy. 4. Social policy.
5. Globalization—Economic aspects. 6. Globalization—Social aspects.
I. Stiglitz, Joseph E. II. Kaldor, Mary.

HN18.3.Q47 2013
361.2'6—dc23

2012048641

Columbia University Press books are printed on permanent and durable
acid-free paper.
This book is printed on paper with recycled content.
Printed in the United States of America

c 10 9 8 7 6 5 4 3 2

Cover design: Fifth Letter

CONTENTS

ACKNOWLEDGMENTS

Many people contributed to the organization of the conference out of which this book grew, and to the book.

At the London School of Economics, we are grateful to the Open Society Institute and the school for financial support and to Dominika Spyratou, who helped with the preparation of the conference and manuscript.

At Columbia, we especially acknowledge Sasha de Vogel and Eamon Kircher-Allen for their indispensable support in compiling this volume. We would also like to acknowledge the contributions of Laura Morrison, Robin Stephenson, and Vighnesh Subramayan, as well as Jill Blackford. We would like to thank those who organized the conference, including Sharon Cleary, Rebekkah Hogan, and Adam Robbins.

We also extend thanks to participants who shared their insights at the 2008 conference "A Manifesto for a New Global Covenant: Protection without Protectionism," but whose work is not included in this volume.

Finally, we thank the Committee on Global Thought at Columbia University and the Civil Society and Human Security Research Unit at the London School of Economics for their on going support of this project.

EDITORS' NOTE

The contributions collected in this volume are the product of the conference "A Manifesto for a New Global Covenant: Protection without
Protectionism," convened December 1–2, 2008, at Columbia University,
organized by Columbia's Committee on Global Thought and the Center
for the Study of Global Governance at the London School of Economics.

While the contributions have been lightly revised to reflect the changes
that have since occurred around the world, the authors have maintained
the perspective and tone of the time at which the conference was convened.

THE QUEST FOR SECURITY

Introduction

The Quest for Global Security

Protection Without Protectionism and the Challenge of Global Governance

MARY KALDOR AND JOSEPH E. STIGLITZ

In countries around the world, ordinary citizens feel under threat. As this book goes to press, citizens in the advanced industrial countries worry about their jobs and about their future and that of their children. Will they be able to retire in comfort? Will governments be able to deliver on the re-tirement benefits they promised? Although those in many of the emerging markets have never had things so good, they understand the precariousness of their fortunes.

For those who see their way beyond the immediacy of the economic crisis, there are more insecurities—from violence, whether the home-bred domestic variety or that of terrorists from abroad. And further into the future lie the risks posed by climate change.

In other parts of the world, this gradation of risk operates the other way round. The threats of violence and climate change are experienced as immediate dangers. In zones of insecurity, people are killed, raped, robbed, expelled from their homes, kidnapped, or taken hostage. And in environ-mentally vulnerable areas, they are the victims of excessive flooding or of famine on an increasing scale. And beyond these immediate dangers, they are often extremely poor, living on less than a dollar a day, without access to clean water and sanitation, healthcare, jobs, or even homes.

To be sure, individuals have always faced risks. Farmers were exposed to the variability of weather. Those in coastal areas worried about marauding pirates. There were always earthquakes, hurricanes, and droughts. But today's risks are unpredictable, with what statisticians call "fat tails," small probabilities of very, very bad outcomes. In the global financial crisis, exports of some countries fell by more than 30 percent. In some countries, youth unemployment has reached 50 percent.

Moreover, many of these risks are global in nature. And this means that they may be beyond the ability of individual countries' coping capacity. In traditional farming communities, the community provided a support system for those who were temporarily facing hardship. As the nation-state formed, responsibility for social protection shifted to the state and for good reason. Some of the most important risks affected virtually everyone in the community; the risks were highly correlated. The nation-state had fiscal resources that were greater than that of the individual or the market.

In some ways, today the small nation-state is like the small rural community. Many of the risks are national in character—such as a national economic downturn. Small countries feel at the mercy of events beyond their control, and they face limited resources. There is little that Greece or Ireland can do to restore their own economy. If the European and global economies prosper, their economy will prosper; and if these economies do not, neither will theirs.

There is, however, a difference: Most of the risks facing farming communities were from acts of nature—a flood or drought. Many of the risks facing countries today are man-made. Policies at the national and global level affect both the risks that individuals and countries face and their capacity to respond.

Globalization has increased the scale and velocity of risk. A problem anywhere in the system can move quickly across borders. We saw how the subprime mortgage crisis in the United States quickly became a global crisis. Avian flu and SARS showed how diseases too could move quickly around the world. Terrorism—al-Qaeda—has become global. Trying to deprive it of a homeland in one country does little good; it quickly shifts its base of operations elsewhere.

Even though globalization has increased risks in these ways, it has simultaneously decreased the ability of the nation-state—the political unit that in the preceding decades had increasingly taken on the role of protection—to perform these roles. Of course, the extent to which this is true varies. Large nations such as the United States or China retain an independent capacity to act. Middle-ranking nations have often ceded sovereignty to larger entities such as the European Union (EU), while some smaller states have become so weak that they are termed fragile or failing states. Globalization has undermined the state's abilities in several ways. First it has, whether intentionally or not, reduced the power of taxation, particularly of capital. As capital became more mobile, it could move more easily from any jurisdiction in which it was (in its view) excessively taxed or regulated to another jurisdiction where it was more favorably treated. Labor, for the most part, did not have that option of easy mobility. But at least part of social protection is protecting the poor and the most vulnerable, and these implicit restrictions on revenue-raising from those most able to contribute left many states bereft of the funds required for an adequate social protection system.

Not only was the state potentially eviscerated through these limitations in taxation, international rules and standards were established that restricted the freedom of the state to act in ways that might protect its citizens. Implicitly, more and more of the legislative power was delegated. Rules for trade and finance were set, at least partially, in the international arena. Trade agreements, for instance, forced governments to substitute tariffs for quotas; and although there are some advantages of tariffication, the change also exposed countries to more risk (Dasgupta and Stiglitz 1977). Until recently, trade agreements and the International Monetary Fund (IMF) pushed countries toward capital and financial market liberalization—the abolition of regulations that helped stabilize cross-border capital flows, resulting in increasing macroeconomic volatility (Stiglitz et al. 2006).

Globalization has also eroded the monopoly of violence—often regarded as the defining characteristic of what makes a state. Only a few large nations such as the United States, Russia, China, or India still retain the capacity to use their military forces unilaterally, although even they are theoretically bound by the UN charter that prohibits the use of force except in self-defense or if authorized by the UN Security Council.[1] For most states, their forces are integrated into collective security arrangements such as NATO or the EU, and their budgets are insufficient to finance all but limited provision of security services. In many states, the capacity to enforce law and order and to protect people even from everyday crime is also greatly weakened and reduced to their only having the capacity to protect the ruling elites.

Of course, governments voluntarily ceded sovereignty, but especially smaller countries felt they had little choice. If they didn't go along with the international agreements, they risked becoming pariahs, or at the very least not partaking of the benefits that would come from global economic integration. They might console themselves that these were agreements made among democratic governments, so that even if their own democratic institutions had had little role in crafting them, at least other democratic voices had been heard. But that was only partially true. Economic agreements were typically negotiated by ministries (such as that of trade and industry) and usually more closely linked to special interests. In the United States, trade agreements were approved on a fast-track basis, which meant that Congress could only vote yes or no, without any say in the provisions that went into them. Only when civil society groups mounted a concerted campaign, for instance, to give poor countries some access to life-saving drugs, was the power of the pharmaceutical companies to dictate the terms of the intellectual property provisions effectively challenged.

In one way or another, the world has long been globalized—to which colonialism and two world wars bear testimony. But globalization only became a subject of controversy—it only became "visible"—after the end of the Cold War. The bipolar order had dominated the way we perceived the world. Growing interconnectedness and the prevalence of new and old risks were obscured by our preoccupation with the East–West conflict. The binary thinking to which we were habituated allowed the collapse of communism to be interpreted as a victory for the United States. This interpretation was also a victory for a particular set of ideas that assumed increasing ascendancy in the years after the Cold War, a period that saw the United States become the sole superpower. American-style capitalism, based on notions that free and unfettered markets were the best form of economic organization, reigned supreme.[2] Unbridled U.S. military power would assure a Pax Americana. America's military machine, triumphant from its victory in the Cold War, faced a slight downscaling under President Clinton, but still, the United States was spending close to 50 percent of what the entire world was spending on defense.[3] Without any apparent enemies, the amounts seemed disproportionate.

The Rising Risk of Protectionism

That easy world has now been irrevocably disturbed. The events of 9/11 brought home the point that all of that spending didn't suffice to protect the United States from a terrorist attack inside its own borders. Iraq showed that all of that spending—and much more—could not assure an easy victory against a fragmented and disorderly set of enemies. Western troops will withdraw from Afghanistan in 2014, but it is unlikely that Afghanistan will be any safer. Indeed, it is fair to say that the United States is yet another country in a long line (which included Russia and the United Kingdom) to have to admit defeat in that mountainous terrain. Increasingly the War on Terror has transmuted to a long-distance campaign of drone strikes, which may be successful in killing the leaders of al-Qaeda but contributes to a pervasive and disorderly sense of insecurity in those regions where the campaigns are conducted. And this war, rather than containing the insecurity presented by al-Qaeda and terrorists, has—at least to some extent— spread it. It has now spilled over to Pakistan, Yemen, and parts of Africa.

And America's economic machine, on which all of its military and other strengths rested, was shown to be more fragile than even its harshest critics had suggested. The economic crisis exposed a dysfunctional financial system that enriched itself at the expense of others by predatory lending and by dishonest and anti-competitive practices—not by feats of economic wizardry that had led to an economy that was truly more productive, as it had claimed. It showed a country where most citizens had seen their income decline for more than a decade; a country that, to maintain internal law and order, had to imprison a larger fraction of its citizens than any other; a country that, as it projected military strength abroad, was marked by high levels of violence at home.

There is no longer confidence in the ability of free and unfettered markets to assure economic security. And there is no longer confidence in the ability of the United States to assure the world of its military security, let alone the security of the rest of the world.

In the absence of this security, inward retreat is a concern. In the economic sphere, what such a retreat would mean is clear. It would almost surely entail a high level of protectionism. In the security sphere, this would result in another kind of protectionism—where groups of individuals turn not to the state as the source of their physical security but to their own devices—that of the private security company in the gated community, the ethnic militias in sectarian conflicts, or the drug cartels or the mafia in many global cities. But the danger is that even when these new privatized groups were originally intended to provide protection against outside threats, they can easily turn against and/or exploit the very people they were supposed to protect. This is what is increasingly happening.

Globalization has brought with it problems, but it has also brought with it benefits. It has contributed to the spread of democracy and human rights. And, when well-managed, globalization has even contributed to economic prosperity. It has contributed to moving hundreds of millions of people out of poverty in the developing world. The worry is that mindless protectionism will be costly to those very people who have gained from globalization—to those in the developing world who have benefited from the unprecedented global growth of the past half century, as well as to those in the developed world, who enjoy the bounty of inexpensive goods even as jobs become threatened. Protectionism means the risk of losing all of this.

Social Protection Without Protectionism

There is an alternative path, a reordering of the global economy and society, which entails social protection without protectionism. By social protection, we mean far more than just an economic safety net for those at the very bottom. That's not good enough for those in the middle who see their life-style in jeopardy. They want some security against any significant loss in living standards.

The issue of protection of society, as we conceive it, goes far beyond economics. Citizens are worried about the environment and their physical security. In the United States, they worry too about access to healthcare. Everywhere, there are worries among all but the very rich about whether citizens will be able to have a comfortable retirement, and whether their children will be able to live as well as their parents.

In many countries, citizens are being told that, although the market may not provide the hoped for security, neither can government. We simply can't afford it. The competition resulting from globalization, it is said, forces us to be meaner and leaner, and that means we have to scale back social protection. But there is a curious irony in such claims. Globalization is defended as enriching living standards; yet, it is said, globalization prevents society from providing one of the essential things individuals care about—security.

We believe that such a conclusion is wrong. Globalization is supposed to have increased GDP, and if so, it should have increased the resources we have available. We have choices about what to do with those resources. We can (as the United States has been doing) devote large amounts to the military and incarceration. We could, alternatively, devote more resources to social protection. If we fail to pursue policies that result in most citizens being better off as a result of globalization, there is likely to be a retreat toward protectionism.

We subtitle this book "Protection Without Protectionism and the Challenge of Global Governance" because the retreat in economics to protectionism is a metaphor for what could happen in these other arenas—in the fiction that by retreating into their own shells, countries can insulate themselves from these risks coming from outside their boundaries. Likewise, the protectionism of local strongmen and private guards can never be more than temporary and will only exacerbate a growing market in violence. The gated communities with their high walls are symbolic of such attempts—and reflect the fact that even though the forces giving rise to insecurity may be global, the impacts and responses are often local.

The Need for Global Responses

Local and national responses will never be fully adequate in dealing with these global problems. This is most evident in the arena of global warming—maintaining the global environment is called a global public good. Everyone, regardless of where they live, is affected by the increase in carbon concentration in the atmosphere, or the emergence of ozone holes. If the global consensus in the scientific community proves correct, America's carbon emissions will have devastating effects on faraway places, from island states that within a century will no longer exist, to a third of Bangladesh that will be submerged. Economists focus on incentives, and under current arrangements, those in the United States do not bear the costs of the "externalities" that their actions have on others, and so they have little incentive to reduce their emissions. There would be large global societal benefits from having individuals and firms in the United States (and other polluting countries) bear the full costs of their actions. Such disparities between social and private benefits and costs provide part of the traditional rationale for collective action.

Sometimes, the effects of the externalities (or the benefits of public goods) are felt only locally. (In the case of public goods, these are referred to as local public goods.) In that case, the natural locus of collective action is local. Sometimes, the effects are felt nationally, and the natural locus of collective action is national. But increasingly, externalities and public goods have a global reach, and so collective action should occur at the global level.

Otherwise, there is the risk of a "free rider." If all countries but the United States were to restrict their emissions enough, the world might avoid at least the worst risks of global warming, yet the United States would be able to continue to enjoy its energy- and its emissions-profligate lifestyle. Others will, of course, view this as unfair, and their citizens might refuse to support emissions reductions. Without a global agreement—a global social contract, a new covenant—at best there will be too many emissions; at worst, there will be no agreement at all for emissions reductions.

The Inadequacies of Current Arrangements

The approach pushed by the United States—where each country announces its own targets for emission reductions, and there is a global agreement on transparency to see that countries live up to their own targets—is likely to prove inadequate. It does not address the free rider problem at all. Worse still, it encourages countries to be modest in their targets—if the locus of criticism is on failing to live up to one's targets, then the easiest way to avoid criticism is to set low targets. This is especially true in a context where there are not even agreed-upon norms. To the developing world (and even among many in the developed world), the only "fair" set of targets would be those where each country has (per capita) the same rights to atmospheric carbon space. For example, if the aggregate amount of emissions that the world could absorb from, say, 1992—when the problem of global warming was formally recognized by the international community—onward in order for global warming of more than two degrees centigrade to be avoided with a probability of 75 percent is so much, then each country should have a share of that space in proportion to what its population was in 1992. This means that because the United States has used up much of its carbon space in the two decades of unrestrained emissions, it should reduce its annual emissions by far more than 90 percent in the future. If it reduces its emissions slowly, then it will have to reduce its emissions in the future even more. But to many Americans, the relevant norm is emissions per dollar of GDP—and in these terms, the United States is "better" than China. With such disparities in how each country conceives of what its "fair" contribution to reducing emissions should be, and with such perverse incentives in announcing targets, an approach where it is left to each country to announce its own commitments for emission reductions is unlikely to work.

The problems confronting the international community in dealing with global warming are illustrative of those that appear in so many other areas. Globalization allowed products produced by one country's financial markets to be sold freely elsewhere. America polluted the world with its toxic mortgages. Inside the United States, there is a principle in environmental economics that says that polluters should pay for the damage that they create. It is called the *polluter pays principle.* It is a matter not just of equity but also of efficiency. If polluters do not bear the consequences of their actions, they have incentives to pollute too much. This principle is the basis of U.S. laws on the clean-up of toxic waste dumps. But America bore none of the costs of cleaning up the consequences of the toxic assets that it dumped around the world. Its bankers made profits; those elsewhere bore the losses. If global rules allow the United States to continue to sell its defective products elsewhere without bearing the consequences—and if buyers elsewhere continue to buy these products—then there is no reason either for American firms not to sell these products or for American regulators to curb its firms. To the contrary, there can be a race to the bottom. The jurisdiction with the least onerous regulations and taxation may garner for itself the most business. Interestingly, in the recent debate on financial regulation (and in particular in discussions on a global bank levy to help pay for the costs imposed by banks on the rest of society), the United States took the same position that it took in climate change: There should be no global rules. Each country (in the position of the American administration) should set its own levies. But that cannot be the basis of standard setting in a world with global competition and free capital mobility—where the race to the bottom results in such adverse effects.

And the same argument can be applied in the security sphere. America's wars in Iraq and Afghanistan against al-Qaeda have had the opposite effect of recruiting more young men to the Islamist cause, and the victims have been primarily Afghans and Iraqis but also, of course, Spaniards, Indonesians, Londoners, and Americans as well. The use of military force in areas where everyday social protection (against violence and material deprivation) is lacking only makes things worse—escalating a range of cross-border risks such as terrorism and organized crime.

There are, of course, realists who say this normative approach is irrelevant; all that really matters is power. Power resides in the nation-state and, in the international arena, in the most powerful of the nation-states. The United States uses international institutions and preaches the gospel of globalization when it is convenient—when that policy advances its own interests. Thus, the global institutions are mainly instruments for the projection and continuation of existing power relationships. Consider, for instance, the issue of development. The UN may be a democratic talk shop, but real power lies in the IMF and the World Bank, still effectively controlled by the advanced industrial countries.

Much of the international discussion over global governance fits within such a mold. In the East Asia crisis, the United States resisted Japan's proposal—and offer of $100 billion—for the creation of an Asian monetary fund, which arguably could have led to a shorter and shallower downturn in the region and enhanced regional stability going forward. It did so presumably out of fear that it would diminish U.S. influence, its hegemony, and that of the IMF, where it had veto power.[4,5]

More recently, the G20 endorsed the idea that the heads of the international organizations be chosen on the basis of merit, rather than the current system, where the head of the World Bank is always an American, and the head of the IMF is always a European. But even key heads of foreign governments who pushed the idea were concerned about why the United States may have gone along. The IMF was more central to U.S. interests than the World Bank, and the new agreement may simply have been paving the way for the World Bank to be headed by someone from the developing world and the IMF to be headed by an American. But in the first two appointments made after the G20 agreement (at the IMF and the World Bank, respectively), the status quo was maintained. A European was chosen to head the IMF and an American to head the World Bank—even though, in the latter case, excellent candidates from the developing world—with far more relevant experience than the American candidate—were nominated. The global economy is changing rapidly, but global governance is changing far more slowly.

Still, institutions, once created, take on a life of their own, whatever the motives of those who were instrumental in their creation. The United States may have seen the World Trade Organization (WTO) as a way of getting other countries to open their markets, but the international rule of law—flawed as it may be—has provided a check on U.S. protectionism. America's cotton subsidies have been declared to be WTO-illegal. And yet, things didn't work out the way that most thought. Rather than eliminating its subsidies, the United States bribed Brazil to accept its subsidies. Brazil was compensated, but the far poorer people in Africa remain victims of the lower cotton prices brought on by America's cotton subsidies.

So too, the euro has taken on a life of its own. The European Union and the eurozone can be viewed as an experiment in economic integration. Things have not gone as predicted. This has been especially clear as the eurozone crisis has unfolded, with Spain and Greece in deep depression and no end in sight. The construction of the euro was fatally flawed— a monetary union was established without a fiscal, banking, or political union. Now there are fears that the euro will collapse, leaving a trail of beggar-thy-neighbor policies that will reduce economic prosperity and contribute to pervasive insecurity not just in Europe but worldwide. The euro will only be saved if European states are ready to cede much more power to collective institutions, a sort of model of global governance.

Global Governance Without Global Government

Today we have a system of global governance without global government— an array of institutions and agreements (global, regional, bilateral) affecting every aspect of life. It is an imperfect system, one which, as we have seen, imperfectly addresses many of the key areas where there is a need for global collective action. Yet in many areas it has been moving in the right direction. Global norms have been or are being established, such as those concerning human rights and civil liberties. In the Great Recession of 2008, even though many countries (including the United States) resorted to protectionism, they did so to a far less extent than they did in the Great Depression, partly because of restraints imposed by the WTO and global pressure brought to bear by the G20.

The silo-like nature of global governance in practice with trade ministers, for instance, negotiating with trade ministers—inhibits the ability to take systemic perspectives and provides excessive scope for special interests to exercise their influence. One result is that we sometimes impose standards where we shouldn't, and we don't have them where we should; and often the standards that are imposed are more reflective of corporate interests than of general interests.

Another major limitation on global governance is the inadequacy of enforcement mechanisms. Yet even here, there has been some progress. The Montreal convention restricting ozone-destroying gases was effective, partly because of the threat of trade sanctions against any country violating the agreement.

Countries have been granted the right to impose tariffs in the interests of global environmental public goods (in the shrimp–turtle appellate decision).[6] European courts have barred extradition to the United States when U.S. punishments are out of line with international norms.

Part of the reason for progress in global governance is the growing recognition that many of the problems are beyond the ability of any single state—even the most powerful and the richest—to solve, especially when it is constrained by new norms, such as on the uses and abuses of that power. Financial constraints too have played a role. If the United States believes that it is providing a global public good in its fight against terrorism, it is no surprise that it should expect others to make a contribution to the costs of this war. The United States has turned to its allies to help in the war in Afghanistan. But it has failed to understand that global cooperation, in a world without global government, is built on trust and on shared understanding. If the United States refuses to respond to concerns, say, of European countries on issues that they view as vital—such as climate change—it will inevitably be more difficult for the United States to elicit support in areas that it views of vital concern to itself, such as in Afghanistan. And if it seeks financial support, the United States must also realize that it will not get that support without ceding some control over decision-making. For instance, many other countries are skeptical that terrorism can be addressed through military force; they fear that the War on Terror is creating terrorists. A move toward global governance must entail a public global discussion about the best ways to deal with the risks and dangers of our contemporary world.

Thus, there are deep contradictions in our current system of global governance that reflect and sometimes conceal the large imbalances in economic, political, and military power and inconsistencies in underlying ideologies. We speak of democracy, and yet few in the advanced industrial countries would support a global system based on one man, one vote. The advanced countries are even reluctant to cede power to those from the emerging markets, even as they seek their financial assistance and even as they recognize the enormous changes in the global balance of economic power that have occurred in recent years. We speak of open markets, and yet we worry about being flooded by products from low-wage countries. We may cover up our distrust of open markets by talking about fair trade, but surely we must understand that changing global comparative advantages will put the wages of highly paid workers in the advanced industrial countries in jeopardy. We speak of human equality, yet the lives of Afghans and Iraqis or Somalis matter less than the lives of Americans or citizens of NATO countries.

Exceptional Times

These are exceptional times. The world is facing a series of cataclysmic events—the financial crisis of 2008, the current euro crisis, the Fukushima nuclear accident, the revolutions in the Middle East. Exceptional times are times that allow us to see new patterns and that open up new ways of understanding the world. They are moments when marginalized groups are able to introduce their ideas into public opinion. A sizeable body of citizenry in the United States and other countries has become cosmopolitan—seeing the world through a lens of global social justice. The activists involved in the Arab awakening and the Occupy movement in Europe and the Americas are widening this lens to a broader population. They are challenging the prevailing orthodoxies and developing a critique of the way in which national political elites are more responsive to global corporate and banking interests than to their own electorates. Even if these movements have not (for a variety of reasons) brought about the political changes that many hoped, it is clear that the current wave of popular mobilization is striking a chord with the mainstream. This is a new global generation that takes interconnectedness and communication across the world for granted. They represent a possible starting point for a new global debate.

Ideas matter, and ideas about what a fair and just world—and a fair and democratic system of global governance—might look like are shaping debates about globalization and about how it could be managed better. Even in comparison with the moment when we organized our conference, we believe that the arguments and proposals in this book are becoming increasingly relevant for any systematic analysis of current global risks and problems. We hope that the ideas presented here will help in articulating the questions that we should be asking and providing at least the beginnings of answers.

This book is part of a rapidly developing new field of globalization and global governance that focuses on the global community and global collective action. It is distinct from international relations, which focuses on relations among nation-states. Nation-states are key actors in globalization, but they are not the sole actors. There is no global government, but there is, as we have noted, a complex system of global governance. At the center, of course, are international institutions, such as the IMF, WTO, the World Bank, and a host of international conventions and treaties, helping to create a global legal framework. International NGOs and social movements help shape global policy. And increasingly, the reach of global law extends down below the level of the nation-state to that of the individual and is reflected in the establishment of the International Criminal Court and the UN agreement on the "responsibility to protect."

This book looks at what has traditionally been one of the central responsibilities of the nation-state—providing security to its citizens, protecting them against risks posed, for instance, by the threat of violence, economic disorder, or environmental hazards. As we have noted, today many of the risks come from beyond the nation-state and have to be addressed globally. This book is unusual in bringing together discussions of three arenas that are typically covered by scholars from distinct fields. Security experts, environmentalists, political scientists, sociologists, and economists seldom break bread together, let alone engage in analytic discussions or in policy debates. We brought these disparate scholars together partly because we believe that there are strong parallels between what is going on in each of these areas—a study in one arena may provide insights into the others. But there is an even more profound reason why these topics need to be addressed together. They are inextricably intertwined. The failure to provide a modicum of economic security is giving rise to extremism, which may manifest itself in violence and physical insecurity. Violence, in turn, impedes growth and leads to economic insecurity. Today, in many parts of the world, climate change is bringing droughts, floods, and unparalleled levels of economic insecurity. And if the consequences of this economic insecurity in places such as Pakistan are not addressed better than they have been, there is more than a little risk that already high levels of violence will worsen.

The problems are intertwined but so too may be the solutions. Insurgencies may be arrested through providing greater economic protection. The attempt to reduce carbon emissions can create new jobs that will be an engine of growth for the global economy for years to come.

We stand at a halfway point. The nation-state still remains at the center, but it is not up to the task of adequately protecting citizens from the threats—economic, physical, environmental, and health—that arise from outside its borders. The international community is not yet at the stage of providing protection or even of adequately mitigating the risks. In some cases, the international institutions that have been created are so flawed that they may even be exacerbating the risks. Yet, there is a beginning. There are nascent institutions; there is a promise that they will rise to the task ahead, or at least do better than they have in the past. The chapters in this volume are descriptive and prescriptive. They describe where we are in global governance today and point to what needs to be done in the future.

The chapters in this volume provide a convincing case that the world can provide "protection without protectionism" in each of the arenas that we examine: That economic, physical, and environmental security can be enhanced best by global cooperation, far better than can be achieved by withdrawing behind closed doors. That this is the better way is clear. Whether it is the path the world will take is less so.

This volume is divided into five parts. The first three parts discuss key areas in which insecurity has manifested itself: economic insecurity, physical insecurity, and climate insecurity. But although the threats that arise in each of these areas can only be addressed through the lens of globalization, they play out at every level. Indeed, it is often at the most local level, within cities, that we see their full effects and also the potential that cities offer for implementing global policies. This is analyzed in the fourth section. Part 4 examines some of the challenges posed to local communities. Finally, part 5 discusses the implications for our evolving system of global governance.

Notes

1. Although the enforcement capability of the UN may be limited, increasingly citizens within countries feel reluctant to engage in war without the sanction of the UN.

2. At the same time, America's dominance of the international scene meant that it no longer had to compete for the hearts and minds of those in the Third World. It could now impose its interests (or more accurately, its corporate and financial interests) on those elsewhere, cloaking them with a free-market rhetoric.

3. In 2000, U.S. military expenditure was 41 percent of world military expenditure in current U.S. dollar reference (World Development Indicators, World Bank, 2010).

4. Even if the United States had not opposed this initiative, it might not have been brought to fruition, but U.S. opposition ensured its failure.

5. So too, the United States opposed the UK's proposal for the creation of a strong Financial Stability Board (FSB) that would help create stronger financial regulatory standards—of the kind that might have avoided the crisis ten years later—because that would cede power to a body that might be pushing in a direction that was the opposite of the dangerous deregulatory agenda that the U.S. Treasury was pursuing. (Instead, a much weaker FSB was created, which helped codify the deregulatory standards.

To be fair, even if a stronger regulatory body had been created, it is unlikely that stronger standards would have been adopted, with the opposition of the Bush administration wedded to a deregulatory philosophy.)

6. See, for instance, the discussion in chapter 6 of J. E. Stiglitz, *Making Globalization Work* (2006).

References

Dasgupta, P. and J. E. Stiglitz, 1977, "Tariffs Versus Quotas As Revenue Raising Devices Under Uncertainty," *American Economic Review*, 67(5):975–981.

Stiglitz, J. E., 2006, *Making Globalization Work,* New York: W. W. Norton.

Stiglitz, J. E., J. A. Ocampo, S. Spiegel, R. French-Davis, and Deepak Nayyar, 2006, *Stability with Growth*, Oxford: Oxford University Press.

World Bank, 2010, World Development Indicators–2010, available at http://data.worldbank.org/data-catalog/world-development-indicators/wdi-2010 (accessed November 5, 2012).

1

Social Protection Without Protectionism

Introduction

The conference at which these papers were presented occurred just months after the collapse of Lehman Brothers. It was clear, at that point, that the world was entering the deepest recession since the Great Depression seventy-five years earlier. Unemployment would inevitably rise. It was unclear how long and how deep the downturn would be—and years later, as this volume goes to press, those uncertainties remain. One out of six Americans who would like a full-time job still can't get one. In Spain, the official unemployment rate exceeds 24 percent, but youth unemployment is twice that.

The Great Recession affected almost every country in the world. Unlike previous crises that came from the periphery (the developing countries), with the developed world striving to insulate themselves from the impact, this was a crisis that came from the United States. It risked bringing down with it countries throughout the world, affecting poor people and countries far less able to withstand these economic vicissitudes.

The Great Recession gives a special poignancy to the papers and discussion of part 1 of this volume—the provision of social protection. The crisis raises questions about the basic capitalist model, and especially its stability, as George Soros emphasizes in his comment in chapter 3. It raises, too, questions about globalization, about how responses to previous crises and the global financial architecture and institutions had contributed to the making of the crisis and its rapid transmission around the world. The policies of financial market liberalization and deregulation were based on notions of market fundamentalism, the view that markets were self-regulating; ideas that had little empirical or theoretical support before the crisis but that have since become thoroughly discredited. But the international institutions (like the IMF and the Financial Stability Forum) had pushed these policies, often on unwilling developing countries, telling them that such policies were necessary for long-term growth and stability. That they did so—and that in the aftermath of the crisis, there was no system of "social protection" in place either for those countries that were adversely affected or for their citizens—suggests some fundamental weaknesses in the system of global governance, a subject touched upon by several of the contributions to part 1. The international financial institutions have been dominated by the advanced industrial countries and by those in the financial sector within those countries. These are issues to which this volume returns in part 5.

Most of part 1, however, is concerned with social protection: how social protection is affected by and affects globalization. Joseph Stiglitz argues that globalization has increased the need for social protection, but that it simultaneously has reduced the capacity of nation-states—still the basic unit of governance in our global economy—to respond. Many of these consequences are not inherent, but are a result of the way globalization has been managed, bringing us back to the critical question of global governance. Of particular concern has been the asymmetric nature of globalization, where there has been greater liberalization of financial markets than of labor markets, weakening workers' bargaining power, with resulting adverse effects on wages. Moreover, a race to the bottom drives tax rates down, with businesses threatening to move elsewhere unless taxes—especially on businesses—are kept low. Many claim that globalization *demanded* the weakening of social protections and wages, leading to a curious contradiction: While globalization was being sold as bringing benefits to all, workers (in response to globalization) were being told that they had to accept these drastic changes that visibly made them worse off (Stiglitz 2006). Presumably, in the long run (the argument went), they (or their great grandchildren) would be better off. As Keynes pointed out, in the long run, we're all dead. Blue-collar workers in the United States had seen their standards of living erode over a quarter century. It was no wonder that so many had turned against globalization. The power of the prevailing paradigm was so strong that most did not reject globalization directly—they only demanded a fair globalization.

Finally, liberalization combined with deregulation has exposed those in developing and developed countries to additional shocks.

Leif Pagrotsky, a long-time member of Sweden's social democratic government, argues that this interpretation underestimates the positive contribution of globalization: The competition to which it gives rise has provided a spur to innovation and economic restructuring that are essential to economic growth. How countries respond to this competition is, of course, one of the central questions addressed by this volume. They may respond by protectionism, closing themselves off, or they may reply by devising systems of social protection. The Scandinavian countries took the latter route.

The chapters in this section—and especially that of Karl Ove Moene—explain why Scandinavian countries took that route and why the system of social protection that they constructed was so effective. The analysis goes beyond narrow economics to a broader understanding of politics and society.

The prevailing wisdom in recent decades has argued for stripping away social protections, lowering taxes, providing greater reliance on individuals to protect themselves—a move away from the state toward markets. This was supposed to lead to higher growth, which would benefit all. Economists have typically depicted a trade-off: One can only get more equality and security by giving up on growth. The Scandinavian model challenges these presumptions. The Scandinavian countries have the highest taxes in the world and the strongest system of social protection; yet, in most metrics, they also have the highest standard of living, with lower inequality, better social indicators, and dynamic economies. They have embraced globalization perhaps more than any other region in the world.

These outcomes are not an accident; stronger social protections have been one key part of their economic strategy. The central message of part 1 is that equality (equity), economic security, efficiency, and dynamism (growth) can be complementary. Societies with greater social protection can be more dynamic and more open to globalization. Of course, it matters how one designs the social protection system. Globalization (and more broadly, the increased pace of technological innovation) should not lead to the stripping away of the system of social protection, but to its redesign.

The economic argument has several components. The first, and most traditional, has been especially relevant recently: Systems of social protection act as automatic stabilizers, sustaining aggregate demand in the face of an economic downturn, and thus contributing to economic (and social) stability.

Second, in countries with better social protection, individuals are more able and willing to undertake risk. Risk-taking is at the center of a dynamic economy. As Moene puts it, stronger social protection facilitates the economy's ability to engage in the Schumpeterian process of creative destruction.

Third, higher minimum wages and—more broadly—a compressed wage structure provide incentives for firms to upgrade the skills of their workers. It shifts comparative advantage toward more skilled sectors, and this too leads to a more dynamic economy. (As an example, some economic historians argue that the imposition of the minimum wage played a critical role in the transformation of the U.S. South from a backward region dependent on very low-wage workers.)

But probably more important than the economic argument is the political and social analysis, which highlights how economic policies affect social cohesion. Voters are more willing to support globalization (with its attendant risks) if good systems of social protection are in place. More broadly, in societies in which there is more equality, there is greater social cohesion and—accordingly—a greater willingness to make efficiency-enhancing public investments.

Moene also argues that there is an "equality multiplier." More social cohesion results in greater support for policies that promote equality and social cohesion, including better social protection. As societies become more egalitarian, they become more sensitive to inequities and work to address them. In short, societies with greater equality do a better job at solving the collective action problem.

Although the success of these countries is widely recognized, there are those who talk of "Scandinavian exceptionalism." These are institutional arrangements that work for these countries, with their high degree of homogeneity and broad social consensus. To the contrary: There are good theoretical reasons why we should expect these outcomes. Scandinavian countries did not always have the degree of social cohesion they have today. What one sees today in these countries results in part from the welfare state.

Of course, there are other aspects of the economic and social policies in Scandinavia that contributed to these successes. Moene emphasizes, for instance, the role of trade associations. Some of the complementary policies can, in fact, be thought of as part of a system of social protection. High investments in human capital (perhaps spurred on by the challenges posed by globalization) enhance the ability of individuals to move from job to job, reducing both private and societal costs associated with job loss. Gender policies—bringing women into the labor force—may have been driven by broader views of what a good society should look like, but families with two wage-earners are far better able to withstand shocks. Moreover, the demand for efficiency, to which globalization gave increased impetus, means that one cannot underutilize half of a country's potential human capital. The Scandinavian countries recognized this and developed policies to ensure greater labor force participation while enhancing the capacity of families to respond to the inevitable strains that resulted. These countries recognized the problems and, in response, devised policies that worked remarkably well.

No country can simply adopt wholesale institutions from another. Each institution is part of an "ecology," and systemic change—altering the entire system—is no easy matter. The particular system of social protection that has worked so well in Scandinavia will have to be adapted to reflect the circumstances and conditions in other countries. The message that comes out of these papers is clear: One can design effective systems of social protection that enhance economic security—an important aspect of individuals' sense of well-being. Well-designed systems of social protection can contribute to a more dynamic and more stable economy—and to a society and economy that are more open to globalization.

These are ideas that should be adopted by the international economic institutions (the IMF and the World Bank) that play such a large role in shaping economic policies in developing and emerging markets. These institutions have been cheerleaders for globalization, but the policies they pushed for a quarter century under the Washington Consensus undermined support for globalization, and for good reason. The failure of these institutions is in part related to deficiencies in global governance and is one of the reasons that reforming global governance (including the governance of the international economic institutions) is so important—a theme we return to in part 5.

Reference

Stiglitz, J., 2006, *Making Globalization Work*, New York: W. W. Norton.

1

Social Protection Without Protectionism*

JOSEPH E. STIGLITZ

The various papers in this volume highlight different dimensions of the rise in insecurity. The increased threat of terrorism may have decreased our sense of physical security. With growing numbers of Americans not covered by health insurance, there is an increase in "health insecurity." In addition, global warming confronts everyone around the world with an important new set of environmental risks. This chapter focuses on one key dimension of insecurity—economic insecurity.

In spite of the social and economic progress of society in recent decades, in many countries—both developed and developing—individuals have less economic security today than they did earlier. This is especially true in the United States. As the International Commission on the Measurement of Economic Performance and Social Progress observed, our measures of GDP do not adequately reflect this important aspect of well-being (Fitoussi,

*Revised version of a paper presented at the Conference on Social Protection Without Protectionism, sponsored by Columbia University's Committee on Global Thought and the London School of Economics, New York, 2008. The author is indebted to the Ford Foundation, Hewlett Foundation, and Rockefeller Brothers Fund for financial support.

Sen, and Stiglitz 2010). If they did, improvements in the standard of living would be less than current measures suggest.[1]

Today the world is immersed in a global financial crisis.[2] The risks and uncertainties are unprecedented. No one is sure how this crisis will evolve. In the years after the Great Depression, we erected in the United States and many other advanced industrial countries a set of social protections. But in the United States and some other countries, the last three decades have seen these social protections weakened—in the name of increased economic efficiency.

The arguments for doing so, at least in some cases, were of dubious merit.[3] For instance, the shift from defined benefits retirement programs to defined contributions has imposed more risk on individuals and, by weakening the economy's automatic stabilizers,[4] increased economic volatility. As markets crashed in 2008 and 2009, many saw their life savings disappear before their eyes. Those who had looked forward to a comfortable retirement now face unprecedented anxieties as they confront their old age.

Other changes have simultaneously decreased equity in our society and increased economic volatility. Social protection programs (relative to the size of the economy) have been scaled down, and the degree of progressivity of the income tax system has been reduced.

The weakening of social protections has, from a macroeconomic perspective, both adverse demand and supply-side effects. Individuals who see their income and (retirement and housing) wealth erode will cut back on consumption—especially in the United States, where the average household savings rate has been near zero. The increased risk (associated not only with retirement but also with unemployment) is also likely to contribute to increased savings—especially in a country where the need for precautionary savings for medical and other emergencies is so great, especially if the safety valve of being able to borrow has been dampened down.

With strong anti-age discrimination laws in the United States, there is a further supply-side effect in labor markets: Many who otherwise would have retired may be forced to work longer. With the supply of labor increasing and the demand for labor decreasing, unemployment (open and disguised) will increase. This will, of course, put more downward pressure on wages, exacerbating the already increasing inequalities in American society.

As the effects of the financial crisis begin to be felt in the real economy, unemployment will increase.[5] The official unemployment rate will underestimate the stress in the labor market—large numbers will drop out of the labor force, others will take part-time jobs simply because no full-time jobs are available, and still others will claim disability benefits. The official un-employment rate is likely to hit 8 percent to 10 percent, the effective ("real") rate will be at least 50 percent higher, and the unemployment rate in certain marginalized groups (youth, minorities) will be greater still.[6]

Unfortunately, in recent years, unemployment insurance has been cut back, to the point that less than 40 percent of the unemployed receive benefits, and the replacement rate (the ratio of benefits to normal income) has fallen, to around a half (compared with three-quarters in some European countries).

Even before the crisis, those in manufacturing were facing problems. The pre-crisis excesses—a bloated financial sector garnering for itself 40 percent of all corporate profits and a real estate sector absorbing forty percent of all investment—will compound the challenges of restructuring the economy. Unless the hoped-for government stimulus package is well constructed,[7] it will do little directly for those in manufacturing, real estate, or even in finance: Those in the financial sector are not likely to retrain themselves to work on road construction crews.

Social changes, including the weakening of unions, have heightened these problems. Job protections are weaker and, in Europe, there is ongoing pressure to weaken them further in the name of labor market flexibility. Enhancing the ability of individuals to move from one job to another has obvious efficiency benefits. However, imposing high costs on individuals by stripping away hard-won protections also has obvious costs—a loss in security, which has received too little attention. The rhetoric of increased labor market flexibility is often just a code for lower wages and fewer job protections. The question (to which we turn later in this chapter) is, can we have more labor market mobility with greater security? Although some countries may have struck the balance too much in favor of security, the United States may have gone too far in the opposite direction.

In many developing countries, matters are even more dire. The consequences of weakening job protections are worse because economic volatility in these countries has been increased as a result of capital, financial, and trade liberalization (see the section "Globalization and Social Protection" later in this chapter).

In the face of these uncertainties, demands for protection are inevitable. So concerned were the G-20 leaders about such demands that one of the few commitments undertaken at their first meeting in Washington in November of 2008 was a commitment to not resort to protectionism in response to the crisis.

This chapter argues that a need for enhanced social protection exists and that this social protection will not only decrease the demand for protectionism but also enhance the efficiency of the economy. This chapter then describes some innovative forms that this social protection might take. First, however, the theory of market failures on which the principle of social protection lies is explained, and how globalization may have made the problem of providing social protection more difficult is described.

The Theory of Market Failures

At least since Keynes, we have understood that markets are not self-regulating, at least in the relevant time frame. The Great Depression led to new insights as to how periods of unemployment could persist. Today everyone (or almost everyone) is a Keynesian[8]—both the Left and Right agree that there is a role for government in maintaining the economy at full employment.

After the Great Depression, a peculiar doctrine prevailed called the neoclassical synthesis, which held that once the market failure of unemployment was corrected, markets could be relied upon to allocate resources efficiently. It was not a theorem, but a simple belief—perhaps held so that all the investments in neoclassical economics would not be thrown by the wayside.[9] The idea was always suspect, though. Why should market failures *only* occur in big doses? Recessions were more like the tip of the iceberg. There were many smaller market failures, harder to detect, lurking beneath the surface; many were related to imperfect information, incomplete markets, and irrational behavior. Indeed, a closer examination of behavior revealed huge inefficiencies, for instance, in the so-called tax paradoxes.[10]

The current crisis is a microeconomic failure leading to a macroeconomic problem. As we have noted, financial markets are supposed to allocate capital and to manage risk. But they misallocated capital and mismanaged risk. Markets did not create financial products that would have enabled individuals to manage the risks they face. Individuals cannot buy insurance against risks associated with their future wages or even against broader macroeconomic risks (such as GDP risks). Instead markets focused their attention on innovations that were, for the most part, perfecting regulatory, accounting, and tax arbitrage. The "innovative" mortgage products, while they succeeded in increasing the transactions costs received by the financial sector, made it even more difficult for individuals to manage the risk of home ownership.[11]

Behind this market failure is a general theorem: Whenever information is imperfect or markets are incomplete (in other words, always), markets are not constrained Pareto efficient. That is, taking into account costs of collecting and processing information or of creating markets, there are government interventions that can make everyone better off (Greenwald and Stiglitz 1986).

Many of the important risks that individuals face are not insured (or insurable) by private markets. The burden of insecurity is placed on individuals. Without government, individuals would have no unemployment insurance. Private retirement programs do not insulate individuals against the risks of inflation; only the government social security program—and some defined benefit programs—do so. The mortgage products that were sold by financial markets forced many individuals to bear huge risks associated with interest rate volatility. Not only were products not provided that helped these individuals mitigate the risks they faced, but markets totally misjudged their ability to bear the risks associated with the financial products (such as mortgages) that they sold them.

Not only did the financial markets fail to provide the products that would have enabled ordinary citizens to better manage the risks they faced, the markets have even resisted innovations to improve risk-bearing. When I was a member of the Council of Economic Advisers, I pushed for the introduction of inflation-indexed bonds. We finally succeeded, despite the opposition of many from the financial markets. When Argentina proposed introducing GDP bonds as part of its debt restructuring, enabling better risk sharing (related to the uncertainties about how much debt the country could reasonably bear), financial markets resisted.

Insurance markets often fail, either as a result of moral hazard or of adverse selection. Nonmarket insurance (e.g., provided by social [nongovernmental] institutions) often make matters worse; they might exacerbate, for instance, the problems of moral hazard and crowd out market insurance with less effective "informal" insurance (Arnott and Stiglitz 1991). In this chapter, however, we are concerned primarily with publicly provided (*social*) insurance for risks such as unemployment, which private markets almost never provide.

One of the reasons that markets often do not provide such insurance is that these are systemic risks—with huge potential losses beyond the ability of any individual or firm to bear.[12]

The failure of individuals to purchase insurance against some of these risks—when insurance is available—is a reflection of moral hazard; they know that in a modern society the government cannot allow individuals or society to suffer excessively from their failure to purchase insurance or to take appropriate actions to mitigate risk. The banks have been particularly guilty; there have been repeated bailouts, and the bailouts have been poorly designed, with the banks (and more particularly, the bankers, the share-holders, and the bondholders) bearing few of the consequences of their bad lending decisions. In most of these cases, society could have been just as well or better protected without the financial sector investors having been bailed out, at least to the extent that they were.

Any provider of insurance needs to be sure that the insured-against event does not occur—or that it occurs with less frequency and severity. That is part of the rationale for regulation. (Not surprisingly, those like the banks, who are beneficiaries of this subsidized social insurance, not only call for more insurance, they also call for less regulation.)

At the same time, the fact that the government will step in if private parties fail to adequately self-insure provides a rationale for compulsory provision of social insurance (social security).

There are additional reasons for (publicly provided) social insurance: Transaction costs may be lower than for privately provided insurance (as in the case of the U.S. Social Security program). One reason transaction costs are lower is the lack of spending on unproductive advertising. Another is that private firms have an incentive to engage in cream skimming—in as-certaining who the low-risk individuals are.

For a societal perspective, under a utilitarian or a Rawlsian social wel-fare function (i.e., a society that maximizes either the sum of the utilities of individuals or the well-being of the worse-off individual), optimal social insurance entails pooling—not discriminating among individuals with different risk categories. But pooling cannot be sustained within private markets.[13]

Finally, social insurance also may be an effective way (with limited costs) to engage in redistributive policies. Some redistribution occurs, for instance, through the U.S. Social Security program.

Effective social protection may have societal benefits not fully appro-priated in private markets. Individuals who feel more secure are willing to engage in more risk-taking. In economies with progressive taxation, the government shares disproportionately in the upside of such risk-taking. By itself, this would discourage risk-taking, but with some downside protection provided, the adverse effects are partially or possibly fully offset. In the New Economy, innovation and risk-taking have taken on special importance. Innovating individuals typically appropriate only a fraction of the social returns from their activities.

There is a final rationale for government intervention in markets, perhaps particularly evident in the recent crisis. Markets behaved in a way that is hard to reconcile with rationality. In a sense, a failure of rationality by itself may not be a persuasive basis for government intervention, if the result was that individuals only harmed themselves. But others have been harmed—and governments have had to take action. The logic against government intervention, however, has been largely predicated on rationality, and the current episode provides convincing evidence of massive departures from rationality, with massive consequences.

For instance, markets used models that were flawed, and flawed in predictable ways. They underestimated systemic risk and obvious correlations. They ignored the fact that an increase in interest rates or that a decrease in aggregate demand would have adverse effects on housing prices across the nation; therefore, the risk of foreclosure would be correlated. And they repeatedly underestimated the significance of fat tail distributions. Events that their models claimed could happen only once in a century were happening once a decade—partly because of the aforementioned results, partly because markets underestimated other systemic effects. They systematically overestimated the value of the insurance they had purchased (coverage from undercapitalized insurance companies was of less value than they thought), and they underestimated potential consequences of conflicts of interest and moral hazard problems, the perverse incentives to which the contracts they had gave rise, and the scope for fraud.[14] Each of these and other problems had been discussed extensively before becoming evident in this crisis; most had manifested themselves in one way or another in earlier crises.[15] It had been noted, for instance, that stock options give rise to incentives for bad accounting. Especially when combined with the bonus incentive system, stock options gave rise to shortsighted behavior and to excessive risk-taking.[16] Yet most market participants ignored the warnings.

Further, there was a kind of intellectual incoherence in many bankers' analyses. They argued that they had created new products that transformed financial markets; their creativity helped justify their high compensation. Yet these bankers based risk assessments on data from before the creation of the new products—data that assumed the new risk products had not changed anything. This is particularly disturbing given that securitization, not surprisingly, reduced the quality of lending (due to the newly introduced asymmetries of information). So too, many in the financial sector argued that financial markets were efficient, and they based pricing on spanning theorems, which infer prices of, say, a new financial product from the prices of existing products. Yet they also argued that they were creating new products that transformed financial markets. If spanning theorems and efficient market hypotheses were approximately correct, then the maximum value of the new products was the savings in transaction costs. Yet expenditures on transaction services were actually increasing—with the financial sector eventually garnering for itself 40 percent of all corporate profits.

Other paradoxes are hard to reconcile with "rational markets."[17] For instance, even if those originating mortgages had flawed incentives, why didn't investors buying mortgages exercise better oversight? If they were rational, they would have understood the obvious risks posed by securitization. Why weren't they more attentive to the perverse incentives provided by the peculiar incentive schemes?

What makes these behaviors so hard to explain is that these problems have been repeated. Evidently markets are slow to learn.

If only those individuals who engaged in these "irrational" behaviors suffered, then the rationale for government action might be debatable. Interventionists would be accused of paternalism. Shouldn't individuals be allowed to make their own mistakes and to suffer the consequences?

There are two answers: The first is that these particular irrationalities have had systemic effects—and that these have occurred systematically. Others have had to bear the consequences. Governments cannot sit idly by when the well-being of the entire economy is at risk. In passing the $700 billion Wall Street bailout, many congresspeople felt that they had a gun pointed at their head. Those who had mismanaged the economy were demanding ransom to save it! Legislators knew that this seemed wrong: They knew that taxpayers would not be happy—but they felt that the downside risk of not doing it was even greater.

The second answer is that individuals—and society more generally—may realize that they (collectively) act irrationally, but know that such behavior cannot *individually* be stopped, at least without regulation. (Some of the instances of collective irrationality are not inconsistent with individual rationality. Some firm managers knew that paying out dividends unnecessarily increased tax payments, but they also knew that—given the beliefs of others—not to pay out dividends would result in a decrease in stock market values.) There may be an understanding that economies are plagued by panics, booms, and busts; individuals suffer from herding, both rational and irrational. This knowledge by itself, however, is not enough. The behaviors that give rise to it have to be circumscribed. Individuals (in their moments of rationality) know this and, in effect, ask government to regulate these behaviors believing that they (individually and collectively) will be better off if the government takes appropriate actions.

Other aspects of financial markets are hard to explain. Markets still have not made mortgages available that would have helped individuals manage the risks that they face; there are obvious welfare-enhancing innovations. Such alternatives have been introduced elsewhere. The Danish mortgage bonds have a proven record of success. Given capital market imperfections, there are advantages of variable rate, fixed payment, and variable maturity mortgages. In the past, government has often had to play an entrepreneurial role in improving risk and capital markets. Prior to government provision of social security, annuity markets were virtually absent. Prior to government provision of mortgages, mortgage markets for most citizens were thin. It was government that pioneered the securitization of mortgages and the provision of student loans.

Today there is a host of lacunae in the private sector's provision of risk mitigation products—some easy to understand (the classical problems of insurance market failure), some harder to explain. One of the reasons for social protection is to fill in these gaps.

Globalization and Social Protection

Globalization has enhanced the need for social protection; unfortunately, it has also often been associated with a decrease in the provision of social protection.

Globalization, at least as it has typically been managed, has exposed countries to new risks. Economic and financial crises have become more frequent. Openness exposes countries to new sources of outside shocks.

Although in principle, one of the arguments for capital market liberalization was that it would enable stabilizing capital flows, for the most part, capital flows have been procyclical. As the old adage has it, bankers do not like to lend to people who need their money. When a country faces a downturn, those who have lent that country money demand it back. The evidence is that, at least for many countries, capital and financial market liberalization has been associated with increased volatility.

Increased volatility imposes particularly heavy burdens on unskilled workers and small businesses. Even when countries respond quickly and effectively to the new shocks, the average unemployment rate increases. When job destruction resulting from trade liberalization is matched by job creation, the job losses are associated with significant wage decreases. But in many countries, job destruction has outpaced job creation, at least for significant periods.

Although globalization has imposed additional burdens for social protection, it has weakened governments' ability and willingness to provide such protections.

Many countries have argued, for instance, that the increased competition associated with globalization requires that they strip away social protections to make the economy more nimble and to help it adapt to changing circumstances. They have argued for more labor market flexibility. Globalization has implied changing comparative advantages, requiring redeployment of workers. Lack of labor market flexibility impedes that process. But globalization has meant that, in effect, unskilled workers in the advanced industrial countries have had to compete with comparable workers in developing countries—workers who are often paid a fraction of the wages received by those in advanced industrial countries. Not surprisingly, employers would like their workers to accept large wage cuts; this is what they often mean by increased labor market flexibility.

Because globalization has proceeded in a very asymmetric way, with financial and capital market liberalization outpacing labor market liberalization, and markets for skilled labor being liberalized more rapidly than markets for unskilled labor, countries have faced increased competition for capital and, in some cases, for skilled labor.

This has had both direct and indirect consequences. It has reduced the bargaining power of labor versus capital and especially that of unskilled labor. Thus globalization has contributed to growing inequality within most countries of the world and to the weakening of social protections. Competition from abroad has lowered the ability of unions to deliver higher wages and better working conditions, and this has weakened unions. There has been a vicious circle in which workers have been the losers.

Asymmetric globalization has also forced countries to lower taxes on capital and to reduce environmental and health protections on unskilled labor. Developing countries have been forced to cut back on tariffs, and they have not been able to make up for the shortfall in tax revenues in other ways. Although government revenues and the scope for progressive taxation have been diminished, globalization has also put pressure on governments to cut back deficits and to redirect spending toward increasing the attractiveness of private investment. All of this leads inextricably to the reduction of government expenditures on social protection.

The argument for globalization has typically been that it would so increase growth that everyone would benefit—an updated version of trickle-down economics. But trickle-down economics has not worked, at least in many countries, perhaps because the increases in inequality have been so large and the benefits in growth have been so small that the adverse effects of the former have outweighed the positive effects of the latter.

There is, indeed, an argument to the contrary: Unbridled globalization has led to increasing inequality and insecurity. Increasing insecurity undermines, as we have noted, the willingness of individuals to undertake high-return risky activity, thereby lowering growth. But there is a further political economy effect: Growing inequality enhances the scope for distributive politics. Rather than a consensus around high-return public investments and social protections that enhance individuals' ability to cope with the risks posed by globalization and, in turn, to increase their willingness to accept the challenges that it presents, politics becomes more divisive. Social justice may demand that more of government revenue go toward redistribution, which the rich resist—except when they benefit from the redistributions themselves (as in the massive bailouts). The rich, worried that a strong state might use its powers to redistribute, work to weaken the power of the state and its ability to perform even its productivity-enhancing role. Especially in democracies like the United States where campaign contributions and lobbying can have a large influence on shaping political outcomes, the perspectives of the rich may come to predominate—or at least to have an influence far outweighing their share in the population. The new equilibrium that emerges may be a relatively smaller state, with less social protections and less productive public investments, in which most citizens are actually worse off.

Designing Social Protection in an Era of Globalization

Countries have approached the problem of social protection differently. Among the advanced industrial countries, the United States is perhaps at one extreme, the Nordic countries at another. Some of the differences may reflect differences in behavior and social cohesion—the likelihood that individuals will take advantage of government-provided benefits.

But even in a country as diverse as the United States, I believe that the current arrangements are Pareto inefficient and that there is a risk that things may be getting still worse. I believe that we could provide more security and increase national output. Doing so requires changing macroeconomic, regulatory, and social protection policies.

Social protection is designed to safeguard individuals from a variety of adverse circumstances—illness, disability, loss of work, and so on. Some of these adverse events are predictable, at least to some extent. As individuals get older, there is a higher risk that they will lose income from work, either from voluntary retirement, incapacity to work, or the loss of a job; employers are reluctant to hire someone over 70. Market investments in which individuals put their money are highly volatile. If they put their money in the stock market, it may lose value. If they put it into short-term Treasury bills, the yield may fall to zero. They may live longer than they expected, so the amount they set aside for retirement may not suffice. Inflation may erode the value of their retirement income. As we have noted, markets provide inadequate insurance against the risks that individuals face. When markets do provide insurance, transaction costs may be unjustifiably high or restrictions may be imposed that make the insurance highly imperfect. Government has had to provide social protection simply because the market has failed.

Here I focus on one aspect of social protection—against unemployment and macroeconomic volatility—but much of what I have to say is equally applicable to other forms of social protection.

Macroeconomic Stability

The first and most important aspect of economic security is to maintain the economy at as close to full employment as possible and to protect individuals from what happens when governments fail to achieve that objective. (Full employment is also an important aspect of physical security: It has a strong effect on crime.) That, in turn, requires (a) moderating exposure to external and internal shocks; (b) ensuring that there are strong, built-in stabilizers; (c) avoiding built-in destabilizers; (d) using effective discretionary policies to compensate for deficiencies in the effectiveness of the automatic and structural policies; (e) having in place active labor market policies to facilitate individuals moving from one job to another, in response to the necessary adjustments to the economy; and (f) protecting individuals who do lose their jobs and can't provide full-time alternatives.

As noted earlier, many of the so-called reforms in recent years have moved in exactly the wrong direction.

Of particular concern are *monetary policies* that focused on inflation, assuming that controlling inflation was necessary and almost sufficient for stability and growth. We now see how wrong that perspective is. As monetary authorities pursued price stability, they supported deregulation and liberalization policies that increased the fragility of the financial system, the consequences of which we are now seeing. There was no excuse: We have seen these problems repeatedly.

An *excessive focus on deficits and debt* (reflected in Europe in the Growth and Stability Pact) constrains the use of discretionary fiscal policy when needed. Not only is this shortsighted from the short-term perspective of stability, it is also misguided from a growth perspective and from that of the country's long-term national debt. What countries should focus on is their balance sheet; borrowing for high-productivity assets improves the economy's long-term prospects.

I described earlier how we have weakened some of the *automatic stabilizers*—those in the private and public sector and in tax and expenditure policies. Automatic stabilizers that provide social protection simultaneously reduce the need for social protection by ensuring that the economy is maintained closer to full employment and by helping individuals cope with the consequences of imperfect macroeconomic policies—the failure to maintain the economy at full employment. Not only have some countries' automatic stabilizers been weakened, we have put in place automatic destabilizers.

Regulatory Policies

Some of the reforms designed to enhance the strength of the financial system approached the problem from a microeconomic perspective—that of a single firm facing a problem—and ignored systemic effects. The result was procyclical automatic destabilizers. Rigid capital adequacy standards or rigid rules about loan-to-value ratios were imposed. The result was that when, say, a property bubble developed so that the nominal value of the assets soared, banks were allowed to lend more (in total and to each property), fueling the bubble.[18] There is an alternative—**macro-prudential regulation**—where the capital adequacy and loan-to-value ratios are adjusted to reflect the state of the economy.

Coping with Instability

Even the best-designed automatic stabilizers, regulatory policies, and discretionary interventions will be imperfect: There will still be some economic volatility. This means that someone should fill the gap. Private markets have failed to provide insurance. Government has had to step in to fill the breach.

At least two reasons for private sector failure illustrate the broader issues raised earlier. The first is that the size of the macroeconomic risk is too large: Unlike death (other than from war and plagues), unemployment is a highly correlated risk. When the economy goes into a deep and prolonged recession, such as the Great Recession of 2008, the requisite payments are simply too great for a private insurance company to bear.

The second reason is the problem of asymmetric information: Individuals most likely to purchase insurance are also those most likely to see themselves unemployed. Those in secure positions would not buy the insurance.

Employers do provide severance pay, but it is typically limited and of minimal effectiveness. If the company provides severance pay if an individual is fired, there will be an incentive to induce individuals to quit, by making the job unpleasant. If the employer provides too large a severance payment, the individual has little incentive to work; indeed, any severance pay increases the compensation that a firm has to pay to ensure that a worker does not shirk his duties (Shapiro and Stiglitz 1984).

Almost all advanced industrial countries recognize that, for these and other reasons, one cannot rely on privately funded unemployment insurance. But different countries have enacted legislation making it harder (or easier) to fire a worker and providing larger (or smaller) benefits, obtainable under more (or less) stringent terms. Many in Europe have proposed redesigning unemployment and job protection systems, and have called for more labor market flexibility, which their proponents emphasize will lead to more employment. These proponents might acknowledge that—incidentally—this could lead to lower wages and to less security.

Such reforms have to be evaluated in terms of the impact that they have on societal welfare. Even if it were true that GDP as measured went up, that does not mean that such reforms are desirable; GDP takes no account of the value of security, and such reforms can markedly lower security. Nor does GDP take into account the impact on distribution: Pressing down already low wages may enhance GDP, but at what cost?

Even in the more narrow terms of GDP and unemployment, however, these reforms may be counterproductive. The fallacy in the standard argument is easy to see. It is argued that individuals have to be motivated to search for a job. Unemployment benefits attenuate incentives to search. There may be some validity to that argument in normal times, when the unemployment rate is 4 percent. More intensive searching might enable us to lower the "frictional" unemployment rate. But today, with dozens of applicants for every job, adding one more individual to every queue will have a miniscule effect on employment levels. Lowering unemployment benefits to motivate searching will, on the other hand, have a significant detrimental effect on societal well-being.

More generally, policies aimed at reducing job projections may actually lead to higher levels of unemployment. In the Shapiro-Stiglitz "no-shirking" incentive model of unemployment, what motivates individuals to work hard is the length of time that an individual is unemployed. That is a function of two variables: the size of the unemployment pool and the rate of flow into (and out of) that pool. Regulations that allow or that encourage easy firing of workers (when, for example, they are not perfectly matched with the needs of the firm) engender faster inflows (and in equilibrium, outflows) from the unemployment pool; therefore, in equilibrium, there will be higher wages and larger unemployment—exactly the opposite of what was intended by enacting more labor market flexibility.[19]

Even with the best of macroeconomic policies, some individuals will lose their jobs and need to find new jobs. Active labor market policies directed at helping individuals move from one job to another have shown that these policies can work—but obviously, only if there are jobs to which the jobless can move.[20] Training workers for a labor market in which there are no jobs is not going to succeed.

Explaining the Changes

Recent years have seen marked changes in perspectives on social protection. Some of these changes were the result of misguided government interventions to increase individual responsibility in the belief that markets work well on their own. Some of these changes were the result of misguided views on the extent of the problems of moral hazard (the adverse effects of providing any insurance). Conceptually it is possible that as individuals get wealthier, they are in a better position to bear risk, or that as markets improve, there is less need to rely on social protections.

A closer look at what has happened provides an alternative, and less benign, interpretation. Markets still do not provide retirees with adequate insurance against inflation. Markets still do a poor job of protecting against market volatility. No private insurance company can provide the kind of security that the U.S. Social Security program provides—and none can do it with anywhere near as low transaction costs.

Fine-tuning of government programs can fully take into account the balancing of risk mitigation and incentives—there is no need to abandon social protection.

Much of the drive for change is coming from a quarter that has no interest in making the economic system work better—especially not for those who need social protection. Rather it is coming from those in the financial sector who see risk management as their domain of competency; and they see a takeover of activities in these sectors as a rich, new opportunity for enhanced fees (i.e., high transaction costs).

The demonstrated incompetency in financial sector risk management and the divergence between their private interests and broader social concerns should give us cause for reflection: Some of the reforms in social protection undertaken in the last ten years may make sense, but some may reflect the success of the self-interested ideology that the financial sector so successfully foisted on much of the world.

Globalization and Changes in Social Protection

Globalization makes the challenge of maintaining economic stability greater—greater potential volatility, greater restraints in responding—but it also requires redesigning social protection and, in particular, shifting the locus of social protection away from corporations to society. The system of social protection that prevailed in the Soviet Union and in the United States—where corporations were responsible not only for production but also for providing welfare services—is no longer viable. It never made a great deal of sense. Institutions should have focus, and this focus should be on their comparative advantage. This increases productivity and allows more efficient sorting (i.e., ensuring that good firms survive and bad firms fail). Today we may not be sure whether U.S. automobile companies are failing because they are inefficient or because they have a legacy of social burdens.

The implication is that the *social* protection role of government is even more important today than it was in the past. An example of this changed role is provided by Denmark's system of "flexicurity."

Such reforms are particularly important in the context of U.S. provision of healthcare. The United States has been pursuing more modest reforms within the current structure, such as facilitating mobility by forbidding provisions that deny coverage for preexisting conditions or reducing vesting requirements in retirement programs and moving toward individual accounts.

Some of these are moves in the right direction; some (like the individual accounts) have weakened social protections and are likely never to work very well. In particular, individual accounts are likely to be marked by high transaction costs and, simultaneously, to provide ineffective social protections (no pooling equilibrium) and to weaken built-in stabilizers.

Improving the Efficiency of Social Protections

The greater competition provided by globalization means, of course, that we have to enhance efficiency in the provision of economic security. One important reform entails integrating social insurance programs (as Singapore did with its Central Provident Fund). This can lead to better security with higher-powered incentives (Stiglitz and Yun 2005). For instance, most episodes of unemployment are short-lived. If capital markets worked better, individuals could self-insure. Allowing individuals to borrow against their pension funds allows for intertemporal smoothing—but then one needs to provide lifetime insurance against the risk of a series of bad outcomes, such as extended unemployment (Stiglitz and Yun 2010b). It should be clear that we have not paid enough attention to the design of social protection systems that reduce the scope for moral hazard and simultaneously allow for greater smoothing of consumption over time and across states of nature.

A Catalytic Role for Government

Social protection is designed to help mitigate the consequences of the risks that individuals face in a market economy. We noted earlier that it is striking how poorly markets have fared in providing risk mitigation products. Earlier I described pervasive market failures in the provision of market insurance. The crisis has brought out the fact that some—perhaps many—of the U.S. financial market's innovations in recent years actually exacerbated the real risks that borrowers faced and exploited borrower ignorance. This should not come as a surprise: The misalignment between private incentives and social returns that led markets to perform so poorly in allocating capital and in managing risk also implied that they had distorted incentives with respect to innovation.

In a sense, though, incentives in innovation are more distorted because of the difficulty of appropriating returns from financial products that actually might succeed in mitigating risks faced by individuals. A good product would simply be imitated, and the innovator would not be able to capture much of the returns.

As a result, the government needs to take a role not only in regulating financial markets (e.g., restricting the kinds of mortgages that they can offer) but also in developing new risk mitigation products. For instance, I have repeatedly made reference to the need for better mortgages. Even with more extensive social security, there is a need for better retirement insurance. The private sector continues to fail to provide protection against inflation and protection against changes in *relative* position. If wages and productivity increase rapidly, a worker who retires at 65 and relies on savings from his own wages is likely to find his level of consumption much lower than that of the rest of society by the time he is, say, 85. Some protection against both of these risks is, of course, included in the current social security program.

More broadly, defined benefit retirement programs have provided protection against risks that cannot be insured in the market. Individuals with defined contribution programs are thus left exposed. If the market cannot or does not provide insurance against these risks, then the government should.

Today many defined benefit programs are in serious economic straits. They put aside money based on beliefs concerning "normal" returns and were allowed to take out some "excess returns." Now, with the deep drop in the markets, they are underfunded. There is a need for government reinsurance for defined benefit programs and for better regulation to ensure that they are adequately funded.[21]

(Of course, with publicly provided insurance, the government must do what it can to reduce the risk of the insured against events occurring; in the case of the financial sector, this entails better, and stronger, regulation and better macroeconomic management.)

We should be broadening social protections *and* enhancing the ability of individuals and families to manage the risks that they face by themselves.

Better educated people are better able to adjust to the shocks they face. They are more mobile and more adaptable. Families with two wage-earners have a built-in shock absorber. Thus family and education policies can be viewed as part of social protection policies.

Such policies can help address a variety of market failures (such as capital market imperfections) and may, at the same time, have positive supply-side and welfare effects. These policies increase individual expected utility and societal well-being (however that term is defined, whether in the utilitarian or in the Rawlsian sense).

Concluding Comments

I want to draw attention to one further aspect of strengthened social protection: Increased social protection may enhance political support for globalization.

Many forces contribute to the growing inequality and decreased social mobility. Globalization is only one of them. But it is one about which individuals think that they can do something. (They can't do anything about changes in technology that alter the relative returns to, say, skilled versus unskilled labor.) Social protections—including adjustment assistance—may make globalization more acceptable.

The old criticism of the welfare state was that it resulted in attenuated incentives. It was based on the presumption that markets by themselves were efficient. The Great Depression undermined that belief, but it was almost resurrected through Keynesian economics and the neoclassical synthesis. Limited government intervention—limited to maintaining the economy at full employment—was all that was required to ensure economic efficiency. The theoretical foundations for this belief in the efficiency of markets—in this more limited sense—were undermined a quarter-century ago. Nonetheless, advocates of market fundamentalism continued with their crusade. Today no one can believe that unfettered markets lead to efficiency or stability.

Of course, ordinary citizens have long understood market failures. They knew that markets did not provide them with insurance against the important risks that they faced. But market fundamentalists argued that interventions in the market to provide insurance were distortionary—or even worse, interventions to require insurance were paternalistic. We have argued that with the irrationalities in the market that have been so evident recently (and so evident repeatedly), citizens may well (and in some sense *rationally*) desire some degree of paternalism. Moreover, the large external effects generated by the failure to provide and obtain appropriate risk protections necessitate collective action.

Globalization and the current economic crisis require that we revisit our system of social protections. There is room for improvement in most countries, but especially in the United States. Appropriately designed social protections cannot only enhance individual and societal well-being as broadly defined, but may even lead to an increase in output and growth.

As the United States and the world confront an economic downturn, we must be mindful of the anxieties of those who will not quickly find jobs. For the United States, this means providing health insurance (perhaps through the Medicare system) for the unemployed and assistance to avoid foreclosures (such as the United Kingdom does).[22] It should be clear that the market has failed to provide insurance against many of the risks that loom most importantly in individuals' lives and that the government so far has not stepped into the breach.

In the run-up to the crisis, the private sector—and some government regulators—demonstrated enormous hubris in their assertions about their (and the markets') ability to manage risk. But advances in economics do mean that we understand the issues far better than we did, say, forty years ago. We have a deeper grasp of moral hazard and adverse selection and of the consequences of incomplete and asymmetric information and imperfect and incomplete risk markets. I believe we can use this knowledge in a way that can generate more security—with less adverse incentive effects—than has been the case in the past.

The Great Recession has reminded millions around the world of the frailty of their prosperity. Life prospects can change dramatically with the loss of a job. The confidence of the young that they can then quickly get a new job after being let go has been shattered. Security is important—very important—for most ordinary citizens. The response of these millions to this new insecurity will be either to reduce the threats to their security—through protectionism—or to improve the system of social protections. In short, the response to globalization should be to strengthen and to improve systems of social protection, not to strip them away.

The future dynamism and openness of the advanced industrial countries will depend on which of these choices they make. I hope it is along the path toward more social protection without protectionism.

Notes

1. While this chapter was written shortly after the collapse of Lehman Brothers and the beginning of the global financial crisis, as this book goes to press, four years later, the global economy is still weak and future prospects uncertain.

2. Actually, in the United States, even in the conventional measure, most individuals have not been doing well. Median household income in the United States in 2011 was nearly 9 percent lower than it was in 1999 (U.S. Census Bureau).

3. The argument for weakening social protections paralleled the argument for stripping away regulations. In both cases, it was contended that there would be overwhelming efficiency gains—gains so large that all would benefit. Deregulation of financial markets may have led to increased short-term profits for that sector, but there is little evidence that there was any relationship between those short-term profits and long-term increases in societal productivity and the well-being of most citizens. Although a small fraction of the financial sector was devoted to financing new innovations (in particular, venture capital firms), most of the so-called innovation was directed at regulatory, accounting, and tax arbitrage. The theory was that deregulation would lead to greater efficiency in the financial sector—to an enhanced ability to manage risk and to allocate capital. But the new innovations increased risk. Capital was misallocated on a massive scale. The sectors' net private returns over a half-decade now appear to be negative—its social returns massively so.

4. Automatic stabilizers inject money into the economy when it is weak.

5. This chapter was written shortly after the collapse of Lehman Brothers, when the unemployment rate was only 6.9 percent (U.S. Bureau of Labor Statistics). The predictions of what would follow from that collapse turned out to be correct: Subsequently, unemployment increased to 10 percent, with one out of six Americans who wanted full-time jobs not being able to get them. As this revision goes to press, the unemployment rate is still stuck at 7.7 percent.

6. Even though the overall unemployment rate reached its peak at 10.6 percent in January 2010, the youth (ages 16–19) unemployment rate soared to 26.9 percent, and the African American unemployment rate was 17.3 percent.

7. A stimulus package of almost $800 billion was enacted in February 2009. It was less effective than it should have been; almost 40 percent of the package was tax cuts. Little of it was directed at restructuring the economy.

8. This moment of universal Keynesianism was short-lived. As this book goes to press, countries around the world are engaged in cutbacks in expenditures and are worried about the large deficits that accompanied the global slowdown.

9. The idea is usually attributed to Paul Samuelson. For an early critique of this idea, see Greenwald and Stiglitz (1987).

10. See, in particular, the dividend tax paradox: Firms can reduce the total corporate plus individual income taxes paid by repurchasing shares rather than paying dividends (Stiglitz 1973).

11. For a fuller analysis of the causes of the crisis, see Stiglitz (2010).

12. This does not provide a full explanation because all that it takes to make a market is differences in views and/or differences in aversion/ability to bear these risks. I have discussed these issues more broadly in Stiglitz (1993).

13. For an analysis of optimal insurance in the presence of adverse selection and moral hazard and an explanation for the role of government, see Stiglitz and Yun (2010a).

14. Among the conflicts of interest were appraisers owned by originating companies and rating agencies paid by those producing products.

15. For instance, in the East Asia crisis, some of the cover for foreign exchange risk that Korean firms thought they had disappeared with the bankruptcy of the firm providing that cover. Many banks thought they had obtained insurance against some of the risks they faced by buying insurance through AIG (e.g., in the form of CDSs), though AIG was clearly over exposed. (In the end, the banks got "insurance" through the government; there is some suspicion that at least some of the banks may have counted on this.) Securitization gave rise to new asymmetries of information. Almost twenty years ago, at the beginning of the securitization movement, I suggested that it would end badly: "…the banks have demonstrated an ignorance of two very basic aspects of risk: (a) The importance of correlation…(b) The possibility of price declines" (Stiglitz 1992:25).

16. In fact, in Stiglitz (2003), I attributed some of the problems of the previous economic downturn to excesses and to distortions created by such incentive schemes.

17. Even earlier, I had called attention to a large number of other such paradoxes—behavior that was hard to reconcile with profit maximization or with value maximization. In particular, firms paid more taxes than they needed to (the so-called tax paradoxes and, in particular, the dividend paradox). There are also compensation paradoxes—ways of providing higher power incentives, with lower taxes and less risk (Stiglitz 1982).

18. The U.S. regulatory authorities behaved in an even worse way: As the bubble developed, they increased the allowable loan-to-value ratios and lowered the capital adequacy standards.

19. These results are robust (See Rey and Stiglitz [1996]). The more general point is that free market solutions, by themselves, are not constrained Pareto efficient (Stiglitz 1974; Shapiro and Stiglitz 1984; Arnott and Stiglitz 1985; Greenwald and Stiglitz 1986, 1988).

20. Again we can ask: Why is government necessary to provide such programs? There are two reasons. First, once individuals are out of a job, they typically face severe financial constraints, which make it difficult for them to finance these training programs. But perhaps more relevant, in many countries (including the United States), for-profit skills-training programs have a disproportionately large number of firms that are scams providing little in benefits. They excel not in education, but in deception.

21. As part of the defined benefits (deferred compensation) provided by firms, there is insurance against certain risks. As in other areas of insurance, the government has to make sure that there is adequate funding so that the promises made will be fulfilled.

22. One of the signal achievements of the Obama Administration was the passage of legislation ensuring access to healthcare for all Americans. It did not, however, build in the Medicare system, but rather was designed as a "patchwork" on the existing healthcare system, marked by high costs associated with private healthcare providers.

References

Arnott, R. and J. E. Stiglitz, 1985, "Labor Turnover, Wage Structure and Moral Hazard: The Inefficiency of Competitive Markets," *Journal of Labor Economics*, 3(4):434–462.

——, 1991, "Moral Hazard and Nonmarket Institutions: Dysfunctional Crowding Out or Peer Monitoring?," *American Economic Review*, 81(1):179–190.

Fitoussi, J.-P., A. Sen, and J. E. Stiglitz, 2010, *Mismeasuring Our Lives: Why GDP Doesn't Add Up: The Report by the Commission on the Measurement of Economic Performance and Social Progress*, New York: New Press.

Greenwald, B. and J. E. Stiglitz, 1986, "Externalities in Economies with Imperfect Information and Incomplete Markets," *Quarterly Journal of Economics*, 101(2):229–264.

——, 1987, "Keynesian, New Keynesian and New Classical Economics," *Oxford Economic Papers*, 39:119–133.

——, 1988, "Pareto Inefficiency of Market Economies: Search and Efficiency Wage Models," *American Economic Review*, 78(2):351–355.

Rey, P. and J. E. Stiglitz, 1996, "Moral Hazard and Unemployment in Competitive Equilibrium," working paper, October 1993. Revised July 1996.

Shapiro, C. and J. E. Stiglitz, 1984, "Equilibrium Unemployment as a Worker Discipline Device," *American Economic Review*, 74(3):433–444.

Stiglitz, J. E., 1973, "Taxation, Corporate Financial Policy and the Cost of Capital," *Journal of Public Economics*, 2:1–34.

——, 1974, "Alternative Theories of Wage Determination and Unemployment in L.D.C's: The Labor Turnover Model," *Quarterly Journal of Economics*, 88(2):194–227.

——, 1982, "Ownership, Control and Efficient Markets: Some Paradoxes in the Theory of Capital Markets," in *Economic Regulation: Essays in Honor of James R. Nelson*, edited by K. D. Boyer and W. G. Shepherd, 311–341. East Lansing, MI: Michigan State University.

——, 1992, "Banks versus Markets as Mechanisms for Allocating and Coordinating Investment," in *The Economics of Cooperation*, edited by J. Roumasset and S. Barr, 15-38. Boulder, CO: Westview. Paper originally presented at a conference at the University of Hawaii, January 1990.

——, 1993, "Perspectives on the Role of Government Risk-Bearing within the Financial Sector," in *Government Risk-bearing*, edited by M. Sniderman, 109–130. Norwell, Mass.: Kluwer. Paper prepared for Conference on Government Risk Bearing, Federal Reserve Bank of Cleveland, May 1991.

——, 2003, *The Roaring Nineties*, New York: W. W. Norton.

——, 2010, *Freefall: America, Free Markets, and the Sinking of the Global Economy,* New York: W. W. Norton.

Stiglitz, J. E. and J. Yun, 2005, "The Integration of Unemployment Insurance with Retirement Insurance," *Journal of Public Economics,* 89:2037–2067.

——, 2010a, "Optimality and Equilibrium in a Competitive Insurance Market under Adverse Selection and Moral Hazard," Columbia University working paper, available at www.josephstiglitz.com.

——, 2010b, "Public Provision of Self-Insurance Against Unemployment," Columbia University working paper, available at www.josephstiglitz.com.

U.S. Bureau of Labor Statistics, historical unemployment rate data, available at http://data.bls.gov/PDQ/servlet/SurveyOutputServlet?data_tool=latest_numbers&series_id=LNS14000000 (accessed October 17, 2012).

U.S. Census Bureau, household income data, available at http://www.census.gov/hhes/www/income/data/historical/household/index.html (accessed October 17, 2012).

2

Scandinavian Equality

A Prime Example of Protection Without Protectionism

KARL OVE MOENE

Going on his nine-month-long trip to North America in 1830, Alexis de Tocqueville[1] was curious about the impact of democratic equality. Summing up his impressions in *Democracy in America,* he was astonished:

> Among the new objects that attracted my attention during my stay in the United States none struck my eye more vividly than the equality of conditions. I discovered without difficulty the enormous influence that this primary fact exerts on the course of society; it gives a certain direction to public spirit, a certain turn to the laws, new maxims to those who govern, and particular habits to the governed (Tocqueville 1835, 1840:3).

What did he see? Based upon his description, Tocqueville must have seen something that in many ways resembles the present Scandinavian model much more than the present American one. The contexts are of course very different, but on the abstract level the mechanisms are rather similar.

In this essay, I argue—in line with Tocqueville's observations—that Scandinavian equality also gives direction to governance, social consciousness, and economic behavior. I show how coordination induces wage compression in the labor market, which in turn leads to an egalitarian welfare state. Together they constitute an institutional equilibrium where equality is both cause and consequence. Faced with fierce competition on the world market, this equilibrium path has produced the smallest wage differentials, the lowest frequency of labor disputes, and the most generous welfare states in the world. It must be the prime example of protection without protectionism—where worker security and free trade have persisted together for more than sixty years despite shifting governments and varying external circumstances.[2]

Just as Tocqueville Saw It

Of the many observations that Tocqueville made on his trip to America, some clearly remind us of Scandinavia today. This is at least true for the following features.

Equality of Opportunity Induces More Equality of Income

Tocqueville explains how "the great are pulled down, while the small rise," including the breakdown of the monopoly powers of small privileged groups by increasing entry into their areas (Tocqueville 1835, 1840:555). As a consequence, the highest wages decline. At the other end of the distribution, the lowest wages rise as workers with new rights "refuse their services when one does not want to accord them what they consider a just reward for work" (Tocqueville 1835, 1840:556). Being less dependent on their masters, "[t]he raise in wages they already have obtained renders them less dependent on their masters each day, and as they become more independent they can more easily obtain a raise in wages" (Tocqueville 1835, 1840:556).

As in Scandinavia today, the pay compression was strongest in the public sector: "In America, officials of secondary rank are paid more than elsewhere, but high officials much less" (Tocqueville 1835, 1840:203). He concludes that "democracy generally gives little to those who govern and much to the governed. The contrary is seen in aristocracies, where the money of the state profits all the classes at the head of affairs" (Tocqueville 1835, 1840:205).

All this has a modern mirror image in Scandinavia as wage compression and empowerment in private and public enterprises. The Scandinavian countries of Denmark, Norway, and Sweden have long competed in having the lowest levels of wage inequality in the world. The Scandinavian countries also have extraordinarily high degrees of social mobility. The comparison with the United States today is enlightening. While the wage gap between the bottom and the top is more than twice as large in the United States as in Scandinavia, the social mobility from the bottom to the top is more than 50 percent higher in Scandinavia than in the United States (Jäntti et al. 2006; Barth and Moene 2011).

Greater Equality Induces New Social Relations Between Bosses and Workers and Between Men and Women

In both public and private enterprises, equal opportunity alters the relation between master and servants: "it changes their spirit and modifies their relation" (Tocqueville 1835, 1840:546). Social cleavages decline and hierarchies are reduced. In addition, social mobility goes up. Neither poverty nor wealth is inherited to the same degree as before, implying that family background means less.

In addition, "[t]he Americans understand the equality of man and woman," Tocqueville insists, and points to how the conditions for women improve. After discussing the many different aspects of American life, Tocqueville concludes, "if one asked me to what do I think one must principally attribute the singular prosperity and growing force of its people, I would answer that it is to the superiority of its women" (Tocqueville 1835, 1840:576).

Today we can say something similar about Scandinavia. There is little difference between workers and bosses, and there is a high worker participation in decision-making in the workplace. Scandinavia is recognized for supporting work organizations that grant employees high levels of autonomy. The unusually flat work organization is evident from the contrasts experienced within Scandinavian companies establishing themselves abroad in an environment that expects more hierarchies and more commands.

Scandinavia is also known for "the superiority of its women." The female workforce participation is record-breakingly high. The World Economic Forum measures gender equality by the gap between man and woman in economic, political, educational, and health spheres. The Nordic countries of Iceland, Norway, Finland, and Sweden are all among the top five in gender equality.

Social Beliefs and Collective Action Depend on Economic and Social Differences

More equality means more social care and stronger social consciousness. The moral norms change, for "as people become more like one another, they show themselves reciprocally more compassionate regarding their miseries, and the law of nations become milder" (Tocqueville1835, 1840:539). Less social distance means stronger social identification: "All feel themselves to be subject to the same weakness and the same dangers, and their interest as well as their sympathy makes it a law for them to lend each other mutual assistance when in need" (Tocqueville 1835, 1840:545). This creates a special state of social harmony, for, as Tocqueville said, by establishing "a state of society in which each has something to keep and little to take, you will have done much for the peace of the world" (Tocqueville 1835, 1840:607).

Social consciousness reduces collective action problems and facilitates local organization in accordance with common interests because "in democratic peoples, associations must take the place of powerful particular persons whom equality of conditions has made disappear" (Tocqueville 1835, 1840:492). Further, he claims that "similar conditions" produce "common opinions," something that enables collective action. In this context, he emphasizes the role played by the media: "Newspapers multiply relative to the more or less repeated need for men to communicate together and to act in common" (Tocqueville 1835, 1840:493).

All this is highly relevant for Scandinavia today. As I shall argue later, Scandinavia has the highest generosity of the welfare state in the world and has a high spending on public goods more generally. It has exceptionally strong collective organizations among employees and among employers. Even the number of newspapers is exceptionally high, particularly in Norway.

Each of the features mentioned here strengthens the impact of the others. This complementarity explains why the 1830 American model deviated so much from the contemporary aristocratic European model, and why northern European countries today deviate so much from other almost equally rich countries. Today the feedbacks between equality in the labor market and equality in welfare spending are particularly strong.

Equality in the Labor Market

A key concept to understanding Scandinavian redistribution in the labor market is coordination among unions and employer associations. A key to how it works is the system of wage determination. Wages are taken out of market competition and placed in a system of collective decision-making. From this, many features of the Scandinavian societies follow, including the small wage differentials and the big welfare states. What is most remarkable, however, is that these egalitarian features have emerged together with a high degree of capitalist modernization in the private sector of the economy and with a high exposure to competition on the world market.

A Noncooperative Approach to Cooperation

In general, interest organizations and other groups of actors who have joined to achieve some common interests compete for power and for influence. They bargain with each other, and they interact in noncooperative ways. At the same time, they need to maintain their internal cooperative structure voluntarily; and they enter into new explicit and implicit coalitions that coordinate their actions. Most labor unions in northern Europe, for instance, are quasi-democratic institutions that consist of membership-based unions at the local level that are merged into larger associations.

Each separate coalition agrees to a course of action in a cooperative fashion, yet it plays noncooperatively toward other coalitions. The functioning of the system is therefore dependent both on the social organization—that is, what coalitions form explicitly as well as implicitly—and on the economic behavior of these organizations. To understand this interaction, we have to apply cooperative reasoning to the formation of coalitions but use a noncooperative approach to predict the actions taken by each coalition toward other coalitions and other players. Which coalitions form depends on the noncooperative equilibrium; and the noncooperative equilibrium depends on which coalitions form.[3]

All this is important in order to grasp the major changes in the system of wage setting that took place in Scandinavia in the 1930s and that have dominated developments ever since. The changes in Sweden and Norway were most distinct. In these two countries, workers of different types were initially organized in separate unions. All workers who were each other's substitutes in production had joined the same union. Organizing all substitutes in the same independent union maximizes worker militancy. It contributed to an unofficial world record in labor disputes as measured by the number of lost working days relative to the workforce, a record that Sweden and Norway shared between World War I and World War II. Unions were not the only guilty parties. Nowhere else did employers fight the unions with lockouts as fiercely as in Scandinavia in this period.

What triggered the change was the crisis in the world economy. This crisis did not hit all sectors equally. Construction workers, for instance, were highly paid, militant, and sheltered from foreign competition. When foreign demand collapsed, comparable to increasing competition in a globalized world today, workers in the export sectors, such as metal workers, accepted large wage reductions in order to stem the decline of employment. Construction workers came under no such pressure, in large part because of increased government spending on housing. Higher wages in construction, however, meant higher living costs for workers in the export sector. When construction unions called a strike in support of higher wages (in 1928 in Norway and in 1932 in Sweden), the National Confederation of Unions intervened to force the strike to an end.

The intervention of the National Confederation of Unions to end the strikes in construction was supported by the employers, who threatened with lockouts if the construction workers did not return to work. The combined efforts of workers in the exporting industries and their employers were the initial steps in what can be thought of as an export-led implicit coalition in the labor market, which would become highly influential in the years to come. First of all, these efforts helped initiate a process of centralization of authority within the union movement in Norway and in Sweden, a process that again was encouraged and supported by employers. Second, they were important for the acceptance of the controversial "basic agreements" between the national associations of unions and of employers, establishing rules for collective bargaining, which were accepted in 1935 in Norway and 1938 in Sweden. Third, these efforts were instrumental in replacing wage bargaining at the industry level with direct negotiations over pay by the national associations of unions and of employers. Finally, as white-collar and professional union confederations joined the centralized negotiations, the impact of the export-led coalition was extended to include most of the working population in the private sector.

Organizing Complements Rather than Substitutes

The economic effects of coordinating wage setting depend on whether the coordination takes place among workers who are each other's complements or each other's substitutes. The separate demands for workers who are complements move in tandem because a wage increase for one group reduces the demand for all. In contrast, the separate demands for workers who are substitutes go in opposite directions because higher wages for one group implies more demand for the labor of the other groups. All this is important because coordination means that negotiators internalize externalities in wage setting.

With central negotiations, wage setting (in actuality) becomes coordinated between workers who are complements in total production. Coordination therefore leads to wage restraint and to employment expansion. The highest wages are held back more than the lowest wages. The central agreements are necessarily general. The details of how the agreement is to be implemented are decided by subsequent bargaining at the industry-wide and at the local level. Once the central agreement is signed, however, work stoppages are illegal according to the basic agreement. Wage increases at the local level are limited to what could be obtained without the threat of a strike.

Coordination across industries also reduces the ability of union leaders to pass on higher wage costs to market prices for goods that their members do not consume. Paradoxically, therefore, a strong and comprehensive union association has less effective monopoly power than a less comprehensive association. Less paradoxically, perhaps, unions simultaneously prevent the utilization of employers' monopsony power over the lowest wages. The exercise of monopsony power by employers can be particularly harmful for low-paid groups. Monopsony is not necessarily the result of having only one single employer. It is a natural result of search frictions that limit the short-run mobility among workers across firms and sectors (Card and Krueger 2000; Manning 2003). With search frictions affecting the flows in the labor market, employers may find it profitable to restrict their demand for labor in order to reduce the wage.

Employers become more restrained in their exercise of monopsony power when they face unions that represent the collective interests of the local workforce. Thus union wage setting has similar implications as an exogenously set minimum pay. When employers face the collective interests of workers, they cannot gain much by attempting to reduce their employment levels in the hope of reducing the lowest equilibrium wages.

In sum, the direct impact of centralizing wage setting is to raise the lowest wages and restrain the highest. Coordinated wage bargaining leads to wage moderation at the top and wage increases at the bottom as the wage setters internalize more of the externalities, including the total employment effects of wage restraint. In fact, it takes wages out of market competition, implying that unions must find ways of sharing the gains from cooperation.

As unions are quasi-democratic institutions, it is difficult to distribute the gains in ways that would mimic the relative wages in unregulated labor markets. Thus fairness norms such as "equal wages for equal work" play a more prominent role. As long as the gains are distributed according to such fairness norms, the level of wage coordination determines the size of the gains and the units over which the fairness norms are applied. When wages are determined at the firm level, unions compress the distribution of wages within the firm. When wages are set at the industry level, unions compress the distribution of wages across firms within the industry. When wages are set at the national level, unions compress the distribution of wages across firms, industries, and occupations throughout the entire nation. The pattern is that more coordination becomes associated with less wage inequality.

In the 1950s, wage compression was adopted as an explicit goal of the unions in Norway and in Sweden under the title of "solidaristic bargaining."

Supporters of Equality

One of the important groups that supported solidaristic bargaining from the start consisted of the employers (Moene and Wallerstein 1997; Swenson 2002). Hence wage compression was in fact supported by actors who had appeared to be skeptical toward equality per se. Yet employers were able to increase aggregate profits by reducing wage inequality relative to the wage schedule associated with decentralized bargaining and even relative to the wage schedule associated with a competitive labor market where employers set wages unilaterally (Moene and Wallerstein 1997). Thus employers much preferred to bargain with the "sensible" leadership of the union confederations rather than with the militant leadership of the shop-floor union bodies.

Another important group that supported the policy of wage compression was the leadership of unions with low-wage workers. Because the union movement was all-encompassing, both low- and high-wage earners had influence on union policy. While the policy of wage compression was controversial among the rank and file of unions of high-wage workers, it was enthusiastically supported by members of unions of low-wage workers. Thus the political coalition composed of the low-wage unions and employers prevailed in the 1950s; and it established the pattern of central-ized and solidaristic bargaining that was to last until the 1980s in Sweden and that still exists in Norway today. The export-led coalition had, in fact, a flavor of the ends against the middle. High-wage unions, in particular those in the sheltered industries, were prevented from leaving the central-ized negotiations by the threat of lockouts.

Both union power and countervailing employer power were important for the egalitarian outcome. It is unlikely that the low-wage unions and the leadership of the union confederation would have been able to force the high-wage unions to accept an egalitarian wage policy without the back-ing of employers and the threat of lockouts against unwilling unions. This balance of countervailing power emerged as each separate coalition agreed to their course of action and each played noncooperatively toward other coalitions. Yet not only were the explicit coalitions (formal organizations) important; implicit coalitions (alliances that easily could be established) were almost equally decisive. They worked as credible threats disciplining the behavior of other organizations.

The wage policy found support in the widespread preference of Scan-dinavian workers for a more egalitarian wage scale. It would be wrong, however, to think of the Scandinavian wage compression that started in the 1930s only as a result of a special commitment to equality. Rather, it should be thought of basically as a result of a conflict within the labor movement between workers in sheltered and in exposed industries. Coalitions that were established in defense of their own sector interests helped sustain a system of wage coordination that compressed wages more as a by-product. In the longer run, the compressed wage structure and the openness to world market competition facilitated the voluntary coalitions in the labor market that were necessary for the system to work. Thus the coordinated wage set-ting led to further wage compression in a gradual process of compression from above and from below. Over time, it generated the most egalitarian distribution of wages and salaries in the capitalist world.

The cumulative impact on the distribution of wages and salaries was dramatic. Douglas Hibbs claims that solidaristic bargaining extended the principle of "equal pay for equal work" from one industry to the entire economy, and then moved toward the goal of "equal pay for all work." To-gether with Håkan Locking, he estimates that the variance of log hourly wages in the mid-1980s in Sweden was only one quarter what it was in 1960 (Hibbs and Locking 2000). That dramatic decrease did not include the equally prominent reduction of the wage differential between blue-collar and white-collar workers. Today the ratio of the wage for a worker at the ninetieth percentile of the wage distribution to the wage for a worker at the tenth percentile is about two to one in Sweden, Norway, and Denmark; these are the lowest ratios in the Organization for Economic Cooperation and Development (OECD). In contrast, the ninety-to-ten ratio is above five to one in the United States.

Consequences of Equality

In addition to the reduction in wage inequality and its political implications, to which we return shortly, the coordinated system of wage setting had two important consequences. The first consequence was the virtual elimination of industrial conflict. From the countries with the highest levels of strikes and lockouts in the world in the interwar years, Norway and Sweden suddenly had the lowest levels of industrial conflict in the postwar period. The encompassing structure of unions and employer associations implied that both faced more of the costs of industrial disputes and work stoppages, making them more responsible. In addition, information among negotiators became more symmetrically distributed. There were no longer reasons for unions to call strikes in order to find out whether their firms actually could pay higher wages or not, nor were there reasons for the employers to call a lockout in order to see whether their unions had strike funds or not. The negotiators at the central level had perhaps less information than local negotiators, but the central negotiators had essentially *the same* information. It therefore became impossible for unions to price discriminate between employers with high and low profitability and for employers to price discriminate between strong and weak unions—as could easily be the case with asymmetric information at the local level.

The second consequence was that conditions in the export industries were allowed to determine the growth of wages throughout the economy. This implied wage moderation and international market orientation. In practice, the centralized system of wage bargaining tied wage growth throughout the economy to the growth of wages in the export sector because the unions in the export sector, the metal workers in particular, were the largest and most influential unions within the national confederations. In this way, the system was conducive to free trade and globalization in accordance with the basic interests of the export-led coalition. It became the foundation for what was to be called pattern negotiations (*frontfagsmodellen*) where the unions in the export sector set the pace for wage increases for all other groups of workers—a typical free-trade institution.

The inherent wage compression also affected innovations and structural change, my next theme.

Equality and Creative Destruction

Wage compression directly encouraged the movement of capital from less productive to more productive activities, but the effect on the incentives for workers to change occupations was mixed. While wage compression would increase job loss in industries with low productivity and job creation in industries with high productivity, employers in highly productive firms lost the ability to attract workers with the offer of higher pay. The government, unions, and employers responded to the problem with an array of active labor market policies that subsidized the movement of workers from one industry to another with training programs and grants to cover moving expenses.

The compression of wage differentials affected the pace of modernization and economic development.

The Promotion of Development

Equalizing wages across Scandinavian firms and industries would promote economic development and efficiency by forcing wages up in low-productivity firms or industries and by keeping wages down in high-productivity firms or industries. In a decentralized bargaining system, wages vary according to the productivity of the firm and of the industry.

In contrast, in a system of coordinated wage setting, wages become relatively insensitive to the profitability of the enterprise. On the one hand, industries with low levels of productivity are prevented from staying in business by paying low wages. On the other hand, workers in industries with high levels of productivity are prevented from capturing much of the productivity differential in the form of higher wages. By reducing profits in low-productivity firms and by increasing profits in high-productivity firms, labor and capital would be induced to move from low-productive to high-productive activities, increasing aggregate efficiency as well as reducing inequality (Rehn 1952; Agell and Lommerud 1993; Moene and Wallerstein 1997).

To see the implication more clearly, we can follow Schumpeter (1942) in attributing the dynamics of capitalist economies to what he denoted the process of creative destruction, where existing productive units are scrapped as new and more productive units are being created. Entering firms introduce new techniques and drive the least efficient of the existing firms out of business. When new techniques are embodied in new plants and equipment, technical progress entails continuing turnover of plants and firms.

A simple representation of this is contained in a vintage model (Moene and Wallerstein 1997). Newer plants are more productive than older plants, but the building of new plants is costly, so older plants are not immediately replaced. Once plants are built, however, investment costs are sunk and firms keep the plants in operation as long as income is higher than the variable production costs. Thus the age of the oldest plant in operation is given implicitly by the condition that current profits in the oldest plant in operation equal zero.

The wage bargaining system affects the firms' decision to build new plants through its effect on the market value of new plants. The higher the market value of new plants, the greater the number of new plants that will be built each period. Wage compression holds down wages in plants when they are relatively new but raises wages relative to local bargaining when plants are older. In other words, a coordinated wage compression prevents less efficient firms from paying lower wages than the most efficient ones. As a result, older plants are shut down earlier than they would have been with decentralized bargaining. At the same time, coordinated wage compression prevents workers in newer, more productive plants from obtaining higher wages. The result for firms is higher profits during the first period of a plant's life.

Whether or not coordinated wage compression is more efficient than decentralized bargaining in the sense of raising productivity, employment and output simultaneously depend on the workers' average share of value added. When this share is below a certain threshold, coordinated wage compression uniquely increases efficiency (Moene and Wallerstein 1997).

The condition for wage compression to raise productivity, employment, and output can be expressed more intuitively as follows: Static efficiency requires equal wages for equal work so that workers are allocated efficiently across the existing plants. Dynamic efficiency requires that the average wage costs over the lifetime of the plant are sufficiently low to generate the profit-induced investments in new plants necessary for full employment.

In fact, both conditions seem to be met in Scandinavia by taking wages out of market competition and moving them into a system of collective decision-making by comprehensive union associations that care suffi-ciently about both jobs and pay. The principle of "equal wages for equal work" was easily achieved by applying union norms of equal treatment of all members. The other principle was equally easily met by the willingness to use wage moderation to achieve full employment.

Clearly, the possibility that so-called monopoly unions can enhance productivity and efficiency stands in sharp contrast to textbook economics.

Beauty or Reality

Unlike what textbook economics claims, participants in decentralized labor markets have unequal power. Some local unions have monopoly power; some employers have monopsony power because insiders have in general more power than outsiders; and there are many frictions that prevent the law of one price from prevailing. The resulting individual wages, even for homogenous workers, vary depending on local conditions. Hence, decen-tralized wage setting does not produce equal wages for equal work and does not fulfill the criteria for static efficiency.

On the contrary, a large empirical literature shows a clear tendency of rent sharing in a decentralized wages setting, suggesting that there is un-equal pay for equal work in the absence of unions (Krueger and Summers 1988; Groshen 1991; Gibbons and Katz 1992; Barth et al. 2010). When this is the case, unemployment easily results. Employers underinvest in new plants as the local workforce tries to expropriate more rents by being less collaborative. Due to such holdup problems, dynamic efficiency can easily be violated as well.

Taking wages out of market competition means eliminating the dif-ferent sources of unequal power and replacing them by wage leveling. As stated, Schumpeter's process of creative destruction is fueled by wage com-pression, implying that equality induces innovation because it suggests higher profits in the most modern enterprises. Average productivity can go up for a given employment level. For instance, each vintage of capital gets "fatter" while the difference between the most productive vintage and the least productive vintage in operation declines.

Without wage compression, the complementarity between heteroge-neous firms and heterogeneous workers might imply a sorting of the most productive workers into the most productive firms. A competitive wage structure would then have a distribution of wages where it would never pay for a firm with lower productivity to compete for workers with higher ability. In some cases, when for instance there is no learning from higher-qualified to lower-qualified workers, the large wage differentials associated with sorting can in fact be efficient. But this is obviously not fair because the distribution of wages easily becomes more unequal than the distribution of talent and of qualifications (Moene and Wallerstein 1997).

While wage compression eliminates part of these magnified wage differentials, at the same time, average productivity may increase. A similar reasoning also shows that wage compression leads more enterprises to approach international markets (Willumsen 2011). Entering international export markets entails fixed entry costs. Thus only the most productive firms find it profitable to go international. Wage equality, however, makes it more profitable for the most productive firms to invest the necessary entry cost to compete abroad. In fact, a compressed wage structure enables more of the firms to enter global markets, and the productivity threshold that divides domestic producers from producers for global markets becomes lower. In this sense, wage equality induces globalization.

Equality in the Welfare State

Equality in the labor market spills over to egalitarian public policies. Internationally, there is a general pattern showing that countries with more wage equality tend to have more generous welfare states (Barth and Moene 2011). For instance, the Scandinavian countries have twice as generous welfare spending as the United States but have only one-third of the U.S. pretax wage inequality. This equality–generosity pattern runs counter to the most prominent theories of welfare spending such as the seminal papers by Romer (1975), Roberts (1977), and Meltzer and Richard (1981), which all predict that higher pretax inequality should be associated with more, not less, generous welfare spending. In contrast, the welfare state seems to be least developed where it is the most needed.

The negative association between wage inequality and welfare spending is a special case of what has been denoted "the Robin Hood paradox":

> Poverty policy within any one polity or jurisdiction is supposed to aid the poor more, the lower the average income and the greater the income inequality. Yet over time and space, the pattern is usually the opposite (Lindert 2004:15.).

The Equality Magnifying Effect

To understand the equality–generosity pattern across countries and over time, and particularly the Scandinavian position in this pattern, it is important to notice that in most countries, pure redistribution of resources has not been so important for the expansion of the welfare state as some claim. It is rather the provision of services and, in particular, the protection against risks that has been the driving force (Baldwin 1990; Barr 1992). Welfare policies that, in addition to providing a more fair distribution, cover social demands for which the market fails to provide are much more likely to be both legitimate and popular. This is particularly relevant for social insurance against loss of income due to sickness, unemployment, and old age (Moene and Wallerstein 2001, 2003; Barth and Moene 2011).

In Scandinavia, countrywide universalism of welfare provision—the provision of basic welfare goods for everybody as a citizen's right—was also an important issue, even for employers. To keep highly productive employers from undermining the policy of wage restraint by offering workers generous benefits (which were harder to monitor at the central level than wages), the Swedish employers' confederation lobbied the government to nationalize the provision of healthcare and pensions (Swenson 2002). Even though everybody was covered by these schemes, they were offered on better terms for the poor than for the rich in the sense that the expected contributions relative to the expected benefits were much higher for high-paid workers than for low-paid workers.

Now, how does the political support for welfare spending relate to the distribution of wages in the labor market? The political competition over voters' support depends on the interests of the majority of voters. These interests, however, are shaped by the pretax distribution of wages. A more compressed wage distribution, for a given mean, makes the majority of workers richer, which in turn raises the political demand for welfare spending on commodities and on services that are normal goods for households. In particular, the political demand for social insurance against the loss of income due to unemployment, disability, sickness, and occupational injury tends to rise as wage inequality declines (Moene and Wallerstein 2003; Barth and Moene 2011). In this way, more wage equality fuels the political demand for generous welfare spending.

There is also another important effect of equality that Tocqueville observed, as hinted at earlier in this chapter. Equality makes people more like one another. Equals show more reciprocity, feel stronger social identification with each other, become "more compassionate regarding their miseries," experience similar weaknesses and dangers, and "their interest as well as their sympathy makes it a law for them to lend each other mutual assistance when in need" (Tocqueville 1835, 1840:545). If this is right, these kinds of social identification easily translate into a higher political demand for welfare generosity.

Political parties compete to attract voters with such interests. When the distribution of wages becomes more compressed, the attitudes within political parties toward welfare spending become more in favor of expansions. Both the Left and the Right shift their welfare platforms toward more generosity. In a separate study of political party programs in twenty-two countries, we find that higher wage equality generates an overall Leftward shift in welfare state programs, yet somewhat more in Left-wing parties than in Right-wing parties (Barth, Finseraas, and Moene 2012).

Clearly it might matter which party or block wins the election, but all parties run on programs that are already adjusted to the wage distribution—to new welfare programs that are still likely to differ across political parties. No wonder that even rather conservative parties in Scandinavia today have become ardent defenders of the welfare state. It is impossible to win elections without a positive attitude toward welfare spending because it is so popular among a majority of voters. The political demand is also fueled by other factors including the income level of the country and economic risks that voters are exposed to such as those generated by fluctuations in the world economy.

In fact, globalization can fuel and be fueled by welfare spending. On the one hand, societies that are particularly exposed to global competition tend to have bigger welfare states, while, on the other hand, globalization is more popular in societies with big welfare states with generous social insurance. The small open economies in northern Europe are typical examples.

Empowering Weak Groups

Pretax equality induces welfare spending, but does welfare spending induce higher or lower pretax equality? One channel goes via empowering low-paid workers. Everybody with pressing economic needs is weak in negotiations and might have to take the first available job. Access to social insurance makes such groups less vulnerable. Their pressing economic needs become less pressing when more of their needs are covered by welfare state arrangements.

Thus welfare benefits strengthen weak groups in the labor market as their fallback position becomes better. Low-paid workers therefore become able to command a higher pay and to improve their relative wage.

Welfare benefits may also set a floor below which wages cannot fall. As a consequence, welfare spending may eliminate bad jobs or turn some bad jobs into good jobs. While a low wage may discourage effort, a high wage may work as a positive encouragement. In accordance with traditional efficiency wage arguments, employers might increase wages in order to raise profits by inducing higher efforts.

Yet in low-productivity jobs, it is also possible to raise profits by *lowering* wages as long as work efforts go down relatively less than the relevant wages. Powerful employers may gain by obtaining a larger share of a smaller pie. This low-wage trap can be costly not only to the workers but also to society at large. Production goes down and poverty increases, as profits go up. Employers simply gain by employing human resources inefficiently. With a generous welfare state, this strategy becomes less attractive as the possibility to offer low wages declines. The result is again a compression of the wage distribution from below—what Erling Barth and I denote as the wage-equalizing effect.

There are also specific features of each social policy that feed back to economic performance and the distribution of earnings. Some of the effects can be surprisingly strong. The rise of subsidized child care in Norway from the 1970s is a good example. By exploring exogenous variation across municipalities, using a comprehensive set of register data, Havnes and Mogstad (2011) show how child care can have large positive effects on children's adult outcomes. Measured by the outcomes later in life, public child care is both productivity enhancing and redistributive. It produces more education, a stronger labor market attachment, and more equality in labor earnings. The effects are particularly strong for girls and for children of disadvantaged families. It seems that good access to subsidized child care levels the playing field by increasing intergenerational mobility and by closing the gender wage gap in a way that raises total productivity.

How Equality Multiplies

Combining the equality magnifying effect and the feedbacks in the form of the wage-equalizing effect we have two links with distinct causal impacts. Together they constitute a simple description of a political economic equilibrium that incorporates the mutual dependence between wage set-ting and welfare spending. More wage equality leads the majority of voters to support a more generous welfare state. More generous welfare benefits in turn reduce wage inequality by strengthening weak groups in the labor market. More equal wages fuel welfare generosity and a more generous wel-fare state fuels wage equality, stimulating further welfare generosity and further wage equality in a cumulative process. In the long run, it adds up to a sizable equality multiplier.

Erling Barth and I have estimated the multiplier by utilizing variations across eighteen OECD countries over a period of twenty-six years to iden-tify the two separate effects (accounting for obvious erogeneity problems and by paying due attention to the fact that countries differ in so many other ways than welfare spending and wage inequality). The effects are strong and robust. Our best estimate shows an equality multiplier of 1.5, implying that exogenous changes are magnified by 50 percent in the long run (Barth and Moene 2011). The estimate does not change much by using only subsamples of countries, indicating that it does not rely on any specific groups of countries.

We have also estimated the equality multiplier by another data set that covers the separate U.S. experience over a longer period, from 1945 to 2002. The results are similar, but the magnitudes are a bit smaller with an (in)equality multiplier around 1.3. According to our estimates, the United States experienced a cumulative process of wage compression and welfare state expansion from 1945 to around 1970 as the equality multiplier mag-nified overall equality. From the 1980s until today, the U.S. multiplier has worked in reverse (as an inequality multiplier) magnifying overall inequal-ity. In this period, the United States has experienced a cumulative process of increasing wage dispersion and stagnating or even declining welfare spending.

In general, our social multiplier seems to magnify structural differ-ences in wage setting, production, and resources. The direction of change depends on the initial stimuli, and the magnitude of change depends on both the size of the stimuli and the strength of the feedbacks.

Inequality Gets Noticed When It's Small

Because the Scandinavian countries today have the smallest wage differen-tials in the world and the most generous welfare states, it may come as a surprise that people there are obsessed by the belief that inequality is steadily on the rise and that domestic levels of poverty are going up. This type of false consciousness should, however, not come as a shock—it is a natural effect of a high level of equality on public spirits and social psychology.

Our psychological capacity to register changes depends on existing differences. When existing differences are small, it becomes easier to recognize rising inequality as compared with a situation where the existing inequalities are large. Similarly, our social reactions to increasing inequality are stronger when differences are small. In other words, we perceive and react to higher inequality in the light of present inequalities. Our reactions to a given increase in disparity are inversely related to its importance. Small differences are important when the absolute differences are small. In this way, existing inequality works as a transformer that magnifies the small and diminishes the large. In egalitarian societies, even the smallest inequalities get noticed, while in inegalitarian societies, the greatest inequalities pass by unnoticed.

Tocqueville said all this much more elegantly: "When inequality is the common law of a society, the strongest inequalities do not strike the eye; when everything is nearly on a level, the least of them wound it" (Tocqueville 1835, 1840:513). This appears to me a sharp observation. If it is right, it has important implications. When the smallest differences get noticed, egalitarian societies become more socially stable than they otherwise would have been. Or, as Tocqueville said: "The desire for equality always becomes more insatiable as equality is greater" (Tocqueville 1835, 1840:513). In other words, the social preference for equality is strongest when inequality is lowest. When the smallest differences get noticed, egalitarian societies can also maintain high work incentives with small wage differentials. Incentives are in this way self-calibrating (Loewenstein and Moene 2006).

Incentives are connected to relative rewards. In situations where rewards normally are large, one cannot expect higher effort by a small rise. In situations where rewards normally are small, however, people might be willing to work hard to achieve a small improvement that helps one move up in the local ranking of remunerations. Tocqueville did not say this explicitly, but he came pretty close when he said that every citizen "always perceive[s] near to him several positions in which he is dominated, and one can foresee that he will obstinately keep looking at this side alone" (Tocqueville 1835, 1840:513).

When the smallest differences get noticed, globalization is less of a threat via the traditional mechanisms of factor price equalization. Globalization may imply, however, that it is no longer the smallest differences that get noticed but rather the largest. The first thing to get globalized may simply be the reference group. When reference groups are global, the local self-calibration of incentives easily gets weaker.

In sum, the income distribution in egalitarian societies becomes relatively stable through the filtering of social perceptions, reactions, and complaints. Equality and efficiency are maintained by the restlessness of citizens, or as Tocqueville said about people's attitudes toward equality: "They see it from near enough to know its charms, they do not approach it close enough to enjoy it, and they die before having fully savored its sweetness" (Tocqueville 1835, 1840:514).

What Are the Lessons?

In contrast to what I have argued earlier, many economists implicitly claim that the Scandinavian model is a recipe for trouble. Wage differences are too small, taxes too high, welfare states too generous, and unions too strong— they might say (and some of them say it loudly). Despite these seemingly harmful excesses, the Scandinavian countries have for decades been doing quite well by accepted measures of economic performance.

What is seen as a recipe for serious economic trouble to a substantial part of the economic profession seems in Scandinavia to be consistent with high growth, low unemployment, low inequality, and a fairly efficient allocation of resources. Thus there must be some lessons both for economics and for politics that can be drawn from the Scandinavian experience with the egalitarian policies of protection without protectionism. I conclude by listing some of them from a methodological perspective.

All-Else-Being-the-Same Is Misplaced

One reason why many economists get it wrong is their overuse of the all-else-being-the-same ("cæteris paribus") assumption. Considering each special feature of Scandinavia's equality in isolation, one easily overlooks how the impact of a simultaneous adjustment in all of them can be quite different from the sum of a partial change in each. To get it right, one has to consider them jointly within a consistent framework that allows mutual adjustments.

Clearly one has to focus on both the benefits and the costs—not just the costs. Social policies can be highly productivity-enhancing. Social policies and participation (by collective interest organizations) can complement the working of a market economy; and well-functioning markets make social policies and participation more, rather than less, feasible.

Not Deviations from a Natural U.S. Model

The wide dissimilarities in institutions, social organizations, and economic outcomes among countries should not be interpreted as deviations from one natural U.S. model. To understand why people in almost equally rich societies are working under different rules, we need to account for how policies, institutions, and behaviors interact in a general equilibrium. A more partial approach, one that neglects institutional complementarities and social spillovers, does not capture such mechanisms and may easily misinterpret the Scandinavian experience and the viability of an equitable society in general.

Rightly interpreted, the general equilibrium effects can be quite different from the sum of the partial equilibrium effects. For instance, the high taxes in Scandinavia (a feature that is often exaggerated) finance a generous welfare state, empower weak groups, help compress the wage structure, turn bad jobs into good jobs, and so forth. To consider the narrow impact of high taxes in isolation from these other effects would lead us astray.

Similarly the process that started with the rising female labor participation in the 1960s had wide-ranging general equilibrium effects. As the woman joined her husband as wage laborer, the household naturally demanded more public care for children and for the elderly. The gradual expansion of the welfare state made it easier for yet more women to enter the workforce.

Equality May Require Double Redistribution

Many economists are obsessed by cost efficiency but neglect the equally important problems of political implementation. But good policies are not always good politics. In Scandinavia, redistribution takes place via wage compression in the labor market and, on top of that, via welfare spending. For an egalitarian economist, it may perhaps be too much of a good thing. Why twice?

If one takes democratic implementation seriously, both optimal policies and good politics depend on the income distribution in society. As
I have argued here, many features of the Scandinavian societies, including the small wage differentials and the big welfare states, follow from the
arrangements that take wages out of market competition and place them in
a system of collective decision-making. The egalitarian public policies are
endogenously determined by the political competition over the votes of a
majority of citizens who have already been made similar to each other via
the compression of their labor earnings.

The resulting equilibrium of double redistribution is simple. While
wage compression affects welfare policies, welfare policies empower weak
groups in the labor market and improve their position in the wage distribution, which again affects welfare policies. The interconnections are strong.
Equality generates more equality, adding up to a sizable equality multiplier. It is highly unlikely that one would have achieved a similar equality
of disposable income simply by voting over taxes and benefits for the entire
income distribution in one setting. The path matters.

Policies and Institutions Must Fit Together

The Scandinavian social model can be distinguished by its major institutions—a large welfare state and encompassing associations of unions and
of employers—and by its institutions' policies—the provision of basic
welfare goods for everybody as a citizen's right and wage leveling through
solidaristic bargaining. In addition, there is at least one other important
institution—the arrangement of routine consultation among government
and interest organizations that is committed to a policy of full employment
(Moene and Wallerstein 1993). Together they constitute an institutional
equilibrium. If institutions and policies do not fit together in this way, they
easily erode each other's impact.

Take the commitment to full employment, for instance: Is it sustainable? Can it be enforced? The commitment can be understood as a mutual
gift exchange between unions and the government; although wage moderation enables the government to follow a full employment policy, the promise of full employment in exchange for wage moderation is important for
the unions to implement wage restraint. This makes it easier to finance
the generous welfare state because high employment rates fuel generosity
because generosity becomes cheaper; and as fewer people need to use the

system, relative to the employed population, the less expensive it is per employed to provide the taxes necessary for higher generosity (Barth and Moene 2012). Government commitments to full employment in countries with a different union structure are often not credible.

Protection Without Protectionism Is Feasible

Systems that combine social policies with free access to international markets have been politically contested on the Left as well as on the Right. Both would insist that radical social reforms and good market performance are substitutes, not complements. While Leftist economists may insist that partial social victories are continually eroded by market forces (Luxemburg 1970:43), Right-wing economists may claim that market forces are steadily eroded by social reform (Lundberg 1985).

Neither view is proven correct because social equality and worker security have persisted in the small open market economies in Scandinavia for decades. The egalitarian features have emerged together with a high degree of capitalist modernization in the private sector of the economy, a high level of innovation, and a strong export orientation by producers. As a result, economic growth has been on par with the United States.

In the United States, rising inequality has gone hand in hand with social cleavages and with lower welfare for at least one-third of the population. In contrast, most of Europe has experienced only a modest rise in inequality but a sharp rise in unemployment. The Scandinavian countries, however, have in the same period combined social equality with good macroeconomic performance and full employment. Hence, protection without protectionism is possible.

Evolution, Not Intelligent Design

Scandinavian equality was implemented gradually whenever a social victory was possible. Thus it is not the result of intelligent design but rather of social and economic evolution. Societal arrangements that are not designed but implemented gradually tend to be more stable toward shocks and toward disturbances than those that originate at the drawing table.

In the case of the small open economies of Scandinavia, the general equilibrium of a large welfare state and encompassing interest organizations

SCANDINAVIAN EQUALITY   71

should be viewed as an equilibrium of free trade institutions. The arrangement provides for a fair sharing of the necessary costs of globalization because, for instance, the sharing of the costs of social insurance required that workers be willing to take jobs, exposed to international competition, on terms that are profitable for employers.

Gradually implemented policies, institutions, and behaviors that fit together and strengthen each other may look ex post facto as if societal arrangements come in packages with different social and economic organization, while they in fact are the results of adjustments in a process of trial and error. In Scandinavia, the results of this evolution seem to negate the commonly presumed conflict between inequality and unemployment and between inequality and good economic performance in general. A system of governance and incentives has evolved, leading private businesses to act in socially desirable ways without altering property rights and without protectionism.

Learning from Other Countries Is Not the Same as Imitating Them

One may wonder whether the Scandinavian lessons are only relevant to small, homogeneous, and affluent societies with an extraordinary commitment to equality. On one level, the answer must be no. The affluence and homogeneity are products, not prerequisites of the model. Yet whether a similar leveling of the playing field has clear relevance for countries that are heterogeneous, conflict-ridden, and poor today is an open question. In poor countries, there can be additional problems of implementation because of the high level of surplus labor (see Moene and Wallerstein 2006 for a discussion).

Neither should one jump directly from the Scandinavian experience to conclusions about what can be achieved by policies that are sufficiently pro-labor. Again, policies are endogenous and institutions need to be maintained. It should also be noticed that Scandinavian equality consists of small wage differentials and big welfare states; it is not a change in the functional distribution of income between wages and profits. Scandinavian social democrats tend to think about capitalists as "saving machines."

While the scope for learning is large, the benefits from imitating might be small for other countries with different histories and initial conditions. The initial conditions that favored the equitable development in Scandinavia throughout the last century include, for instance, features that are unheard of in most developing countries today. In Scandinavia, there was a high level of educational attainment in the adult population; the state apparatus was efficient and basically honest and, most importantly, the countries should not be known for the strength of unions only—employers also achieved an extraordinary level of organization. All these aspects helped in sustaining the wage compression via the ends-against-the-middle coalition in the labor market and the huge expansion of the egalitarian welfare state via democratic political competition.

Even though no local system is exportable to other countries, with different histories and initial conditions, all countries can learn much more from each other than they seem to today. They can also learn from the long process of trial and error in the Scandinavian countries.

Notes

1. Elster (2009) provides an elegant discussion of Tocqueville's contributions more generally.

2. This chapter arose from research conducted under the auspices of the ESOP, a research center funded by the Research Council of Norway. I'm grateful for comments from Mary Kaldor, Trine Nickelsen, Atle Seierstad, and Joseph Stiglitz.

3. One way to analyze these interactions is to combine cooperative and noncooperative game theory—cooperative games for the formation of coalitions, noncooperative games for the equilibrium actions. The theoretical literature is sparse on these issues except for the contributions by Leif Johansen (1982) and by Debraj Ray and various coauthors further elaborated in Ray's recent book from 2008. See also Moene (2012).

References

Agell, J. and K. E. Lommerud, 1993, "Egalitarianism and Growth," *Scandinavian Journal of Economics, 90*(4):559–579.

Baldwin, P., 1990, *The Politics of Social Solidarity: Class Bases of the European Welfare State, 1875–1975*, Cambridge: Cambridge University Press.

Barr, N., 1992, "Economic Theory and the Welfare State: A Survey and Interpretation," *Journal of Economic Literature, 30*:741–803.

Barth, E., A. Bryson, J. C. Davis, and R. Freeman, 2010, "The Contribution of Dispersion Across Plants to the Increase in the U.S. Earnings Dispersion," Paper presented at the 2010 National Bureau of Economic Research Summer Institute, Cambridge, Mass.

Barth, E., H. Finseraas, and K. O. Moene, 2012, "Wage Inequality and Welfare Policy Platforms," Equality, Social Organization and Economic Performance (ESOP), University of Oslo, and Institute of Social Research, Oslo.

Barth, E. and K. O. Moene, 2011, "The Equality Multiplier," working paper, ESOP, Department of Economics, University of Oslo.

——, 2012, "Employment as a Price or a Prize of Equality: A Descriptive Analysis," *Nordic Journal of Working Life Studies*, 2(2):5–33.

Card, D. and A. B. Krueger, 2000, "Minimum Wages and Employment: A Case Study of the Fast-Food Industry in New Jersey and Pennsylvania: Reply," *American Economic Review*, 90(5):1397–1420.

Elster, J., 2009, *Alexis de Tocqueville: The First Social Scientists*, Cambridge: Cambridge University Press.

Gibbons, R. and L. Katz, 1992, "Does Unmeasured Ability Explain Interindustry Wage Differentials?" *Review of Economic Studies*, 59:515–535.

Groshen, E., 1991, "Sources of Intra-Industry Wage Dispersion: How Much Do Employers Matter?" *Quarterly Journal of Economics*, 106(3):869–884.

Havnes, T. and M. Mogstad, 2011, "No Child Left Behind: Subsidized Child Care and Children's Long-Run Outcomes," *American Economic Journal: Economic Policy*, 3(2): 97–129.

Hibbs, D. A. Jr. and H. Locking, 2000, "Wage Dispersion and Productive Efficiency: Evidence for Sweden," *Journal of Labor Economics*, 18(4):755–782.

Jäntti, M., B. Bratsberg, A. Björklund, T. Erisson, R. Naylor, K. Røed, O. Raaum, and E. Österbacka, 2006, "American Exceptionalism in New Light: Intergenerational Earnings Mobility in the Nordic Countries, the United Kingdom, and the United States." IZA Discussion Paper No. 1938.

Johansen, L., 1963, "Marxism and Mathematical Economics," *Monthly Review: An Independent Socialist Magazine*, 14(9):505–514.

——, 1982. "Cores, Aggressiveness and the Breakdown of Cooperation in Economic Games," *Journal of Economic Behavior and Organization*, 3(1):1–37.

Krueger, A. B. and L. J. Summers, 1988, "Efficiency Wages and the Inter-industry Wage Structure," *Econometrica*, 56:259–293.

Lindert, P. H., 2004, *Growing Public: Social Spending and Economic Growth since the Eighteenth Century*, Cambridge: Cambridge University Press.

Loewenstein, G. and K. O. Moene, 2006, "On Mattering Maps," in *Understanding Choice, Explaining Behaviour*, edited by A. Hylland, O. Gjelsvik, J. Elster, and K. Moene, 153–176. Oslo: Oslo Academic Press.

Lundberg, E., 1985, "The Rise and Fall of the Swedish Model," *Journal of Economic Literature*, 23:1–36.

Luxemburg, R., 1970, *Reform or Revolution*, New York: Pathfinder.

Manning, A., 2003, *Monopsony in Motion, Imperfect Competition in Labor Markets*, Princeton: Princeton University Press.

Meltzer, A. H. and S. F. Richard, 1981, "A Rational Theory of the Size of Government," *Journal of Political Economy*, 89:914–927.

Moene, K. O., 2012, "The Bargaining Society," *Nordic Journal of Political Economy*, (Forthcoming).

Moene, K. O. and M. Wallerstein, 1993, "What's Wrong with Social Democracy," in *Market Socialism*, edited by P. Bardhan and J. E. Roemer, 219–235. New York: Oxford University Press.

——, 1997, "Pay Inequality," *Journal of Labor Economics*, 15:403–430.

——, 2001, "Inequality, Social Insurance, and Redistribution," *American Political Science Review*, 95(4):859–874.

——, 2003, "Earnings Inequality and Welfare Spending: A Disaggregated Analysis," *World Politics*, 55(4):485–516.

——, 2006, "Social Democracy as a Development Strategy," in *Globalisation and Egalitarian Redistribution*, edited by P. Bardhan, S. Bowles, and M. Wallerstein, 148–168. Princeton: Princeton University Press.

Ray, D., 2008, *A Game-Theoretic Perspective on Coalition Formation*, New York: Oxford University Press.

Rehn, G., 1952, "The Problem of Stability: An Analysis of Some Policy Proposals," in *Wage Policy under Full Employment*, edited by R. Turvey, 30–54. London: W. Hodge.

Roberts, K. W. S., 1977, "Voting over Income Tax Schedules," *Journal of Public Economics*, 8:329–340.

Romer, T., 1975, "Individual Welfare, Majority Voting, and the Properties of a Linear Income Tax," *Journal of Public Economics*, 14:163–185.

Schumpeter, J. A., 1942, *Capitalism, Socialism and Democracy*, New York: Harper Perennial.

Swenson, P., 2002, *Capitalists Against Markets*, Oxford: Oxford University Press.

Tocqueville, A. de, 1835, 1840 [2000], *Democracy in America*, Chicago: University of Chicago Press.

Willumsen, F., 2011, "Trade and Wage Equality," working paper, ESOP, Department of Economics, University of Oslo.

3

Further Considerations on Social Protection

KEMAL DERVIS, LEIF PAGROTSKY, AND GEORGE SOROS

The following commentaries are adapted from the transcript of the Social Protection panel of the conference on which this volume is based. Karl Ove Moene and Joseph E. Stiglitz's presentations preceded a discussion between the other panelists. These commentaries were originally delivered on December 1, 2008. In an effort to preserve their tone and reflect the perspectives of that time, they have only been minimally revised for clarity in a few places.

Commentary

KEMAL DERVIS

Let me start with a general comment: I do hope that the current crisis will get us to a new equilibrium between two things that are desirable; one is competition and efficiency, and the other is robustness and security. I think as Karl Ove Moene and Joseph Stiglitz explained, the two are not always trade-offs.

I believe that if you have on one axis competition and efficiency, and on the other robustness and security, then in the beginning, by increasing competition and efficiency, you probably increase the robustness and security of a society. In other words, a society where there is very little competition and very little efficiency is unlikely to be robust in the medium term. We saw this in the old societies of Eastern Europe; they had many defects and there were political problems. There was a great deal of wage compression. There was a great deal of equality, and there was a great deal of paternalism. Indeed, even in East Germany, if you walk around today, you have some people kind of saying that in the good old days we didn't have to worry about being unemployed. But as these societies have shown in the past, when these conditions are extreme they actually reduce not only efficiency, which is already clear, but even long-term robustness and security because you invite a collapse.

On the other hand, if you go further and further in seeking efficiency as the only goal, then you reach the other side of the trade-off. You severely reduce robustness and security, and you get to a point—a point some Western societies and particularly the United States may have reached in 2007–2008—such that the search for ever-greater returns, efficiency above all, leads to forgetting about robustness and security. You actually reach a different type of collapse, which unfortunately we are living today, through the financial and economic crisis.

My son, who is an aeronautical engineer by training, once told me, "You know, we don't build airplanes to be superefficient. We have to seek always the balance between efficiency and robustness with respect to tail-end events—catastrophic events—that are unlikely but not impossible." Looking in general at human society and economies and social systems, we have to keep in mind that desirable element of robustness, and that is what both Stiglitz and Moene's presentations gave us. There are many ways of constructing robustness and security that will actually improve efficiency and growth in the long run.

Of course, one cannot look at all of this in a one-country model. The recent events have shown us how interdependent we are. There was recently an article in the *Financial Times* that said General Motors and Ford are talking to Sweden because their Saab and Volvo affiliates are in trouble—clearly what went wrong in Wall Street and in the United States has repercussions everywhere.[1] I heard about this Norwegian little town, Narvik, where people had bought subprime mortgages and half the town is bankrupt right now.

Clearly one has to look at all of these things in an international context. When we look at the literature, what I would call the excess competition model or the excess free market model has been pushed very hard since the late 1990s. There was this recurrent comparison between Europe and the United States in terms of productivity growth and employment levels. One of the key arguments for the totally free market model was that U.S. productivity was actually increasing very rapidly during that period. It was not true in the 1970s and 1980s, but during the 1990s it was quite a bit faster than European productivity, and European unemployment was significantly higher than in the United States.

A lot of the literature discussing this was microeconomic literature and looked at the microeconomic characteristics, but I think one thing that the literature forgot or didn't carefully examine is that this happened to be a period in which the United States built up a huge current account deficit and imported a huge amount of capital, and that of course helped the employment and short-term growth situation. I do not think that got a lot of attention. But we see that this macro imbalance—the big current account deficit—was one of the reasons why we landed in the situation we're in today. Having to import all this capital from abroad led to additional incentives to devise financial products and apparently extremely profitable investments, which are part of the reason we're having the financial crisis. So when comparing Europe and the United States, one cannot forget the macroeconomic dimension in that comparison.

Finally, looking more broadly at the world, there is the whole problem, which Stiglitz's paper mentions, of a possible race to the bottom. Do globalization and international competition lead to limits as to what kind of social welfare model and social protection model you can have in one particular country? Since Moene reminded us of Rosa Luxemborg, we can also remember that in the old days some said you cannot have socialism in just one country. I think in this debate, I will take a centrist position again. I do believe that there is a danger of a race to the bottom in terms of tax rates, tax shelters, environmental standards, all kinds of things that attract capital to the least costly location. Therefore, to build strong social protection systems, one should worry about the international dimensions. Even in the Scandinavian countries, this is part of the debate.

On the other hand, one should not go too far in that direction either because the general environment in which you live, the quality of life, the quality of the air you breathe, the quality of the traffic, are also all attractions. To take an extreme example, if a society does not spend much on protection of citizens, if there is a very high crime rate because of high unemployment, drugs, lack of police, and so on, then clearly the tax rate in that society may be low and in that sense you would think that enterprises would want to migrate to that society. On the other hand, if there is no security in the streets, then that is a disincentive. When one looks at this tax competition, one also has to remember that the quality of life is another important element of attracting capital and entrepreneurship. In fact, here again you could have a positive correlation between the degree of social protection or environmental protection that a society gives and the amount of capital or skilled labor that it attracts.

It is a complex topic but I think there are these two dimensions, which at times are complementary and at times may be competitive. Finally, coming from the UN Development Programme, I would like to stress that in this globalized world, there is also a dimension of social protection that has to reach across borders and particularly to the developing countries. The developing countries again and again have been hit by events beyond their control and some of the poorest people suffer the most because of these events. Think back to the late 1970s to early 1980s, when the United States finally decided to reduce its inflation rate. Paul Volker's extremely high interest rates and anti-inflation policies were very successful in the United States and got the inflation down, although at the cost of a fairly severe recession. There had been countries that faced negative real interest rates in capital markets, and all of a sudden they had to face 6 to 8 percent real interest rates. The shift in monetary policy in the United States created huge problems for Latin American countries, for developing countries that had one decade of no growth because of the adjustment to the debt overhang and the debt problems they faced. This is one example of how policy in one country affects everyone else.

In 2008, we have another example of this. The financial and economic crisis had a huge impact on the developing countries. It was not caused by the developing countries and yet there were hundreds of millions of people whose wages fell as employment fell, through no fault of their own, or of their own countries', but because of policies in richer countries.

Climate is another essential subject to address. We are already seeing climate refugees in some countries. If climate change is not seriously dealt with over the next years and decades, we will have very substantial disruptions of people in the most vulnerable parts of the world. Again, policies—in this case climate policies—in the rich and most powerful countries have a huge impact on the poor countries.

When we talk of social protection and of human protection, it is important to remember how the world is now integrated. Clearly sovereign states face their own electorates and much of this protection policy has to be focused on citizens; that will not change for a long time. Nonetheless, given this interaction in the world economy, for moral and ethical reasons but also in the end for security reasons, there is need for solidarity. Disruption and poverty and unfairness in the world create security problems. Some of these protection policies have to be extended beyond the borders of the rich countries to the poorest countries—for the sake of poor countries' citizens but also for the sake of citizens in rich countries.

Another point is that there are many countries in the developing world where more redistributive policies are necessary. I have two points here I want to make that I think go a little bit against what Moene said.

One is that, in India for example, there is no way that through taxation you can get rid of poverty, even the extreme poverty of two dollars a day. The population living below two dollars per day in India is more than 600 million.[2] There is no way that you can tax rich Indians and thereby get rid of that kind of poverty. You have to do it through growth, and there are many other parts of the world where that is the case.

Also, two dollars a day is very poor, but frankly three dollars a day is also very poor. Depending on where you draw the poverty line, things get even more difficult.

The second point is that this crisis was exported to developing countries from the rich center. I do believe there is both an ethical and a political argument that the rich center has to act. If it does not act and hundreds of millions of people lose their jobs in developing countries, it is going to lead to a very nasty political reaction. For those reasons, the responsibility lies squarely with the rich countries. Of course, the policies in developing countries can help, but reacting to the crisis only with policies in the developing countries will not work.

Commentary

LEIF PAGROTSKY

When I use the word globalization, just like I know that Joseph Stiglitz does, I also include effects of technological change. I believe that when we talk about globalization, the main driving force behind the things that actually happen are changes in technology, not changes in tariffs or other similar factors. But they are lumped together under the word globalization, which is the threat that looms over us. So when I use the word globalization, it's with this slightly different connotation.

I think that Stiglitz is a bit too negative when he talks about globalization. He only talks about bad things: risks, race to the bottom, jobs being shipped away or the fear of jobs being moved, and eroded labor standards and all kinds of things. I think this reflects the view from the United States. People here have an impression of the world as a threat. But the world is bigger than the United States. If this is the drama in the United States, there may be other dramas going on elsewhere.

I think globalization offers not only risks and dangers but also opportunities. It offers opportunities for countries with entirely different starting points, such as China or Brazil. If we talk about globalization, we must do it in a globalized way, meaning that we look at its effects all over the world.

We should look not only at very different countries but also other advanced countries like the Nordic states that were discussed in this chapter. I realize I was invited here because I represent a Nordic country, Sweden, with our very different experience, so I will look a bit further at what globalization can do to another kind of advanced industrialized country that is not the United States. The image of globalization here in the United States does not have to be its universal image.

In the past decade, my country, like the other Nordic countries, was more exposed to globalization than the United States. We not only encountered new competition from countries like China and India, we also had very close neighbors entering the world economy—close neighbors with high education but with extremely low wages. Poland and the Baltic republics are our closest neighbors. Tallinn, the capital of Estonia, is closer to Stockholm than Helsinki, Oslo, or Copenhagen. Their wages were about one-tenth of our wages, and they had an education standard that was very high. It is unique for very poor countries to be that well-educated. They were introduced into the European Union with no tariffs and fully integrated in our single market. So I argue that we were more exposed to the threats and risks of globalization than the United States, and still this past decade, our blue-collar workers' jobs were not exported—not yet at least.

In fact, over the past ten years, the number of blue-collar jobs increased rather substantially. Not only that, blue-collar workers' real wages increased more than at any time since the 1960s. Productivity increased more than in the United States during this period. The United States is considered to be the strongest, the most flexible, and the most productivity-driven economy on the planet, at least among the developed countries, but our companies reported faster productivity growth than the United States. All this was done with stable prices and with an enormous current account surplus.

If you have this enormous diversity in development, it cannot be attributed to one common, external factor called globalization. There must be something different here. And as Stiglitz said, and now I must start agreeing, it has to do with politics and policies. This does not have to do with invisible hands or laws of God or something else. It is policy-driven and man-made.

Globalization means change. Faster globalization means more rapid change. The better you are at dealing with change, the more flexible you are, and the more likely you are to be a winner in globalization. I argue here, in line with what Karl Ove Moene explains in more detail, that the Nordic countries are more flexible than the United States, most countries in Europe, and other places, in spite of what we are doing that goes in the opposite direction to what we learn in the textbooks.

In fact, we are more flexible not in spite of going against the textbooks but because we do. The first basis of our strategy is transferring cash transfers to individuals. Transfers mean that when economies and the structure of the economy change, and when individuals are affected by change, then the entire society shares the burden of adjustment through supporting the livelihoods of those affected. This means that resistance to change is still there but to a much lesser extent than elsewhere. This is a very important side effect. If you have generous and effective unemployment insurance, you do not need to insure or bail out the banks. You do not need to use the British method of insuring the mortgages, because if people who are unemployed can maintain their incomes, they can continue to service their debt to their local banks, so that they don't have to go bust. That is a very important but overlooked consequence of having strong unemployment insurance. You can even argue that the more important effect of unemployment insurance is that it protects the society and its banks against some of the banking crises that affect other countries.

The second basis of our greater flexibility is education. Knowledge is the currency of the globalized economy. Periods of unemployment can be used for generous and ambitious education and training programs, not six weeks learning the new cash register at the local grocery but perhaps a three-year university education or a two-year education to augment what you already have, so that you can use it somewhere else. That is extremely important but also, we must remember, extremely expensive. These things do not come for free, but economists often talk about the costs of high taxes, the cost to productivity, to incentives, to growth, and they overlook the revenues of what the taxes are used for. If taxes are used for things that promote growth, this can outweigh the negative effects of higher taxes. Now I am talking about economic effects. As a politician, I must also realize that taxes have some effects on voter behavior, so I have to be a little bit cautious there.

A third basis of our flexibility, apart from cash transfers and education, is that we have done away with the old-fashioned corporate-based security and benefit systems that exist in the United States and elsewhere, for instance in Germany and France. These corporate-based systems lock up labor in individual firms. People cannot move easily between firms, and it promotes rigidity, not flexibility. Look at General Motors now: They have expenses for retired workers who worked for them from the 1950s to the 1980s that now cost, I think, $10,000 per car. This is old-fashioned. This is against every economic interest there is. We don't have it in Sweden, and it's a main competitive asset for us.

The result of what I'm saying is that the general attitude in the Nordic countries to globalization is very positive. The general attitude in the United States is very negative. The Pew Institute in Washington, D.C., which makes surveys about attitudes to globalization, ranked the United States at the bottom together with Egypt when it comes to attitudes about globalization. No other country is more negative to globalization than the United States and Egypt. At the top of the scale you'll find Sweden and China. The other Nordic countries are somewhere around there as well. I think it is obvious that these attitudes toward globalization are man-made. This is not caused by God, religion, or tradition; this is a result of our policies.

So my conclusion about the theme of this volume—protection without protectionism—is that without protection, you will have protectionism.

When it comes to identifying bubbles, national accounts and current accounts are good enough to see some of the risks. If you have countries like Iceland, Estonia, Latvia, or Argentina that accumulate 15 to 20 percent of GDP in current account deficits year after year, you don't need new national accounts to understand that they would run into problems; but the United States is just so different, because they can print dollars and the rest of the world will accept them. That is a truly unique gift.

I do not follow the line that a crisis every now and then is a price worth paying for financial innovation. On the contrary. A few years ago when I was minister for trade, I actually went to Parliament with a bill proposing that in our development assistance, we should give priority to improved banking supervision in developing countries, which is aimed at the elevation of standards of living in developing countries over the long term. Just as it is important to raise growth levels, it is important to prevent recurrent falls in GDP due to financial crises every now and then. Learning from the Asian crisis, I proposed that we should allocate more of our development assistance to banking supervision. Maybe we should have done that for the United States.

I do not agree with the idea that this is a price worth paying, because if you fall back like this once every decade, it does not matter how much you grow the nine years in between. The long-term rise in prosperity that you need will not happen. We focus too little on these risks. The financial risk and bubbles may now be the main risks, and the financial sector is now the main source of instability in the past decades, more than other markets, and more than other external shocks that I have heard of. The financial market is the engine for instability. It is not, as Greenspan used to say, that they are so good at controlling risks because they have such talented mathematicians employed that we could all trust them better than any low-paid bureaucrat. I do not agree with him. In fact, I think the opposite.

Commentary

GEORGE SOROS

The commentaries in this section are about the relationship between social protection and globalization. They offer two rather different perspectives. One is from the Nordic countries arguing that the welfare state is compatible with globalization and flourishes in globalization. The other view from Joseph Stiglitz is that while globalization has increased the need for social protection, it has also decreased the capacity of governments to respond, so globalization interferes with social protection.

I definitely side with Stiglitz, and I'm much more radical than he is, which is not an easy thing to be. First of all, I think we have to clarify what we mean by globalization. To me, globalization means the globalization of financial markets, and I consider that to be a market fundamentalist project. I date the globalization of financial markets to 1980. When Ronald Reagan was elected president and Margaret Thatcher was prime minister in England, market fundamentalism became the dominant creed. I would argue that market fundamentalism is responsible for the enormous financial crisis and economic crisis that we are currently in. This crisis had its origin in the financial markets, but it is now enveloping what you might call the real economy. I think this is a serious crisis. In fact, one could argue that it's more serious than the crisis that we lived through in the 1930s. I base this on a statistic that was brought to my attention today that says that credit, as a percentage of GNP, was 265 percent at its peak in 1929, and it was 365 percent at its peak in the current crisis. So the magnitude of the problem is actually greater today than it was in the 1930s.

I hope we will be able to deal with this crisis better because maybe we understand things better. But it is still a very serious problem, and I attribute it to this belief that financial markets should be given free reign because they can correct their own excesses. That belief is false, and it is responsible for three things: globalization, deregulation, and financial innovation. Those three factors are the factors that are at work in the current financial crisis.

I have put forward a different view of financial markets in which I claim that financial markets don't necessarily tend toward equilibrium. The prevailing view and the basis for all the financial engineering that has become so pervasive is that financial markets tend toward equilibrium, that deviations are random and caused by external factors—shocks that are so severe that markets have difficulty adjusting to them. Now, that view has to be false because the events of the last two years[3] demonstrate that the crisis did not originate outside, from some external exogenous force. It was generated by the market itself.

My theory differs fundamentally in two important respects. One, I claim that financial markets never give an accurate picture of the so-called fundamentals that market prices are supposed to reflect. It is always biased or distorted in some way. And secondly, I claim that the prevailing bias or distortion can on occasion and in special ways actually affect the fundamentals that market prices are supposed to reflect. So there's a two-way connection. Markets are not a passive reflection of fundamentals but are connected with the fundamentals in a two-way feedback mechanism, which I call reflexivity. They both affect and reflect. Because the prevailing view is always biased, it is possible for a deviation to be self-reinforcing, or at least initially self-reinforcing, until the bias becomes so pronounced that it becomes unsustainable, leading to a reversal. That creates a process of initially self-reinforcing, then reversing, boom and bust. Or the currently fashionable word, bubbles.

Now let me focus particularly on globalization, because the important feature of globalized financial markets is that they don't provide a level playing field. There is an asymmetry between the position of the developed world and what I call the periphery countries. This is reflected in the fact that the system is governed by institutions that are controlled by the countries of the developed world. If you look at the IMF, the United States has veto rights. The three Benelux countries—Belgium, the Netherlands, and Luxembourg—have as much voting rights as China. Because this belief that markets are self-equilibrating is false, since it has become the dominant creed, we have had a number of financial crises. Each time, the authorities intervened. It was not the markets that corrected their excesses; it was the authorities who took the appropriate measures to prevent the system from collapsing. When the system was endangered, consideration of moral hazard or market discipline went out of the window. And rightly so. I think we actually have to make every effort to protect the system, not to repeat the mistake of the 1930s, in which the banking system effectively broke down.

In the past, we have had a number of financial crises. If the crisis occurs in the periphery countries, then the Washington consensus prevails and you impose market discipline. But when it threatens the center, then you intervene and you merge away the failing institution; you provide fiscal stimulus, monetary stimulus, so effectively the center remains unscathed.

That has had an interesting effect of allowing the country at the center, the United States, to suck up the savings of the rest of the world. Over the last 25 years we have been living with an ever-increasing current account deficit, which reached nearly 7 percent of the GNP at its peak in the first quarter of 2006. That allowed us to consume more than we produced. Very beneficial. We liked it. So did China, because they and the other Asian tigers were happy to produce more. So the system worked very well and it was of great benefit to the United States.

I had the pleasure of dining with Alan Greenspan a few months ago. I asked him to read my book and discuss it and we agreed to disagree, because he said that the benefits of financial innovation in terms of increased efficiency are so great, that having occasional breakdowns where you have to pick up the pieces is a relatively small price to pay. At the time we had dinner, before the full impact of the financial crisis was apparent, he had actually some good grounds to justify this belief because we have had 25 years of almost uninterrupted economic prosperity and certainly a growing GDP, although we have also had ever-increasing differences in income. It depends on how you measure economic prosperity. If you take the aggregate amount, we certainly prospered. If you take the average income, it's more questionable. But nevertheless, it was pretty good.

Today that view is no longer valid. Greenspan, himself previously a serious analyst, admitted as much before Congress. He said there was some flaw there. So this is where we are now: We have this flaw that the markets are prone to create bubbles and that the system is unfair, asymmetric, and favors the center to the detriment of the periphery.

Because of this flaw, the international financial institutions need a new mission to protect the periphery against the financial storm that has originated at the center. This is a new task. Whether the authorities are going to be equal to that task will determine whether the system actually survives or not. Because if they are not, I don't think the system can actually be sustained. This is a tremendous challenge. I hope that we will be equal to it.

With my theory, I anticipated this crisis, but I did not anticipate that the system would actually melt down. That is something else that you have to recognize, that with the bankruptcy of Lehmann Brothers, it was a new ball game. It happened September 15, 2008. Actually the system melted down and went into cardiac arrest. The authorities in the developed world realized that they have to pull out all stops, and they effectively announced and have reiterated the position that no institution that is of systemic importance will be allowed to fail.

Now, the countries at the periphery are not in a position to give a similar assurance. The result is that the markets have responded with a new flight of capital from the periphery to the center. Brazil, for instance, which was until that moment a beneficiary of globalization and was doing particularly well, suddenly had a crash: Their currency dropped 40 percent, the stock market dropped, and the banking system is suddenly in danger. Of course, it happened to coincide with the crisis in Iceland, which is a Nordic country. Hungary was immediately in trouble as well.

So you have a problem with the banking system: how to protect the banks of the periphery countries. More importantly the countries at the periphery are not in a position to engage in countercyclical policies, because they cannot finance their fiscal deficits. Finding a way to enable them to engage in countercyclical policies is essential for their benefit but also essential for the global economy because the U.S. consumer, who had been the motor of the global economy, has been knocked out by the housing crisis and cannot continue to be the motor. Therefore you have to have some domestic growth in other countries. China has actually announced a very serious program. Brazil has also announced a program. Still, it is very hard to do it on a sufficiently large scale unless there is a way to finance that fiscal deficit.

Finally it is important to reform regulation. My main conclusion is that since markets are prone to produce bubbles, it becomes the objective of regulators to prevent bubbles from growing too big. That is a responsibility that they have expressly rejected, and they now need to accept it. Now they have very good reasons for objecting to it. The main reason is that it's very difficult to identify a bubble. Regulators are no better than markets in predicting the future. In fact they are, generally speaking, worse than markets. So how can they deal with it?

The main lesson is that it is not enough to control the money supply. You have also got to control credit availability—the amount of leverage that market participants are allowed to use. That used to be the case, but it was largely abandoned and needs to be reintroduced. This means minimum margin requirements and minimum capital requirements. Those requirements need to be varied. There should not be fixed requirements for all, but the rules should allow for the fact that markets have moods. You have to counterbalance those moods. If markets are euphoric, you have to tighten credit and vice versa. That is where the problem of judgment comes in. The regulators are bound to be wrong, but they get feedback from the market. If they move a little bit and it is not enough, then they can move a little more, or if they moved too much, then they can reverse it. The feedback becomes a cat and mouse game. That cat and mouse game is actually being played and has been played. The greatest artist has been Alan Greenspan himself with his Delphic utterances, except that he did not admit that he was manipulating the markets; he kept that as a state secret.

We need more regulation. At the same time, I hope that we do not go back to the very tight regulations that we had after the 1930s. While markets are imperfect, regulators are even more imperfect, because they are bureaucratic and subject to political interferences. You want to rely on the market to the greatest possible extent.

Notes

1. Saab Automobile AB later declared bankruptcy in December 2011.

2. Updated for 2011 based on Oxford Poverty and Human Development Initiative Country Briefing: India, available at www.ophi.org.uk/wp-content/uploads/India.pdf?cda6c1.

3. At the time of publication, the financial crisis and the economic malaise that followed were in their fifth year.

2

Protection from Violence

Introduction

At the heart of a global social covenant is a commitment by political authorities at all levels—global, national, regional, and local—to protect individual human beings from life-threatening harms. The first part of this book focused on social protection; this part is about protecting people from violence—the domain we usually describe as security even though, as these chapters stress, protection from violence is difficult to disentangle from protection from other kinds of risks.

Four themes run through this part of the book. The first theme is the changing nature of the sources of insecurity. In the past, the most important external security threat was considered to be an attack by a foreign state. That threat has all but disappeared since the end of the Cold War. Now the sources of insecurity are usually identified as a range of global risks. Some have to do with potential or actual violence: terrorism, war and counter insurgency, ethnic cleansing, the spread of weapons of mass destruction, massive human rights violence, and organized crime. Others have to do with natural disasters: famines, pandemics, cyber warfare, and even financial crises. Many of these sources of insecurity have always been around; they have just become visible in the aftermath of the Cold War. Because an East–West conflict seemed like the worst possible eventuality, other sources of insecurity were accorded a low priority.

Some sources of insecurity are new or have new features that are the consequence of growing interconnectedness, such as new forms of communication that speed up mobilization and that facilitate long-distance violence, or weak states that are the legacy of the collapse of dictatorships, or the drying up of superpower aid to clients and of neo-liberal economic strategies.

A second theme is the interrelatedness of different types of global risk. A transformation in the way we conceive and implement security is a precondition for addressing other global challenges and vice versa. Take the global economic crisis, for example. At present our security capabilities consist largely of conventional military forces designed to meet the threat of a foreign attack. High levels of military spending primarily by the United States, which accounts for half of all global military spending, are an important explanation for the huge public deficit and consequently for external imbalances. Yet military forces do not make us more secure. On the contrary, the use of military force in Iraq and Afghanistan greatly exacerbated levels of violence in those countries and served as recruiting grounds for extremist Islamist terrorists. At the same time, the consequences of economic crisis—high levels of joblessness, increased migration, climatic pressures, severe global inequalities, rapid urbanization, and weak rule of law—all can contribute to the spread of radical ideologies, the growth of criminality, and the growing privatization of violence.

A particular concern in these chapters is the blurring of criminal and political violence. Much contemporary violence inflicted in the name of a political cause is criminal in the sense that it violates international law, including the laws of war and human rights law. Organized crime, traced by Misha Glenny, has flourished in zones of generalized insecurity both because it offers a way of financing political violence and because the lawlessness associated with political violence provides a favorable environment for organized crime. In many such zones, the state monopoly of organized violence has been eroded, and it is often difficult to distinguish warlords, private militia, and criminal gangs from legitimate forces. Soaring crime rates are often associated with stagnant or negative rates of growth, as desperate people seek alternative ways of surviving.

A third theme is the interconnectedness of global risks. It is no longer possible to maintain domestic security merely through the protection of borders, despite the fact that border security has become more and more elaborate. Insecurity travels through refugees and displaced persons; through the spread of ideologies that arise out of resentment and fear in the inner cities of the industrial world and not just in the more insecure part of the world; and through the long-distance projection of violence through the new techniques ranging from suicide bombers to advanced drones. A critical factor alluded to by all the authors in this section is the dramatic improvement in communication. On the one hand, this makes it possible for the entrepreneurs of violence to link up with each other and mobilize support through publicizing what they do via Web sites, videos, and even radio. On the other hand, it has led to an increased human rights consciousness, whereby people in advanced countries are no longer willing to stand by while they observe atrocities inflicted in faraway places.

Finally, the fourth theme has to do with the need for a new approach to security. Such an approach has to comprise three elements:

First of all it is a cooperative or comprehensive approach to security. It is comprehensive both in the sense of covering a broad range of risks and in the sense of being globally shared. Mary Kaldor uses the term "human security" to refer to the shift from national, that is, state-based security, to the security of individual human beings and the communities in which they live. Such a comprehensive approach is law-based rather than war-based. It is about extending the kind of security that is supposed to operate in well-ordered societies to the whole world; it involves a blurring of the internal and the external.

Second, such security requires a new set of institutions. Although nation-states are primarily responsible for human security within their borders, external institutions are required as agencies of last resort when states themselves are the source of insecurity or when states lack the necessary capabilities. Global institutions that guarantee legal arrangements and that watch over the behavior of states are needed; so are local security providers—cities, for example—that are capable of mobilizing the trust needed to maintain security.

Third, there needs to be a transformation of security capabilities. John Ikenberry writes about a protective infrastructure that would be the equivalent of global social services. Part of that infrastructure is the capabilities required to cope with security in a classic sense. Such capabilities would need to include a combination of military and civilians as global emergency services. The military would be required for very violent situations but they would operate quite differently—more like police than military—aiming to tamp down violence and to protect civilians rather than to defeat enemies. Kaldor spells out the kind of principles that would guide their use.

4

Global Security Cooperation in the Twenty-First Century*

G. JOHN IKENBERRY

In the twenty-first century, the United States confronts a complex array of security challenges—diffuse, shifting, and uncertain. This is good news and bad news. The good news is that the old sources of violence and insecurity that plagued the last century—great power war and a superpower nuclear arms race—have become less salient. We live in the longest era of great power peace. The United States is the leading global power. China is rising, but the United States is still unchallenged by a coalition of balancing states or by a superpower wielding a rival geopolitical ideology. Most of the great powers are democracies and are tied to the United States in alliances. State power is ultimately based on sustained economic growth, and no major state today can modernize without integrating into the globalized capitalist system. What made the fascist and communist threats of the twentieth century so profound was not only the danger of arms races and territorial aggression but that these great power challengers embodied rival political and economic systems that could generate growth, attract global allies, and create counterbalancing geopolitical blocs. Measured in terms of the security threats of the past, the United States lives in an extraordinarily benign security environment.

*This essay adapts and builds on Ikenberry (2008), Ikenberry (2011), and the Final Report of the Princeton Project on National Security (Ikenberry and Slaughter 2006).

The bad news is that new and decentralized threats lurk around the world. No singular "enemy" looms on the horizon. Instead, there is a sprawling array of diffuse threats to international peace and security, including nuclear proliferation, weapons of mass destruction (WMDs), terrorism, global warming, health pandemics, energy and food scarcity, and the weakening and collapse of political order in states and regions around the world. In effect, the sources of violence and insecurity have shifted and diffused. There is a greater variety and more widely dispersed array of threats to worry about. Nuclear proliferation is a danger driven by insecurity, nationalism, and geopolitical competition, but many of the new dangers, such as health pandemics and transnational terrorist violence, stem from the weakness of states rather than from their strength. Technologies of violence are evolving, providing opportunities for weak states or nonstate groups to threaten others at a greater distance. Threats can also interact in new and complex ways. Natural disasters, perhaps caused by long-term global environmental shifts, can trigger or exacerbate food and energy crises, which in turn can undermine or destabilize weak states, radiating instability and insecurity worldwide.

In the background, not only are the sources of violence and insecurity changing but so too are our societal and international understandings of what it means to be safe and secure. Homeland security and the physical safety of citizens are the traditional notions, yet over the last century, states have assumed greater and greater responsibility for protecting not just the lives and property of citizens but also for maintaining social and economic standards and upholding human rights. The postwar human rights revolution and the more recent emergence of norms such as "responsibility to protect" have expanded our notions of what it means to be free of violence. Dignity, minimal living standards, protection again state oppression—these are part of the expanding global political aspirations for peace and security.[1]

If the world of the twenty-first century were a town, the security threats faced by its leading citizens would not be organized crime or a violent assault by a radical mob on city hall. It would be a breakdown of law enforcement and social services in the face of constantly changing and ultimately uncertain vagaries of criminality, nature, and circumstance. The neighborhoods where the leading citizens live can only be made safe if the security and well-being of the beaten-down and troubled neighborhoods are also improved. No neighborhood can be left behind. At the same time, the town will need to build new capacities for social and economic protection. People and groups will need to cooperate in new and far-reaching ways.

This chapter argues that, confronted with a new and changing security environment, the overriding task of U.S. foreign policy in the years ahead is to rebuild and to expand the authority and capacities of the international community to engage in multi faceted collective action—ongoing tasks that include arms control, state building, economic assistance, conflict prevention, WMD safeguarding, disaster relief, and technology sharing. The United States will also need to lead in rebuilding its own authority to operate in these complex and extended forms of security cooperation. Indeed, the greatest threat to U.S. national security today is not a specific threat but the erosion of the institutional foundations of the global order that it commanded for half a century and through which it has pursued its interests and national security. In the recent past, America's leadership position and authority within the global system has been in serious crisis, and this has put U.S. national security at risk. The United States needs to restore its role as a global security provider and rebuild the global institutions and partnerships upon which this leadership position rests. It is only from this position of leadership that the United States can expand global capacities to protect and to secure the planet, and by so doing protect and secure itself.

The United States needs to lead in the re-creation of the global architecture of governance, rebuilding its leadership position and the institutional frameworks through which it pursues its interests and cooperates with others to provide security. Above all, it needs to create resources and capacities for the collective confrontation of a wide array of dangers and challenges. That is, the United States needs a grand strategy of "liberal order building"—creating shared capacities to respond to a wide variety of contingencies. In the twenty-first century threat environment, a premium will be placed on mechanisms for collective action and sustained commitments to an expanding agenda of security-related problem-solving.

In what follows, I offer three arguments. First, I look at the changing character of America's security environment. I suggest that the fundamental driver of change is a profound deepening of "security interdependence." Second, I look at the various forms of security cooperation that are needed in this complex environment of shifting, diffuse, and uncertain threats. I suggest that the most important way to pursue security in this environment is to focus on the building of cooperative security institutions. Rather than direct attention to one threat or one enemy, the United States needs to pursue a "milieu-oriented" security strategy. Finally, I look at the underlying principles and norms of a twenty-first century global security system. Notions of "national" security will need to yield to notions of "comprehensive" and "cooperative" security. Importantly, the United States will need to lead the way in bringing other states into a global system of security cooperation that fashions bargains and institutions to a new reality with both great promise and great peril.

A Changing Security Environment

The challenge of the modern state to protect its citizenry from foreign threats has changed over time because its "security environment" has constantly changed. The threat of great power conflict in the nineteenth century gave way to a new twentieth-century reality of advanced industrial world war (the so-called age of "total war"), which in turn gave way to the existential threat of nuclear mass destruction. The threats to national states shifted over the centuries with changes in the technologies of violence, the character of states, and the distributions of power. Sometimes threats would evolve slowly but at various moments, such as in the mid-twentieth century in the wake of the nuclear revolution, when states found themselves in radically transformed security environments. Along the way, the political meaning of "security" has also been changing. If the security challenge in the nineteenth century was "military defense," during the Cold War it had become "national security." In the twenty-first century, some observers talk about "human security" and other more extended and comprehensive notions that move the state's challenge from the protection against physical violence to the protection against a wider array of social and political degradations.

What is the threat environment in which the United States finds itself? In contrast to earlier eras, there is no single enemy or source of violence and of insecurity that frames America's choices. The United States and the wider world face a diffuse array of threats and of challenges. Global warming, health pandemics, nuclear proliferation, jihadist terrorism, energy scarcity, and other dangers loom on the horizon. Any of these threats could endanger American lives and way of life either directly or indirectly by destabilizing the global system upon which American security and prosperity depend. Pandemics and global warming are not threats wielded by human hands, but their consequences could be equally devastating. Highly infectious disease has the potential to kill millions of people. Global warming threatens to trigger waves of environmental migration, food shortages, and further destabilize weak and poor states around the world. The world is also on the cusp of a new round of nuclear proliferation, putting mankind's deadliest weapons in the hands of unstable and hostile states. Terrorist networks offer a new specter of nonstate transnational violence. The point is that none of these threats is, in itself, so singularly preeminent that it deserves to be the centerpiece of U.S. national security in the way that antifascism and anticommunism did in an earlier era.[2]

What is more, these various threats are interconnected, and it is the possibility of their interactive effects that multiplies the dangers. This point is stressed by Thomas Homer-Dixon:

> It's the convergence of stresses that's especially treacherous and makes synchronous failure a possibility as never before. In coming years, our societies won't face one or two major challenges at once, as usually happened in the past. Instead, they'll face an alarming variety of problems—likely including oil shortages, climate change, economic instability, and mega-terrorism—all at the same time (2006:16–17).

The danger is that several of these threats will materialize at the same time and interact to generate greater violence and instability.

> What happens, for example, if together or in quick succession the world has to deal with a sudden shift in climate that sharply cuts food production in Europe and Asia, a severe oil price increase that sends economies tumbling around the world, and a string of major terrorist attacks on several Western capital cities (Homer-Dixon 2006:16–17)?

The global order itself, as well as the foundations of U.S. national security, would be put at risk.

We can add to these worries the rise of China and more generally the rise of Asia. It is worth recalling that it was China that preoccupied the U.S. national security community in the years before the September 11 terrorist attacks. China's rapid economic growth and active regional diplomacy are already transforming East Asia, and Beijing's geopolitical influence is growing. The United States has no experience managing a relationship with a country that is potentially its principal economic and security rival. It is unclear, and probably unknowable, how China's intentions and ambitions will evolve as it becomes more powerful. We do know, however, that the rise and decline of great powers—and the problem of "power transitions"—can trigger conflict, security competition, and war. The point here is that, in the long run, the way that China rises up in the world could have a more profound impact on U.S. national security than incremental shifts up or down in the fortunes of international terrorist groups.

The larger point is—and it is a critical assumption here—that today the United States confronts an unusually diverse and diffuse array of threats and challenges. When we try to imagine what the premier threats to the United States will be in 2015 or 2020, it is not easy to say with any confidence what they will be. Moreover, even if we could identify a preeminent threat around which all others turn, it is very likely it will be complex and inter-linked with lots of other international moving parts. Global pandemics are connected to failed states, homeland security, international public health capacities, and other issues. Global warming is related to food supplies, water shortages, and the prospects for economic development and politi-cal stability in poor parts of the world. Terrorism is related to the Middle East peace process, economic and political development, non proliferation, intelligence cooperation, and European social and immigration policy, among others. The rise of China is related to alliance cooperation, energy security, democracy promotion, the World Trade Organization (WTO), management of the world economy, and so on.

It is the diffuse and uncertain character of threats that drives the need for new forms of global governance and cooperative security. In a world of mul-tiple threats and uncertainty about their relative significance in the decades to come, it is useful to think about security protection as an "investment" problem. Where do you invest your resources, build capacities, and take action so as to maximize your ability to be positioned to confront tomorrow's unknowns? National security is about discerning threats and setting priori-ties, but it is also about diversifying risks and avoiding surprises.

The Shifting Sources of Violence and Insecurity

If America's security threats and challenges are diffuse, shifting, and uncer-tain, it is because the underlying sources of violence and of insecurity are themselves shifting. We can identify four major shifts or transformations in the underlying character of the security problems that the United States and other countries face.

The first is the most basic: the intensification of "security interdepen-dence." This notion is really a measure of how much a state's national secu-rity depends on policies of other actors.[3] A security-independent country is capable of achieving an acceptable level of security through its own actions. Others can threaten it, but the means for coping with these threats are within its own national hands. This means that the military intentions and capacities of other states are irrelevant to a state's security. This is true either because the potential military threats are too remote and too far removed to matter, or because, if a foreign power is capable of launching war against the state, that state has the capability to resist the aggression. In a world of security independence, the measure of security is relatively simple. It is as Ian Bellamy characterizes it: "Security itself is a relative freedom from war, coupled with a relatively high expectation that defeat will not be a consequence of any war that should occur" (Buzan 1991:16). This is an old and traditional notion of security. It is also one that the United States, separated from the other great powers by vast oceans, has embraced for much of its history. The Reagan-era vision of missile defense reflected an aspiration to reestablish security independence. To be able to shoot down any incoming missile assault is to regain the state's ability to protect itself, regardless of the policies and intentions of others.

Security interdependence is the opposite circumstance. The state's security depends on the policy and choices of other actors. Security is established by convincing other actors not to attack. During the Cold War, the United States and the Soviet Union were in a situation of intense security interdependence. Each had nuclear weapons that could destroy the other. It was the logic of deterrence that established the restraints on policy. Each state knew that to launch a nuclear strike on the other would be followed by massive and assured retaliation. There are actually two aspects to security interdependence. One is that states cannot protect themselves or achieve national security without the help of other states. There is no "solution" to the security problem without active cooperation, even if that cooperation is based on mutual deterrence. The other aspect of security interdependence is the security dilemmas. That is, in attempting to defend itself, a state can take steps that make other states more insecure, triggering responses that make the original state less secure. In his classic statement of the security dilemmas, John Herz noted that

> Striving to attain security from such attack, they are driven to acquire more and more power in order to escape the impact of the power of others. This, in turn, renders the others more insecure and compels them to prepare for the worst . . . and a vicious circle of security and power accumulation is one (1950:157).

In seeking protection, states risk generating insecurity in others that creates spirals of action and reaction that leave both states worse off.

What this means is, as Zbigniew Brzezinski argues, "[t]he traditional link between national sovereignty and national security has been severed" (2004:13). When states are in a situation of security interdependence, they cannot go it alone. They must negotiate and cooperate with other states and seek mutual restraints and protections. During the Cold War, security interdependence manifested itself primarily in the existential threats of superpower nuclear arms competition. In the current era, it is the diffusion of threats away from the great powers and away from states that make security interdependence more profound and the solutions to it increasingly complicated and politically challenging.

The second major shift in America's security environment is the privatization of war. Increasingly, nonstate conflict groups are the wielders of violence. Insurgents, terrorist groups, and breakaway factions are the actors that threaten to gain access to technologies of violence and project it near and far. In previous eras, it was hostile great powers and territorial aggression by revisionist states that threatened the United States. Hostile and revisionist states have not disappeared completely, but now nonstate terrorist groups pose growing threats. This is a transformation in the ways and means of collective violence in international politics that is driven by technology and by the political structure of the system itself. The effect of this transformation is to render more problematic old norms of sovereignty and the use of force. It raises troubling new questions about the relationship between domestic politics and international relations and raises parts of the world that previously could be ignored to greater national security significance. It also creates new functional challenges that inevitably will influence patterns of security cooperation.

This new development might be called the rise of "informal violence." In the past, only states—primarily powerful states—were able to gain access to violence capabilities that could threaten other societies. Now we can look out into the future and see the day when small groups or transnational gangs of individuals might be able to acquire weapons of mass destruction. The technologies and knowledge almost inevitably will diffuse outward. Determined groups of extremists will increasingly be in a position to obtain a WMD.

There are actually two shifts at work here. One is the rise of nonstate transnational actors as wielders of violence. Robert Keohane argues,

Effective wielding of large-scale violence by nonstate actors reflects new patterns of asymmetrical interdependence, and calls into question some of our assumptions about geographical space as a barrier. . . . Geographical space, which has been seen as a natural *barrier* and a locus for human barriers, now must be seen as a *carrier* as well. (2011:78–80)

The other is the empowerment of these groups with increasingly lethal violence technologies. Fewer and fewer numbers of people are needed to project more and more violence across longer distances. Robert Wright (2007) has called this the "growing lethality of hatred." The actual number of individuals in the world who are willing to inflict harm on others may not be growing. What is growing is the capability. In the past, groups that were willing to use violence to express their hatred were limited in the damage they could cause. In the future, this limitation may well drop away.

A third shift follows from the previous ones. As security interdependence grows, and as conflict groups become more disaggregated, dispersed, and lethal, there is an inevitable transformation in the security implications of geography and political space. Put simply, there are more people in more places around the globe who can matter to American security. So what these people do and how they live matter in ways that, in earlier eras, were irrelevant to national security. The ability of states in all parts of the world to maintain the rule of law, to uphold international commitments, and to engage in monitoring and enforcement of security agreements matters. The presence of weak or failed states in remote regions of the world matters. The socioeconomic fortunes of states—that is, the abilities of states to satisfy their citizens—matter.[4]

Again, there are two aspects to this shift. One is the expansion of the world's "security space." What this means is that there is more territorial space around the world that matters for security because these territories can be the sites and launching points for transnational violence. Order and governance in remote and troubled parts of the world matter for security in the United States. The other aspect is the growing interaction effects between sources of instability and insecurity. Global warming or health pandemics interact with energy or food shortages to destabilize countries and to radiate violence and insecurity outward to other parts of the world. It is harder to hide or to protect oneself from these transnational and interactive dynamics.

Finally, the fourth long-term shift is in the norms and ideas about security and national sovereignty. It is striking how global understandings of what it means to be secure have evolved over the last century. The core of security remains the state's protection of the physical security of its citizens. But security has come to mean much more. Prevailing global norms about security are now increasingly tied to social and economic security and human rights. This grand shift has been driven in large part by the postwar human rights revolution, and the resulting erosion of norms of sovereignty.

One part of this long-term shift in global norms is the evolution of what might be understood as minimum standards of human rights and welfare. Implicit in these changing norms is a linkage between human rights and socioeconomic well-being on the one hand, and international peace and security on the other. Elizabeth Borgwardt argues that the 1941 Atlantic Charter captured this liberal vision:

> . . . this Anglo-American declaration was soon best known for a reso-
> nant phase about establishing a particular kind of postwar order—a
> peace "which will afford assurance that all the men in all the lands
> may live out their lives in freedom from want." To link antifascist
> politics and economic well-being was unusual in an international
> instrument, but to speak explicitly of individuals rather than state
> interests—to use the phrase "all the men in all the lands" in place of a
> more traditional reference to the prerogatives of nations—was posi-
> tively revolutionary. The phrase hinted that an ordinary citizen might
> possibly have some kind of direct relationship with international law,
> unmediated by the layering of a sovereign state. Though oblique, this
> hint that ideas about dignity of the individual were an appropriate
> topic of international affairs was soon to catalyze groups around
> the world committed to fighting colonialism and racism as well as
> Nazism. It marked a defining, inaugural moment for what we now
> know as the modern doctrine of human rights (2004:4).

This transformation in global expectations really took off in the decades after World War II. Global activists, wielding liberal internationalist assumptions about world order, pushed forward the human rights agenda. The breakthrough was probably the Universal Declaration of Human Rights adopted by the UN General Assembly in December 1948. Championed by liberals such as Eleanor Roosevelt and others, this document articulated a notion of universal individual rights that deserved recognition by the whole of mankind and not simply left to sovereign governments to define and enforce (Glendon 2002). A steady stream of conventions and treaties followed that together constitute an extraordinary new vision of rights, individuals, sovereignty, and global order (Donnelly 2002).

The postwar transformation in global norms and expectations has entailed two sorts of shifts. One is the expansion of notions of rights and obligations. To be secure, individuals need protection against socioeconomic deprivation and political oppression. The array of rights that the international community "recognized" in treaties and conventions steadily expanded over the decades. These rights were also increasingly seen as not just necessary for purposes of social justice but also a necessary condition for stability and peace. After the Cold War—and certainly after September 11—the perceived linkages between socioeconomic well-being, political rights, and international peace and security have only intensified. The other shift is the simultaneous erosion of norms of state sovereignty. As notions of individual social and political rights have grown, the norms of Westphalian sovereignty have weakened. The international community increasingly is seen to have a legitimate interest in what goes on within countries. Sovereignty is more contingent, increasingly a legal right that must be earned.

Taken together, the global setting in which the United States seeks security has undergone a grand transformation. There are still threats and challenges from traditional sources, such as the proliferation of nuclear weapons in states that are hostile to the United States or its allies. But the wider security environment has been profoundly altered. Globalization and the privatization of violence have expanded the national security field of play. More people and places matter for U.S. security than in past eras. At the same time, there is a new security premium attached to how people live—their life prospects—and for how they operate across borders. The United States needs to worry as much about the weakness of states—that is, the inability of states to provide social well-being and govern under the rule of law—as it does the power of states. Fundamentally, it is the growing intensity of security interdependence that is the defining feature of America's twenty-first-century security environment. This, more than anything else, will drive the agenda for security cooperation in the years ahead.

A Global Strategy of Cooperative Security

How does the United States pursue security in this changing global environment? The answer is that it needs to pursue a strategy of building global capacities and cooperative frameworks to cope with the threats and insecurities that emerge from it and to also pursue long-term policies to help improve the developmental prospects of troubled states and societies. I call this overall strategy "liberal order building" (Ikenberry 2008). This is essentially the strategy that the United States pursued after World War II and in the shadow of the Cold War. The United States takes the lead in the creation of a system of global governance, in providing public goods, and in helping to solve collective action problems. The United States pursues grand bargains with other major states to create institutionalized arrangements for stable order. American power is put in the service of an agreed-upon system of rule-based global cooperation.

To clarify the idea of liberal order building, it is useful to distinguish two types of security strategies: positional and milieu-oriented. A positional security strategy is where a great power seeks to counter, undercut, contain, and limit the power and threats of a specific challenger state or group of states. Nazi Germany, Imperial Japan, the Soviet bloc, and perhaps—in the future—greater China are examples. A milieu grand strategy is where a great power does not target a specific state but seeks to structure its general international environment in ways that are congenial with its long-term security. This might entail building the infrastructure of international cooperation, promoting trade and democracy in various regions of the world, and establishing partnerships that might be useful for various contingencies. The point I want to make is that in a world of diffuse threats and growing security interdependence, and with pervasive uncertainty over what the specific security challenges will be in the future, this milieu-based approach to security is needed. In the pursuit of security, the United States needs to make long-term and systematic commitments to a liberal international order that fosters expanding forms of security cooperation.

This strategy needs to be pursued in five ways. The first way is to build a stronger protective infrastructure of international capacities to confront an array of shifting, diffuse, and uncertain threats and catastrophes; this is, in effect, creating an infrastructure of global social services. The second method is the rebuilding of a system of cooperative security, reestablishing the primacy of America's alliances for strategic cooperation and with the global arms control regimes. The third way is the reform of global institutions that support collective action and multilateral management of globalization, such as the United Nations and multilateral economic institutions, thereby creating greater institutional capacities for international decision-making, for the provision of public goods, and for integrating rising states into governance institutions. The fourth method is to shift the long-term focus of security to global economic development and to the building of stable and accountable governments around the world. Finally, the United States should endeavor to reestablish its hegemonic legitimacy; this preeminent objective must be pursued with policies and with doctrine that signal America's commitment to rule-based order and to leadership in the pursuit of global peace and security.[5] We can look more closely at this security agenda.

Build Protective Infrastructure

The United States needs to lead in the building of an enhanced protective infrastructure that helps prevent the emergence of threats and limits the damage if those threats do materialize (Ikenberry and Slaughter 2006:10). Many of the threats mentioned earlier are manifest as socioeconomic backwardness and failure that generate regional and international instability and conflict. These are the sorts of threats that are likely to arise with the coming of global warming and epidemic disease. What is needed here is institutional cooperation to strengthen the capacity of governments and the international community to prevent epidemics or food shortages or mass migrations that create global upheaval or to mitigate the effects of these upheavals if they, in fact, occur.[6]

It is useful to think of a strengthened protective infrastructure as an investment in global social services, much as cities and states invest in such services. It typically is money well spent. Education, health programs, shelters, and social services—these are vital components of stable and well-functioning communities. The international system already has a great deal of this infrastructure in the form of institutions and networks that promote cooperation with regard to public health, refugees, and emergency aid. But in the twenty-first century, as the scale and scope of potential problems grow, investments in these preventive and management capacities will also need to grow. Early warning systems, protocols for emergency operations, standby capacities, and so on are the stuff of a protective global infrastructure.

Revive Cooperative Security

In the 1980s and 1990s, U.S. security specialists articulated the notion of cooperative security. The vision was of ongoing cooperative engagement among various groupings of states in regulating and controlling military technology and deployments. Between the United States and its allies, this meant extensive cooperation in planning and operation of combined forces. Between the United States and the Soviet Union, this meant ongoing consultation between the two superpower defense establishments, building on the experience of the detente era of arms control.[7] After the Cold War, leading security experts have suggested that cooperative security is the sort of security orientation that best fits the new era of threats. As Ashton Carter and his colleagues argue, cooperative security is

> . . . in essence a commitment to regulate the size, technical composition, investment patterns, and operational practices of all military forces by mutual consent for mutual benefit. The resulting cooperative form of security offers the best prospect of addressing the new problems of the post-Cold War world (Carter et al. 1992:6).

The strategy of cooperative security directly responds to the problem of post-Cold War security interdependence. With the diffusion of WMD technologies to more states, the United States cannot meet new threats exclusively, or even primarily, through deterrence and readiness. As Carter and his colleagues argue, "The new security problems require more constructive and more sophisticated forms of influence that concentrate more on the initial preparation of military forces than on the final decision to use them" (Carter et al. 1992:6). The key point of cooperative security is that states get involved with each other on an ongoing basis to discuss and agree on how to make military forces predictable, controllable, defensive, and as safe from accident or misuse as possible. Cooperative security makes sense as a tool to reduce the arms race potential in regional and global security dilemmas. It also makes sense as a tool to reduce the risks of proliferation of WMD technologies.[8]

In particular, security threats coming from the diffusion of violent technologies into the hands of terrorist groups will continue to generate incentives for more intrusive international arms control and counterproliferation capacities. The International Atomic Energy Agency (IAEA) is the leading-edge organization of these international efforts. In the last two decades, the IAEA has developed scientific and technical competence and legal frameworks for monitoring and inspection of nuclear programs around the world. As nuclear, biological, and chemical weapons technologies grow more sophisticated and diffuse into troubled parts of the world, governments will no doubt seek to expand IAEA-type capacities for monitoring, inspection, verification, and safeguarding. Pressures will grow for norms of Westphalian sovereignty to continue to incrementally give way to intrusive international security regimes.[9]

Rebuild Alliances

The United States should recommit to and rebuild its security alliances. The idea would be to update the old bargains that lie behind these security pacts. In NATO, but also in the East Asia bilateral partnerships, the United States agrees to provide security protection to the other states and to bring its partners into the process of decision-making over the use of force. In return, these partners agree to work with the United States, providing manpower, logistics, and other types of support, in wider theaters of action. The United States gives up some autonomy in strategic decision-making, although this is a more informal than legally binding restraint, and in exchange it gets cooperation and political support. The United States also remains "first among equals" within these organizations, and it retains leadership of the unified military command. The updating of these alliance bargains would involve widening the regional or global missions in which the alliance operates and making new compromises over the distribution of formal rights and responsibilities.[10]

There are several reasons why the renewal of security partnerships is critical to liberal order building. One is that security alliances involve relatively well-defined, specific, and limited commitments; this is attractive for the leading military power and its partners. States know what they are getting into and what the limits are on their obligations and liabilities. Another reason is that alliances provide institutional mechanisms that allow accommodations for disparities of power among partners within the alliance. Alliances do not embody universal rules and norms that apply equally to all parties. NATO, at least, is a multilateral body with formal and informal rules and with norms of operation that accommodate the most powerful state and provide roles and rights for others as well. Another virtue of renewing the alliances is that they have been institutional bodies that are useful as "political architecture" across the advanced democratic world. The alliances provide channels of communication and of joint decision-making that spill over into the wider realms of international relations. They are also institutions with grand histories and records of accomplishment.

The United States is a unipolar military power, but it still has incentives to share the costs of security protection and to find ways to legitimize the use of its power. The postwar alliances, renewed and reorganized, are an attractive tool for these purposes.[11]

Reform Global Institutions

The United States also needs to lead in the reform of global security institutions that foster and legitimize collective action. The first move here should be to reform the United Nations, starting with the expansion of the permanent membership on the Security Council. Several plans have been proposed. All of them entail new members—such as Germany, Japan, India, Brazil, South Africa, and others—and reformed voting procedures. Almost all of the candidates for permanent membership are mature or rising democracies. The goal, of course, is to make them stakeholders in the United Nations and thereby strengthen the primacy of the United Nations as a vehicle for global collective action. There really is no substitute for the legitimacy that the United Nations can offer to emergency actions, such as humanitarian interventions, economic sanctions, uses of force against terrorists, and so forth. Public support in advanced democracies grows rapidly when their governments can stand behind a UN-sanctioned action.

Beyond this, the reform of these institutions will offer an opportunity for the United States to help bring rising states into a more direct role in global governance. The International Monetary Fund, the World Bank, and the G8 are all global governance institutions that need to redefine their missions and to open their doors to new leadership. China, India, Brazil, and other emerging powers are eager for seats at the high tables of governance. Russia is also a country that seeks to reestablish its authority and its presence as a great power. Part of the purpose of reforming these multilateral governance institutions is to bring states that are increasingly important to the management of the world economy into management positions. Another part of the purpose is to make these states serious stakeholders by granting them status and authority in institutions that currently are heavily weighted in favor of the United States and Europe (Ikenberry and Wright 2007).

At the end of this cycle of governance reform, the preeminent objective is to retain what might be called "one world" political architecture.

The danger is that as emerging powers rise, dissatisfaction and grievances will lead these countries—particularly China and Russia—to reject or work outside of Western-oriented global institutions. Major and emerging non-Western powers must be integrated into the core mechanisms for global collective action. A world that is split between democratic and autocratic states will undercut America's long-term interest in building cooperative institutions and capacities to address emerging security imperatives.

The American-led postwar institutions are generally formal-based global multilateral institutions. These institutions will not disappear, but two alternative forms of governance are likely to grow in importance. One is the informal steering committee, such as the G8 and G20. These institutions have advantages for rising states. They are easier to join (particularly in contrast to the UN Security Council), and they do not entail direct diminishment of sovereignty. Another alternative form is regional governance institution. These institutions also provide advantages for rising states. They give these states greater authority than they might have within global institutions. Regional institutions also allow for cooperation on specific problems that are particularly pressing for these states, so that the balance of governance institutions will be redrawn. But through the reform process, the United States will want to keep all the major states operating within the overall complex of global security institutions. In a world of growing security interdependence, all states must be at the table and be willing to cooperate in generating protective capacities and in managing threats.

Renew American Hegemonic Authority

This "crisis" of American authority is perhaps the most serious threat to the ability of the United States to secure itself in the decades ahead. U.S. foreign policy in the first decade of the new century severely eroded America's global position and endangered its ability to lead and facilitate collective action. The proximate cause of this crisis might be traced to the Bush administration's failure to operate within its own postwar liberal hegemonic order. The Bush administration's Iraq War and its disrespect of global rules and institutions—seen most clearly in President Bush's first term—reduced America's global authority and prestige. But there are deep shifts in the global system that make it harder for the United States to act as it did in the past—as a global provider of goods and as a liberal hegemon willing to restrain and to commit itself. If the United States is going to lead the world in the establishment of expanded capacities for security cooperation, it will need to rehabilitate itself (Ikenberry 2011).

The reestablishment of U.S. authority is best accomplished by pursuing liberal order building. As it did in an earlier era, the United States should step forward and offer to lead the way in the provision of public goods, such as international security, rules and institutions, and economic openness. At the heart of a renewal strategy for American hegemonic leadership is a set of renegotiated bargains with other states. In some sense, this is what is already happening today (Drezner 2007). The United States would continue to provide functional services for the wider system, and in return, other countries would acquiesce to the rules and institutions championed by Washington.

This goal of rehabilitating America's hegemonic authority has been embraced by the Obama administration. This is seen in its efforts to reaffirm the U.S. commitment to operate within agreed-upon rules and institutions. Speaking to the doubts raised in the Bush years regarding this key component of the hegemonic leadership, President Obama has asserted that "America cannot insist that others follow the rules of the road if we refuse to follow them ourselves." In the use of military force, "we have a moral and strategic interest in binding ourselves to certain rules of conduct" (Obama 2010b). In his 2010 West Point commencement address, President Obama again claimed that "America has not succeeded by stepping out of the currents of cooperation—we have succeeded by steering those currents in the direction of liberty and justice" (Obama 2010a).

In a reformed international order, the United States would give up some of its hegemonic rights and privileges but retain others. In economic and political realms, it would yield authority and accommodate rising states. The United States would share authority within the reformed Bretton Woods institutions. In security realms, however, the United States would retain its hegemonic position. It would offer security to other states in a worldwide system of alliances. The U.S. economy would remain a leading source of markets and growth, even if its relative size declined. The United States would remain positioned to support and uphold the renegotiated rules and institutions of the liberal order.

If the United States wants to remain at the center of a one-world security order built around cooperative security, it will need to make difficult decisions about restraint and commitment. The question remains whether the United States will actually be willing to cede authority back to the international community and accommodate itself to a system of more binding rules and institutions. Short of a radical shift in the international distribution of power, the United States will remain the world's most powerful state for several decades to come, so there is reason to think that other countries would be willing to see the United States play a leading role and provide functional services if the terms are right. Under almost any circumstances, these terms would entail a reduction in America's hegemonic rights and privileges while it operated within agreed-upon rules and institutions. The United States might also come to believe that this renegotiated hegemonic arrangement is better than any of the alternatives. So the question is: Could the United States in fact make the political commitments implicit in this renegotiated liberal international order?

Conclusion

Looking out toward the distant decades of the twenty-first century, it is very difficult to discern threats and enemies. There is much we do not know about our future security environment, but we do know some things. We know there will be more people living on a, figuratively speaking, smaller planet. We know the global political hierarchies will be shifting. We know that technologies of violence will diffuse outward from established great powers to other states and to nonstate conflict groups. We know that groups that we have not yet heard of might eventually gain access to weapons of mass destruction and wield this capacity for violence in horrific ways. We know that our socioeconomic systems will be increasingly interdependent, and that disruptions and instabilities in one part of the world will threaten stability and well-being elsewhere. We know that it will be impossible for countries to hide from other countries. In a world of increasing security interdependence, there is no escape; there is only a march forward into a new sort of globally governed and protected system.

Two sorts of security imperatives follow from this depiction of the coming decades; one involves international cooperation and the other political development. First, the United States and its partners will need to invent evermore complex and extended forms of security cooperation. It is impossible to look at the fundamentals of technological change and not see that American security is going to require much more intensive forms of cooperation—global, institutionalized, and intrusive. Laboratories and scientific knowledge are dangerous if they fall into the wrong hands, so the states of the world will need to increasingly find ways to guard laboratories and scientific knowledge. This needs to become the core of a new system of global cooperative security. There is every reason to believe that the vast majority of states and peoples can find common interest in this endeavor. It does require compromise and new forms of cooperation. The idea is to work preventively to tie down and to lock up capabilities for violence.

In addition, the United States and its security partners will need to begin constructing a more comprehensive and elaborate protective infrastructure. International capacities need to be developed to cope with the global problems that inevitably follow from growing security interdependence: infectious disease, environmental degradation, refugee flows, food shortages, energy crises, and so on. The world needs to develop a new layer of "social services" for the system. Moreover, if conflict groups that threaten to unleash violence across longer distances become more dispersed and more lethal, the world will need to have standby capacities to cope with the damage they inflict.

The second implication of the foregoing depiction of threats and insecurity is that the United States and the other major states will need to invest much more in global political and economic development. In a world of intensifying security interdependence, no state can be left behind. That is, the world is only as safe as its weakest link. The world needs to worry less about powerful states and more about weak states in the periphery. It needs to worry about how to orchestrate the knowledge and resources of the developed countries to bring along peoples and societies in troubled regions.

If all of this is to be accomplished, our very notion of security will need to evolve as well. In many ways, it already has. It was in the mid-twentieth century that the notion of national security emerged. This was an advance on older notions of national defense, and it meant that a country had to worry not just about territorial invasion but about deploying a wider array of political, economic, and technological assets. Within advanced industrial societies, a parallel shift occurred in the notion of domestic economic security. The government was increasingly called upon to provide full employment and social protections. States became more than shells for private capitalists and for workers. They became social protection units. Our notions of security broadened: Social security and national security were terms that denoted a new era of challenges and of aspirations for modern societies. Today, these advanced countries need to lead the way in the next phase of security development. This entails extending further the notion of what security is. National security needs to be defined as comprehensive and cooperative security. The ideas are clear. But the political challenges of building a new system of global cooperative security are daunting indeed.

Notes

1. States are, above all else, "protection organizations." What states protect and how they do so has changed over the centuries. Charles Tilly argued that the earliest states in sixteenth-century Europe offered protection to mercantile capitalists in exchange for taxes and for political allegiance. National states became the dominant form of political organization because they succeeded in gaining a monopoly of the means of organized violence. Along the way, states assumed the responsibility for regulating the economy, for protecting civic rights, and for maintaining public order. In the modern age of democracy, the state—its legitimacy and raison d'être—is based fundamentally on its ability to deliver security to its citizens. At home, this has meant the provision of social and economic security, and abroad this has meant the pursuit of national security. See Tilly (1990).

2. This is our judgment in the Final Report of the Princeton Project on National Security. See Ikenberry and Slaughter (2006).

3. For a major study of the logic of security interdependence and its implications for international cooperation, see Deudney (2007).

4. As Robert Cooper puts it: "The world may be globalized but it is run by states. Spaces with no one in control are a nightmare for those who live there, a haven for criminals, and a danger to the rest of us" (2008:17).

5. The Obama administration's focus on reviving the Non-Proliferation Treaty and its agenda for radical reductions in nuclear weapons, together with its emphasis on development, human security, and multilateral cooperation, are markers in that administration's attempt to orient American foreign policy toward an era of escalating security interdependence.

6. For an important statement of these ideas, see Jones, Pascual, and Stedman (2009).

7. See Larson (2002) and Sigal (2000).

8. One can contrast cooperative security with collective security. Collective security is cooperation among states in order to respond to unsanctioned aggression. It is meant to be a deterrent against state use of force or to roll it back once it has occurred. Cooperative security is meant to forge understandings and agreements between states at an earlier stage in the security cycle. Between allies, it is meant to build strategic ties and foster agreement on threats and on use of force contingencies. Between potentially threatening states, it is meant to reduce uncertainty and suspicion. Among all states, it is meant to lock down and to protect technologies from getting into the hands of rogue states or terrorist groups.

9. For discussions of the evolving technical and legal frameworks for arms control monitoring and enforcement, see Cirincione, Wolfshal, and Rajkmar (2005) and Kessler (1995).

10. The case for renewal of NATO is made in Ikenberry and Slaughter (2006).
11. This argument is discussed in Ikenberry (2001).

References

Borgwardt, E., 2004, *A New Deal for the World: America's Vision for Human Rights*, Cambridge: Harvard University Press.

Brzezinski, Z., 2004, *The Choice: Domination or Leadership*, New York: Basic.

Buzan, B., 1991, *People, States, and War: An Agenda for International Security Studies in the Post-Cold War Era*, New York: Harvester-Wheatsheaf.

Carter, A. B., W. J. Perry, and J. D. Steinbrunner, 1992, *A New Concept of Cooperative Security*, Washington, D.C.: Brookings Occasional Papers.

Cirincione, J., J. B. Wolfshal, and M. Rajkmar, 2005, *Deadly Arsenals: Nuclear, Biological, and Chemical Threats*, 2nd ed. Washington, D.C.: Carnegie Endowment for International Peace.

Cooper, R., 2008, "Picking Up the Pieces," *Financial Times*, October 25–26.

Deudney, D., 2007, *Bounding Power: Republican Security Theory from the Polis to the Global Village*, Princeton: Princeton University Press.

Donnelly, J., 2002, *Universal Human Rights in Theory and Practice*, Ithaca: Cornell University Press.

Drezner, D., 2007, "The New New World Order," *Foreign Affairs*, 86(2):34–46.

Glendon, M. A., 2002, *A World Made New: Eleanor Roosevelt and the Universal Declaration*, New York: Random House.

Herz, J. J., 1950, "Idealist Internationalism and the Security Dilemma," *World Politics*, 2(2):171–201.

Homer-Dixon, T., 2006, *The Upside of Down: Catastrophe, Creativity, and the Renewal of Civilization*, Washington, D.C.: Island.

Ikenberry, G. J., 2001, *After Victory: Institutions, Strategic Restraint, and the Rebuilding of Order after Major War*, Princeton: Princeton University Press.

——, 2008, "Liberal Order Building," in *To Lead the World: American Strategy after the Bush Doctrine*, edited by M. P. Leffler and J. Legro, 85–108. New York: Oxford University Press.

——, 2011, *Liberal Leviathan: The Origins, Crisis, and Transformation of the American World Order*, Princeton: Princeton University Press.

Ikenberry, G. J., and A. Slaughter, 2006, *Forging a World of Liberty under Law*, Princeton: Woodrow Wilson School.

Ikenberry, G. J., and T. Wright, 2007, "Rising Powers and Global Institutions," in *Policy Report*, New York: The Century Foundation.

Jones, B., C. Pascual, and S. J. Stedman, 2009, *Power and Responsibility: Building International Order in an Era of Transnational Threats*, Washington, D.C.: The Brookings Institution.

Keohane, R., 2011, "The Globalization of Informal Violence, Theories of World Politics, and 'The Liberalism of Fear,'" in *Understanding September 11*, edited by C. Calhoun, P. Price, and A. Timmer, 77–91 New York: New Press.

Kessler, J. C., 1995, *Verifying Nonproliferation Treaties: Obligations, Process, and Sovereignty*, Washington, D.C.: National Defense University Press.

Larson, J. A., ed. 2002, *Arms Control: Cooperative Security in a Changing Environment*, Boulder: Lynne Rienner.

Obama, B., 2010a, "Remarks by the President at the United States Military Academy at West Point Commencement," May 22, 2010.

Obama, B., 2010b, "Remarks of the U.S. President in Oslo," December 10, 2010.

Sigal, L. V., 2000, *Hanging Separately: Cooperative Security between the United States and Russia, 1985–1994*, New York: The Century Foundation.

Tilly, C., 1990, *Coercion, Capital, and European States, AD 990–1992*, Malden, Mass.: Blackwell.

Wright, R., 2007, "The Neocon Paradox," *The New York Times*, April 24.

5

Restructuring Global Security for the Twenty-First Century*

MARY KALDOR

Introduction

In today's world, many people lead intolerably insecure lives. They risk being killed, kidnapped, raped, robbed, or expelled from their homes; they fear earthquakes or cyclones, the spread of disease, or losing their life's savings; they may not have enough to eat or clean water to drink; they may lack access to healthcare. In today's conflicts, civilians are targeted with impunity. Moreover, the insecurities generated by political violence are inextricably linked to insecurities resulting from transnational organized crime, environmental degradation, food shortages, or financial crises. No country, not even the United States, is immune from these insecurities any longer; some insecurities—such as Hurricane Katrina, house repossessions, or the terrorist attacks of 9/11—are experienced directly, and others are experienced indirectly through our humanitarian concerns, the concerns of diaspora groups, or our generalized fears about the future.

Yet our security capabilities largely designed for the Cold War seem incapable of addressing these everyday sources of insecurity. In Europe, there

*I am grateful to Marika Theros for help with the section on Afghanistan, which draws heavily from her paper for the Human Security Study Group, convened by Mary Kaldor.

are 1.8 million men and women under arms, yet Europe only has the capacity to deploy some 20,000 troops to crisis zones. The war in Iraq has cost U.S. taxpayers some $3 trillion, according to Joseph Stiglitz, yet the war has not increased the security of either Iraqis or Americans (Bilmes and Stiglitz 2008). The Russian intervention in Georgia resulted in greater polarization between the West and Russia and between Georgia and Russia and has led to increased insecurity in Ossetia and in parts of Georgia; some 130,000 people have been made homeless, and the new BP oil pipeline running through Georgia was closed for the duration of the conflict. In Afghanistan, despite a hugely expensive military effort, security deteriorates daily both within the country and among neighbors, especially Pakistan.

The gap between the everyday experience of security and our actual security capabilities erodes the legitimacy of our political institutions. We trust our institutions if we believe they will protect us in times of crisis, and that trust, in turn, is essential for security. What Ulrich Beck (1992) calls the "master narrative" of the modern state was constructed around its role in protecting people against risk: the dangers posed by nature, personal risks of ill health and unemployment, as well as threats posed by foreign enemies. Indeed, the idea of defense against a foreign enemy has become a metaphoric umbrella term for security in general. This explains the importance attached to the War on Terror by the Bush administration—a conflict that continued under another name during the Obama administration.

In this chapter, I will suggest that it is important to make the case for a profound restructuring in the global security sector away from a preoccupation with national and bloc security, largely based on conventional military forces, toward a strengthened global security system with greatly enhanced integrated civilian–military capabilities aimed at addressing the everyday insecurities experienced in the world today. I use the term "human security" to describe the goals and methods of such a new global security system. We need such a term to provide a way of framing security that mobilizes popular support and that establishes a cohesive concept that could help to bring together diverse and complex multilateral institutions. In particular, "human security" offers a clear alternative to the War on Terror as an organizing narrative for global security.

My focus is on protection from violence, although I stress the interrelated nature of security. This chapter complements the chapter by John Ikenberry by elaborating what a "protective infrastructure" (as he and Anne-Marie Slaughter have put it) might mean in practice and, in particular, what steps a future U.S. administration would need to take to begin to implement an alternative security approach (Ikenberry and Slaughter 2006). I start by describing some of the key characteristics of contemporary forms of violence. I then outline what a human security approach would involve. And in the final section, I make some recommendations for the strategy in Afghanistan, which I believe could make or break a human security approach.

Contemporary Forms of Organized Violence

War no longer exists. Confrontation, conflict, and combat undoubtedly exist all round the world . . . and states still have armed forces, which they use as symbols of power. Nonetheless, war as cognitively known to most combatants, war as battle in a field between men and machinery, war as a massive deciding event in a dispute in international affairs: such war no longer exists.

General Sir Rupert Smith, former Commander of UNPROFOR in Bosnia,
former Deputy Supreme Allied Commander NATO (2006:1)

When General Sir Rupert Smith talks about war, he is referring to our image of war, drawn from the experience of twentieth-century wars. We think of war as a conflict between states, carried out by regular armed forces, in which the aim is the military capture of territory and the decisive encounter is battle. In our image of war, the entire resources of a state are mobilized for victory.

This type of war resulted from the emergence of the modern states system in Europe in the eighteenth and nineteenth centuries. During this period, states established a monopoly of legitimate violence. They eliminated private armies, brigands, and privateers. Only those who wore the uniform of the state were allowed to kill. The term *bellum*, war between states, was viewed as legitimate, while *duellum*, war between individuals or private parties, was outlawed. A distinction was drawn between the police, who enforced the law at home, and soldiers, who were trained for war against other states.

The brilliant strategist Carl von Clausewitz was the first to point out that this kind of war has an extremist logic (von Clausewitz 1997). Developments in science and technology combined with the mobilization of populist patriotic sentiments made the machinery of war more deadly and more total. This extremist logic reached its apex in World War I and

World War II. Some 20 million people died in World War I and 70 million in World War II. The discovery of nuclear weapons and the Cold War arms race in the second half of the twentieth century threatened the world with extermination.

Contemporary forms of organized violence are very different. They range from military intervention and air strikes, through ethnic conflict, terrorism, human rights violations, organized crime, and urban gang warfare. They are less extremist but more pervasive and longer lasting than classic war. There are three characteristics that are relevant in addressing these different forms of violence.

Civilians as Victims

First, civilians are the main victims. Already in the two world wars, the mobilization of whole societies meant that the distinction between the military and civilians was beginning to break down. In World War I, three-quarters of the casualties were still military, if the figures for the Ottoman Empire are excluded. In the Ottoman Empire, some 4 million civilians died during World War I because of disease and the deliberate genocide of Armenians. In World War II, civilian casualties were much higher, both because of aerial bombing and because of the Holocaust. During that war, some 65 percent of casualties were civilians.

Today, the ratio of civilian to military deaths is probably even higher, although the statistics are notoriously poor. Indeed, one of the shocking aspects of contemporary violence is that we have exact numbers of military deaths in places like Iraq and Afghanistan but no decent statistics on civilian deaths. Civilian casualties are both a consequence of deliberate attacks and of the indirect effects of war, such as lack of access to healthcare or humanitarian assistance. Four or five million have died in the Democratic Republic of Congo as a consequence of the war there. Hundreds of thousands have died in Iraq and tens of thousands in Afghanistan, but the numbers are hotly disputed. By contrast, we know that as of February 2012, 4,804 coalition soldiers have lost their lives in Iraq and 2,916 in Afghanistan.[1]

We do have reasonably good statistics on population displacement. The huge rise in population displacement as a consequence of violence is one of the most striking features of our times. According to the United Nations High Commissioner for Refugees (UNHCR), the global refugee population has increased from 2.4 million refugees in 1975 to around 15 million in 2010.

According to the Internal Displacement Monitoring Centre in Geneva (2012), the number of internally displaced people increased from 17 million in 1998 to 27.5 million in 2010. It should be noted, of course, that these numbers are cumulative unless displaced people are repatriated. Also, methods of estimating numbers of internally displaced persons have greatly improved, so the earlier figures may be underestimated. Nevertheless, there does seem to be a trend toward increasing displacement per conflict (Kaldor 2012).

In the "new wars" in the Balkans, Africa, and the Middle East, the killing of civilians is deliberate. It is a central component of military strategies that evolved over the past few decades as a way of getting around concentrations of advanced military technology and the diminishing utility of conventional military force. Instead of trying to control territory militarily, by defeating an opposing army, paramilitary groups or a combination of regular and irregular forces try to control territory politically by using violence to control the population. Whereas revolutionaries like Mao Zedong or Che Guevara aimed to control territory by winning the support of the local population by appealing to "hearts and minds," today the aim is to sow fear and hatred by expelling or killing those of a different ethnicity or religion, or even just dissidents and intellectuals.

This is how, for example, Serb forces controlled territory in Bosnia. Regular Serb forces would shell a village to create an atmosphere of panic. Then paramilitary groups with names like "Tigers," "Chetniks," or "Scorpions" would enter the village. Men would be separated from women and killed, especially if they were rich or intellectual, or imprisoned in detention camps. Women would be raped and/or expelled; the argument was that Muslim women would feel so ashamed of having been raped, they would never want to return to their homes. Symbols of culture and historic buildings would be destroyed.

The Janjaweed in Darfur and Chad use similar tactics. Reports speak of systematic and often race-related rape raids, with some women having been branded on the hand to permanently stigmatize them. Abductions of girls and boys, random killings of civilians, and the destruction of private property as well as water sources and other essential civilian properties are common. In places such as West Africa or Uganda, hideous atrocities have been carried out, including beheadings, throat cutting, and cutting off of limbs, ears, lips, and noses. In Iraq, Sunni suicide bombers attacked crowded Shiite areas, and Shiite militias organized death squads. And a 2007 report by Amnesty International documents a dramatic increase in deliberate attacks on civilians by Afghan insurgent groups, primarily Taliban and Hezb-e Islamic forces.

Suicide bombings, as have been carried out by terrorists in New York, Madrid, and London, as well as in Palestine, Iraq, and Afghanistan, are another tactic for avoiding direct confrontations with superior military forces. Suicide bombing is sometimes intended to create fear and panic among the civilian population. It is also sometimes used as a cost-effective way of attacking heavily protected strategic targets, such as the Twin Towers of the World Trade Center in Manhattan, American forces in Iraq and Afghanistan, or political figures, such as the assassinated Rajiv Gandhi. But because civilians are unprotected, they are usually the main victims.

Counterterrorism is supposed to counter those tactics, but actually counterterrorist tactics have the same effects. Because combatants cannot be separated from noncombatants, supposed attacks on insurgents mainly kill or displace civilians; examples include counterattacks by the United States in Iraq, Afghanistan, and Pakistan; by Russia in Chechnya; and by Israel in Lebanon and Palestine. This is particularly true of air strikes, including the recent drone campaign, which are a way of minimizing military casualties while attacking strategic targets or combatants. Even though Western governments claim to minimize so-called collateral damage, air strikes are not always as precise as claimed, and there are often targeting mistakes; they are also terrifying for those on the ground. Indeed this is the point of tactics such as "shock and awe." Cluster munitions—bombs that explode into tiny fragments that have been used by, for example, the Israelis in Southern Lebanon or Gaza—leave large amounts of territory unusable and result in casualties, especially children, long after the bombs have been dropped. Moreover, air strikes often provoke counterattacks either against civilians, since military targets are harder for insurgents to hit, or attacks in which civilians get killed as collateral damage.

Privatization of Violence

Second, contemporary organized violence usually involves a transnational combination of state and nonstate actors: regular and irregular forces. Nonstate actors include:

- Groups that call themselves revolutionary or resistance groups, such as the PKK in Turkey, the FARC in Colombia, or Hezbollah in Lebanon;
- Paramilitary groups that formed around particular leaders, such as Arkan's Tigers and Frenki's Boys in the former Yugoslavia, or Moqtada Sadr's Mahdi Army in Iraq;

- Party militias such as the Badr brigade attached to SCIRI (the Shi'ite religious party in Iraq), or Hamas and the Al Aqsa brigades (Fatah) in Palestine;
- Extremist Islamist groups such as the various cells that have called themselves al-Qaeda;
- Or self-defense forces that spring up to defend their localities in Iraq, Bosnia, and even Rwanda.

Often governments establish these groups in order to distance themselves from more extreme manifestations of violence. This was probably the case for Arkan's Tigers in the former Yugoslavia, or so Arkan himself insisted (Kaldor 2012). Likewise the pre–1994 Rwandan government recruited unemployed young men to a newly formed militia linked to the ruling party; they were given training by the Rwandan army and a small salary. Sometimes these groups are composed of redundant soldiers or even whole units of redundant or breakaway soldiers, such as in Iraq where groups of soldiers dismissed in the immediate aftermath of the U.S. invasion formed groups such as the 1920s Revolutionary Brigades, the Black Anger Brigades, or the Mujahedeen of the Victorious Sect. Something similar has happened in Syria. Whole units have defected from the army because they refuse to attack civilians. They have established independent brigades with names like the Hamza Al-Qatib Brigade or the Salaheddine Al-Ayoubi Brigade; the names come from victims of the repression or historical figures.

These groups can also include common criminals, such as in the former Yugoslavia where many were deliberately released from prison for that purpose and in Iraq where Saddam Hussein released criminals just before the invasion. Unemployed young men also join these groups in search of a living, a cause, or an adventure.

Foreign mercenaries or volunteers are another growing phenomenon in areas of violence. They include individuals on contract to particular fighting units such as the former Russian officers working with new post-Soviet armies; British and French soldiers made redundant by post-Cold War cuts who train, advise, and even command armed groups in Bosnia, Croatia, and various African countries; foreign volunteers such as American Armenians who went to fight in Nagorno-Karabakh in the name of Armenian identity; and German Croats who went for the weekend to join the war in Bosnia Herzegovina. The most prominent example is the Mujahedeen; originally veterans from the Afghan resistance to the Soviet Union in the 1980s, they are generally to be found in all conflicts involving Islam and are funded by the Islamic states, most notably Iran and Saudi Arabia. Many went to fight in Iraq and Afghanistan and now seem to be appearing in Syria.

There has been a huge increase in the use of private security contractors in the wars in Iraq and Afghanistan. In Iraq, the United States employed more than 180,000 private contractors, more than the total number of troops. And these contractors "perform the full spectrum of functions once carried out by U.S. personnel" (Elsea and Sarafino 2007). Some sixty companies are employed including well-known names such as Blackwater USA, DynCorp LLC, and Triple Canopy Inc., who mainly undertake protection and intelligence functions, as well as British companies such as Aegis Defense Services Limited and Armour Group International. The number is smaller in Afghanistan but still large in relation to the Afghan army. Two-thirds of the contractors employed are local Iraqis and Afghans. A number of concerns have been expressed. These contractors are not bound by such tight rules of engagement as military personnel; they receive much higher rates of pay and therefore make recruitment into the military difficult; and, above all, they create a substantial constituency inside Iraq and Afghanistan and in other countries that profit from war.

Political Violence and Organized Crime

Third, political violence is often difficult to distinguish from organized crime. Today's political violence takes place in a context of state "un-building." Regular forces are, by and large, still financed by taxation, but in some places defense budgets no longer cover the costs of the military, and the military engage in various licit and illicit entrepreneurial activities. In the case of the United States, as has been exposed in the financial crisis, the wars in Iraq and Afghanistan have been accompanied by tax cuts, so the huge defense budget has been financed by borrowing largely from abroad. Despite the huge budget, however, low pay and inadequate equipment have made recruitment difficult; hence the growth of private contractors.

Even before the end of the Cold War, illicit economic activities were flourishing within authoritarian regimes. In fact, the demise of Soviet Communism and South Africa's apartheid system was associated with the explosion of organized crime that had its roots in the shadowy interstices of authoritarianism. In South Africa, the Goldstone Commission and the Truth and Reconciliation Commission revealed the extraordinary range of criminal activities in which security forces were engaged: running of drugs, ivory, precious gems, and minerals; bank robbery, embezzlement, and money laundering; falsification of records, illegal sales of licenses, and fabrication of evidence. And as any visitor to the Soviet Union in the last days of communism will testify, smuggling, black-market exchanges, trafficking, and other activities were rampant.

During the Cold War, irregular forces were often financed by the opposing super powers. The Soviet Union and China often supported revolutionary groups, while the United States supported the Mujahedeen in Afghanistan and the Contras in Nicaragua. When superpower patronage dried up, various methods of financing were developed, most of which are related to violence. What Carolyn Nordstrom calls "shadow networks" are the underside of the growth of the global market (Nordstrom 2004:11). The "new wars" have provided a fertile zone for nurturing these transnational networks of state and nonstate actors, which are engaged in a range of violent illicit activities: looting, pillaging, and hostage-taking; establishing checkpoints to control the flow of necessities and charging "customs duties"; "taxation" of humanitarian aid; and, of course, transnational crime. Remittances, illegal trading, and humanitarian assistance all provide ways of recycling foreign exchange so that local actors can purchase weapons and equipment (as well as luxuries) on international markets.

Remittances from abroad have become an increasingly important source of finance. In Kosovo, for example, the shift in diaspora funding from the nonviolent movement to the Kosovo Liberation Army (KLA) was a key development in the descent toward war in the late 1990s. An organization such as Hezbollah in Lebanon depends on support from its members working in places like the Gulf and Western Europe, as well as support from outside powers like Iran and Syria. In Southern Sudan, fighters gained access to remittances sent to poor families from family members working in the Gulf by controlling the price of food at checkpoints.

Other increasingly important sources of finance are smuggling goods such as cigarettes, alcohol, and drugs as well as human beings (illegal immigrants or abducted women and children) and illegal trading in valuable commodities such as oil and diamonds, endangered species, and valuable hardwood. Countries that are dependent on valuable primary commodities have been shown to be particularly prone to violence (Collier and Hoeffler 2004). This is partly because of geopolitical competition for control over the sources of valuable commodities. But it is also because such countries develop rentier societies in which different groups or individuals struggle for access to the state because that means access to oil or to diamond revenues and because commodity revenues can be used to finance wars. In Chechnya, local warlords sold oil drawn from backyard oil wells to Russian generals who, in turn, sold the oil they had received from the government on the Moscow market in order to finance soldiers' wages. In Colombia, different irregular forces have developed different techniques for accessing oil revenues: blowing up pipelines, taking oil workers hostage, controlling municipalities that receive oil revenues, and "protecting" oil enclaves. In the war in Angola, the government was financed by oil revenues and the rebels by diamond revenues (Kaldor, Karl, and Said 2007).

In other words, in place of the national formal economy with its emphasis on industrial production and state regulation, a new type of globalized informal economy is being established in which external flows, especially humanitarian assistance, remittances from abroad, transnational smuggling, and trade in valuable commodities, are integrated into a local and regional economy based on looting, pillaging, hostage-taking, and on forced manipulation of local prices. Some argue that these new types of violence are actually motivated by private gain. It is certainly true that, in conditions of conflict where the rule of law breaks down, there are many opportunities for criminal activity. In Iraq and Gaza, much hostage-taking is for ransom rather than to achieve political goals. In the former Yugoslavia, many paramilitary fighters were able to take control of new homes and small businesses. But it is also true that many politically motivated fighters and terrorists engage in economic crime in order to finance political violence. Moreover, many of the forms of violence are also criminal in the sense that they violate international law. Rather, the point is that the differences between organized crime, markets, and war are breaking down in our contemporary era.

This new type of predatory political economy has a tendency to spread. A variety of factors reproduce the conditions that nurture the new forms of violence: the cost of war in terms of lost trade, especially where sanctions or communications blockades are introduced or where borders are closed, either deliberately or because of fighting; the burden of refugees, since generally it is the neighboring states that accept the largest numbers; the spread of illegal circuits of trade; and the spillover of identity politics. It is possible to identify what Misha Glenny calls the "badlands"—a "thick belt of instability" that stretches "all the way across the Caucasus and the so-called *stans* of Central Asia and on to the western edge of China and the northwest frontier of Pakistan" (Glenny 2008:6). These are regions where weak states are further weakened by the spread of the globalized informal economy. Similar "badlands," characterized by a toxic combination of political violence and organized crime, can be found in places such as West Africa, Central Africa, and the Horn of Africa as well as the Middle East. Indeed the piracy in the Arabian Gulf represents yet another "silk route—a multilane criminal highway" (Glenny 2008:6).

Protecting Individuals from Violence

These three characteristics—civilians as victims, the privatization of violence, and the blurring of the distinction between political violence and organized crime—need to be taken into account in any new approach to security. Of course, it is already the case that the protection of civilians has entered the security lexicon, especially in the United Nations (Holt and Berkman 2006). Concern with protection was evident in the 2006 U.S. Counter insurgency Manual prepared by General David Petraeus and General James F. Amos (Department of the Army and United States Marine Corps 2006). General Petraeus's "new thinking" emphasized the protection of civilians over and above force protection—a radical turnaround in the way U.S. forces are used. Instead of technology and firepower, the emphasis has been on bottom-up local security. His "Counter insurgency Guidance" (published July 8, 2008) includes instructions such as "Secure and Serve the Population," "Live Among the People," "Promote Reconciliation," "Walk," "Build Relationships," "Employ Money as a Weapons System," and "Empower Subordinates."

Moreover, the interrelated nature of security has also been increasingly emphasized. The term "population security," for example, was used to describe operations during the surge in Iraq. Secretary of State Condoleezza Rice (2008) defined population security as "addressing basic needs for safety, services, the rule of law, and increased economic opportunity." Another term is "stabilization," defined (Department of Defense 2009) as the effort to "create a secure and stable environment and to provide for the basic needs of the population to include food, water, sanitation and shelter." The European Union refers to crisis management and possesses a "stability instrument" (Development and Cooperation—Europeaid 2012). The State Department uses the term "civilian security" and has established an Under Secretary for Civilian Security, Democracy, and Human Rights.

But, by and large, these approaches are seen as adjuncts to the main security tasks—a means to an end, especially in the case of the United States.

The main purpose of military forces is the protection of the nation and defeat of enemies. The U.S. Counter insurgency Manual is still couched in the framework of national security, of war between the United States and its enemies. This is why air strikes continued for so long in Iraq and detention rates continued to climb. Moreover, despite the language of civilian protection, the United Nations lacks the capacity to implement civilian protection, which has become all too clear in the failure to address crises in the Democratic Republic of Congo or Syria and to ensure the protection of civilians in Iraq and Afghanistan. The European Union is developing an array of appropriate instruments, albeit a small one, but lacks the political cohesiveness to adopt this approach at a political as well as a practical level.

This is why I favor the adoption of a term like "human security" both as an organizing framework and as a new global security narrative. I define human security as follows:

First, it is about the security of individuals and the communities in which they live rather than the security of the state. In other words, it is about protecting civilians.

Second, it is about the interrelated nature of security, the link between freedom from fear and freedom from want. In other words, it is about protecting civilians from violence and other related insecurities including crime and economic predation.

Third, it is about the global nature of security and the blurring of the distinction between internal security, which is supposed to be guaranteed through the rule of law, and external security, which is guaranteed through defense policies. A human security approach extends the internal security worldwide; it is about shifting from a war paradigm to a law paradigm. In other words, it is about protecting people through the framework of law, dealing with violence as crime rather than war, and reestablishing a monopoly of legitimate violence.

There are, of course, many versions of human security. The original United Nations Development Program (UNDP) version, known as the broad version and supported by the Japanese government and promulgated in the 1994 *Human Development Report*, put the emphasis on the interrelated nature of security and the urgency of considering development as a security priority. The Canadian version expressed in the *Human Security Report* is closely associated with the "Responsibility to Protect" and focuses on protection from violence. My version of human security is somewhere between the two definitions. It is the version put forward by the Human Security Study Group that reported to Javier Solana (Glasius and Kaldor 2005). The focus is on insecurity as a consequence of violence (both political and criminal), but it emphasizes the interrelatedness of different types of insecurity.

Human security is about both ends and means. There is currently a lot of discussion about the conditions under which it is right to use military force—to prevent genocide, for example, or for regime change—but there is much less discussion about how military forces should be used in such a role. As Holt and Berkman point out, protecting civilians is different both from classic war fighting, which was about defeating enemies, and from peacekeeping, which was about separating sides (Holt and Berkman 2006). There are discussions about how civilian elements of crisis management are to be used to provide basic services or to help strengthen the rule of law but much less about how and when they work together with the military. Human security is not just the goal of operations; it also offers operational guidance.

Two reports undertaken by the Human Security Study Group, which reported to Javier Solana when he was High Representative for Common Foreign and Security Policy of the European Union (hereafter referred to as the Barcelona and Madrid reports) spelled out a set of principles that would guide security capabilities in contemporary crises. Among these principles are:

The Primacy of Human Rights

The primacy of human rights is what distinguishes the human security approach from traditional state-based approaches. What this principle means is that the primary goal is protecting civilians rather than defeating an adversary. Of course, sometimes it is necessary to try to capture or even defeat insurgents, but it has to be seen as a means to the end of civilian protection, rather than the other way around. Torturing suspects who have been arrested is also illegitimate and illegal. Causing greater human suffering as a result of an intervention would seem questionable. So-called collateral damage is unacceptable. At the same time, the application of this principle to saving life directly under threat from other parties may require a greater readiness to use force and to risk the lives of soldiers or aid workers—a shift in the balance between force protection and civilian protection. Human rights include economic and social rights as well as political and civil rights. This means that human rights such as the right to life, the right to housing, and the right to freedom of opinion are to be respected and protected even in the midst of conflict.

Legitimate Political Authority

Human security can only be guaranteed by a rule of law that depends on the existence of legitimate institutions that gain the trust of the population and that have some enforcement capacity. This applies to physical security, where the rule of law and a well-functioning system of justice are essential, as well as to material security, where increasing legitimate employment or providing infrastructure and public services require state policies. Legitimate political authority does not necessarily mean a state; it could consist of local government (a city, for example) or regional or international political arrangements such as protectorates or transitional administrations. Since state failure is often the primary cause of conflict, the reasons for state failure have to be taken into account in reconstructing legitimate political authority. Measures such as justice and security sector reform; disarmament, demobilization, and reintegration (DDR); extension of authority; and public service reform are critical for the establishment of legitimate political authority (Wulf 2005).

This principle explicitly recognizes the limitations on the use of military force. The aim of a human security operation is to stabilize the situation, so that a space can be created for a peaceful political process, rather than to win through military means alone.

Effective Multilateralism

This principle is related to legitimacy and distinguishes a human security approach from neocolonialism. Human security means a commitment to working with others, including international institutions, by creating or complying with existing common rules and norms and solving problems through rules and cooperation, as well as working with individual states, regional actors, and non governmental organizations (NGOs). It also means a better division of tasks and agreeing on the appropriate means to resolve conflict and to build peace. It is also closely related to international law and the need to operate within an international legal framework.

The Bottom-Up Approach

Notions of partnership, local ownership, and participation are already key concepts in development policy, while soldiers often refer to the "ground truth" or to knowledge of the "human terrain." Decisions about the kind of security and development policies to be adopted, and whether or not to intervene with military forces or through various forms of conditionality and how, must take into account the most basic needs identified by the people who are affected by violence and insecurity. This is not just a moral issue; it is also a matter of effectiveness. People who live in zones of insecurity are the best source of intelligence and are best able to sustain long-term security. Thus, communication, consultation, and dialogue are essential tools for human security. These tools are effective not simply to win hearts and minds, nor even to gain knowledge and understanding, but to empower those who will have to be responsible for security in the long run.

Particularly important, in this context, is the role of women. The importance of gender equality for development, especially the education of girls, has long been recognized. The same may be true when managing violence. Women play a critical role in dealing with the everyday consequences of the violence and in overcoming divisions in society. Involvement and partnership with women's groups could be a key component of a human security approach.

Regional Focus

The tendency to focus attention on areas that are defined in terms of statehood has often meant that relatively simple ways of preventing the spread of violence are neglected. Time and again, foreign policy analysts have been taken by surprise when, after considerable attention had been given to one conflict, another conflict would seemingly spring up out of the blue in a neighboring state. The war in Sierra Leone could not be solved without addressing the cause of conflict in Liberia, for example. Today's war in Afghanistan can only be contained if the neighboring states, especially Pakistan, are involved.

Clear, Transparent Civilian Command

In human security operations, civilians are in command. This means that the military must operate in support of law and order and under rules of engagement that are more similar to those of police work than to the rules of armed combat. Everyone needs to know who is in charge, and leaders must be able to communicate politically with local people as well as with people in the sending countries. It is very difficult to undertake civilian military operations unless civilians are in charge because civilians fear, often rightly, that they will become targets.

The world needs human security capabilities able to address a range of crises from natural disasters to pervasive violence. These capabilities should involve a mix of military and civilian elements that can be tailored to very different situations. Civilian elements could include police, legal experts, engineers, medical staff, and development experts in a state of readiness for deployment in crisis areas, as well as partnerships with NGOs and private contractors.

There is often resistance from civilians to integration with the military. Civilians insist on preserving what they call humanitarian space, involving the neutrality and impartiality of humanitarian agencies. The notion of humanitarian space, originally developed by the Red Cross, arose in very different circumstances of classic wars or insurgencies, where it was possible to define the "sides" and where the "laws of war" were at least known if not always applied. In contemporary conflicts or indeed other forms of violence, where civilians are often the main targets, humanitarian space no longer exists. The job of the military is first and foremost to create secure spaces with the help of civilians to protect communities from violence, and this means acting in very different ways from classic military operations. Both the military and civilians need to operate according to shared human security principles. Essentially, in human security operations, the military need to act more like robust law enforcement officers than like soldiers. Because the aim is the establishment of legitimate political authority, political considerations are paramount. In operational terms, this means that there needs to be a single commander, political or military, who understands politics and who has access to political authority.

These security forces would have to operate on behalf of a global multilateral system, as outlined in John Ikenberry's chapter in this volume. There is also a need to develop a multilateral legal framework covering international human security missions, which would tackle deficits in the international legal system. This should clarify the legality of international deployments and the legal regimes that govern deployed personnel (military and civilian) and locals in zones of insecurity and build on the domestic law of the host state, the domestic law of the sending states, and the rules of engagement, international criminal law, human rights law, and international humanitarian law.

Perhaps the biggest challenge for a human security approach is cognitive. It is the challenge of accepting that the lives of Africans and Asians are equal in value to the lives of Americans and Europeans. While this seems obvious on paper, it is by no means obvious in practice. Soldiers and aid workers in violent zones are protected in ways that the people, including women and children, who live in those zones can only dream of.

A good example of a human security approach is the British role in Northern Ireland, despite the problems and mistakes. The British did manage to contain the conflict until a political agreement could be reached using a combination of policing and development assistance, although it required a massive resource effort. They did this because the people of Northern Ireland are British citizens; they could not bomb insurgents and inflict collateral damage. A human security approach treats everyone as a world citizen.

What Would It Mean to Apply This Approach to Afghanistan?

In Afghanistan, there is a huge tension between the War on Terror, the goal of militarily defeating U.S. enemies, and the goal of stabilization and protection of the Afghan population. This tension is reflected in the two military commands—the American forces, known as Operation Enduring Freedom, and the NATO forces (the International Security Assistance Force, or ISAF) authorized by the United Nations—even though a single commander has been put in charge of both. Despite the fact that top officials in the U.S., NATO, and UN administrations frequently declare that the war in Afghanistan cannot be won militarily and despite the adoption by NATO and the United States of a comprehensive and "whole of government" approach that brings together civilian and military efforts to address the range of causes of insecurity for ordinary Afghans, the thrust of the international intervention has remained within a traditional security narrative that focuses on stabilizing the state militarily and that prioritizes the hunt for terrorists and insurgents over the protection of civilians.

As Iavor Rangelov and Marika Theros point out, the paradox is that despite pouring more money and troops into Afghanistan, violence has steadily escalated, reflected in the growing number of attacks and the growing number of civilian casualties every year since 2005 (Rangelov and Theros and 2012). At the time of writing, the only alternative to continued intervention on this model is considered withdrawal, if possible accompanied by reconciliation with the Taliban. It is hoped that Afghan security forces will be able to take over the international role. Yet ordinary Afghans view withdrawal and reconciliation as a frightening scenario. They expect a return to the kind of chaos and repression they experienced in the 1990s.

So is there something between classic military intervention and withdrawal? This is the aim of a human security approach. Of course it would be much less militarized than now and would reorient the intervention from a predominantly military mission with a political component to a political mission with a military component. This would still require a substantial international presence, but international personnel (military and civilian) would operate according to the six principles outlined earlier. What might this mean in practice?

The Primacy of Human Rights

In recent years, the focus of Allied forces has been on killing or capturing al-Qaeda and the Taliban. The use of air strikes and other heavy-handed measures, such as torture, arbitrary searches, and detentions, have greatly damaged the credibility of the multinational forces. General McCrystal, the former commander in Afghanistan, ordered troops not to pursue Taliban fighters at the risk of civilian casualties; nevertheless, civilian casualties have steadily mounted year by year. It is true that fewer are killed by allied forces because of greater attentiveness to minimizing civilian casualties, but the intensification of violence has necessarily entailed higher casualties. The effort to eliminate the Taliban has merely provoked more violence and more recruitment.

Other human rights violations experienced by Afghans include violations by the government, the police, and governors, who rule in a corrupt, repressive, and predatory way within a weak rule of law and with an absence or perversion of justice; domestic violence including widespread violations of women's rights; criminality, especially the drug trade, which now accounts for a large share of the total economy; unemployment, poverty, lack of access to healthcare and education, clean water and sanitation, and other violations of economic and social rights.

The drug economy represents one of the most difficult challenges Afghanistan faces, cutting across and negatively impacting security, governance, and development. Cultivation, production, and the trade of opium have increased over the course of the insurgency. The drug economy contributes to endemic corruption at all levels of government, greatly undercutting public confidence in the government, and it purportedly funds more than one-third of Taliban operations. It has become the single largest source of revenue for warlords, insurgents, criminal organizations, and members of the government, threatening to turn Afghanistan into a narco-state (UNODC 2007).

A focus on human rights would mean a dramatic reduction in combat and a focus on protection rather than on defeat of enemies. And it would also mean addressing directly other types of human rights violations, including the drug economy.

Legitimate Political Authority

The key to addressing human rights violations is the establishment of legitimate political authority. The Karzai government, established through the Bonn process, has failed to deliver effective or legitimate governance at the local level. Indeed, the sway of the Karzai government does not extend much beyond Kabul. Decisions to co-opt warlords, forgo justice, and under-resource key institutions responsible for law and order in the early years of the intervention had far-reaching implications for the legitimacy of the government and for its ability to deliver essential public goods.

The growing power of former commanders, whose brutality and abuses precipitated the Taliban takeover in the 1990s, has created a climate of fear, terror, and lawlessness. The U.S.-led Coalition forces' reliance on anti-Taliban militias to defeat the Taliban in 2001 led to the empowerment of these factional commanders. During the Bonn process, they were rewarded with positions in the government. This has entrenched a culture of impunity and has effectively surrendered the state. The fraudulent elections of 2009 have only made things worse.

One of the main obstacles to effective governance in Afghanistan has been lack of attention to rule-of-law institutions. Nowhere is this more evident than with the Afghan police force, which has been infiltrated by the former commanders and their militias, and which ordinary Afghans increasingly view as a tool of oppression and predation. Multinational forces and their civilian counterparts never put in the technical and financial resources necessary to establish a fully functioning law-and-order institution with the proper vetting processes, internal affairs, oversight, and operating rules. The objective was to "stand up" a police force as quickly as possible.

These mistakes have been compounded by the international forces retasking the police units to counterinsurgency operations rather than to law enforcement and by the creation of a number of militia programs at local levels. This shift in priorities has undermined the police's main task of protecting civilians and of supporting the rule of law and has led to their widespread mistrust.

Similar to the police, the justice system suffers from rampant corruption and a lack of human capital and remains sensitive to outside political pressure. This has led to a vacuum that the Taliban, in many areas, is only too eager to fill with the establishment of parallel administrations. Their harsh, but often welcome, system of courts offers a greater degree of predictability and reliability than the corrupt, slow, and ineffectual formal courts. They issue prompt rulings on a number of criminal and civil matters, including land disputes, family disputes, loan disputes, robbery, and murder. Essentially, they are delivering the basic governance tasks that the police and judiciary should be providing.

A focus on legitimate political authority might include the arrest of some of the most corrupt formal and informal powerholders (many of whom carry U.S. passports), an effective system of vetting for security and justice systems, as well as elections and serious efforts to build rule-of-law institutions.

A Bottom-Up Approach

The construction of a legitimate political authority must take into account another principle of a human security doctrine—the bottom-up approach. This would require the participation and empowerment of the broadest possible range of Afghans, especially women. There is a case for seeking political reconciliation but not just among those who are armed. There has been a consistent tendency to neglect those social actors (tribal and religious leaders, middle class professionals, women and youth, community organizers) who could potentially represent the basis for constructing legitimate authority.

Effective Multilateralism

At the operational level, the international effort in Afghanistan remains fragmented and suffers from a lack of coherence and unity of effort. This confused international structure has proved to be one of the greater obstacles to operations in Afghanistan. The divisions, rivalries, and "organizational tribalism" of the international community have prevented the development of a coherent strategy guiding and integrating the different elements of the stabilization and reconstruction effort. The sheer number of actors complicates efforts to enhance structures for coordination. There are two separate military operations, whose troops operate according to different missions and rules of engagement. In addition, there are several UN agencies, three special civilian representatives (UN, EU, and NATO), dozens of bilateral development agencies, and thousands of NGOs and contractors involved in rebuilding the country.

The UN must be mandated to act as the main strategic coordinating body, providing guidance, direction, and authority to the multiple actors comprising the international community. Moreover, the U.S.-led Operation Enduring Freedom should sign a status-of-force agreement with the Afghan government and be brought within the framework of the UN mandate. This legal vacuum has left U.S. forces unrestrained, creating significant problems regarding detention practices, the use of torture, and the lack of accountability for civilian deaths. This has not been remedied by the recent signing of a strategic partnership agreement in May 2012, which allows U.S. forces to continue to enjoy immunity from the Afghan legal system for any crimes they commit on Afghan soil.

Regional Focus

For decades, the nature of the Afghan conflict has been transnational, drawing in neighboring states directly and through local proxies. Despite having signed a pledge of noninterference at the Kabul Declaration in 2002, the six neighboring states retain their links to client networks in Afghanistan that are capable of destabilizing the country as an insurance policy. The insurgent sanctuary and recruiting base within Pakistan remains one of the biggest challenges to stability in Afghanistan.

With the exception of the Kabul Declaration, the Allies—mainly led by the United States—have sought to engage with the neighbors, namely Pakistan, bilaterally. Recent initiatives such as the Istanbul Process—a conference on regional security and cooperation that took place in November 2011—are a step in the right direction but still fall short of shifting the predominant framework of involvement away from merely an

Afghan–American partnership. Without a multilateral approach to building regional cooperation, panregional projects such as the New Silk Road advanced by the West are likely to fail, negatively impacting Afghanistan's economic outlook. Even worse, it is increasingly difficult to resist the perception that Afghanistan is steadily becoming a crucial area once again for geopolitical rivalries and renewed "proxy wars."

Clear Civilian Command

The final principle is clear civilian command. Counterinsurgency is a military strategy. A human security approach needs to be led by a powerful civilian, such as a UN special representative. Even though the late Richard Holbrooke was supposed to be the civilian counterpart to General Petraeus, at that time the commander in Afghanistan, he was much less visible in the region and internationally. The military need to be thought of as contributing to a civilian strategy rather than the other way round. Civilian control is necessary if the needs of people are to be put at the top of the agenda in practice as well as in theory. Civilian control would have to mean different rules of engagement, based on human rights rather the "laws of war," and it would also create more space for economic, social, and political development.

Summary

To summarize, a human security strategy in Afghanistan would:

- Reduce the international military presence, end air strikes, and reorient military tactics away from attacking insurgents toward protection and engagement at local levels.
- Rebalance economic and military efforts and give priority to the provision of basic services and legitimate ways of making a living by promoting agricultural alternatives to drug production or through legalization of drug production.
- Help establish a legitimate political authority through effective vetting for election candidates in national and provincial elections and for members of security and legal services, especially police, and through more resources for rule-of-law institutions and end the culture of impunity through arrests of prominent criminals.

- Involve the Afghan population, especially women, in the political process and in international deliberations including the "reconcilable" members of the insurgency.
- Bring U.S. forces within a UN mandate and establish a single strategic coordinating body led by the UN.
- Establish a multilateral regional framework involving governments and civil society.
- Establish a UN special representative as overall person in charge of both the civilian and military effort.

Conclusion

The Strategic Partnership Agreement signed by presidents Karzai and Obama on May 1, 2012, will govern the relations between the two countries up to 2024. It will allow the United States to keep some troops in Afghanistan after the withdrawal in 2014. Could this offer a moment in which to reorient the overall approach from the classic geopolitics that underpin the War on Terror and its successor toward something like human security? Or has the whole experience of the wars in Iraq and Afghanistan reduced the space for a humanitarian approach?

An ambitious rethinking of security would require:

- A U.S. commitment to strengthening the multilateral system and, in particular, the UN's capacity to protect people from violence.
- A profound restructuring of the defense sector away from big systems such as missile defense or sophisticated platforms toward the capacity for human security, which requires both military and civilian personnel, who train and work together and who operate in new ways according to human security principles. Such capabilities do require some technology, mainly transport and communications, that are usually interoperable with civilian requirements.
- Rebalancing military priorities versus development and climate change programs.
- A human security approach to the Middle East where the human security not only of Palestinians and Israelis but also all those engaged in the Arab Awakening comes before state security considerations and where a regional approach to conflicts, energy and development, weapons of mass destruction, human rights, and democracy is needed.

- An intensive dialogue with other countries about how to develop appropriate capabilities It should involve China, India, and Russia as well as the EU. The dialogue should recognize that, in some cases, especially the EU and to some extent India, thinking about alternative security approaches is already well advanced.

The tragedy is that a new approach to Afghanistan could have demonstrated that this new thinking is not just words, and this could have made possible other changes. The War on Terror has been associated with the wars in Iraq and Afghanistan. President Obama emphasized the importance of Afghanistan during his 2008 campaign and, indeed, suggested that he was against the war in Iraq because it diverted attention from Afghanistan. For this reason, Afghanistan became a sort of litmus test of his administration's approach to security policy. Unfortunately, this administration has retreated from some of the ideas that were debated during the Afghan war and has reverted to a campaign of long-distance air strikes, especially drones, that is likely to exacerbate growing violence in places such as Pakistan, Somalia, and Yemen not to mention in Afghanistan. Something dramatic is required to prevent a slow slide toward global insecurity. If withdrawal from Afghanistan were to be associated with a very different approach, one based on human security, this would signal a profound change of direction and, if it worked, could help to underpin a new covenant at a global level, establishing trust in multilateral institutions.

Note

1. See www.icasualties.org for updated figures on Coalition casualties.

References

Barcelona Report, 2004, *A Human Security Doctrine for Europe: the Barcelona Report of the Study Group on Europe's Security Capabilities*, 15 September, available at: eprints.lse.ac.uk/40209/, accessed December 2012

Beck, U., 1992, *Risk Society: Towards a New Modernity*, London: Sage.

Bilmes, L. J. and J. E. Stiglitz, 2008, *The Three Trillion Dollar War: The True Cost of the Iraq Conflict*, New York: Norton.

von Clausewitz, C., 1997, *On War*, trans. J. J. Graham, *Wordsworth Classics of World Literature*, Hertfordshire, UK: Wordsworth Editions.

Collier, P. and A. Hoeffler, 2004, "Greed and Grievance in Civil Wars," *Oxford Economic Papers*, 56:563–595.

Department of the Army and United States Marine Corps, 2006, *Counterinsurgency Field Manual No. 3–24*, Marine Corps Warfighting Publication No. 3–33.5, Washington, D.C.

Department of Defense Instruction Number 3000.05, September 16, 2009, available at www.dtic.mil/whs/directives/corres/pdf/300005p.pdf (accessed October 22, 2012).

Development and Cooperation—Europeaid, "Instrument for Stability," available at http://ec.europa.eu/europeaid/how/finance/ifs_en.htm. Updated May 11, 2012. (accessed July 27, 2012).

Elsea, J. K. and N. M. Serafino, 2007, "Private Security Contractors in Iraq: Background, Legal Status, and Other Issues," Congressional Research Service Report for Congress, Washington, D.C., updated July 11, (available at http://fpc.state.gov/documents/organization/88030.pdf, (accessed October 22, 2012).

Glasius, M. and M. Kaldor, eds., 2005, *A Human Security Doctrine for Europe: Project, Principles, Practicalities,* London: Routledge.

Glenny, M., 2008, *McMafia: A Journey Through the Global Criminal Underworld,* London: Bodley Head.

Holt, V. K. and T. C. Berkman, 2006, *The Impossible Mandate? Military Preparedness, the Responsibility to Protect and Modern Peace Operations*, Washington, D.C.: The Henry L. Stimson Center.

Ikenberry, J. G. and A. M. Slaughter, 2006, *Forging a World of Liberty Under Law: US National Security in the 21st Century: Final Report of the Princeton Report on National Security,* Princeton: Princeton University Press.

Internal Displacement Monitoring Centre Geneva, available at www.internal-displacement.org (accessed October 22, 2012).

Kaldor, M., 2012, *New and Old Wars: Organized Violence in a Global Era*, 3rd ed., Cambridge: Polity.

Kaldor, M., T. Karl, and Y. Said, eds., 2007, *Oil Wars,* London: Pluto.

Madrid Report, 2007, *A European Way of Security: The Madrid Report of the Human Security Study Group*, November 8, available at www.world-governance.org/IMG/pdf_0078_A_European_Way_of_Security.pdf, (accessed October 22, 2012).

Nordstrom, C., 2004, *Shadows of War: Violence, Power, and International Profiteering in the Twenty-First Century*, Berkeley: University of California Press.

Rice, Condoleeza, 2008, "Rethinking the National Interest: American Realism for a New Century," *Foreign Affairs,* July/August, available at http://www.foreignaffairs.com/articles/64445/condoleezza-rice/rethinking-the-national-interest (accessed October 30, 2012).

Rangelov, I. and M. Theros, 2012, "Abuse of Power and Conflict Persistence in Afghanistan," *Conflict, Security, and Development* (Special Issue: Persistent Conflict), 12(3):227–248.

Smith, R., 2006, *The Utility of Force: The Art of Making War in the Modern World*, London: Allen Lane.

United Nations Development Programme (UNDP), 2006, *Evaluation of UNDP Support for Conflict Affected Countries*, available at www.lse.ac.uk/Depts/global/ Publications/UNDP_Human%20Security%20Report2006.pdf (accessed October 22, 2012).

United Nations Office on Drugs and Crime (UNODC), 2007, "Fighting Corruption in Afghanistan: A Roadmap for Strategy and Action"; informal discussion paper, Feb 16, available at www.unodc.org/pdf/afg/anti_corruption_roadmap.pdf (accessed October 22, 2012).

Wulf, H., 2005, "The Challenges of Re-Establishing a Public Monopoly of Violence," in *A Human Security Doctrine for Europe: Project; Principles; Practicalities*, edited by M. Glasius and M. Kaldor, 20–40. Oxford: Routledge.

6

Recent Developments in Global Criminal Industries

MISHA GLENNY

Introduction

The evolution of global criminal markets, involving every country in the world (including those such as North Korea that purportedly aspire to autarky), has been one of the most striking developments of the past thirty years.

The global financial meltdown and the consequent economic crisis triggered by the collapse of Lehman Brothers in the fall of 2008 have had several indirect effects in the pattern of transnational organized crime. Although some of these would appear to be merely conjunctural, others indicate a shift in the longer-term strategies of global criminal communities. They further confirm the gradual transfer of global economic power away from the United States, Western Europe, and Japan in favor of Latin America and South and East Asia.

In principle, the dramatic rise in organized crime during the 1990s represented a systemic change, but it was made even more forceful by certain conjunctural advantages. After a high point reached from 1995 to 1997, criminal activity leveled out before becoming a more predictable and even integrated part of the global economy.

Since the millennium, the main sectors of criminal activity have fallen into a more predictable pattern largely in line with the growth rates of G8 countries. There has been one significant deviation from this—the organized use of the Internet and other cyber instruments to commit serious economic crimes.

The two main causes of systemic change in the 1990s were the collapse of communism in Eastern Europe and the former Soviet Union on the one hand and the rapid liberalization of markets in a wide variety of territories characterized by an equally eclectic spread of political strategies and ideologies. The latter included not only China and East Asian countries such as Thailand and Vietnam but also India, the Gulf States, and large parts of Latin America.

The consolidation of criminal networks across and between continents was aided greatly by an older and well-tested part of the financial system that experienced a spectacular growth as part of the licit economy in this period. This was the offshore banking system through which as much as a third of international financial transactions are processed. Multinational companies and wealthy individuals from the super rich class exploit loopholes in the system as a means to evade and avoid taxes.[1]

The existence of offshore banking systems and mechanisms designed specifically to conceal the true origin of taxable income generated by individuals and by companies has proved an invaluable tool in the expansion of global organized crime. The laundering of illicitly procured funds through any number of jurisdictions witnessed an unprecedented boom during the 1990s as new criminal networks around the world successfully reaped the fruits of their activities. Despite a rhetorical commitment on the part of the G8 to act against banking centers[2] that facilitate tax evasion on a monumental scale and the profitability of criminal business, there has been no significant dip in the volume or nature of their trade since 2009. On the contrary, they represent a part of the global economy that continues to grow, perhaps in line with the early recovery of the oligarchs and multinationals that make up the bulk of their customers.

The Fall of the Berlin Wall

The collapse of communism played a major role in the expansion of cross-border criminal activity for two reasons. The failure of the planned economies not only led to the end of a state ideology it also inflicted a massive blow against the state itself. The dramatic downturn in economic activity that accompanied the collapse combined with exceptional political instability throughout Eastern Europe and the former Soviet Union led to a precipitous fall in tax revenue and state subsidies in every social and economic area.

The criminal and commercial justice systems (which were fundamentally different from those regulating market economies) were deprived of funding, forcing their partial dismantling just at a time when they had to adapt to very new conditions. In Bulgaria, for example, between 1989 and 1991, security forces were pruned by some 20 percent, resulting in 14,000 highly trained officers seeking employment (Glenny 2007:14).

The state, which had dominated the industrial sector, quickly lost the authority to maintain its grip; its ownership of industrial and social facilities throughout the country was challenged by a new class of entrepreneurs, many of whom had strong links with the previous regime and who were able to exploit key political and economic networks.

This new elite included many individuals previously dependent on the state—such as former policemen and soldiers, sportsmen (especially wrestlers, boxers, and weightlifters), and in Russia, Afghan veterans—whose skills now enabled them to take the law into their own hands. They quickly established relations with the criminal classes that had existed under the previous regime (especially in Soviet jails), and together they filled the vacuum left by the collapsing criminal justice system.

The aim, in part conscious and in part intuitive, was to establish and to build monopoly positions in the new market economy. Key sectors targeted were those whose value had temporarily collapsed but that had every prospect of reviving later on: mineral resources, metallurgy, and large-scale service industries such as air transport, travel, and leisure, as well as key commodities such as sugar. By contrast, agriculture—the mainstay of many Eastern European economies—was allowed to decline.

The criminal and violent character of many involved in this new grab for market share, along with the lack of clarity regarding the nature of contract law, produced the remarkable side effect of nurturing powerful criminal groups across the region. This is best summed up in Vladimir Volkov's description of this hybrid class as "violent entrepreneurs," alluding to the fact that the failure of the security services and of the courts to police contract law led to the development of groups whose primary resource was violence—violence they would deploy if contracts with businessmen they represented were not satisfactorily honored (Volkov 2002). In earlier periods, these groups were referred to as "mafia" or "protection rackets," but some scholars have argued they would be better described as "violent entrepreneurs," in Volkov's words, or as "protection service providers."

With the substantial withdrawal of the state as social and economic arbiter while a new economic system was emerging, the issue of what constituted a licit product and what an illicit product temporarily disappeared. For the first few years after the collapse of communism, there were few if any effective sanctions on what traders could sell. (This explains the astonishing appearance of hard-core pornography in most Eastern European countries, where it was openly sold in kiosks in broad daylight and in full view of the entire population.) In this anarchic atmosphere, everything was considered licit, so the new business class found itself able and willing to sell anything. This of course included trafficking in drugs and in women for sexual purposes, as well as in food, furniture, and rolled steel.

The withering of the state also affected borders. The year 1989 saw the creation of a series of lawless states that stretched from the Baltics in the north to Central Asia in the south and from Slovenia in the west to the Chinese border in the east; before long China would also engage in some of that lawless activity.

Nonetheless, the criminal markets in Eastern Europe and in the Soviet Union were very small. The economic collapse meant that consumer spending power was negligible. Similarly, for all its faults, communism had at least ensured that the market for narcotics, for example, was very underdeveloped. (Within a few years, cultural shifts started to change this.) The weakness of the local markets meant that the new criminal networks sought out more vigorous markets beyond their borders, integrating quickly into a global chain of production, distribution, and consumption of illicit goods and services.

The Advent of Globalization

In the first few years after the fall of communism, Western countries started to emerge from the torpor of recession. The European Union and the United States were now at the beginning of a significant increase in growth that was not the consequence of improved efficiency or of productivity, but of a series of speculative bubbles, each one outdoing its predecessor. Even Japan, still recovering from the damaging effects of the "bubble economy" of the late 1980s, started to revive a few years after the United States, and European economies began to pick up.

Western consumers, encouraged by unprecedentedly low interest rates found themselves with more income at their disposal than ever before in history. The sale of white goods and of products from the newly expanding high-tech industry began to increase rapidly.

But other industries were also prospering. The early 1990s saw a significant rise in the global drug market. Police forces in Western Europe, Canada, and the United States reported being overwhelmed by the increase in usage of heroin, cocaine, and synthetic drugs such as Ecstasy that were associated with the rave culture that attracted not just European but global youth during this period. One of *The Guardian*'s most respected columnists, Decca Aitkenhead (2003), actually wrote a book at the time detailing her pilgrimage to clubbing hot spots around the world, during which she tested and compared the rich culture of narcotics as it conquered an ever greater number of territories.

Meanwhile, in those countries where markets were opening up but where the chaotic political transition that characterized the fall of communism had been avoided, businessmen and traders were learning that liberalization also enabled them to expand their portfolio to include criminal goods and services, especially if they were close to the origin of the products or to the people (usually women) providing those services.

The flooding of Western markets with cocaine from Colombia and with heroin from the poppy fields of Afghanistan was in part caused by the political instability in these two countries.

For criminal markets, the world was becoming divided into three broad geographic sectors—zones of production, zones of distribution, and zones of consumption—which necessitated the emergence of logistics regimes that were every bit as efficient (if not more so) than those in the licit world. Central and Southeast Asia (narcotics, the sex industry, endangered species, and counterfeit goods), Africa (mineral resources—especially illegally mined or "blood" diamonds and coltan, and the sex industry), and South America (narcotics) were the main areas of production. Russia, Eastern Europe (particularly the Balkans), South and Central America, and, later, West Africa were the major distribution zones. Consumers were concentrated in Western Europe, the United States, Japan, Australasia, and later in hybrid economic areas such as the Middle East and South Africa.

In general, the closer to the zone of production, the more unstable and violent the social and political circumstances. Producer areas tend to have the highest number of states whose authority is contested at virtually every level and whose reach is often restricted to only a few urban areas. In Colombia, for example, there are large areas where the peasantry rarely, if ever, encounters institutions of the state (Thoumi 2003).

In the distribution zones, the primary aim of criminal groups is to influence the positions of customs and police, as well as to corrupt politicians. These countries often boast more complex social and economic relations through which the state is able to exert greater influence, meaning that violence perpetrated by informal or criminal groups is not as pronounced as in the producer zones. The great exception to this was in the Balkans where it can be argued that the wars of the 1990s were integral to the successful development of criminal groups.

In the consumer zones, organized crime acts as retailers trying to ensure that their products reach and satisfy a discerning consumer. This requires a very different strategy from the corrupt practices and indeed domination of political structures that is so common in producer and distribution zones. Criminals need to keep well under the radar to avoid detection from one of their two serious business risks—law enforcement.[3]

Of course, the delineation of these three zones is not hard and fast. Levels of violence in two distribution countries, Mexico and Venezuela, are now outstripping anything reported elsewhere in the world aside from one major producer zone, the eastern Democratic Republic of Congo. There are also one or two sectors where the zone system is reversed; duty-not-paid cigarettes and illegal weapons, for example, tend to be produced in traditional consumer zones and consumed in traditional producer zones.

Under this system, the functions of individual Eastern European states were sometimes highly differentiated. The Balkans became a major global transit or distribution zone for goods and services from all over the globe, straining to reach the world's most lucrative market, that is, the European Union. Russia was a major producer of services, especially of women being trafficked into Western Europe's sex industry, but it also created a powerful criminal class associated with its vast mineral wealth and even with its endangered species, such as the sturgeon responsible for producing caviar. Furthermore, it became a central transit route for Afghan heroin heading toward Western European markets. The Visegrad countries, Poland, the Czech Republic, Slovakia, and Hungary, became bridgeheads for Russia's mighty criminal syndicates as they sought to make inroads into Western Europe, with the aim of setting up money-laundering operations in key districts such as the City of London and enjoying the fruits of their wealth in Europe's main cultural centers.

Stabilization and the Return of the State

From the late 1990s, the volatility of criminal markets settled to a large degree. The impact of reforms stipulated by aspiring members of the European Union did much to bolster the delicate criminal justice systems across most of Eastern Europe. There was a reduction in large-scale criminal activities recorded in the Visegrad countries in particular, although both Poland and Hungary continue to face serious problems as centers of the duty-not-paid cigarette and money laundering industries, respectively.

The changes wrought by improving economic circumstances were most obviously visible in the provision of female sex workers for the Western European market. In the first half of the 1990s, the majority of women being trafficked or smuggled to service this market were from Poland, the Czech Republic, and Slovakia. In the second half of the 1990s, this flow has diminished to a trickle due to the greatly improved economic circumstances in these states. (There is a demonstrable linkage between the number of women entering the sex industry, whether willingly or not, and national poverty levels.) Instead, they have been replaced by women from Moldova (including Transnistria), Ukraine, Belarus, and Russia and, to a lesser degree, from the Baltic States.

The prospect of EU membership also exerted massive force in the former Yugoslavia and in other Balkan countries. Above all, it underpinned a host of other efforts to stabilize the former Yugoslavia, transforming a turbulent region that had experienced high levels of violence and armed conflict into one that has been increasingly characterized by regional cooperation and, if not economic prosperity, then certainly by reconstruction. The improving governmental, economic, and social ties between Croatia and Serbia have given considerable impetus to much of that regional cooperation. It has been striking how a joint assault on the corrosive twinned cultures of corruption and organized crime has informed every aspect of the improving relations between the two countries, as both aspire to demonstrate to the European Union their commitment to the Justice and Home Affairs chapters of the accession package (Glenny 2012). In several parts of the region, this commitment has been more rhetorical than practical, but extracting corruption from political culture, once it has become thoroughly rooted, can take decades, especially in states such as Kosovo where adult unemployment rates are running between 40 and 50 percent.

In Russia, there was no equivalent pull from Europe. Here a different shift took place after Vladimir Putin established himself as the most powerful political figure in the country. His rule saw a revival of the residual influence of the state. This was achieved partly by a powerful reassertion of central government at the expense of the provinces, but it was also accompanied by the retrenchment of the security services, the Federal Security Bureau (FSB), and other state organs at the expense of the oligarch class and their "violent entrepreneurs." Under Yeltsin, the oligarchs and organized crime groups controlled the state. Putin reversed this relationship, so that the state now determined the role of the oligarchs and of organized crime. The political aim of this strategy was clear: the restoration of order as a means of defusing the powerful popular discontent that had been growing in the final years of Yeltsin and the early part of Putin's administration.

In certain industries and sectors, the influence of criminal activity and corruption continued to destabilize markets, notably in the licit sector of energy distribution. The smooth supply of gas to Western Europe through Ukraine continues to be periodically disrupted as the various criminal organizations and corrupt political groupings in Russia and Ukraine argue over the distribution of vast illegal payments associated with this trade, which has been effectively institutionalized (Global Witness 2006). Of course, throughout Eastern Europe and Russia, rising prosperity has seen the development of new consumer markets for illicit goods and services, as these countries edge away from their role in the zones of production and distribution and toward the consumer zone.

The Drug Trade

Elsewhere in the world, the problem of criminal markets, mainly associated with the narcotics industry, became considerably more severe in the first decade of the new century.

The War on Drugs has continued to inflict immense collateral damage on several key countries. The Taliban secures hundreds of millions of dollars in funding annually from its taxation of the heroin trade and it also gains political support by protecting the poppy crop. Furthermore, the

Afghan government itself is greatly influenced by corrupt money generated from the production and export of the drug that in the latest United Nations estimate accounts for 47 percent of GDP. Equally devastating has been the impact in Mexico and in other Latin American countries, including Venezuela, where the death rate since 2008 has actually exceeded that recorded in Mexico.

In consequence, global drug policy is in flux, and the consensus that has characterized international policy since before World War II is now breaking down. Several Latin American governments, including Mexico and Colombia, have decriminalized the possession of narcotics for personal use. In addition, a group of influential elder statesmen led by Brazil's former president, Fernando Henrique Cardoso, have called for the full legalization of drugs. The proliferating calls for the legalization of drugs in Latin America reflect the growing independence of the region from the United States, where consumer demand for narcotics has always driven the violence and political instability associated with the cocaine, marijuana, and heroin trades. Washington's ability to influence drug policy in the region appears to be slipping.

At the same time, there is a growing challenge to the drug policy consensus within the United States. The use of marijuana as a prescription medicine in fourteen states and the District of Columbia has led to a huge growth in the regulated narcotics industry, especially in California where finding a doctor prepared to prescribe the drug rarely poses any great challenge to consumers. California has accrued benefits from the development of the medical marijuana industry through its taxation and regulation. Although Proposition 19—which argued for the full legalization of the drug in 2010—failed, there are likely to be further attempts in the near future. Already the federal government and the state laws on medical marijuana have created some conflict; federal law enforcement officers have made several arrests of marijuana growers who are licensed locally but not by Washington.

The significance of this and similar moves in some parts of Europe and Canada cannot be underestimated. The legalization of marijuana will bring a very lucrative industry out of the shadows and under control of the state. In the long term, the importance of this lies in the fact that the illegal drug industry remains the primary entry point for organized criminal syndicates; should the consensus on the prohibition of drugs fracture, this will greatly alter and disempower the global criminal community.

The Rise of Cyber Crime and Financial Fraud

In the spring of 2001, a new Web site, CarderPlanet, went live on the World Wide Web. Developed by a group of young men in Odessa, Ukraine, CarderPlanet was the first structured criminal site on the Internet. It acted as a department store or "one-stop shop," as U.S. law enforcement agencies have described it, for those engaged in criminal activity on the Web, chiefly relating to the fraudulent use of credit cards (Glenny 2011).

This marked the beginning of a remarkable growth in a sector of criminal activity that did not exist a decade ago. The low-hanging fruit of the industry involves the theft and resale of credit and debit card data, which is then used to fraudulently withdraw money either through ATMs or by purchasing goods over the Internet. There are, however, a whole range of further crimes being committed on a daily basis over the Web, including cracking bank accounts, roaming databases of corporations following successful phishing attacks launched via spam, and pumping and dumping schemes, whereby hacking is used to manipulate share prices. Just as there is no end to creativity on the Web, so there is no end to criminal activity in the same medium.

One of the most lucrative activities so far has been the sale of so-called scareware. Hackers distribute a virus onto the Web that infects people's computers before triggering a pop-up on their browser warning them that their computer has been contaminated by viruses. People can spare themselves the infection, the Web page continues, by purchasing a particular type of antivirus software. This software has in fact been developed by the criminal group, who charges money for it. The software does not in fact protect the computer on which it is installed; on the contrary, it renders the machine vulnerable to a whole host of new infections. One case currently under investigation by the FBI is believed to have netted its perpetrators an astonishing $500 million.

Simple cybercrime is now estimated as being worth just over $110 billion annually. This, however, is based primarily on reported crime, and it does not include crimes committed against companies and corporations. A coalition of computer security firms estimated that the direct and indirect economic damage inflicted by cybercriminal activity amounts to some $1 trillion.

In some but not all respects, the structures behind this phenomenon differ markedly from traditional organized crime groups. The industry is characterized by a much greater degree of fragmentation; individuals or small groups with an advanced technical ability can already generate huge sums of money through digital crime. Traditional organized groups are identified as being active on the Web, but they are not the sole or indeed primary community.

Nonetheless, with the economic recession, those crime groups engaged in the sale and distribution of traditional illicit commodities and services have witnessed a downturn in their trade. The explanation for this is relatively straightforward: Consumers have less disposable income, and items such as narcotics and the purchase of services from sex workers are among the first markets to suffer. By contrast, there has been a dramatic rise in another major criminal industry—the sale and distribution of counterfeit goods, which are now found not only in every sector of consumer goods but also in industrial goods as well. But the most dramatic expansion, as registered by Western European and U.S. law enforcement agencies, has been in financial fraud and in computer crime. For the foreseeable future, these are likely to remain the major growth industries for criminal groups around the globe.

Notes

1. For details of the offshore industry, see Shaxson (2011).

2. Contained within Clause 15 of the Final Declaration of the G20 Summit in London, this promised an end to banking secrecy worldwide and sanctions against uncooperative jurisdictions. See text at www.economicsummits.info/2009/10/document-london-summit-communique.

3. The other risk is competition; however, all criminal groups are dissuaded from allowing competition to break down into violence among themselves because this tends to make their operations less efficient and to draw the attention of their first risk, that of law enforcement.

References

Aitkenhead, D., 2003, *The Promised Land: Travels in the Search for the Perfect E*, London: HarperCollins UK.

Glenny, M., 2007, *McMafia: A Journey Through the Global Criminal Underworld*, New York: Vintage.

———, 2011, *DarkMarket: Cybercops, Cyberthieves, and You*, London: Bodley Head.

———, 2012, *The Balkans: Nationalism, War, and the Great Powers—1804–2012*, rev. ed., New York: Penguin.

Global Witness, 2006, *It's a Gas: Funny Business in the Turkmen-Ukraine Gas Trade*, London: Global Witness.

Shaxson, N., 2011, *Treasure Islands: Tax Havens and the Men Who Stole the World*, London: Bodley Head.

Thoumi, F. E., 2003, *Illegal Drugs, Economy, and Society in the Andes*, Washington D.C.: Woodrow Wilson Center.

Volkov, V., 2002, *Violent Entrepreneurs: The Use of Force in the Making of Russian Capitalism*, Ithaca, N.Y.: Cornell University Press.

3

Environmental Protection

Introduction

Today one of the major threats to individuals' security—economic and physical—around the world arises from the danger of global warming and climate change associated with the increased atmospheric concentration of greenhouse gases. Changes in weather affect those whose livelihood is dependent on agriculture, and extreme weather events—such as floods and cyclones—have left thousands, in some cases millions, homeless. Insecurity going forward is even greater: Rising sea levels will inundate low-lying coastal areas. As an example, rising sea levels are predicted to displace millions of people in Bangladesh.

Global warming is the quintessential global public good (or bad): It arises from carbon emissions everywhere in the world. America's carbon emissions adversely affect Bangladesh and the United States alike. The carbon molecules don't carry passports and they don't require visas as they move into the global atmosphere.

Although all may benefit from reducing carbon emissions, everyone would like others to bear the costs. This is a classic "free rider" problem. What makes the problem particularly difficult is the uneven incidence of the costs of climate change as well as of the costs of reducing emissions. The latter is likely to be especially large for the big polluters, such as the United

States, although the costs of climate change are disproportionately felt by poor countries in the developing world.

While in Copenhagen in December 2009, the international community agreed to reduce global emissions to prevent (or more accurately to reduce the likelihood of) a two-degree Celsius increase in temperature; however, they could not agree on how to share the burden or on how to enforce any agreement that might be reached. Indeed to many the agreement was a step back from the Kyoto Protocol, which had at least negotiated targets for emission reductions, though there was no enforcement mechanism and a large fraction of the world's pollution did not come within the ambit of that agreement. The Copenhagen Accord only committed countries to set out their own national agendas. It seemed to rely on peer pressure. Peer pressure had been remarkably successful in calling forth significant efforts at emissions reduction, but peer pressure had been totally unsuccessful in getting countries to reach an agreement or in getting the U.S. Congress to pass any bill to significantly curtail U.S. emissions. These failures—and the disarray evident at the Copenhagen summit—symbolized the failures of global governance. Clearly, an agreement could not be reached even in an arena that represented a real threat to the entire planet.

The two chapters in part 3 lay out some of the critical issues. The second, by Joseph Aldy and Robert Stavins, describes the key challenges facing the international community, the obstacles to reaching an agreement, and four alternative approaches going forward.

The first chapter in this part, though, focuses more narrowly on one of the obstacles—how to share the burden of saving the world—and borrows ideas from the analogous literature on how to share the burden of financing public goods within a country. Joseph Stiglitz expresses considerable pessimism—justified by the failures in international negotiations—about the current dominant approach, which focuses on reaching an agreement about emission reduction targets. The reason is that the allocation of emission rights is little different from allocating money. And the Kyoto Protocol—which effectively gave more emission rights (money) to those that had polluted more in the past—is, and should be, unacceptable to most in the developing world. Some (such as Lord Nicholas Stern) are hopeful that, nonetheless, a global deal can still be reached. The developing countries gain sufficiently from a reduction in emissions that even if they are granted, say, emission rights that are "unfairly small," they might nonetheless agree to a deal (Stern 2009). Stiglitz is less sanguine that a deal that is unfair—in effect, giving the rich greater rights to the atmosphere's "carbon space" than the poor—will be acceptable to those in the developing world. He suggests that an approach based on "common measures"—an agreed-upon tax on carbon emissions, agreed-upon standards for automobiles or electricity generation—will be more acceptable, especially if accompanied by assistance to developing countries to help meet the additional burdens.

Reaching an agreement on enforcement also faces three obstacles. It would be nice if one could just trust others to live up to their commitments, but, as Stiglitz points out, what has happened since 1992 in the arena of climate change provides reason not to have such faith. Most of those signing on to the Kyoto Protocol did not achieve the reductions that had been promised; and to a large extent, some of the advanced industrial countries now seem to be trying to renegotiate the commitments they made as part of the 1992 Rio agreement to finance the incremental costs associated with emission reductions for developing countries. (China and India, for instance, remain developing countries, according to the World Bank, even though they are large countries with many well-off individuals.)

The first obstacle to achieving an enforceable agreement is that any enforceable agreement entails, in effect, a derogation of sovereignty. It is one thing to agree to a principle that there ought to be reductions in global emissions, so long as doing so imposes no direct obligations, or, if there are obligations, so long as those obligations cannot be enforced. It is quite another matter to give others—the international community—the right to impose one form of sanction or another if one fails to live up to one's commitments. The second obstacle—related to the first—is that there is no confidence in the international community's ability to adjudicate disputes. China may, for instance, worry that the United States might accuse it of not reducing emissions in the way agreed, and any international tribunal, composed largely of those from the advanced industrial countries, will side with the United States. Moreover, any international agreement involves multiple obligations, and developing countries worry that there may be more rigor in enforcing the obligations on them to reduce their emissions than the obligations on the developed countries to make technology or finance available to the developing countries. Thirdly, there are problems of devising effective enforcement mechanisms. The standard mechanism is trade sanctions (part of the Montreal Convention aimed at reducing ozone-destroying gases). But such sanctions are more effective against poor countries than against rich, and developing countries worry that with the possibility of such sanctions advanced industrial countries will impose "green tariffs" accusing the developing countries of violating their commitments, even if they have not.

Developing countries worry, moreover, that any system, even if it were de jure fair, de facto might not be: Bringing and defending cases is costly. Rich countries can bear these costs far more easily than can poor countries. All of these fears on the part of developing countries find partial justification in what has happened in trade and investment agreements. Yet, there are some reasons for optimism. Although there was much to-do about the loss of sovereignty when the United States signed on to the WTO agreement, such concerns are seldom voiced today. There is a general consensus that countries gain by such agreements and that any agreement that is credible must have some enforcement mechanism. The benefits of the agreement, with its limited loss of sovereignty, are seen to be worth the costs (at least if the other problems described here can be solved). And there have been some instances of success—especially in the environmental area, for example, with the Montreal Convention.

What is at stake in climate change is much larger, as are the distributive consequences. That makes not only the benefits of achieving an agreement greater but also the difficulties. If the global community can make progress in this arena, it will enhance confidence in global governance. If it fails, the entire planet—and the security of all of its citizens—will be at risk.

Reference

Stern, N., 2009, *The Global Deal: Climate Change and the Creation of a New Era of Progress and Prosperity*, New York: Public Affairs.

7

Sharing the Burden of Saving the Planet: Global Social Justice for Sustainable Development

*Lessons from the Theory of Public Finance**

JOSEPH E. STIGLITZ

Introduction

The risks of climate change resulting from the increase in the atmospheric concentration of greenhouse gases have been well documented. There are likely to be especially adverse effects on developing countries and particularly the poor within these countries. There is a global consensus that strong actions need to be taken to ensure that the world does not face *excessive* risk from an increase in the atmospheric concentration of greenhouse gases that would, say, lead to an increase in average global temperatures of more than 2 degrees Celsius. This chapter is concerned with how the global community should respond to this global risk and in particular how the burden of preventing global warming—or, more accurately, reducing the

*Earlier versions of this paper were presented at the World Congress of the International Economic Association, Istanbul, June 2009, and at a meeting on Equitable Burden Sharing in Responding to Climate Change hosted by Brooks World Poverty Institute, Manchester, and jointly sponsored by the Initiative for Policy Dialogue on June 17–18, 2009. The author is indebted to the Ford, Mott, and Macarthur Foundations for financial support. The author served as a member of the 1995 assessment panel of the International Panel on Climate Change (IPCC).

risk—should be shared, especially between developed and less-developed countries. Almost surely, no matter what we do, there will be the necessity for adaptation, with significant costs borne especially by developing countries. How those costs should be shared is an important question that is beyond the scope of this chapter.

There are five other points of consensus that form the background for this chapter:

1. Global warming is a global problem, and it needs to be addressed globally. Unless all countries participate, there is a danger of leakage; reductions in emissions in one country may be more than offset by increases elsewhere (Stern 2007).
2. Global warming is a long-run problem. We are concerned not so much with the level of emissions in any particular year as with the long-run levels of atmospheric concentrations of greenhouse gases.
3. The costs of reducing the level of emissions (limiting the increases in atmospheric concentration of greenhouse gases) will be much lower if it is done efficiently. Efficiency implies *comprehensiveness*—we need to address all sources of emissions and explore all ways of reducing atmospheric carbon concentrations, including carbon storage and carbon sequestration.
4. There is considerable uncertainty about the level of "tolerable" increases in greenhouse gas concentrations and about the impact of particular policy interventions.
5. Global warming is a public good problem, so there is a risk of free riding. This means that there will have to be some system of credible enforcement.

There are five important corollaries of these points of consensus:

1. We need a global agreement, and a global agreement will require equitable burden sharing. Much of this chapter is concerned with exploring what this entails.
2. The shadow price of carbon should be approximately the same *in all uses, in all countries, and at all dates.* Current arrangements deviate in important ways from this principle. The (shadow) price of carbon in those countries that signed on to the Kyoto Protocol is higher than in other countries. The (shadow) price of carbon associated with deforestation is lower than in other uses. In many countries, the price

of carbon (reductions) associated with renewables and, especially, ethanol is higher than in other uses.

3. The costs of adjustment will be smaller if the adjustment is done efficiently, which means that the adjustment will be spread out over time. But that does not mean that the prices need to adjust slowly. An immediate adjustment in prices to reflect the true scarcity will result in a gradual adjustment in behaviors, reflecting an efficient response to the costs of adjustment. If there is an argument for gradual adjustment of prices, it is based on distributive concerns.

4. The fact that this is a long-run problem with considerable uncertainty means that whether we work through emission targets or prices, there will need to be adjustments over time. In an emission targets system, we will have to adjust the targets. In a carbon tax system, we will have to adjust the tax. Thus, the standard argument that, in the face of certain types of uncertainties, quantity targets are preferable to price interventions is of limited relevance.

5. We need to differentiate between systemic risk and risk faced by market participants. Uncertainties—and differences in beliefs about the nature of the risks—in fact provide an argument for mixed instruments, such as the safety valve, where, in the short run, there is a cap on the price faced by firms. Market participants are risk averse, and there is a cost to imposing risk on them. Intertemporal adjustments allow firm and individual risks to be spread out over time, and this greatly mitigates those risks. The fact that what matters is the long-run atmospheric concentrations means that the environmental costs of any limited temporary deviations from prespecified targets is likely to be small.

Insights from Public Finance

There are two more introductory remarks. The first problem we are discussing has many of the features of those addressed within classical public finance. The preservation of our common atmosphere (preventing global warming) is a global public good.[1] It has to be financed. Standard theories of public finance provide clear formulations concerning equitable and efficient taxation.

Alternatively, we can think of carbon emissions as generating a global externality, and again, standard public finance theories discuss efficient and equitable ways of controlling an externality-generating activity—including the relative merits of corrective taxation and of regulatory interventions. Much of the literature has focused on the equivalence of the two systems of interventions, under certain conditions, and much of our analysis will make use of that equivalence. We will first analyze tax interventions because in doing so, the efficiency and equity implications become more transparent. We will then provide the interpretation for quantity interventions.

Theory of Second Best

Second, policy in this area—even more than in many other areas of economics—is a matter of the *economics of the second best*. Even governments that are committed to reducing emissions have limited control. Emissions are the by-product of every economic activity. Emissions are not just a matter of industrialization: The methane produced by animals is a major contributor to emissions. We have increasingly become concerned with deforestation, which contributes 20 percent of the world's emissions. But moving to building materials other than lumber may not help: 5 percent of the world's emissions come from the production of cement. Not only can't we control emissions perfectly, we cannot even measure emissions perfectly.

There is a second important second-best consideration. There are, in fact, two important unpriced (or imperfectly priced) resources: (clean, fresh) water and (carbon in the) air. Many of the reform proposals involve, implicitly or explicitly, putting a price on carbon. But this may increase the importance of other distortions.

Biofuels provide an illustration of what is at issue. One of the responses in many parts of the world to the threat of global warming is to increase the production of biofuels, the production of which, in some parts of the world, makes extensive use of already very limited supplies of water.[2] At the very least, we need to be aware of this distortion.

Moreover, the increase in biofuels has contributed to the increase in the price of food. In this case, the *incidence* of the (hidden and implicit) tax on carbon is borne disproportionately by the poor in the world because they spend a larger fraction of their income on food, whereas the rich biofuel producers and corn producers in the United States are actually better off. This compounds the inequities already imposed by global warming: Those in the tropics—where a large fraction of the poorest live—are likely to be most adversely affected by global warming; but this response puts the burden of adjustment disproportionately on them.

One of the reasons that the economics of the second best is especially important in this context is that enforcing a global carbon regime will not be easy. Imagine the difficulties of enforcing a global income tax. Tax evasion would be rife. Whether we have a global carbon tax or a system of emission permits, carbon will have a price, and there will be incentives to avoid paying that price. Over the years, we have come to understand how better to enforce taxes; we will need to transfer some of these lessons to controlling carbon emissions.

Key Insights

This chapter has three parallel themes. The most important concerns burden sharing between developed and less-developed countries.[3] Any agreement has to be crafted in such a way that it does not adversely affect growth and poverty alleviation within the developing world. Beyond the normative perspective (in virtually any ethical framework, an agreement that put the burden of mitigation on developing countries to such an extent that it increased poverty—while the rich in the developed countries continued to consume in their current profligate style—would seem an anathema), it would be hard for any developing country to muster support for an agreement that was perceived to put their development agenda in jeopardy. This would be so even if the developed countries didn't have a historical responsibility for the increases in greenhouse gases that have occurred during the past two centuries, or even if the developed countries didn't bear special culpability for their failures to live up to prior commitments.

All of this means that the costs of mitigation ought to be borne by the developed countries and that the developed countries ought to help the developing countries bear the costs of adaptation. Resources devoted to limiting emissions or to adapting to climate change are resources that could have been spent reducing poverty or promoting growth.

In a sense, it is unlikely that what emerges from any agreement is truly a "fair deal," given the "climate change" that has already been built into the system.

By now, there is a broad consensus that equitable distribution of the required global emission reductions—especially taking into account the imperatives for developing country growth and poverty alleviation—requires very large reductions by the developed countries, by 80 percent, 90 percent, or more below 1990 levels by 2050. Delay in large reductions by the developed countries has large implications for equity: It means that, other things being equal, the developed countries will have "consumed" an even larger share of the "atmospheric pie," the total amount of cumulative emissions that are consistent with, say, two degrees Celsius global warming. And if these inequities are to be avoided, it means that the developed countries' cuts by 2050 will have to be all that much deeper. (And if the developed countries do not cut their emissions, there will be strong and inequitable adverse effects on developing countries.)

The second theme is methodological. One aspect, already noted, entails using insights and tools from public finance to provide insights into the merits of alternative approaches to addressing the problems posed by global warming. The second methodological insight is to view the problem of carbon management through the lens of the basic *carbon conservation equation*—which says that carbon molecules must either be in the atmosphere or in storage (below the ground, in the ocean, or in trees or other forms of terrestrial carbon). What is of concern (at least for global warming) is the carbon in the atmosphere. Individuals and firms have to be charged for putting carbon into the atmosphere, or rewarded for keeping carbon molecules in one of the other locations.

The third is substantive, the result in part of applying these methodologies. Four central insights (beyond those already described) are:

1. Distributive issues are central, within and between countries; issues of efficiency cannot be fully separated from those of equity.
2. Under standard normative approaches, fair burden sharing under a system of emissions rights would give more emission permits per capita to developing countries than to developed countries.
3. Because equal per capita emissions is thus the minimal acceptable allocation from the perspective of developing countries but is beyond the "maximal" acceptable allocation from the perspective of developed countries, achieving an agreement within the emissions rights framework is likely to prove elusive. A carbon tax may provide a better approach to achieving an equitable global agreement than the allocation of emission rights. We suggest one particular approach to the design of a carbon tax—carbon-added tax—that may have some advantages in implementation.
4. A concern for distributive consequences provides a rationale for at least partial reliance on regulatory measures. Although such measures may be less efficient than a uniform carbon price (achieved through a carbon tax or emission permits), the distributive impacts may be less severe.

Lessons from Public Finance: Tax Equivalence
and Implementation

Public finance theory focuses on three key aspects of taxation: (1) efficiency—does the tax distort resource allocation (or how to design taxes to minimize distortions); (2) equity—how does the tax affect different groups (what is its *incidence)* and is the burden of the tax, in some sense, fair; and (3) administration—is the tax effectively enforced, at reasonably low transaction costs, and relatively immune from corruption.

There is, in general, a cost to raising taxes—as the old adage has it, there is no such thing as a free lunch. But taxes on polluting activities are an exception, for they increase economic efficiency at the same time that they raise revenues. Such taxes are referred to as corrective or Pigouvian taxes.[4] Such taxes are consistent with a basic principle of environmental economics, called the polluter pay principle: Making polluters pay for the pollution that they create is fair and efficient.

That is why economists have begun with the presumption that the best way to incentivize individuals and firms not to emit greenhouse gases is to impose a tax on their emissions, a carbon tax. Surprisingly, however, attention has shifted to another mechanism of reducing emissions, emission permits, which can be bought and sold. To emit, one must have an emission permit. This results in the imposition of a marginal cost associated with emissions, just as the case is with a carbon tax. As we will explain later in the chapter, the two systems can be made fully equivalent; in practice, though, they are not likely to be because of how emission permits are granted. This has large distributional consequences. These in turn have strong implications for the prospect of reaching an agreement. Before turning, however, to a comparison of these different instruments for reducing emissions, it is instructive to understand better the lessons of standard public finance.

In a world with perfect competition, it makes little difference whether we impose a tax on producers or consumers. The incidence of the tax (i.e., who pays the costs) is the same, and the general equilibrium that emerges (i.e., the output of each sector, the income of each individual) is the same. Public discussions, however, typically make a great deal of difference, partly because markets are not perfectly competitive and partly because transitions from one equilibrium to another are not instantaneous: How the tax is levied can make a great deal of difference in the transition.

In the case of carbon, the focus has been totally on production. China is being "credited" with exceeding the United States in emissions (though its carbon emissions per capita are still markedly smaller). However, many of the goods that are produced in China and that account for considerable amounts of its emissions are consumed in the United States. In terms of "consumption" accounting, America is still in the lead.

Whether one uses consumption- or production-based accounting makes a great deal of difference in the case of carbon, for two reasons. If one levies a tax (or imposes a system that is equivalent to a tax), the way that the tax is levied can have large distributional consequences. If a tax is levied on consumption, revenues are generated at the point of consumption; if levied on production, at the point of production. In a closed economy, it makes no difference. In an open economy, it can make a great deal of difference, because it affects who gets the tax revenues.

Second, if taxes are imposed on production, and some countries are more effective in enforcement—or impose a lower tax—then production, particularly of carbon-intensive goods, will gravitate to where it is, in effect, taxed less. This impedes efficiency: Production will occur not where it is most efficient but where taxes are the lowest. In the case of carbon, this is of particular concern because the objective of imposing the tax (restriction) is a *global* reduction. With such "evasion," total carbon emissions could actually increase as production shifts from locales with lower emissions but higher (effective) taxes to locales with higher emissions but lower effective taxes. (This is called the problem of "leakage.")

A Carbon-Added Tax

In the design of tax systems, problems of *enforcement* have taken on first-order importance. The argument for the value-added tax (VAT) in the advanced industrial countries is that the system is self-enforcing, and thus there is greater compliance. Collection efforts can be focused on large firms that generate a large fraction of value added. Each firm in the production chain has an incentive to claim a deduction for goods purchased from others, which helps ensure that they reveal their purchases, forcing others to reveal their sales.

At the same time, the difficulty of enforcing the VAT *uniformly* in developing countries—it is virtually impossible to collect VAT revenues from the informal sector, including agriculture, which comprises a large share of GDP—has provided one of the strongest criticisms for its adoption there. Even though with full enforcement, such a tax is efficient, in practice, it is highly distortionary—moving resources out of the "formal sector," the very sector that most developing countries wish to encourage (Emran and Stiglitz 2005).

A *carbon-added tax* (CAT) levied at each stage of production would have some of the same advantages that a value-added consumption tax has. Each producer would have to show receipts for the carbon tax paid on inputs into its production. (We frame the discussion in terms of a carbon tax; later, we will reframe the discussion in terms of a regime of emission permits.) The taxes levied at each stage of production would be passed on to consumers. It is *as if* the tax were imposed on consumers, but the problem with levying a tax directly on consumers is that there may be many ways of producing a good. We cannot look at a good and infer how much carbon was used in its production. A carbon value-added tax will discourage production in more carbon-intensive ways and discourage the consumption of carbon-intensive goods.

If a firm could not produce receipts for carbon taxes on inputs, then a tax would be levied on the input, assuming it was made in the least carbon-efficient way. This would provide strong incentives for each firm to make sure that its suppliers complied with the carbon tax regime.

It would be easy to incorporate countries that failed to go along with the international regime. Producers in those countries would not be able to show carbon tax receipts. One could follow the procedure just described: A tax would be imposed on the input based on the assumption that it was produced in the most carbon-intensive way possible. This by itself would provide a strong incentive for the country to impose a carbon tax, at least on exports. The cost to outside buyers would be the same, but the producing country's government would garner the revenue.[5]

Because most firms are unlikely to have two production lines—one for exports, one for domestic consumption—the tax would provide an incentive for reducing carbon emissions. But if exports are a small fraction of total production, the incentive is limited. This suggests a more aggressive approach, with a compensatory tax on the input designed to make up for the failure to impose the tax on output that is not exported.

Intergovernmental Distributional Implications

We noted earlier that the allocative effects of taxing consumers and producers are the same, but if production occurs in a different jurisdiction from consumption, then the two taxes will differ in who receives the tax revenues. With a CAT, taxes are collected at each stage of production. This implies that the revenues go to the producing countries.

Because most carbon emissions are related to the burning of fossil fuels, it might seem that an efficient way of collecting the tax would be to have a global tax on fossil fuels, corresponding to the greenhouse gases that are emitted when they are used. There are many fewer points of production of oil, coal, and gas than there are points of usage (one of the arguments for the VAT).

It would thus seem efficient to have the taxes collected by the producers of fossil fuels; and obviously, these countries would prefer such a system because they would reap virtually all of the tax revenue—a tax in addition to the market price. As the tax increased, the market price (the "rents" they receive from their natural resources) would go down. But their total revenues would be essentially unaffected.[6] Interestingly, although the fossil fuel producers have been major opponents of doing something about global warming, under this regime, they would be fully compensated; but with their incentives for producing effectively unchanged, it is clear that such a system would do little for global warming.

Thus, even though it might seem *administratively* simpler to impose the tax at the point of production of coal, oil, or gas, or at the cutting of the forest, and so on, and such a tax would, in effect, capture most of the "carbon added" into the global system, any carbon tax system will have to focus on usage, that is, imposing the tax on the *use* of carbon (oil, coal, gas) at each stage of production.[7]

As we have noted, much of the policy debate has focused not on the question of the best way to implement a carbon tax but on whether a carbon tax (administered as a CAT or in some other way) is superior to a system of emission permits. Later in this chapter, we have a word to say about the relative merits of the two systems. For now, we note that the standard approach on emission permits is based on the "value-added" approach—that is, emission permits are required at each stage of production. There has been less attention to the enforcement issue than in the context of taxation, but the same logic can easily be extended to emission permits, as both systems have the advantage of decentralized enforcement. Permits would be required at each stage of production. Each firm would be responsible for verifying that those from whom they bought inputs did so "legally," that is, holding the requisite carbon permits. If the supplier did not have valid permits, the firm would be "charged' for using carbon on the assumption that the most carbon-intensive method of production had been used.

Equitable Burden Sharing

The key problem today in reaching an agreement is not the science: As we have noted, there is a growing consensus about the minimum that needs to be done—and that the minimum is much greater than what the world is doing today. The problem is how to share the burden of adjustment—and adjustment costs are likely to be large.

A scarce resource—carbon in the atmosphere—has been treated as if it were a free good. The market equilibrium that has emerged is, as a result, greatly distorted. Many of the key decisions that affect carbon emissions are long-run, such as power plants, housing, and transportation systems. Many of the decisions themselves are not totally market-driven; for example, land usage patterns are affected by zoning.

It is, of course, not just a matter of adjustment costs. Charging the social cost for something that has been treated as free will change relative prices. There will be winners and losers: The losers will want to be compensated; the winners will be reluctant to do so. In a sense, any change in the scarcity value of any factor of production has similar consequences; when these changes in relative prices are driven by market forces, we come to accept them—though those hurt are again more demanding of help than those who benefit are willing to share their newfound gains. But this seems somehow different because it is a political decision (though no less than the enclosure of common land or common knowledge[8] is a political decision).

If, say, through a high carbon price we succeed in ensuring that fossil fuels remain below the ground, then those who otherwise would have sold those fuels are clearly worse off.[9] With a credible program on global warming, the owners of oil and coal reserves will see the value of their assets diminish—regardless of the design of the program. The wealth of the oil exporters will also diminish. To be sure, there may be limited sympathy—they have done very well in the last few years, and unlike wealth that is the result of hard work, ingenuity, or savings, it appears to be largely the result of luck. We should expect that countries with large endowments of these resources will do everything they can to make sure that there is no agreement.

The same thing is true, of course, not just for countries but for companies—though companies have more of a choice. An important part of their asset base is their skills and knowledge. BP, with its slogan *Beyond Petroleum,* has suggested that a company can transform itself from an oil producer to an energy producer that is not dependent on fossil fuels. Still, responding to global warming will result in a decrease in the value of certain assets (just as *not* responding to global warming will result in the decrease in the value of other assets).

It is worth bearing in mind these *within*-country distributive effects because they play an important role in determining policies. America's response to global warming may be more determined by the impact on its oil companies and on its automobile industry, which has been geared toward high oil-consuming vehicles, than by a more balanced consideration of the country's national interest. As a major oil importer, America would benefit from the lower price of oil that a global agreement would bring about.

Still, for most of this chapter, as important as these within-country distributive effects are for political economy, I shall focus my attention on the cross-country distributive effects.

Externalities and Pareto Improvements

The fact that there are externalities means, of course, that there is scope for a "deal" that makes everyone better off. In principle, there is a "Coasian" agreement by which those injured by the polluters pay the polluters not to pollute, leaving the polluters and those suffering from the pollution better off. In this perspective, it should be easy to reach an agreement, and because the developing countries, on average, are those harmed by global warming, it would entail the developing countries paying off the rich countries not to pollute, in contradiction to the principle of polluter pay. That the world is unlikely to reach agreement based on such a perspective seems obvious.

The Insufficiency of Improved Energy Efficiency

Much attention has been placed on the inefficiencies in energy usage in developing countries. Increasing energy efficiency will, it is widely believed, reduce emissions. This is presented as a win–win situation: The global environment benefits at the same time that the developing country saves on scarce resources. Such increases in energy efficiency are likely to go only a little of the way toward meeting the requisite reductions in emissions. Indeed, whether increases in energy efficiency lead to an overall increase or decrease in emissions depends on whether achieving "economic" energy efficiency leads to an increase or decrease in energy usage, which in turn depends on whether the demand for energy has an elasticity that is greater or less than unity. More energy efficiency will lead to the price of energy falling; if the demand for energy is price elastic, then there will be a more than proportionate increase in energy usage so that emission levels will increase. Achieving energy efficiency is desirable, but it will not suffice.[10]

A Global Carbon Tax

The basic insight of public finance theory is that the global societal costs associated with reducing energy emissions can be minimized by the imposition of a global carbon tax. The current price of carbon is zero. Increasing the price of carbon from zero to the optimal price will, however, adversely affect some countries (carbon exporters). But the notion that it is inefficient to allow global warming means that the revenue generated by this corrective tax is more than sufficient to compensate them for the increase in the price of carbon. In appendix A, we provide an analytic framework within which one can calculate the amount of compensation each country must receive to make itself better off.

Indeed, there are many allocations of the tax revenues that can make every country better off, and much of the fight going on can be viewed as how to allocate the *typically implicit* tax revenues.

A system of carbon trading, with grants of emission permits based on, say, 1990 levels of emissions (as the Kyoto Protocol of 1997 effectively did), in effect gives emission tax revenues in proportion to 1990 levels of emissions. It does not, of course, directly give tax revenues; but it does grant emission permits, which have a market value, and the value of what each country receives is proportional to their emission allowances, which are roughly proportional to past emissions.[11] That means that the United States not only gets the single largest allocation but also gets the largest allocation on a per capita basis.

There is no ethical basis for such an allocation. Indeed, developing countries argue that because the North contributed disproportionately to the current build-up of greenhouse gases, their future allocations should be commensurately reduced.

The compensation on which attention has been focused is the direct extra costs associated with the higher price (inclusive of the tax) of fossil fuels. The discussion so far has not shifted to the broader issue of compensation for the implied changes in consumption prices, for example, for food.[12] It is thus worth noting that some developing countries could be worse off after the imposition of a global carbon tax in which they were fully compensated for the increased price of their direct purchases of fossil fuel. Because the country might have to pay more for its imports of foods, it would have less money at its disposal for development.

The benefits of having a distorted global economy, where the price of carbon was zero, are distributed in complex ways, so much so that—not surprisingly—correcting this distortion will have ramifications for developed and developing countries. But allocating so much of the implicit tax revenues from the global carbon tax to the developed countries means that there is a much greater likelihood that more developing countries will see themselves worse off, once full account is taken of the indirect consequences for food as well as energy, which comprise such a large fraction of their market basket.[13] (Some of these, of course, will still be better off than they are in a regime with global warming; a full analysis also needs to take into account the benefits from reduced global warming.)

Financing a Global Public Good

The earth's atmosphere is a global public good. Thus, avoiding global warming—in other words, preserving the health of the atmosphere—is also a global public good, and given the large disparities between the rich and the poor countries, all (or at least most) of the costs of providing this public good *should* be borne by rich countries.[14] In this perspective, developing countries should be compensated for providing valuable environmental services—carbon storage—and for the additional costs of reducing carbon—of going beyond energy efficiency to carbon efficiency.

An Agreed-Upon Carbon Tax

One proposal that has received some attention is that the countries of the world agree upon a carbon tax level that would achieve the desired reduction in emissions. Each country would then keep the revenue for itself. In effect, a carbon tax would substitute for taxes on work and savings; and under the principle that it is better to tax bad things than good things, such taxes would yield a double dividend.

Appendix B explains why, for most countries, we should expect this to suffice to provide adequate compensation—so that all countries are better off. In a sense, the distributional impacts are likely to be small. The "cost" of the carbon tax is the *difference* between the dead weight loss[15] of the carbon tax and the alternative tax (say, a wage tax). This number is likely to be small. But the *differential* incidence is the difference in this difference across countries—a number that is likely to be even smaller. In short, the advantage of the common carbon tax is that distributive consequences can be shunted aside.

Emission Permits

The alternative to a common global carbon tax is a set of agreed-upon emission limits. Efficiency can be obtained if these emission allowances (or permits) are tradable (i.e., can be bought and sold). Later in this section, I will discuss some of the relative merits of the two systems. But one disadvantage of the emission permits is that they bring to the fore the distributive conflict.

We have already discussed the implicit—and unacceptable—allocation of emission permits under the Kyoto Protocol, in which those who had polluted the most get the most emission permits. The question of the allocation of emission permits is, of course, isomorphic to the question of the allocation of tax revenues.

Equal Emissions per Capita

One alternative, widely discussed principle is equal emission permits per capita—that is, distributing the revenues equally among all the citizens of the world. This seems more philosophically acceptable than allocations based on past emissions. But there are two criticisms.

Most theories of social justice argue for a more progressive distribution of the revenues generated from the "sale" of a global natural resource—the right to emit carbon in the atmosphere—than equal per capita. Arguing that those who polluted more in the past have the right to pollute more in the future is, to say the least, perverse; and because past levels of pollution are related to income, such a rule is clearly highly regressive.

The question can be viewed another way, from a property rights perspective: How should property rights in the atmosphere be allocated? Ronald H. Coase (1960) argued that it did not matter how one assigned property rights; all that mattered for economic efficiency was that there was a clear assignment. Though that proposition has come to be questioned, to achieve a global agreement among all the countries will require that the developing countries believe that the implicit assignment of property rights is, in some sense, fair, or at least acceptable.

Within democratic developing countries today, a property rights allocation that gives citizens any less than a proportionate claim is not likely to be acceptable. Indeed, there is an alternative approach that suggests that the developed countries get markedly smaller allocations on a per capita basis. The world has now agreed that carbon concentration should be limited to make it unlikely that the world will experience an increase in temperature of more than two degrees Celsius. This implies a maximum level of greenhouse gases in the atmosphere, that is, there is a limited amount of "carbon space." Developing countries are now arguing that each should be given a claim on this carbon space in proportion to their population. But, they add, the developed countries have already used up much of their carbon space, so that their remaining carbon space is much less (on a per capita basis); this implies that, going forward, they must have lower levels of emissions per capita.

Developed countries have two responses: First, any system based on population rewards countries for failing to limit their population; and second, why should they be held accountable for emissions that occurred before the risks of global warming were known? In American jurisprudence, firms are held liable for damages that occur before a particular risk is known because in doing so it provides strong incentives for firms to find out about the risks associated with their actions.

Both concerns may fairly be addressed by providing an allocation of the carbon space as of 1992, on the basis of population as of that date. Because the United States has used so much of its carbon space since then, it is still the case that under this normative principle the United States, going forward, would have fewer emission permits per capita than developing countries.

This approach has a positive incentive effect: It provides an incentive for the United States to reduce its emissions quickly. In the current circumstances, it is as if the United States and some other developed countries are trying to "steal" as much of the global carbon space as they can before an agreement is reached.

The "problem" with even a rule based on the more modest allocation of equal per capita emission permits is the fear that it will lead to high levels of payments from developed to developing countries—at least for the foreseeable future. To be sure, as developing countries develop, differences in per capita emissions will be reduced, and so the scope for transfers will be reduced. A slow enough pacing-in of emission reductions might hold out the possibility that transfers could be kept to a moderate level. But, by the same token, a slow pace of emission reductions increases the inequities in the usage of the global carbon space.

But projections made on the basis of current rates of increases in emissions, say in China, may be misleading for at least two reasons: (1) Rapid paces of technological adaptation may lead to rapid increases in energy efficiency—the government is committed to making these changes; and (2) China has been (and will for some time continue to be) going through a resource-intensive phase of its development—focused on expanding housing and cars. It will eventually follow the pattern of other countries, shifting to the less resource-intensive service sector. Already, China is discouraging output in energy-intensive sectors, particularly energy-intensive exports (this, in turn, may in part be due to the system of attribution that "credits" China with emissions for products consumed elsewhere).

Corruption and Emission Permits

There is another problem with most systems of emission permits *within* countries: Any system in which the government allocates permits (which is equivalent to allocating money) is subject to corruption, either overt corruption or the more subtle form, campaign contributions to induce the political process to adopt a "rule" that benefits particular parties.

There is an alternative—auctioning off emission permits. If the auction is held internationally, the system is identical to a system of global taxation in which the revenues are pooled together—and the international community must then decide on the allocation of revenues (see the earlier discussion). If the auction is held at the national level, it is equivalent to the system of an agreed-upon tax level, with revenues retained by each country.

Of course, the auction undoes one of the reasons given for the permit system: The possibility of receiving large amounts of money has provided political support for (or reduced opposition to) taking actions to reduce emissions.[16] But these political economy arguments *for* tradable emission permits are, at the same time, the main arguments against them; allocating a disproportionate number of permits to those currently engaged in polluting is the very reason that those who are not currently polluting—as much, on a per capita basis—will oppose it.

Risk, Permits, and a Carbon Tax

There is a second reason (besides its ability to "buy" support) that the emission permit approach has been in favor: Environmentalists like the seeming certainty that it provides. Given the agreed-upon level of emission permits, one knows the level of emissions. With a carbon tax, one can't be sure what the level of emissions will be.

However, what we are concerned about is climate change. Emissions translate into increased carbon concentrations, and carbon concentrations translate into climate change; there is uncertainty at each stage, so that there is a high likelihood that any agreed-upon emission levels will be revised as our scientific knowledge improves. So too, if we see that the agreed-upon tax is producing higher levels of emissions than desired and anticipated, we can increase the tax. In both cases, there will be sequential revisions.

Why Granting Emission Permits on the Basis of Past Emissions Overcompensates

There are other arguments for not granting emission permits on the basis of past levels of emissions, besides the obvious one that it rewards those with bad behavior, going precisely against the "polluter pay" presumption. In dynamic competitive markets, it *over-rewards* these past polluters; new firms entering the market will, for instance, not have these permits. It is their marginal costs—including the costs of buying the requisite pollution permits—that will determine market price. Prices will rise to reflect the marginal cost of pollution, so *efficient* firms are fully compensated in equilibrium. Thus, granting them pollution permits on the basis of past levels of pollution overcompensates them. This may help explain the active support for these initiatives by these firms.

Distortionary Approaches to Mitigation

So far, we have considered two alternative, efficient ways of reducing emissions: a global carbon tax and a system of tradable emission permits. Both guarantee that there will be a single price of carbon, in all uses, in all countries. In fact, almost every country has deviated from this general principle by introducing, for instance, regulations on minimal usage of ethanol (United States), minimum fuel efficiency standards (United States), or providing subsidies to renewables (many developed countries).

How can these deviations be justified—particularly in the United States, even by administrations seemingly committed to free market principles? There are two bases for arguing for these distortionary interventions.

Distributive Concerns

The first argument focuses on distributive concerns, a worry about the magnitude of price changes (say, induced by the carbon tax) required to elicit the requisite behavioral responses. When there are low demand or supply elasticities, large price changes may be required to elicit the desired changes in usage. A high enough price of carbon would lead to the requisite changes in carbon emissions; but the effect on the poor could be devastating. To be sure, one could offset these adverse effects using, for instance, revenues raised by the carbon tax or the auctioning of emission permits. But it is never possible to target perfectly, and many may be hurt in the process. And if the revenues have been committed to "buying off" politically powerful potential opponents of emission reductions (for instance, by providing emission permits on the basis of past levels of emissions), additional taxes will have to be levied to compensate those hurt indirectly; and there is a deadweight loss to these taxes.[17]

Regulatory approaches may be able to achieve large reductions in emissions with much smaller changes in equilibrium prices and, accordingly, with much smaller distributive impacts.

Part of the argument (for and against) these regulatory approaches may be that the impacts are less transparent. Requiring the use of renewables increases costs of production and leads to higher consumer prices; but it may be harder to directly link the price increase with the regulation than in the case of a tax.

Market Failures

The second argument is that markets, by themselves, are not efficient, and government intervention is required to achieve efficiency. There may, for instance, be a coordination failure: Builders do not install energy-efficient light bulbs as standard equipment; if they do, they know that consumers will be unhappy because they cannot easily replace them in local stores. And local stores do not stock these light bulbs because there isn't the demand. A government regulation requiring all new buildings to have energy-efficient light bulbs solves the coordination problem. Stores will quickly perceive the demand and will stock them.

Innovation is based not only on prices today but on beliefs about future prices. Market expectations may not be rational. Each market participant may believe that there will be a technological breakthrough that will allow the economy to achieve its emission reductions with a low carbon tax. With a low carbon tax in the future, it does not pay most firms to invest heavily in carbon-reducing innovation. (It is clear that American automobile manufacturers misjudged the probability distribution of future gasoline prices. Shareholders have borne some of the costs of this mistake—but so too does the rest of society when, as a result, there are excessive emissions. Of course, if they had to pay the full costs—through a carbon tax—society would have been compensated. But when a whole industry makes a correlated mistake, it may be too big to fail, and not only will there be a reluctance to impose the full carbon costs, there may even be a bail-out.)

Of course, innovation almost always entails externalities—there are learning spillovers, so that without government support or government mandates, there may be insufficient incentives to innovate.

For all of these reasons (and perhaps others) price signals alone often fail to induce sufficient shifts in investments—particularly research and development investments—so complementary policy measures such as regulations (agreed-upon standards across countries) can play an important role in responding to the challenges of global warming.

There is one arena where price signals explicitly play a more limited role: public investments. For instance, not only is there a need for more public transportation, but cities also need to be redesigned and zoned to induce greater reliance on public transportation. This is an example where market mechanisms by themselves will not suffice: There is a need for collective action, and prices may even give the *wrong* signal for what should be done. Changes in the design of cities can, themselves, lead to changes in preferences. There were changes in lifestyles (and almost surely preferences) in the United States in the 1950s following the construction of the superhighways; but more recently, there has been another change in lifestyle—an increased preference for urban living. Reducing emissions will require changes in the way we live and work—including where we live and work and the structures in which we live and work. And government policies may facilitate such changes.[18]

Global Agreements Around Standards

Perhaps a more hopeful approach (than a common tax or agreed-upon emission permits) to reaching a global agreement that will reduce emissions significantly is based on reaching an accord on standards, that is, for electricity generation, automobile emissions, cement, and so on. Such standards could embrace a large fraction of all emissions.

One of the reasons that an agreement can be reached is that the distributive impacts are less transparent and probably smaller, and compliance may be easier. An example is an agreement that no coal electricity generating plant will be constructed without offsetting carbon storage. Of course, there are still distributive consequences: Countries that rely more heavily on coal may face greater increases in energy prices. They will be disadvantaged relative to those who have hydroelectric resources.

If such agreements are not to have adverse effects on development, the incremental costs faced by developing countries of such carbon-efficient technologies should be borne by the developed countries. The magnitude of the compensation would, however, be limited and be relatively easy to calculate. The magnitude of the compensation required would be reduced if the advanced developed countries fulfill their commitments to the transfer of technology.

Access to Technology

Efficient utilization of knowledge requires that it be made freely available. Knowledge is a quintessential global public good. But the patent system, of course, tries to restrict the usage of knowledge as one way of compensating innovators.

The deficiencies in the patent system (especially as currently designed in the United States) are becoming increasingly recognized: Not only does it lead to an underutilization of knowledge, it may even have adverse effects on the pace of innovation.[19] Here, however, we are concerned with another aspect—the distributive impact and its effect on global warming and reaching an agreement. The refusal of the United States or other advanced industrial countries to transfer technology to developing countries may have large distributive consequences.

If developing countries sign on to a convention requiring them to reduce their emissions by a certain amount, by a certain date, they are thereby committing themselves to an increase in demand for emission reduction innovations. If certain countries have a comparative advantage in the production of these innovations, such a convention can induce large transfers from developing countries to developed countries—and it is understandable that the developing countries would object.[20]

With the developing countries feeling that they have repeatedly been shortchanged, not just by colonialism but also by international agreements (the poorest countries were actually made worse off by the Uruguay round), it is not surprising that they feel reluctant to sign on to an agreement that might result in large transfers from the developing countries to the developed.

Any equitable approach to global warming and to the financing of technological innovations that will succeed in reducing emissions requires that the financial burden rest on the developed countries.

In the 1992 Rio agreement, the developed countries made a commitment to the transfer of technology and to pay the incremental costs associated with carbon emission reductions. There was also a provision for compulsory licenses, so that the developing countries could not be "held up" in the manner described earlier. But there has been little (if any) use of the compulsory license provisions, and the developed countries have basically reneged on commitments to technology transfer and funding.

Developing countries also worry that any funding they do receive will, in effect, come out of existing aid budgets, that is, aid donors will in effect demand that the money that they had previously been providing to promote development be used to reduce emissions.[21] In effect, their growth will be sacrificed to provide a global public good.

Knowledge itself is a global public good, and knowledge to address a global public good is, in a sense, even more of a global public good. This chapter has been concerned with the question of how to finance the costs of reducing global emissions. There is a similar question of how to share the burden of financing research to reduce the costs of addressing this public good and of what institutional arrangements will most facilitate the production and dissemination of knowledge. Incentivizing research through the patent system imposes a risk that the full benefits of any innovation will not be realized. Other mechanisms—including public support and a prize system—should be at the center of these research efforts (Henry and Stiglitz 2010).

National Security, Energy Independence, and Emission Reductions

The analysis so far has focused on conventional economic goods. Energy, however, is so important that many countries—including the United States—have expressed concern about energy independence. A cutoff of supplies of energy would have a disastrous effect on the country. Countries can take actions to ensure that there is no cutoff of supplies within their boundaries, but there is little they can do to protect themselves against external shocks. These concerns are not just a matter of the imaginations of security experts, entrusted with thinking through worst-case scenarios. There have been oil boycotts in the past. Sea lanes for shipping oil are vulnerable. Ukraine has interrupted the supply of gas traveling through the country from Russia on the way to the rest of Europe. Countries rightly worry about their vulnerability.

The problem is that different kinds of energy are not quickly substitutable. China and India have large coal stocks but must import oil and gas. Developing an economy that relies on imported oil and gas leaves the country vulnerable. Restrictions on emissions (or a global carbon tax) can impose a particularly large burden on such countries by forcing them to rely more on external energy sources.

It will be much easier to reach a global agreement on global warming if we can make progress in achieving greater international security.[22]

Terrestrial Carbon and Carbon Conservation

Terrestrial carbon—carbon that is embedded in trees, in agriculture, in meadows, and so on—provides a particularly difficult challenge, conceptually and in terms of implementation.[23] Conceptually, it forces us to think through clearly stock/flow distinctions. Much of the discussion focuses on emissions—the flow of carbon into the atmosphere and how to limit it. Some scientists are hoping that the development of carbon storage technology will allow fossil fuels to be burned and the resulting carbon to be returned back below the ground. Carbon can, of course, enter into the atmosphere in a variety of ways—the melting of the tundra presents a major risk today.

What is of concern is the stock of carbon in the atmosphere. And that is affected not only by the flow into the atmosphere but also the flow out, for example, through the activities of plants.

We can thus look at the problem of the atmospheric concentration of carbon in two ways: at the dynamics—a flow into and out of the atmosphere—or at the stocks—the amount of carbon "stored" below the ground (fossil fuels), in the ground (terrestrial carbon, carbon sequestered in trees), and in the atmosphere.

It is hard to monitor all of the flows into or out of the atmosphere. Consider deforestation. It occurs at millions of points on the globe. Moreover, only part of the wood from a tree that has been harvested will be used as fuel, and therefore contributes directly to amounts of carbon in the atmosphere. Carbon stored in wood used for furniture or construction enters the atmosphere only slowly, through decay. At the same time, cutting down a forest may lead to far more carbon entering the atmosphere than the carbon from the burning itself; carbon can be released from the soil (from the roots). Further, forests are major absorbers of carbon through photosynthesis; thus the elimination of trees also contributes indirectly to increases of atmospheric carbon. Those using wood as fuel should be charged for these indirect releases of carbon into the atmosphere; those using wood for long-lasting construction should be given some credit for the carbon storage.

It may be useful to think about how one might design a system if perfect monitoring were possible. When a tree is cut down, a charge would be made for the indirect emissions into the atmosphere. When the wood is burned, a charge would be made for the carbon entering the atmosphere. And when wood is used for construction, a charge would be imposed as the wood rots and the carbon enters the atmosphere.

In other words, given that our focus is on carbon *in the atmosphere,* a "toll" would be imposed on the individual responsible every time a carbon molecule enters the atmosphere—on those whose action "accounts" for the entry. (The charge would take into account the expected duration of the carbon in the atmosphere—which is sufficiently long that it may be approximated by infinity.[24])

Alternatively, we could impose charges and provide payments based on "stocks." Those maintaining stocks of carbon below or on the ground would be rewarded. Thus, those maintaining forests (in which carbon is sequestered) would be paid for keeping their carbon molecules there, rather than in the atmosphere. The flow and stock systems could be made equivalent: An owner of fossil fuels would be rewarded for maintaining his carbon beneath the ground; the present discounted value of reduced payments, as a result of burning the fossil fuel, is equivalent to the "charge" for emissions. Of course, from a property rights perspective, the systems are quite different: One implicitly assigns the right to the owner of the forest to pollute and pays him not to pollute; the other gives him no rights to pollute and forces him to compensate should he pollute.

It should be clear that the "ideal" monitoring required for the implementation of either of these schemes is impossible. We will be looking for second-best approximations. One approximation that may do well—at least in the long run—focuses on the steady state, making use of the fact that forests are renewable. A forest takes out carbon from the atmosphere and stores it (not only in the tree itself but in the root system). In steady state, the tree and its products are decaying at the same rate that carbon is being taken out of the atmosphere. The problem with current biofuel policies is that, while recognizing that we are failing to take account of the cost of carbon in fossil fuels and the advantages of biofuels, we fail to take account of the carbon storage opportunity costs. *But if we give the forest "credit" for the carbon that it has stored (carbon that is not in the atmosphere)—including carbon that is stored in post-cutting uses (construction, furniture), we ameliorate this to some degree.* Over time, such a credit will incentivize switching land from its current production patterns (that pay no attention to carbon storage) to patterns that recognize the social value of carbon storage. Simultaneously, this entails an increase in the price of energy and in the tax on carbon. These price signals induce more and more land to be switched into uses that do better in carbon sequestration, and lead to less reliance being placed on fossil fuels for energy production. As we set lower limits on the levels of acceptable carbon concentration in the atmosphere, the switch from fossil fuels to renewables will occur more rapidly.

In appendix C, we contrast the optimal pattern of extraction of fossil fuels with the patterns actually observed, while in appendix D, I provide a detailed analysis of the carbon conservation equation, including its implications for switching from fossil fuels to renewables.

Global Governance and Climate Change

The failure of the international community to reach a global agreement on climate change is, perhaps, the most vivid demonstration of the inadequacies in global governance. During the late nineteenth and twentieth centuries, the nation-state succeeded in protecting its citizens against some of the central risks that they faced. Global warming is a quintessential global risk. And delay in taking action may prove very costly. Effective action has to be global; but given the deficiencies in the current system of global governance, action adequate to what needs to be done has yet to be taken.

Perhaps worse still, the way negotiations and agreements—not just in the context of climate change but in other arenas of concern to developing countries—have proceeded so far may have actually undermined the kind of trust that is so necessary to reaching a global agreement. Distrust builds on itself, thereby compounding the difficulties of reaching global accords in areas of common concern.

For instance, in the trade arena, there was a widely perceived Grand Bargain leading to the Uruguay Round agreement in 1994. This entailed the developing countries giving the developed countries what they wanted—bringing into the ambit of trade agreements intellectual property agreement (the Agreement on Trade Related Aspects of Intellectual Property Rights, or TRIPS) and financial services; and the developed countries in turn giving the developing countries what they wanted—elimination of agricultural subsidies and trade restrictions on textiles (the multi-fiber agreement). The developed countries got what they wanted; the developing countries had to wait a decade for the full elimination of the multi-fiber agreement and are still awaiting meaningful concessions in agriculture—especially on cotton. By the same token, at Doha, the developing countries reluctantly agreed to another round of trade negotiations, but in return, the developed countries agreed that it would address the imbalances of the past and called the round of negotiations that began a "development round." But within a few years, the development content was largely removed, so much so that it no longer deserved to be called a development round (Charlton and Stiglitz 2005). And the notion that it was supposed to redress the imbalances of the past was soon forgotten, and the developed countries demanded concessions from the developing countries commensurate with those that they were making. Moreover, the developing countries seemed to have to negotiate anew reductions in, say, cotton subsidies—even though the WTO had already ruled that the U.S. cotton subsidies were WTO-illegal.

So too, the failure of the developed countries to live up to the obligations they undertook earlier in climate change has undermined a sense of trust. In the 1992 Rio agreement, for instance, the developed countries agreed to make transfers of technology and to finance the incremental costs of emission reductions for developing countries. Yet in recent negotiations, the developing countries have had to renegotiate—as if these agreements had not previously been made. Rebuilding that trust is important, perhaps even necessary, for any meaningful negotiations going forward. One way in which that could be done would be for developed countries to undertake ambitious reductions domestically,[25] and to make and follow through on explicit, quantified, and binding commitments to technology transfer and to resources. So too, the institutional arrangements for the disbursement of funds must have the confidence of developing countries, which means, at a minimum, that they must have adequate voice within these arrangements.

Concluding Remarks

The world is engaged in a risky experiment, increasing to dangerous levels the atmospheric concentrations of greenhouse gases. Though we may not yet know the full consequences of this experiment, the risks are sufficiently great that there is a growing consensus that there must be marked reductions in the level of emissions. And given developing countries' aspirations of growth—and increasing evidence that many of these aspirations will be realized—the reductions within the developed countries will have to be all the greater. The total costs of meeting the requisite reductions will depend, to a large extent, on advances in technology. For the last two hundred years, much of the innovation in the West has been directed at saving labor; little has been directed at reducing emissions. This outcome is hardly surprising: With the atmosphere treated as if it were a free good, there were no incentives in place. This suggests that there may be ample opportunities for technological advances.

But the pace of innovation is uncertain, and it would be foolhardy to rely on such advances. It is imperative that wealthy countries change, as well, patterns of consumption—patterns that regrettably are all too often emulated in the developing world. There is a need for a new economic model, one that centers less on the production of emission-intensive goods and more on other things that individuals and societies value. Changes in relative prices, reflecting the scarcity value of air and water, will help facilitate these changes but so too will other government policies.

This chapter has focused on how the burden of saving the planet should be shared between rich countries and poor and how reaching an agreement may be affected by the "framework," that is, whether the negotiations are over a common set of standards, a common tax, or a set of emission rights.

There is no question that there will have to be *global* reductions. Rather, the question is, upon whom should the incidence of the cost of adjustment be imposed? Avoiding global warming is a global public good. Standard public finance theory provides clear guidance about how to achieve such reductions in the most efficient way and how the burden should be shared. Clearly, the brunt of the burden (under virtually any welfare criterion) should lie with the advanced industrial countries. Indeed, these standard ideas suggest that even the approach often taken by developing countries—that there should be equal emissions permits per capita—puts an excessive burden on developing countries.

One way out of a political gridlock is to pass the costs on to someone not at the table—in this case, future generations. And that is what is at issue: whether we will continue to consume and produce as we have, preserving current living standards, at the expense of future generations. In the past, inequities in the global balance of power would have provided an easy alternative way out of the current global impasse: Pass the costs on to those too weak to defend themselves. The trade-offs are stark: between the living standards of the well-off today and those of the poor in the developing countries. The world has changed in the past decade, and this last strategy is not available.

One of the advantages of an agreed-upon common tax rate (with each country keeping its tax revenues) is that it reduces the scope for redistributive deadlock; most countries will, in fact, be better off moving from labor or savings taxes to a carbon tax—and the differences in the welfare costs are likely to be small.

A carbon tax may be the best way of avoiding the impasse confronting the world in addressing climate change, so evident in the failure to reach an effective agreement at the Copenhagen meeting. Unless some effective agreement is reached, the world will be facing enormous risk in the coming years.

Notes

1. A public good is something from which everyone benefits (consumption is "nonrivalrous"). It was first precisely defined by Paul Samuelson in 1954. The concept of global or international public goods—goods from which everyone in the world benefits—was first articulated in J. E. Stiglitz (1995).

2. More generally, many of the attempts to encourage renewables are far from well designed. They are designed as much to increase the profits of the firms lobbying for them as they are to address the problems of global warming.

3. The views in the following paragraphs reflect the consensus reached at the Brooks World Poverty Institute/IPD Meeting in Manchester, June 2009.

4. After the great Cambridge economist, A.C. Pigou, who first discussed them.

5. There is, of course, a problem of implementation, verification, and credibility: How can one be sure that the level of emissions against which the tax was collected was accurately assessed?

6. In fact, in equilibrium with a fixed supply of oil with zero extraction costs, the price paid by consumers would remain unchanged—all of the oil will be extracted, with more of the value of the oil going to the government in the form of taxes and less in rents. In practice, with some private ownership and upward sloping supply curves, there will be some impact on total extraction.

7. Indeed, as we shall argue here, because we are concerned about long-run concentrations, we will almost surely want to keep large amounts of fossil fuels beneath the ground—with the optimal tax, rents will be zero for much of the existing supply. It is not surprising that owners of large amounts of fossil fuels are unhappy about this outcome. And most of the interventions discussed here do not focus on ensuring that they are fully compensated. There is, I suspect, widespread sentiment that it was luck that resulted in their wealth—the good luck of being born on land under which there was oil—and it is similarly the bad luck of the reality of global warming that is now taking that wealth away from them. Without this oil wealth, they may, of course, need assistance.

8. As a result of poorly designed intellectual property rights.

9. Although their economic losses may be partially offset by benefits arising from reduced global warming.

10. It is, of course, more likely that imposing a price on carbon will lead to reduced emissions of carbon. This will be the case so long as the "aggregate emissions curve" is downward sloping.

11. I say roughly because some countries have agreed to somewhat larger reductions from their base than others.

12. Nor have we accounted for the decreased rents received by owners of fossil fuels.

13. This is likely to be especially so in the future, as the increased importance of biofuels may result in food prices being more highly correlated with energy prices.

14. This is, of course, a normative statement, based on widely accepted normative assumptions, such as that the burden of taxes should be placed disproportionately on the rich.

15. A tax reduces the well-being of the taxed party at the same time as it increases the revenue of the government. Most taxes distort behavior, and thus impose a burden on the taxed party that goes beyond the value of the money transferred to the government. This is the *dead weight loss*.

16. We can look at these payments in two different ways—as political bribes not to oppose the legislation to curb emissions, or as payments to ensure that the outcomes are Pareto superior. As we will explain, however, granting emission permits on the basis of past emissions provides overcompensation.

17. The problems may be exacerbated if monetary authorities subscribe to simplistic rules of inflation targeting; the large increases in energy prices then induce large increases in interest rates, which in turn lead to a slowing down of the economy and an underutilization of resources, with especially adverse effects on the poor.

18. There are other ways that government may affect the level of emissions. Standard welfare theory begins with the *assumption* of exogenous preferences. Yet we know that preferences themselves are endogenous, affected, for instance, by advertising and social processes. Government policies can help shape the evolution of preferences.

19. See, for instance, J. E. Stiglitz (2006b), *Making Globalization Work,* chapter 4. The adverse effects arise from several sources: (a) the patent system gives rise to monopoly power, which lowers levels of production, reducing incentives to innovate; (b) the patent system increases the cost of the most important input into innovation—knowledge; and (c) the patent system gives rise to a high risk of patent litigation, especially in the context of the patent thicket—where there is some probability that any innovation will trespass on others' intellectual property.

20. Assume, for instance, that with existing technologies, emission per unit of output is e_0. Assume the country signed an agreement to reduce emissions below the level of E^*, that the international agreement has sufficient sanctions that the country will comply, and that in the absence of commitment, it would have produced an output of Q_0 and emissions of $Q_0 e_0$. To comply with its commitment, the country would have to restrict output to E^*/e_0. If the new technology lowers emissions per unit of output to e_1, sufficient that at Q_0 the country can meet its obligations, then the owner of the new technology can extract a rent up to $[Q_0 - E^*/e_0]$.

21. Confidence that the developed countries will live up to their commitments is undermined too by the fact that most have not lived up to previous commitments to provide 0.7 percent of their GDP for development assistance.

22. See appendix A for how we can incorporate these security costs into the analysis.

23. The equations and explanation of my conclusions for this section of the paper are included in appendix D.

24. That is, a carbon molecule can be thought of as renting space in the atmosphere. If the rent per unit time were c, and there were a decay rate of μ, and the interest rate is r, then the entry charge would be $c/(\mu + r)$. Of course, we don't care about how long any particular molecule stays in the atmosphere; we don't have to track each. We care about the average. If $\mu = 0$ (a molecule never leaves), then the entry charge is c/r.

25. Many of the developed countries did not live up to the commitments on reductions that they had made earlier; the United States has increased its emissions since 1992 almost unabated.

Sharing the Burden of Saving the Planet: Global Social Justice for Sustainable Development: Appendixes

Appendix A

Calculating the Incidence of a Carbon Tax

The imposition of a carbon tax will affect each country differently. The following calculations illustrate how the impacts can be computed.

Assume that the efficient carbon tax (needed to achieve the agreed-upon reductions in global emissions) is t^*. Then the expenditure function for country j, giving the minimum level of income required to attain a given level of utility, provides a money-metric for assessing the impact of the tax. Let $\Pi(t, \mathbf{p}(t))$ be aggregate producer profits when the carbon tax is t^* and the vector of prices is $\mathbf{p}$. Let $B(t^*)$ denote the cost of the tax.

$$B(t^*) = E(\mathbf{p}(t^*), t^*, U_o, G(t^*)), \Pi(t, \mathbf{p}(t), G(t))$$

$$- [E(\mathbf{p}(o), o, U_o, G(o)), \Pi(o, \mathbf{p}(o), G(o))] \tag{A1}$$

where $\mathbf{p}(t)$ is the general equilibrium price vector that emerges when the price of carbon is t^*, U_o is the initial level of utility, and $G(t)$ is the "climate" associated with carbon tax t^*—a global public good.[1] Clearly, different countries will be affected differently, both as consumers and producers.[2]

Compensation

Denote the revenue raised by the carbon tax by $T(t)$. Assume country i gets T_i, with

$$\Sigma_i T_i = T(t).$$

Then (under the assumption that it is desirable to have some carbon tax), for t^*, there exists an allocation such that

$$B_i(t^*) + T_i(t^*) > 0. \tag{A2}$$

Such considerations argue that, at a minimum, developing countries should be compensated for the additional costs of production associated with the increase in the price of carbon

$$T_i(t) \geq \Pi_i\ (0, \mathbf{p}(0), G(0)) - \Pi_i(t, \mathbf{p}(t), G(t)). \tag{A3}$$

With the new focus on terrestrial carbon, it is argued (correctly) that, in addition, they should be compensated for maintaining their forests. Currently, they receive benefits from their forests only if they cut them down, which results in an inefficient (from a global perspective) use of land. Thus,

$$T_i(t) \geq \Pi_i\ (0, \mathbf{p}(0), G(0)) - \Pi_i\ (t, \mathbf{p}(t), G(0)) + rtV_i \tag{A4}$$

where V_i stands for the amount of carbon stored in their forests and $c(t)$ $V_i = rtV_i$ now stands for the compensation for maintaining a forest with carbon storage V_i when the price of carbon emissions is t. (See note 4.)

The additional compensation that may be required to remunerate developing countries for their extra security costs can be captured in our model by positing another public good, S, security; the costs of attaining S can be dependent on t:

$$B(t^*) = E\ (\mathbf{p}(t^*), t^*, U_0, G(t^*), S(t^*)) + \Pi(t, \mathbf{p}(t), G(t))$$

$$- [E\ (\mathbf{p}(0), 0, U_0, G(0), S(0)) + \Pi(0, \mathbf{p}(0), G(0))].$$

Appendix B

A Simple Model Illustrating the Double Dividend

With the increasing debate about global warming, and with attention shifting from the Kyoto approach of agreed-upon target levels for reduction to agreed-upon levels of taxation for emissions (Stiglitz 2006a), the debate over the "double dividend" has arisen once again. See Sancho's 2010 and Saunders's 2006 critiques of Stiglitz (2006a). Several political leaders, on both sides of the political spectrum, have argued that it makes more sense to tax bads, like pollution, than goods, like work and savings. The double dividend argument holds that not only will pollution be reduced but that there is an additional dividend from the reduced burden of taxation from other sources.

The issue has sometimes been incorrectly framed: The claim is not that *measured* GDP would actually increase, but that there is a welfare gain in the reduced burden of taxation. Whether there is this additional benefit, of course, it is still the case that corrective taxation is desirable; it is part of an optimal tax structure (Atkinson and Stiglitz 1972: Sandmo 1976; Stiglitz 1998). The discussion over the double dividend is really a debate about the *interpretation* of the welfare benefits associated with positive taxation of, say, carbon.

In this appendix, I construct a simple but general model that demonstrates the existence of *both* the direct benefit from the reduction in pollution and the indirect benefit from the lowering of a distortionary income tax—so long as labor is elastically supplied (so that the wage tax is in fact distortionary). To highlight the issues, we use a model and notation that is somewhat different from that of the text of the chapter.

We assume an aggregate production function of the usual form, where output is a function of labor, L_Q, and energy, E:

$$Q = F(L_Q, E). \tag{B1}$$

Energy output is a function of labor input, L_E, and environmental degradation, z:

$$E = G(L_E, z). \tag{B2}$$

Firms maximize profits. If we choose output as the numéraire, w is the (real) wage, and p is the price of energy, this means

$$F_L = w, \tag{B3}$$

$$F_E = p, \tag{B4}$$

$$pG_L = w. \tag{B5}$$

Initially, no charges are imposed for environmental degradation, so

$$G_z = 0. \tag{B6}$$

The representative individual has a utility function of the form

$$U(Q, L, z) \tag{B7}$$

where L is the total labor supply, so in equilibrium

$$L = L_E + L_Q. \tag{B8}$$

Individuals maximize their utility, and we assume that initially there is a tax on labor at the rate t_w, so that

$$U_Q w(1 - t_w) + U_L = 0. \tag{B9}$$

We can solve this set of equations for the equilibrium outputs $\{Q, L, z\}$, prices $\{w, p\}$, and labor allocations $\{L_E, L_Q\}$.

We now wish to calculate the effect on utility of a tax on environmental degradation, at the rate of v. To do this, we substitute into (B7) to obtain

$$U = U(F(L - L_E, G(L_E, z)), L, z) \tag{B10}$$

so that

$$
\begin{aligned}
dU/dv = U_Q\{-F_L + F_E\, G_L\}\, dL_E/dv \\
+ \{U_Q\, F_E\, G_z + U_z\}\, dz/dv \\
+ \{U_Q\, F_L + U_L\}\, dL/dv.
\end{aligned}
$$

Using the envelope theorem, we obtain

$$
\begin{aligned}
dU/dv &= U_z\, dz/dv && \text{the direct environmental impact} \\
&\quad + [U_Q\, F_L + U_L]\, dL/dv && \text{the double dividend effect} \\
&= U_z\, dz/dv \\
&\quad + U_Q\, t_w\, F_L\, dL/dv && \text{by Eq. (B9)}
\end{aligned}
$$

using equations (B1) through (B8). The first term, $U_Q\{-F_L + F_E\, G_L\}$, drops out because of the envelope theorem. $G_z = 0$ by (B6).

In short, so long as the supply curve of labor is upward sloping,[3] there is a benefit to introducing a pollution tax that goes beyond the reduction in pollution itself, from the reduction in the level of distortionary taxation. This is so even given the maxim about not taxing intermediate goods. But pollution is both an input into an intermediate good and something that is "consumed" as a final good.

Appendix C

Optimal and Equilibrium Patterns of Extraction

Optimal resource extraction requires that fossil fuels for which the costs of extraction are the lowest be extracted first.

For a fossil fuel with extraction costs ξ, rents, when the tax rate on fossil fuels is t, are

$$p_1 - t - \xi$$

and, denoting time by τ, the rate of increase of rents is

$$[dp_1/d\tau - dt/d\tau]/[p_1 - t - \xi].$$

It is easy to show that in equilibrium, rents must increase at the rate of interest, r, so

$$[dp_1/d\tau - dt/d\tau]/[p_1 - t - \xi\,(CF)] = r(\tau)$$

Let CF represent the cumulative amount of fossil fuels extracted. If CF has been extracted, the marginal extraction costs are $\xi\,(CF)$. At date τ, fossil fuels with extraction costs $\xi\,(CF)$ will be extracted, where

$$[dp_1/d\tau - dt/d\tau]/[p_1 - t - \xi\,(CF)] = r(\tau)$$

where r is the rate of interest. From the pricing and emissions tax functions, we can solve for the carbon utilization (and fossil energy supply) time profiles.

The patterns we have just described do not, of course, accord with observed patterns of fossil fuel usage. We should be extracting oil first from Saudi Arabia (low extraction costs) before we turn to higher extraction cost oil (say, from Alaska). The fact that we do not do so reflects in part the complexity of the oil industry—the risk that we associate, for instance, with reliance solely on the low-cost provider; the fact that Saudi Arabia may feel that investments not inside its boundaries are risky—and hence has an incentive to keep some of its assets below ground; or that a private oil company with the right to extract oil elsewhere does not feel its property rights are secure, and so has an incentive to extract oil more quickly.

It reflects, too, the uncertainty associated with discovery. The latter uncertainty would remain, even if we resolved the other political risks. It would mean, for instance, that should a low-cost supply of oil be discovered at some time in the future, we would want to make use of it. If we are to do that—and to obey our carbon conservation equation—it means that we have to anticipate that we may want to extract some fossil fuels in the future (i.e., given our prior beliefs about the discovery of oil of different extraction costs, we set a reservation extraction costs, ξ_R, such that we only extract oil with extraction costs that are lower than that level). Assume we believed, for instance, that we will be able to continue to discover an amount of oil with low extraction costs every period for the next hundred years, after which there will be no more (cheap) oil to be discovered. Then we set our reservation extraction level to reflect the fact that we believe we will add an additional amount of cheap oil over the next hundred years. If it turns out that we discover less "cheap" oil than we expected, then we adjust our reservation extraction level.

Appendix D

The Carbon Conservation Equation

To a first-order approximation, we can think of the stock of carbon being fixed, and

$$CA + CF + CS + CT + CO = C^*. \tag{D1}$$

The world's stock of carbon is either in the atmosphere (CA) (which is what we are worried about), under the ground, either in the form of fossil fuels (CF) or in storage (CS), stored on Earth (as terrestrial carbon) (CT), or in the ocean (CO). Our concern is to keep CA under control.

A forest takes out carbon from the atmosphere and stores it. In steady state, the trees (and their products) are decaying at the same rate that carbon is being taken out of the atmosphere. We give the forest "credit" for the carbon that it has stored (carbon that is *not* in the atmosphere)—including carbon that is stored in post-cutting uses (construction, furniture). Denote by V_i the volume of carbon stored in a particular forest ($CT = \Sigma_i V_i$, terrestrial carbon is the sum of the carbon stored in all the forests, plus the carbon stored in wood cut down from the forest). Focusing for the moment on just terrestrial carbon (in steady state, CF and CO are fixed)

$$dCA/d\tau = -\Sigma_i \, dV_i/d\tau = \Sigma_i \, (e_i - s_i), \tag{D2}$$

the increase in atmospheric concentration of carbon (from this forest) is the emissions *minus* the absorption (storage) of carbon. In steady state,

$$dV_i/dt = 0, \tag{D3a}$$

or

$$e_i = s_i, \tag{D3b}$$

emissions are equal to the amount stored. There is no net contribution.

Assume there were a charge per unit of time for a molecule being stored in the atmosphere of rc. That would imply that the charge for a molecule being permanently stored in the atmosphere would be c, or, equivalently, the payment for a molecule not being put into the atmosphere (being sequestered in a tree) per unit time is rc. Were this carbon to be transported into the atmosphere, there would be a charge of cV, where c is the price of carbon and V is the amount. In terms of economic incentives, it makes no difference whether we charge someone cV for transporting V units into the atmosphere or pay him rcV every period for not transporting it into the atmosphere. If he never transported it into the atmosphere, he would receive (in present discounted value terms) cV.

Land should be used in the most efficient way possible. Assume that there is a flow of lumber of L, and $\alpha_1 L$ is used for energy, with a value of $\alpha_1 \, p_1 \, L$; and α_2 is used for furniture (or other decaying uses) with a value of $\alpha_2 \, p_2 \, L$. Thus this particular use of land generates a (flow) value of

$$rc[V + \alpha_2 \, mL] + \alpha_1 \, p_1 \, L + \alpha_2 \, p_2 \, L - z \tag{D4}$$

where z is the (non-energy, non-carbon) cost of maintaining the forest, m represents the carbon stored in the furniture, and r is the real interest rate. (The energy used in the production of energy from the forest is netted out in α_1.)

It should be clear that increasing carbon payments (c) increases the return to forest usage with high storage. A higher price of energy shifts production toward uses that result in more "bio fuels." Higher prices of lumber shift production toward uses that result in more lumber output. Better preservatives increase the longevity of carbon stored in furniture, so increase m and hence the incentives for using lumber for furniture.

There is some controversy about whether land should be devoted to forests with the highest V or the highest growth rates. Some forests with large, mature trees (and thus high V) are slow growing and thus may take out much less carbon from the atmosphere per unit time than a fast-growing forest. Equations (D3) and (D4) provide an easy resolution of this controversy—and suggest neither view is quite right. In steady state, the amount of carbon taken out is equal to the amount of emissions, so the *pace* of storage is not directly relevant. (It is only that we typically do not fully measure all of the decay.)

On the other hand, the rate of growth may be relevant for another reason. Assume that the amount of lumber (biomass) that we can take out (per acre) from a forest is related to the stock of carbon by the growth rate:

$$L = gkV. \tag{D5}$$

Some forests have a higher growth rate, g, than others. Then the flow of value from this forest is

$$rcV[1 + \alpha_2\, mgk] + \alpha_1\, p_1\, gkV + \alpha_2\, p_2\, gkV - z. \tag{D6}$$

Other things being equal, a forest with a higher growth rate will generate more energy and usable lumber and thus be more valuable.[4] But, of course, typically, things are not equal. Equation (D6) makes clear that we have to evaluate each plot of land for the carbon that can be stored on it, for its generation of energy, and for its generation of other lumber products (as well as for the cost of maintenance).

But equation (D6) also makes clear that it may be a mistake to cut down a tropical forest (with a high V), to be replaced by sugarcane, even if sugarcane grows more quickly.

Note that if the price of fossil fuels rises (as Hotelling's formula predicts), then more and more land will shift toward forests with a higher renewable energy usage. In a general equilibrium model, the effect will be mitigated by the reduced output of grain, which will raise the price of grain.

What is critical, however, is that in changing land usage, the carbon cost is correctly included. Let π_i denote the private returns to land usage (per hectare).

$$\pi_i = \alpha_{1i} L_i p_1 + \alpha_{2i} L_i [p_2 + rc\alpha_2 \, m] - z_i \qquad \text{(D7)}$$

where in this generalized formulation, z_i is the costs from activity i, $\alpha_{1i} L_i$ is the energy outputs, valued at p_1; and $\alpha_{2i} L_i$ is the non-energy outputs, valued at p_2. Furniture producers receive a payment for the value of their carbon storage activities, providing them with incentives for increasing durability, that is, increasing m.

Then, the (flow) net social returns are

$$S_i = rcV_i + \pi_i. \qquad \text{(D8)}$$

A change in land usage from i to j induces a change in (total) social profit of

$$\Delta S_{ij} = rc\,\Delta V_{ij} + \Delta \pi_{ij} = rc \int \delta V_{ijt} + \Delta \pi_{ij} \qquad \text{(D9)}$$

where the change in the level of carbon storage in moving from one steady state (i) to the other (j) is just equal to the integral of the flows into or out of carbon storage, denoted by δV_{ijt}.

$$\int \delta V_{ijt} = \Delta V_{ij} \qquad \text{(D10)}$$

The problem with current biofuel policies is that, while recognizing that we are failing to take account of the cost of carbon in fossil fuels and the advantages of bio fuels, we fail to take account of the carbon storage opportunity costs, which we have represented by ΔV_{ij}, and, unless we take these into account, we will not obtain socially efficient resource allocations.

Limiting Value

Controlling climate change entails controlling the limiting value of CA at or below some level CA^*. To simplify, let us ignore the amounts of carbon that can be absorbed into the ocean or reinjected through carbon storage into the earth. Then, from equation (D1), we can solve for

$$CF^* = C^* - CA^* - CT^*.$$ (D1')

This means that in long-run equilibrium (ignoring technological change), all energy needs are met by renewables, and the rents associated with the carbon remaining underground are zero. Equation (D1') has some other obvious implications. The more carbon sequestered in forests (the greater CT^*), the less carbon needs to remain in fossil fuels (i.e., the higher the level of extraction of fossil fuels). If extraction costs for fossil fuels are low, this means lower costs for energy (in the intermediate run, at least—in the long run, we will still have to rely on renewables).

Since costs of extraction increase the more fossil fuel that is extracted, the (long-run) tax (per unit of equivalent energy) on fossil fuel must be t^*, such that

$$p_1^* = t^* + \xi\,(CF^*)$$ (D11)

where $\xi\,(CF^*)$ is the marginal cost of extraction when CF^* fossil fuel is left in the ground. Letting CT^* be the equilibrium terrestrial carbon ($= \Sigma_i V_i^*$), a function of the prices for energy, nonenergy uses of "lumber," and the carbon charge t, then, from equation (D6), if each parcel of land is allocated to its best use, that is, the use for which[5]

$$rt^* V_i + \alpha_1 p_1^* g_i kV_i + \alpha_2 p_2 g_i kV_i - z_i$$

is maximized, then we can solve

$$CT^* = \Sigma V_i = \chi\,(p_1^*, p_2^*, t^*)$$ (D12a)

and

$$D_1\,(p_1^*, p_2^*, \ldots) = \Sigma_i g_i \alpha_1 V_i = \varsigma\,(p_1^*, p_2^*, t^*, \ldots)$$ (D12b)

where D_1 is the demand for energy, ς is the aggregate supply of energy, a function of prices and taxes. In the long run, all of the demand for energy must be met by renewables. We can solve simultaneously for the long-run equilibrium price of energy and the equilibrium carbon tax.

This analysis assumes that there are static demand and supply functions. If over time the demand for energy increases, and if nothing else changed, it would imply that (if p_2 and other prices remained unchanged) p_1 would increase, which would shift land use to more energy production and less nonenergy uses and carbon sequestration. Thus, if we wish to keep CT^* fixed, for the carbon equilibrium condition equation (D1) to continue to be satisfied, there would have to be an offsetting increase in t^*.[6]

Knowing the long-run value of p^*_1 and t^*, we can solve backward for prices of energy and the equilibrium carbon tax at each moment of time. Consider the simplest case where there are zero extraction costs, and where we normalize our units so the price of fossil fuels is per unit energy, p_1. Then at each date τ,

$$p_1(\tau) = t(\tau). \tag{D13}$$

In the long run, there can be no rents to fossil fuels, and that means that at every date, there can be no rents (otherwise, there would be an incentive to extract all the oil at the moments when it had positive rents). Equilibrium is described by a tax function and a price function $\{t(\tau), p_1(\tau)\}$ (as before, we take p_2 and other prices as given; it is an easy matter to expand the analysis to incorporate the simultaneous solution for these as well), such that:[7]

(a) the optimal tax (which in the absence of the taxation would be just the rent) is increasing at the rate of interest, r: $dlnt/d\tau = r$.

(b) At each date, demand for energy equals the supply, the sum of terrestrial energy plus fossil fuel energy

$$D_1(p_1(\tau)), \ldots) = \varsigma_\tau (\ldots) + \kappa c_F \tag{D14}$$

where $\varsigma_\tau (\ldots)$ reflects the supply of terrestrial energy based on optimal land usage and where κc_F is the fossil fuel energy, and c_F is the addition to atmospheric carbon from burning fossil fuel:

$$dCF/dt = - c_F \tag{D15}$$

and

(c) the sum over time of atmospheric carbon concentration from the usage of fossil fuel energy equals that required by the carbon conservation equation

$$\int c_F(\tau) \, d\tau = CF^* - CF(0). \tag{D16}$$

Over time, land is switched from its current production patterns (which pay no attention to carbon storage) to patterns that recognize the social value of carbon storage. Simultaneously, this entails an increase in the price of energy and the tax on carbon. More and more land is switched into uses that do better in carbon sequestration, and less reliance is placed on fossil fuels for energy production and more reliance on renewables.

Notice that in this formulation, setting a tighter atmospheric target means that we switch from fossil fuels to renewables more rapidly. This in turn enables us to calculate the upper bound of the cost: An amount of energy equal to $\kappa \Delta CF$ would have been produced at zero social costs (zero extraction costs). Now this energy will be produced at a cost of $p_1(\tau) + v(\tau)$, where v is the implicit renewable subsidy per unit energy produced at time τ. Hence, the upper bound of the cost is just

$$\int [p_1(\tau) + v(\tau)]cF(\tau)\exp\{-\int r\,dz\}\,d\tau$$

over the period during which fossil fuels would have been used under the looser regime, and not under the tighter regime.

Notes

1. This analysis simplifies in a key way: The impacts of changes in emission levels will be (mostly) felt only over the long run. We thus need a more complete dynamic model.

2. These effects are evidenced in recent years as higher fuel prices have led to higher food prices. Producers of fossil fuels are large beneficiaries of today's high oil prices but would be large losers under a carbon tax.

3. Actually, what is required is somewhat more complex: The total derivative of labor with respect to the environmental tax rate is given by

$$dL/dv = (\partial L/\partial w)\,[(1 - t_w)\,dw/dv - w\,dt_w/dv\,] + (\partial L/\partial z)\,(dz/dv).$$

where we have assumed that as we increase the environmental tax (v), we reduce the tax on labor. The increase in the pollution tax leads (normally) to a lower tax on labor, which, if there is a positive elasticity of labor supply, leads to an increased labor supply. There are also general equilibrium effects on the level of pollution (it is designed to reduce it) and on wages. Labor supply is obviously sensitive to the level of wages, and possibly to the level of pollution. Our analysis simply requires that

$$(\partial L/\partial w)\,[(1 - t_w)\,dw/dv - w\,dt_w/dv] + (\partial L/\partial z)\,(dz/dv) \geq 0.$$

Ignoring for the moment the effect of the environment (or assuming that an improvement in the environment leads to an increase in labor supply), this means that if the real wage rises, labor supply unambiguously increases. But it is possible that the real wage could fall, if the pollution tax leads (as expected) to a reduction in the production of energy, and the reduced input of energy has an enormously negative effect on the marginal product of labor. While it is clear that there may be circumstances in which the double dividend does not appear, these would appear to be unusual. Of course, when the "double dividend" term is negative, it simply means that the optimal tax on pollution is less than it otherwise would have been. The general point is that one does have to pay attention to effects of the reduced tax on labor; it is only that the combination of a tax on pollution and a reduced tax on labor could, perversely, somehow lead to a reduction in the labor supply so that revenue that was previously generated by the income tax is reduced.

4. This analysis may exaggerate the benefits from rapid growth for two reasons: Slow-growing forests may be able to sustain a higher bio-mass in steady state per acre (the trees are taller, the wood is denser, and the roots deeper, and hence there is more carbon sequestration), and slow-growing trees may decay more slowly. Assume the decay rate for non energy lumber from forest i is d_i. Then the flow of value from this forest is $rcV[1 + \alpha_2\, gk/d] + \alpha_1\, p_1\, gkV + \alpha_2\, p_2\, gkV - z$. Assume for a slow-growing forest $d = g$ (the rate of decay after the tree is cut down is the same as the rate of growth before it is cut down), and that slow-growing trees are used just for furniture, while a fast-growing forest is used just for biofuel. Then denoting the former forest with a superscript a and the latter forest with a superscript b, it pays to keep the forest as a slow growing forest for furniture so long as

$$rcV^a\, [1 + k^a] + p_1\, g^a\, k^a\, V^a - z^a > rcV^b + p_2\, g^b\, k^b\, V^b - z^b.$$

(In addition, fast-growing forests may need more frequent replanting, so $z^b > z^a$).

5. The full dynamic equation is somewhat more complicated than this, since there cannot be an instantaneous shift from one land use to another and since trees are long-term investments. Hence, at each moment of time, a decision has to be made, say, about terminating its current use (based on the current rate of growth of existing trees) and switching to an alternative use, based on projections on future prices (including prices for carbon storage) and taxes (and future interest rates).

6. In the general equilibrium, the reduced supply of nonenergy outputs would lead to an increase in p_2 as well.

7. These results can be derived more formally from an intertemporal maximization problem, using a standard Hamiltonian formulation. We assume that there is no short-run impact of climate change.

References

Atkinson, A. B. and J. E. Stiglitz, 1972, "The Structure of Indirect Taxation and Economic Efficiency," *Journal of Public Economics*, 1:97–119.

Charlton, A. and J. E. Stiglitz, 2005, *Fair Trade for All*, New York: Oxford University Press.

Coase, R., 1960, "The Problem of Social Cost," *Journal of Law and Economics*, 3:1–44.

Emran, S. and J. E. Stiglitz, 2005, "On Selective Indirect Tax Reform in Developing Countries," *Journal of Public Economics*, 89:599–623.

Henry, C. and J. E. Stiglitz, 2010, "Intellectual Property, Dissemination of Innovation, and Sustainable Development," *Global Policy* 1(3):237–251.

Sancho, F., 2010, "Double Dividend Effectiveness of Energy Tax Policies and the Elasticity of Substitution: A CGE Appraisal," *Energy Policy*, 38(6):2927–2933.

Sandmo, A., 1976, "Optimal Taxation: An Introduction to the Literature," *Journal of Public Economics*, 6(1–2):37–54.

Saunders, H. D., 2006, "Letter: What Will Stiglitz's Global Warming Remedy Really Cost?" *The Economists' Voice*, 3(8):1.

Stern, Nicholas, 2007, *The Economics of Climate Change: The Stern Review*, Cambridge, UK: Cambridge University Press.

Stiglitz, J. E., 1995, "The Theory of International Public Goods and the Architecture of International Organizations," background paper No. 7, Third Meeting, High Level Group on Development Strategy and Management of the Market Economy, UNU/WIDER, Helsinki, Finland.

——, 1998, "Pareto Efficient Taxation and Expenditure Policies, With Applications to the Taxation of Capital, Public Investment, and Externalities," presented at conference in honor of Agnar Sandmo.

——, 2006a, "A New Agenda for Global Warming," *The Economists' Voice*, 3(7):3.

——, 2006b, *Making Globalization Work*, New York: Norton.

——, 2008, "A New Agenda for Global Warming," in *The Economists' Voice: Top Economists Take on Today's Problems*, edited by A. Edlin, and J. B. DeLong, 22–27. New York: Columbia University Press.

8

Designing the Post-Kyoto Climate Regime

JOSEPH E. ALDY AND ROBERT N. STAVINS*

Diverse aspects of human activity around the world result in greenhouse gas (GHG) emissions that contribute to global climate change. Emissions come from coal-fired power plants in the United States, diesel buses in Europe, rice paddies in Asia, and the burning of tropical forests in South America. These emissions will affect the global climate for generations because most greenhouse gases reside in the atmosphere for decades to centuries. Thus, the impacts of global climate change pose serious, long-term risks.

Global climate change is the ultimate global commons problem: Because GHGs mix uniformly in the upper atmosphere, damages are completely independent of the location of emissions sources. Thus, a multinational response is required. To address effectively the risks of climate change, efforts that engage most if not all countries will need to be undertaken. The greatest challenge lies in designing an *international policy architecture* that can guide such efforts. We take "international policy architecture" to

* We are indebted to the research teams of the Harvard Project on Climate Agreements, who contributed to Aldy and Stavins (2009, 2010); Robert Stowe, project manager; and the Doris Duke Charitable Foundation, the major funder of the project. Additional funding was provided by Christopher Kaneb, the James and Cathleen Stone Foundation, Paul Josefowitz and Nicholas Josefowitz, the Enel Endowment for Environmental Economics at Harvard University, the Belfer Center for Science and International Affairs, and the Mossavar-Rahmani Center for Business and Government at the Harvard Kennedy School.

refer to the basic nature and structure of an international agreement or other multilateral (or bilateral) climate regime.

The Kyoto Protocol to the United Nations Framework Convention on Climate Change (UNFCCC) marked the first meaningful attempt by the community of nations to curb GHG emissions. This agreement, though a significant first step, is not sufficient for the longer-term task ahead. Some observers support the policy approach embodied in Kyoto and would like to see it extended—perhaps with modifications—beyond the 2012 end date of the first commitment period. Others maintain that a fundamentally new approach is required and support the emergence of a pledge-and-review system at the 2009 Copenhagen and 2010 Cancun climate talks. Still others, unsatisfied with these two options, call for new ideas to inform the design of climate policy beyond 2020 under the "Durban Platform for Enhanced Action" agreed at the 2011 climate talks.

Whether one thinks the Kyoto Protocol was a good first step or a bad first step, everyone agrees that a second step is required. A way forward is needed for the post-Kyoto period. The Harvard Project on Climate Agreements was launched with this imperative in mind. The project is a global, multiyear, multidisciplinary effort intended to help identify the key design elements of a scientifically sound, economically rational, and politically pragmatic post-Kyoto international policy architecture for addressing the threat of climate change. This chapter draws extensively on the project's research, the results of which are described in much greater detail elsewhere (Aldy and Stavins 2009, 2010).

By "scientifically sound" we mean an international agreement that is consistent with achieving the objective of stabilizing atmospheric concentrations of GHGs at levels that avoid dangerous anthropogenic interference with the global climate. By "economically rational" we mean pursuing an approach or set of approaches that are likely to achieve global targets at minimum cost—that is, cost-effectively. And by "politically pragmatic" we mean a post-Kyoto regime that is likely to bring on board the United States and engage key, rapidly growing developing countries in increasingly meaningful ways over time.

Learning from Experience: The Kyoto Protocol

It is helpful to reflect on the lessons that can be learned from examining the Kyoto Protocol's strengths and weaknesses. Among the Protocol's strengths is its inclusion of several provisions for market-based approaches that hold promise for improving the cost-effectiveness of a global climate regime. We refer, for example, to the well-known flexibility mechanisms, such as Article 17, which provides for emissions trading among the Annex I countries[1] that take on commitments under the Protocol. More specifically, this provision allows the governments of Annex I countries to trade some of the assigned emission allowances that constitute their country-level targets. Second, the Protocol's Joint Implementation provisions allow for project-level trades among the Annex I countries. Finally, the Protocol established the Clean Development Mechanism (CDM), which provides for the use of project-level emission offsets created in non-Annex I countries (the developing countries of the world) to help meet the compliance obligations of Annex I countries.

A second advantage of the Kyoto Protocol is that it provides flexibility for nations to meet their national emission targets—their commitments— in any way they want. In other words, Article 2 of the Protocol recognizes domestic sovereignty by providing for flexibility at the national level. The political importance of this provision in terms of making it possible for a large number of nations to reach agreement on emission commitments should not be underestimated.

Third, the Kyoto Protocol has the appearance of fairness, in that it focuses on the wealthiest countries and on those responsible for a dominant share of the current stock of anthropogenic GHGs in the atmosphere. This is consistent with the principle enunciated in the UNFCCC of "common but differentiated responsibilities and respective capabilities."

Fourth and finally, the fact that the Kyoto Protocol was signed by more than 180 countries and subsequently ratified by a sufficient number of Annex I countries for it to come into force speaks to the political viability of the agreement, if not to the feasibility of all countries actually achieving their targets.

In the realm of public policy, as in our everyday lives, we frequently learn more from our mistakes or failures than from our successes; so, too, in the case of the Kyoto Protocol. Therefore, we also examine some key weaknesses of the Protocol and explore what potentially valuable lessons they may hold for the path forward.

First, it is well known that some of the world's leading GHG emitters were not constrained by the Kyoto Protocol. The United States—until recently the country with the largest share of global emissions—did not ratify the agreement. Also, some of the largest and most rapidly growing economies in the developing world did not have emission targets under the agreement. Importantly, China, India, Brazil, South Africa, Indonesia,

South Korea, and Mexico are not listed in Annex B of the Kyoto agreement. Rapid rates of economic growth in these countries have produced rapid rates of growth in energy use, and hence carbon dioxide (CO_2) emissions. Together with continued deforestation in tropical countries, the result is that the developing world has overtaken the industrialized world in total GHG emissions. China's industrial CO_2 emissions have already surpassed those of the United States; moreover, China's emissions are expected to continue growing much faster than U.S. emissions for the foreseeable future (Blanford et al. 2010:822–856).

These realities raise the possibility that the Kyoto Protocol was not as fair as originally intended, especially given how dramatically the world has changed since the UNFCCC divided countries into two categories in 1992. For example, approximately fifty non-Annex I countries—that is, developing countries and some others—now have higher per capita incomes than the poorest of the Annex I countries with commitments under the Kyoto Protocol. Likewise, forty non-Annex I countries ranked higher on the Human Development Index in 2007 than the lowest ranked Annex I country.

A second weakness of the Kyoto Protocol is associated with the relatively small number of countries that were asked to take action. This narrow but deep approach may have been well-intended, but one of its effects was to drive up the costs of producing carbon-intensive goods and services within the coalition of countries taking action. (Indeed, increasing the cost of carbon-intensive activities was the intention of the Protocol and is fully appropriate as a means to create incentives for reducing emissions.) Through the forces of international trade, however, this approach also led to greater comparative advantage in the production of carbon-intensive goods and services for countries that do not have binding emissions targets under the agreement. The result can be a shift in production and emissions from participating nations to nonparticipating nations—a phenomenon known as emission "leakage." Because leakage implies a shift of industrial activity and associated economic benefits to emerging economies, there is an additional incentive for nonparticipants to "free ride" on the efforts of those countries that are committed to mitigating their emissions through the Protocol's narrow but deep approach.

This leakage is not one-for-one (in the sense that increased emissions in non-Annex I countries would be expected to fully negate emission reductions in Annex I countries), but it does reduce the cost-effectiveness and environmental performance of the agreement and, perhaps worst of all, it pushes developing countries onto a more carbon-intensive growth path than they would otherwise have taken, thereby rendering it more difficult for these countries to join the agreement later.

A third concern about the Kyoto Protocol centers on the nature of its emission trading elements. The provision in Article 17 for international emission trading is unlikely to be effective (Hahn and Stavins 1999). The entire theory behind the claim that a cap-and-trade system was likely to be cost-effective depended upon the participants being cost-minimizing entities. In the case of private sector firms, this is a sensible assumption because if firms do not seek—and indeed succeed in—minimizing their costs, they will eventually disappear, given the competitive forces of the market. But nation-states can hardly be thought of as simple cost-minimizers; many other objectives affect their decision-making. Furthermore, even if nation-states sought to minimize costs, they do not have sufficient information about marginal abatement costs at the multitude of sources within their borders to carry out cost-effective trades with other countries.

There is also concern regarding the CDM. This is not a cap-and-trade mechanism but rather an emission-reduction-credit system. That is, when an individual project results in emissions below what they would have been in the absence of the project, a credit, which may be sold to a source within a cap-and-trade system, is generated. This approach creates a challenge: comparing actual emissions with what they would have been otherwise. The baseline—what would have happened had the project not been implemented—is unobserved and fundamentally unobservable. In fact, there is a natural tendency, because of economic incentives, to claim credits precisely for those projects that are most profitable and that hence would have been most likely to go forward even without the promise of credits. This so-called additionality problem is a serious issue.

Fourth, the Kyoto Protocol, with its five-year time horizon (2008 to 2012), represented a relatively short-term approach to what is fundamentally a long-term problem. GHGs have residence times in the atmosphere of decades to centuries. Furthermore, to encourage the magnitude of technological change that will be required to meaningfully address the threat of climate change, it will be necessary to send long-term signals to the private market that stimulate sustained investment and technology innovation (Newell 2010:403–438).

Finally, the Kyoto Protocol may not have provided sufficient incentives for countries to comply (Barrett 2010:240–272). Some countries' emissions have grown so fast since 1990 that it is difficult to imagine those countries being able to undertake the emission mitigation or to muster the political will and resources necessary to purchase enough emission allowances or CDM credits from other countries, so as to comply with their targets under the Protocol. For example, Canada's GHG emissions in 2008 and 2009 exceeded that country's 1990 levels by about 33 percent on average, making it very unlikely that Canada could comply with an emissions target set at 6 percent *below* 1990 levels, averaged over the 2008–2012 commitment period. As a result, Canada formally initiated the process to withdraw from the Kyoto Protocol in 2011, as it is permitted to do under Article 27 of the Protocol. In short, the enforcement mechanism negotiated for the Kyoto Protocol does not appear to induce policy responses consistent with agreed-upon targets.

Alternative Policy Architectures for the Post-Kyoto Period

We characterize potential post-Kyoto international policy architectures as falling within three principal categories: targets and timetables, harmonized national policies, and coordinated and unilateral national policies (Aldy and Stavins 2007).

The first category—targets and timetables—is the most familiar. At its heart is a centralized international agreement, top-down in form. This is the basic architecture underlying the Kyoto Protocol: essentially country-level quantitative emission targets established over specified time frames. An example of an approach that would be within this realm of targets and timetables, but would address some of the perceived deficiencies of the Kyoto Protocol, would be a regime that established emission targets based on formulas rather than specified fixed quantities (Frankel 2010a:31–87). In lieu of ad-hoc negotiations over emission caps, this formula approach would establish principles that could be translated into quantitative metrics for determining emission obligations. These formulas could be structured to have some of the appealing properties of indexed growth targets: setting targets as a function of a country's gross domestic product (GDP) per capita, for example (Aldy 2004:89–118). As countries become wealthier, their targets would become more stringent.[2] Conversely, when and if countries face difficult economic periods, the stringency of their targets would be automatically reduced.

Such an approach does not divide the world simply into two categories of countries, as in the Kyoto Protocol. Rather, it allows for a continuous differentiation among countries. In this way it reduces, if not eliminates, problems of emission leakage, yet still addresses the key criterion of distributional equity and does so in a more careful, sophisticated manner.

The second category—harmonized domestic policies—focuses more on national policy actions than on goals and is less centralized than the first set of approaches. In this case, countries agree on similar domestic policies. This reflects the view that national governments have much more control over their countries' policies than over their emissions. One example is a set of harmonized national carbon taxes (Cooper 2010:151–178).[3] With this approach, each participating country sets a domestic tax on the carbon content of fossil fuels, thereby achieving cost-effective control of emissions within its borders. Taxes would be set by nations, and nations would have complete discretion over the revenues they generate. Countries could design their tax policies to be revenue-neutral—for example, by returning the revenues raised to the economy through proportional cuts in other distortionary taxes, such as those on labor and capital. In order to achieve global cost-effectiveness, carbon taxes would need to be set at the same level in all countries. This would presumably not be acceptable to the poorer countries of the world. Therefore, significant side deals would most likely need to accompany such a system of harmonized carbon taxes to make it distributionally equitable and hence politically feasible. This could take the form of large financial transfers through side payments from the industrialized world to the developing world, or agreements in the trade or development agenda that effectively compensate developing countries for implementing carbon taxes.

The third and final category that we have used to classify potential post-Kyoto climate policy architectures is coordinated and unilateral national policies. This category includes the least-centralized approaches that we have considered: essentially bottom-up policies that rely on domestic politics to drive incentives for participation and compliance (Pizer 2007:280–314). Although these approaches are the least centralized, they should not be thought of as necessarily the least effective. One example of a bottom-up approach—linking independent national and regional tradable permit systems—may already be evolving (Jaffe and Stavins 2010, 119–150).

Lessons for the International Policy Community

The nations of the world confront a tremendous challenge in designing and implementing an international policy response to the threat of global climate change that is scientifically sound, economically rational, and politically pragmatic. It is broadly acknowledged that the relatively wealthy, developed countries are responsible for a majority of the anthropogenic GHGs that have already accumulated in the atmosphere, but developing countries will emit more GHGs over this century than the currently industrialized nations if no efforts are taken to alter their course of development. The architecture of a robust international climate change policy will need to take into account the many dimensions and consequences of this issue with respect to the environment, the economy, energy, and development.

We present a set of principles that our research teams have explicitly or implicitly identified as being important for the design of post-Kyoto international climate policy architecture. We then go on to highlight four potential architectures, each of which is promising in some regard and raises important issues for consideration.

Principles for an International Agreement

These principles constitute the fundamental premises that underlie various proposed policy architectures and design elements; as such they can provide a reasonable point of departure for ongoing international negotiations.[4]

Climate change is a global commons problem, and therefore a cooperative approach involving many nations—whether through a single international agreement or some other regime—will be necessary to address it successfully. Because GHGs mix uniformly in the atmosphere, the location of emissions sources has no effect on the location of impacts, which are dispersed worldwide. Hence, it is virtually never in the economic interest of individual nations to take unilateral actions. This classic free-rider problem means that cooperative approaches are necessary (Aldy and Stavins 2008a).

Because sovereign nations cannot be compelled to act against their wishes, successful treaties should create adequate incentives for compliance, along with incentives for participation. Unfortunately, the Kyoto Protocol seems to lack incentives of both types (Barrett 2010:240–272; Karp and Zhao 2010:530–562; Keohane and Raustiala 2010:372–402).

Because carbon-intensive economies cannot be replicated throughout the world without causing dangerous anthropogenic interference with the global climate, it will be necessary for all countries to move onto much less carbon-intensive growth paths. Even reducing emissions in the currently industrialized world to zero is insufficient (Blanford et al. 2010:822–856; Bosetti et al. 2010:715–752; Cooper 2010:151–178; Hall et al. 2010:649–681; Jacoby et al.

2010:753–785). With appropriate negotiating rules (Harstad 2010:273–299), more countries can be brought on board. The rapidly emerging middle class in the developing world seeks to emulate lifestyles that are typical of the industrialized world and may be willing to depart from this goal only if the industrialized world itself moves to a lower-carbon path (Agarwala 2010:179–200; Schmalensee 2010:889–898; Wirth 2010:xxxiii–xxxviii). Moving beyond the current impasse will require that developed countries achieve meaningful near-term emission reductions, with a clear view to medium- and long-term consequences and goals (Agarwala 2010:179–200; Harstad 2010:273–299; Karp and Zhao 2010:530–562).

A credible global climate change agreement must be equitable. If past or present high levels of emissions become the basis for all future entitlements, the developing world is unlikely to participate (Agarwala 2010:179–200). Developed countries are responsible for more than 50 percent of the accumulated stock of anthropogenic GHGs in the atmosphere today, and their share of near-term global mitigation efforts should reflect this responsibility (Agarwala 2010:179–200). In the long term, nations should assume the same or similar burdens on an equalized per capita basis (Agarwala 2010:179–200; Cao 2010:563–598; Frankel 2010a:31–87). However, if the goal is a more equitable distribution of wealth, approaches based on metrics other than per capita emissions can be better (Jacoby et al. 2010:753–785; Posner and Sunstein 2010:343–371). It is also important to recognize and acknowledge that in the short term, developing countries may value their economic growth more than future, global environmental conditions (Victor 2010:618–649).

Developing countries face domestic imperatives for economic growth and political development. More and better research is needed to identify policies that promote mitigation and adaptation, while accommodating development. At the same time, developing countries should not "hide behind the poor" (Agarwala 2010:179–200); the burgeoning middle class in the developing world is on a path to exceed the population of developed countries, and, as we have already noted, its lifestyle and per capita emissions are similar to those in much of the developed world. While not exclusively a problem of developing countries, tropical forests, in particular, are one important dimension of the larger interplay between development and climate change policy. Because of the enormous impacts that natural and anthropogenic changes in forests have on the global carbon cycle, it is important to provide a meaningful, cost-effective, and equitable approach to promoting forest carbon sequestration in an international agreement (Plantinga and Richards 2010:682–714).

A credible global climate change agreement must be cost-effective. That means it should minimize the global welfare loss associated with reducing emissions (Aldy and Stavins 2008b; Ellerman 2010:88–118; Jaffe and Stavins 2010:119–150) and also minimize the risks of corruption in meeting targets (Agarwala 2010:179–200; Somanathan 2010:599–617).

A credible global climate change agreement must bring about significant technological change. Given the magnitude of the problem and the high costs that will be involved, it will be essential to reduce mitigation costs over time through massive technological invention, innovation, diffusion, and utilization (Aldy and Stavins 2008c; Blanford et al. 2010:822–856; Bosetti et al. 2010:715–752; Clarke et al. 2010:786–821; Newell 2010:403–438; Somanathan 2010:599–617; Wirth 2010:xxxiii–xxxviii). Rapid technology transfer from the developed to the developing world will be needed (Hall et al. 2010:649–681; Keeler and Thompson 2010:439–468; Newell 2010:403–438; Somanathan 2010:599–617; Teng et al. 2010:469–492; Wirth 2010:xxxiii–xxxviii).

Governments should work through a variety of channels to achieve a credible global climate change agreement that uses multiple ways to mitigate climate change risks. Although a post-2012 agreement under the UNFCCC may be part of a post-Kyoto regime, other venues—whether bilateral treaties, or G20 accords, or under the Montreal Protocol—should continue to be explored, as additional agreements and arrangements may be necessary (Hall et al. 2010:649–681; Schmalensee 2010:889–898).

An effective global climate change agreement must be consistent with the international trade regime. A global climate agreement can lead to conflicts with international trade law, but it can also be structured to be mutually supportive of global trade objectives (Frankel 2010b:493–529; Harstad 2010:273–299).

A credible global climate change agreement must be practical, realistic, and verifiable. That means it needs institutional mechanisms for effective implementation (Agarwala 2010:179–200). Because tremendous start-up costs are usually incurred in creating new institutions, consideration should be given, whenever appropriate, to maintaining existing institutions, such as the Clean Development Mechanism, and improving them rather than abandoning them (Hall et al. 2010:649–681; Karp and Zhao 2010:530–562; Keeler and Thompson 2010:439–468; Teng et al. 2010:469–492). In addition, it should be recognized that most parts of the industrialized world have signaled their preference for the use of cap-and-trade mechanisms to meet their domestic emissions commitments (Jaffe and Stavins 2010:119–150), and it would be *politically* practical to build upon these institutional and policy preferences. Whatever institutions or mechanisms are used to implement policy commitments, they should promote emission abatement consistent with realistic technological innovation to avoid risking costly and ineffective outcomes (Agarwala 2010:179–200; Blanford et al. 2010:822–856; Bosetti et al. 2010:715–752; Jacoby et al. 2010:753–785). The best agreements will be robust in the face of inevitable global economic downturns (McKibbin et al. 2010:857–888). Finally, various metrics can be employed to judge the equity and integrity of national commitments, including measures of emissions performance, reductions, and cost (Fischer and Morgenstern 2010:300–342). An international surveillance institution could provide credible, third-party assessments of participating countries' efforts.

Promising International Climate Policy Architectures

We highlight four potential architectures—each with advantages as well as disadvantages—because each is promising in some regards, raises key issues for consideration, and to a considerable extent is exemplary of the types of architectures we consider.

One architecture follows a targets-and-timetables structure, using formulas to set dynamic national emissions targets for all countries. Two fall within the category of harmonized domestic policies: a portfolio of international treaties and harmonized national carbon taxes. The fourth architecture summarized here is based on a set of coordinated, unilateral national policies and involves linking national and regional tradable permit systems.

TARGETS AND TIMETABLES: FORMULAS FOR EVOLVING EMISSION TARGETS FOR ALL COUNTRIES

This targets-and-timetables proposal[5] offers a framework of formulas that yield numerical emissions targets for all countries through the end of this century (Frankel 2010a:31–87). National and regional cap-and-trade systems for greenhouse gases would be linked in a way that allows trading across firms and sources (Jaffe and Stavins 2010:119–150), not among nations per se (as in Article 17 of the Kyoto Protocol). Such a global trading system would be roughly analogous to the system already established in the European Union, where sources rather than nations engage in trading (Ellerman 2010:88–118).[6]

The formulas are based on what is possible politically, given that many of the usual science- and economics-based proposals for future emission paths are not dynamically consistent; that is, future governments will not necessarily abide by commitments made by today's leaders.[7] Several researchers have observed that when participants in the policy process discuss climate targets, they typically pay little attention to the difficulty of finding mutually acceptable ways to share the economic burden of emission reductions (Bosetti et al. 2010:715–752; Jacoby et al. 2010:753–785).

This formula-based architecture is premised on four important political realities. First, the United States may not commit to quantitative emission targets if China and other major developing countries do not commit to quantitative targets at the same time. This reflects concerns about economic competitiveness and carbon leakage. Second, China and other developing countries are unlikely to make sacrifices different in character from those made by richer countries that have gone before them. Third, in the long run, no country can be rewarded for having "ramped up" its emissions well above 1990 levels. Fourth, no country will agree to bear excessive cost. (Harstad adds that use of formulas can render negotiations more efficient [2010:273–299].)

The proposal calls for an international agreement to establish a global cap-and-trade system, where emission caps are set using formulas that assign quantitative emissions limits to countries in every year through 2100. The formula incorporates three elements: a progressivity factor, a latecomer catch-up factor, and a gradual equalization factor. The progressivity factor requires richer countries to make more severe cuts relative to their business-as-usual emissions. The latecomer catch-up factor requires nations that did not agree to binding targets under the Kyoto Protocol to make gradual reductions to account for their additional emissions since 1990. This factor prevents latecomers from being rewarded with higher targets and is designed to avoid creating incentives for countries to ramp up their emissions before signing on to the agreement. Finally, the gradual equalization factor addresses the complaint that rich countries are responsible for a majority of the accumulated anthropogenic GHGs currently in the atmosphere. In the second half of the century, this factor moves national per capita emissions in the direction of the global average of per capita emissions.[8]

The caps set for rich nations would require them to undertake immediate abatement measures. Developing countries would not bear any cost in the early years, nor would they be expected to make any sacrifice that is different from the sacrifices of industrialized countries, accounting for differences in income. Developing countries would be subject to binding emission targets that would follow their business-as-usual (BAU) emissions in the next several decades.[9] National emission targets for developed and developing countries alike should not cost more than 1 percent of GDP in present value terms, or more than 5 percent of GDP in any given year.

Every country under this proposal is given reason to feel that it is only doing its fair share. Importantly, without a self-reinforcing framework for allocating the abatement burden, announcements of distant future goals may not be credible and so may not have desired effects on investment. The basic architecture of this proposal—a decade-by-decade sequence of emission targets determined by a few principles and formulas—is also flexible enough that it can accommodate major changes in circumstances during the course of the century.

HARMONIZED DOMESTIC POLICIES: A PORTFOLIO OF INTERNATIONAL TREATIES

The second proposal we highlight is for a very different sort of architecture than that of the Kyoto Protocol. Rather than attempting to address all sectors and all types of GHGs under one unified regime, this approach[10] envisions a system of linked international agreements that separately address various sectors and gases, as well as key issues, including adaptation and technology research and development (R&D), plus last-resort remedies, such as geoengineering and air capture of greenhouse gases.

First, nations would negotiate sector-level agreements that would establish global standards for specific sectors or categories of GHG sources. Developing countries would not be exempted from these standards but would receive financial aid from developed countries to help them comply. Trade sanctions would be available to enforce agreements governing trade-sensitive sectors. Such a sectoral approach could have the advantage that it protects against cross-contamination: If policies designed for a given sector prove ineffective, their failure need not drag down the entire enterprise. Similar arguments can be made for separate approaches to different types of GHGs.

In general, sectoral approaches in a future climate agreement can offer some advantages (Sawa 2010:201–239). First, sectoral approaches could encourage the involvement of a wider range of countries because incentives could be targeted at specific industries in those countries. Second, sectoral approaches can directly address concerns about international competitiveness and leakage: If industries make cross-border commitments to equitable targets, this would presumably mitigate concerns about unfair competition in energy-intensive industries. Third, sectoral approaches could be designed to promote technology development and transfer. It should also be recognized, however, that sectoral approaches have some significant problems (Sawa 2010:201–239). First, it may be difficult to negotiate an international agreement using this approach if negotiators are reluctant to accept the large transaction costs associated with collecting information and negotiating at the sector level. Countries that are already participating in emission trading schemes may tend to avoid any approach that creates uncertainty about their existing investments. Second, a sectoral approach would reduce cost-effectiveness relative to an economy-wide cap-and-trade system or emission tax. Finally, it is difficult for a sectoral approach to achieve high levels of environmental effectiveness because it does not induce mitigation actions by all sectors.

Recognizing the technology challenge implicit in successfully addressing climate change, a second component of this suite of international agreements could focus on research and development. Specifically, it could require participants to adopt a portfolio of strategies for reducing barriers and increasing incentives for innovation in ways that maximize the impact of scarce public resources and effectively engage the capacities of the private sector (Newell 2010:403–438).[11] Research and development obligations could be linked with emission reduction policies. For example, an agreement could require all new coal-fired power stations to have certain minimum thermal efficiency and ready capacity to incorporate carbon capture and storage, as the latter becomes technically and financially feasible, with these obligations binding on individual countries as long as the treaty's minimum participation conditions were met. Such an agreement would reduce incentives for free-riding and could directly spur research and development investments in areas where countries and firms might otherwise be likely to underinvest.

Third, an international agreement should address adaptation assistance for developing countries. All nations have strong incentives to adapt, but only rich countries have the resources and capabilities to insure against climate change risks. Rich countries may substitute investments in adaptation—the benefits of which can be appropriated locally—for investments in mitigation, the benefits of which are distributed globally. If so, this would leave developing countries even more exposed to climate risks and widen existing disparities. Critical areas for investment include agriculture and tropical medicine. Policy design to leverage such investment can improve developing countries' resilience to climate shocks while facilitating their economic development.

A fourth set of agreements would govern the research, development, and deployment of geoengineering and air capture technologies.[12] Geoengineering could serve as an insurance policy in case refinements in climate science over the next several decades suggest that climate change is much worse than currently believed and that atmospheric concentrations may have already passed important thresholds for triggering abrupt and catastrophic impacts. Geoengineering may turn out to be cheap, relative to transforming the fossil-fuel foundation of industrial economies. While no one country can adequately address climate change through emissions abatement, individual nations may be able to implement geoengineering options. The challenge may lie in preventing nations from resorting to it too quickly or over other countries' objections.

This portfolio approach to international agreements could avoid the enforcement problems of a Kyoto-style targets-and-timetables structure, while providing the means to prevent climate change (through standards that lower emissions), become accustomed to climate change (through adaptation), and fix it (through geoengineering). By avoiding the enforcement problems of an aggregate approach and by taking a broader view of risk reduction, the portfolio approach could provide a more effective and flexible response to the long-term challenges posed by climate change.

HARMONIZED DOMESTIC POLICIES: A SYSTEM
OF NATIONAL CARBON TAXES

This architecture[13] consists of harmonized domestic taxes on GHG emissions from all sources. The charge would be internationally adjusted from time to time, and each country would collect and keep the revenues it generates (Cooper 2010:151–178). Because decisions to consume goods and services that require the use of fossil fuels are made on a daily basis by more than a billion households and firms around the world, the most effective way to reach all these decision-makers is by changing the prices they pay for these goods and services. Levying a charge on CO_2 emissions does that directly.

Carbon taxes could have several advantages over a cap-and-trade system. First, the allocation of valuable emission allowances to domestic firms or residents under a cap-and-trade scheme could foster corruption in some countries. A carbon tax would avoid such problematic transfers. Likewise, a carbon tax minimizes bureaucratic intervention and the necessity for a financial trading infrastructure (Agarwala 2010:179–200). Second, a carbon charge would generate significant revenues that could be used to increase government spending, reduce other taxes, or finance climate-relevant research and development, though it should be noted that the same is true of a cap-and-trade system that auctions allowances. Third, a carbon tax may be less objectionable to developing nations than an emission cap because it does not imply a hard constraint on growth (Pan 2007).[14] Fourth, any international climate regime requires some means for evaluating national commitments and performance (Fischer and Morgenstern 2010). A carbon tax system provides a straightforward and useful metric because the marginal cost of abatement activities is always equivalent to the tax rate itself.

Because several economies, most notably the European Union, have embarked on a cap-and-trade system, Cooper (2010:151–178) investigates whether cap-and-trade systems and tax systems can coexist. He concludes that the answer is "yes," provided that several conditions are met. First, allowance prices under the cap-and-trade system should average no less than the internationally agreed-upon carbon tax. Second, if the allowance price fell below the agreed-upon global tax for more than a certain period of time, trading partners should be allowed to levy countervailing duties on imports from countries with a low permit trading price. Third, countries could not provide tax rebates on their exports, and cap-and-trade systems would have to auction all of their allowances.

The tax should cover all the significant GHGs, insofar as is practical. The initial scheme need not cover all countries, but it should cover the countries that account for the vast majority of world emissions. All but the poorest nations should have sufficient administrative capacity to administer the tax at upstream points in the energy supply chain—that is, on the carbon content of fossil fuels.[15] The level of the tax would be set by international agreement and could be subject to periodic review every five or ten years.[16]

A carbon tax treaty would need to include monitoring and enforcement measures. The International Monetary Fund could assess whether signatory nations have passed required legislation and set up the appropriate administrative machinery to implement the tax (Agarwala 2010). If a country were significantly and persistently out of compliance, its exports could be subject to countervailing duties in importing countries. Nonsignatory countries could also be subject to countervailing duties. This possibility would provide a potent incentive for most countries to comply with the agreement, whether or not they were formal signatories.

Cost-effective implementation at a global level would require the tax to be set at the same level in all countries. The abatement costs incurred by key developing countries would likely exceed by a considerable margin the maximum burden they would be willing to accept under an international agreement, at least in the near term. This could be addressed through transfers (side payments) from industrialized countries to developing countries, thereby enhancing cost-effectiveness and distributional equity. These transfers would be from one government to another, raising concerns about possible corruption, as well as political acceptability in the industrialized world. Alternatively distributional equity could be achieved by pairing the carbon tax agreement with a deal on trade or development that benefits these emerging economies.

COORDINATED NATIONAL POLICIES: LINKAGE OF NATIONAL AND REGIONAL TRADABLE PERMIT SYSTEMS

A new international policy architecture may be evolving on its own, based on the reality that tradable permit systems, such as cap-and-trade systems, are emerging worldwide as the favored national and regional approach.[17] Prominent examples include the European Union's Emission Trading Scheme (EU ETS); the Regional Greenhouse Gas Initiative in the northeastern United States; AB32 cap-and-trade in California; a hybrid form of carbon pricing in Australia; and systems in Norway, Switzerland, New Zealand, and other nations; plus the existing global emission-reduction-credit system, the CDM.

The proliferation of cap-and-trade systems and emission-reduction-credit systems around the world has generated increased attention and increased pressure—from governments and from the business community—to link these systems. By linkage, we refer to direct or indirect connections between and among tradable permit systems through the unilateral or bilateral recognition of allowances or permits.[18]

Linkage produces cost savings in the same way that a cap-and-trade system reduces costs compared with a system that separately regulates individual emission sources; it substantially broadens the pool of lower-cost compliance options available to regulated entities. In addition, linking tradable permit systems at the country level reduces overall transaction costs, reduces market power (which can be a problem in such systems), and reduces overall price volatility.

There are also some legitimate concerns about linkage. Most important is the automatic propagation of program elements that are designed to contain costs, such as banking, borrowing, and safety valve mechanisms. If a cap-and-trade system with a safety valve is directly linked to another system that does not have a safety valve, the result will be that both systems now share the safety valve. Given that the European Union has opposed a safety valve in its emission trading scheme, and given that a safety valve could be included in a future U.S. emission trading system, this concern about the automatic propagation of cost-containment design elements is a serious one.

More broadly, linkage will reduce an individual nation's control over allowance prices, emission impacts, and other consequences of their systems. This loss of control over domestic prices and other effects of a cap-and-trade policy is simply a special case of the general proposition that nations, by engaging in international trade through an open economy, lose some degree of control over domestic prices but do so voluntarily because of the large economic gains from trade.

Importantly, there are ways to gain the benefits of linkage without the downside of having to harmonize systems in advance. If two cap-and-trade systems both link with the same emission-reduction-credit system, such as the CDM, then the two cap-and-trade systems are indirectly linked with one another. All of the benefits of linkage occur: The cost-effectiveness of both cap-and-trade systems is improved and both gain from more liquid markets that reduce transaction costs, market power, and price volatility. At the same time, the automatic propagation of key design elements from one cap-and-trade system to another is much weaker when the systems are only indirectly linked through an emission-reduction-credit system.

Such indirect linkage through the CDM is already occurring because virtually all cap-and-trade systems that are in place, as well those that are planned or contemplated, allow for CDM offsets to be used (at least to some degree) to meet domestic obligations. Thus, indirectly linked, country- or region-based cap-and-trade systems may already be evolving into the de facto, if not the de jure, post-Kyoto international climate policy architecture.

Of course, reliance on CDM offsets also gives rise to concerns, especially as regards the environmental integrity of some of those offsets. Some have recommended that a system of buyer liability (rather than seller or hybrid liability) would endogenously generate market arrangements—such as reliable ratings agencies and variations in the price of offsets according to perceived risks—that would help to address these concerns, as well as broader issues of compliance (Keohane and Raustiala 2010). These features would in turn create incentives for compliance without resorting to ineffective interstate punishments. In addition, a system of buyer liability gives sellers strong incentives to maintain permit quality so as to maximize the monetary value of these tradable assets.

While in the near term, linkage may continue to grow in importance as a core element of a bottom-up, de facto international policy architecture, in the longer term, linkage could play several roles. A set of linkages, combined with unilateral emissions reduction commitments by many nations, could function as a stand-alone climate architecture. Such a system would be cost-effective but might lack the coordinating mechanisms necessary to achieve meaningful long-term environmental results. Another possibility is that a collection of bottom-up links may eventually evolve into a comprehensive, top-down agreement. In this scenario, linkages would provide short-term cost savings while serving as a natural starting point for negotiations leading to a top-down agreement.[19] The top-down agreement might continue use of linked cap-and-trade programs to reduce abatement costs and improve market liquidity.

A post-Kyoto international climate agreement could include several elements that would facilitate future linkages among cap-and-trade and emission-reduction-credit systems. For example, it could establish an agreed trajectory of emissions caps (Frankel 2010a:31–87) or allowance prices, specify harmonized cost-containment measures, and establish a process for making future adjustments to key design elements. It could also create an international clearinghouse for transaction records and allowance auctions, provide for the ongoing operation of the CDM, and build capacity in developing countries. If the aim is to facilitate linkage, a future agreement should also avoid imposing "supplementarity" restrictions that require countries to achieve some specified percentage of emission reductions domestically.

Conclusion

Great challenges confront the community of nations seeking to establish an effective and meaningful international climate regime for the post-Kyoto period, but we have identified some key principles and promising policy architectures.

Climate change is a global commons problem, and therefore a cooperative approach involving many nations will be necessary to address it successfully. Because sovereign nations cannot be compelled to act against their wishes, successful treaties must create adequate internal incentives for compliance, along with external incentives for participation. A credible global climate change agreement must be: (1) equitable; (2) cost-effective; (3) able to facilitate significant technological change and technology transfer; (4) consistent with the international trade regime; (5) practical, in the sense that it builds where possible on existing institutions and practices; (6) attentive to short-term achievements, as well as medium-term consequences and long-term goals; and (7) realistic. Because no single approach guarantees a sure path to ultimate success, the best strategy may be to pursue a variety of approaches simultaneously.

We have highlighted in this chapter four potential frameworks for a post-Kyoto agreement, each of which is promising in some regards and raises important issues for consideration. One calls for emissions caps established using a set of formulas that assign quantitative emissions limits to countries through 2100. These caps would be implemented through a global system of linked national and regional cap-and-trade programs that would allow for trading among firms and sources. A second potential framework would instead rely on a system of linked international agreements that separately address mitigation in various sectors and gases, along with issues such as adaptation, technology research and development, and geoengineering. A third architecture would consist of harmonized domestic taxes on emissions of GHGs from all sources, where the tax or charge would be internationally adjusted from time to time, and each country would collect and keep the revenues it generates. Fourth, we discussed an architecture that, at least in the short term, links national and regional tradable permit systems only indirectly, through the global CDM. We highlight this option less as a recommendation and more by way of recognizing the structure that may already be evolving as part of the de facto post-Kyoto international climate policy architecture.

Notes

1. We use Annex I and Annex B interchangeably to represent those industrialized countries that have commitments under the Kyoto Protocol, though we recognize that a few countries are included in one annex but not the other.

2. Such a mechanism was proposed by Frankel (2007) and is similar to the graduation mechanism proposed by Michaelowa (2007). As developing countries realize growth in per capita income and per capita emissions on par with Annex I countries, they would be expected to take on binding emission targets.

3. McKibbin and Wilcoxen (2007) advance the idea of parallel, unlinked domestic cap-and-trade programs as a way to move forward in international climate policy.

4. Aldy, Barrett, and Stavins (2003) present six criteria for evaluating potential international climate policy architectures that map closely to most of these principles.

5. This proposed architecture was developed by Frankel (2010a), and supplemented by Aldy and Stavins (2008b), Harstad (2010), Cao (2010), Ellerman (2010), and Jacoby et al. (2010). Bosetti et al. (2010) provide an economic analysis of this and several other potential architectures.

6. For an examination of the possible role and design of cap-and-trade and other tradable permit systems as part of an international policy architecture, see Aldy and Stavins (2008b).

7. It is worth nothing that Harstad's (2010) game-theoretic analysis supports the efficacy of using formulas to calculate national obligations or contributions. This is because if the distribution of contributions or obligations is determined by a formula, it is fundamentally more difficult for a country to renegotiate its own share of the burden. Enhancing its bargaining position is then less useful, and investments in research and development increase.

8. This is similar to Cao's (2010) "global development rights" (GDR) burden-sharing formula and is consistent with calls for movement toward per capita responsibility by Agarwala (2010). On the other hand, it contrasts with the analyses of Jacoby et al. (2010) and Posner and Sunstein (2010). Under Cao's GDR formula, the lion's share of the abatement burden would fall on the industrialized world in the short term, with developing countries initially accepting a small but increasing share over time, such that, by 2020, fast-growing economies such as China and India would take on significant burdens.

9. Somanathan (2010) would argue against including developing countries in the short term, even with targets equivalent to BAU, as recommended in this proposal. We discuss alternative burden-sharing arrangements here.

10. This proposed architecture was developed by Barrett (2010) and supplemented by Newell (2010) on research and development policies, by Sawa (2010) on sectoral approaches, and by economic modeling from Bosetti et al. (2010).

11. In the section following on key design issues, we focus on technology transfer as a key design issue for any international climate policy architecture. Bosetti et al. (2010) analyze the costs and effectiveness of research and development strategies compared with alternative architectures.

12. Geoengineering strategies attempt to limit warming by reducing the amount of solar radiation that reaches the earth's surface—the most commonly discussed approach in this category involves throwing particles into the atmosphere to scatter sunlight. Air capture refers to strategies for removing carbon from the atmosphere. Possible options include fertilizing iron-limited regions of the oceans to stimulate phytoplankton blooms or using a chemical sorbent to directly remove carbon from the air.

13. This proposed architecture was developed by Cooper (2010) and supplemented by Fischer and Morgenstern (2010) on measurement issues, McKibbin et al. (2010) on a hybrid of this approach, and economic modeling by Bosetti et al. (2010).

14. China's 2007 National Program on Climate Change indicated that any near-term emissions reductions in that country will be accomplished using domestic policies designed to address energy efficiency, renewable and nuclear energy, and energy security. The document also indicated that in the longer term, China might be willing to place a price on carbon emissions using more direct mechanisms such as an emissions tax or cap-and-trade system (Jiang 2008). This policy approach is reinforced in Part III of China's October 2008 White Paper on climate change (Information Office of the State Council 2008).

15. For example, the carbon content of oil should be taxed at refineries, natural gas should be taxed at major pipeline collection points, and coal should be taxed at mine heads or rail or barge collection points.

16. For a thorough economic assessment of the implications of a system of harmonized domestic carbon taxes, see Bosetti et al. (2010).

17. This proposed architecture was developed by Jaffe and Stavins (2010), and supplemented by Ellerman (2010) on the European approach as a potential global model, Keohane and Raustiala (2010) on buyer liability, Hall et al. (2010) and Victor (2010) on the importance of domestic institutions, and by economic modeling from Bosetti et al. (2010).

18. As Ellerman (2010) explains, to some degree the EU ETS can serve as a prototype for linked national systems.

19. Carraro (2007) and Victor (2007) also describe the potential for trading to emerge organically as a result of linking a small set of domestic trading programs. This evolution would be analogous to the experience in international trade in goods and services, in which a small number of countries initially reached agreement on trade rules governing a small set of goods. As trust built on these initial experiences, trading expanded to cover more countries and more goods, a process that eventually provided the foundation for a top-down authority in the form of the World Trade Organization.

References

Agarwala, R., 2010, "Towards a Global Compact for Managing Climate Change," in *Post-Kyoto International Climate Policy: Implementing Architectures for Agreement*, edited by J. E. Aldy and R. N. Stavins, 179–200. New York: Cambridge University Press.

Aldy, J. E., 2004, "Saving the Planet Cost-Effectively: The Role of Economic Analysis in Climate Change Mitigation Policy," in *Painting the White House Green: Rationalizing Environmental Policy Inside the Executive Office of the President*, edited by R. Lutter and J. F. Shogren, 89–110. Washington, D.C.: Resources for the Future.

Aldy, J. E., S. Barrett, and R. N. Stavins, 2003, "Thirteen Plus One: A Comparison of Global Climate Policy Architectures," *Climate Policy*, 3(4):373–397.

Aldy, J. E. and R. N. Stavins, 2008a, "Climate Policy Architectures for the Post-Kyoto World," *Environment, 50*(3): 6–17.

———, 2008b, "Economic Incentives in a New Climate Agreement," Prepared for The Climate Dialogue, hosted by the Prime Minister of Denmark, May 7–8, 2008, Copenhagen, Denmark. Cambridge, Mass.: Harvard Project on Climate Agreements.

———, 2008c, "The Role of Technology Policies in an International Climate Agreement," Prepared for The Climate Dialogue, hosted by the Prime Minister of Denmark, September 2–3, 2008, Copenhagen, Denmark. Cambridge, Mass.: Harvard Project on Climate Agreements.

———, 2009, *Post-Kyoto International Climate Policy: Summary for Policymakers*, New York: Cambridge University Press.

Aldy, J. E. and R. N. Stavins, eds., 2007, *Architectures for Agreement: Addressing Global Climate Change in the Post-Kyoto World*, New York: Cambridge University Press.

———, 2010, *Post-Kyoto International Climate Policy: Implementing Architectures for Agreement*, New York: Cambridge University Press.

Barrett, S., 2010. "A Portfolio System of Climate Treaties," in *Post-Kyoto International Climate Policy: Implementing Architectures for Agreement*, edited by J. E. Aldy and R. N. Stavins, 240–270. New York: Cambridge University Press.

Blanford, G. J., R. G. Richels, and T. F. Rutherford, 2010, "Revised Emissions Growth Projections for China: Why Post-Kyoto Climate Policy Must Look East," in *Post-Kyoto International Climate Policy: Implementing Architectures for Agreement*, edited by J. E. Aldy and R. N. Stavins, 822–856. New York: Cambridge University Press.

Bosetti, V., C. Carraro, A. Sgobbi, and M. Tavoni, 2010. "A Quantitative and Comparative Assessment of Architectures for Agreement," in *Post-Kyoto International Climate Policy: Implementing Architectures for Agreement*, edited by J. E. Aldy and R. N. Stavins, 715–752. New York: Cambridge University Press.

Cao, J., 2010, "Reconciling Human Development and Climate Protection," in *Post-Kyoto International Climate Policy: Implementing Architectures for Agreement*, edited by J. E. Aldy and R. N. Stavins, 563–598. New York: Cambridge University Press.

Carraro, C., 2007. "Incentives and Institutions: A Bottom-Up Approach to Climate Policy," in *Architectures for Agreement: Addressing Global Climate Change in the Post-Kyoto World*, edited by J. E. Aldy and R. N. Stavins, 161-172. New York: Cambridge University Press.

Clarke, L., K. Calvin, J. Edmonds, P. Kyle, and M. Wise, 2010, "Technology and International Climate Policy," in *Post-Kyoto International Climate Policy: Implementing Architectures for Agreement*, edited by J. E. Aldy and R. N. Stavins, 786–821. New York: Cambridge University Press.

Cooper, R., 2010. "The Case for Charges on Greenhouse Gas Emissions," in *Post-Kyoto International Climate Policy: Implementing Architectures for Agreement*, edited by J. E. Aldy and R. N. Stavins, 151–178. New York: Cambridge University Press.

Ellerman, A. D., 2010, "EU Emission Trading Scheme: A Prototype Global System?" in *Post-Kyoto International Climate Policy: Implementing Architectures for Agreement*, edited by J. E. Aldy and R. N. Stavins, 88–118. New York: Cambridge University Press.

Fischer, C. and R. Morgenstern, 2010, "Metrics for Evaluating Policy Commitments in a Fragmented World: The Challenges of Equity and Integrity," in *Post-Kyoto International Climate Policy: Implementing Architectures for Agreement*, edited by J. E. Aldy and R. N. Stavins, 300–342. New York: Cambridge University Press.

Frankel, J., 2007, "Formulas for Quantitative Emission Targets," in *Architectures for Agreement: Addressing Global Climate Change in the Post-Kyoto World*, edited by J. E. Aldy and R. N. Stavins, 31–56. New York: Cambridge University Press.

———, 2010a, "A Proposal for Specific Formulas and Emission Targets for All Countries in All Decades," in *Post-Kyoto International Climate Policy: Implementing Architectures for Agreement*, edited by J. E. Aldy and R. N. Stavins, 31–87. New York: Cambridge University Press.

———, 2010b, "Global Environmental Policy and Global Trade Policy," in *Post-Kyoto International Climate Policy: Implementing Architectures for Agreement*, edited by J. E. Aldy and R. N. Stavins, 493–529. New York: Cambridge University Press.

Hahn, R. W. and R. N. Stavins, 1999, *What Has the Kyoto Protocol Wrought? The Real Architecture of International Tradable Permit Markets*, Washington, D.C.: American Enterprise Institute.

Hall, D., M. Levi, W. Pizer, and T. Ueno, 2010, "Policies for Developing Country Engagement," in *Post-Kyoto International Climate Policy: Implementing Architectures for Agreement*, edited by J. E. Aldy and R. N. Stavins, 649–681. New York: Cambridge University Press.

Harstad, B., 2010, "How to Negotiate and Update Climate Agreements," in *Post-Kyoto International Climate Policy: Implementing Architectures for Agreement*, edited by J. E. Aldy and R. N. Stavins, 273–299. New York: Cambridge University Press.

Information Office of the State Council, 2008, "China's Policies and Actions for Addressing Climate Change," white paper published by the government of the People's Republic of China, available at http://china.org.cn/government/news/2008-10/29/content_16681689.htm (accessed October 3, 2012).

Jacoby, H. D., M. Babiker, S. Paltsev, and J. M. Reilly, 2010, "Sharing the Burden of GHG Reductions," in *Post-Kyoto International Climate Policy: Implementing Architectures for Agreement*, edited by J. E. Aldy and R. N. Stavins, 753–785. New York: Cambridge University Press.

Jaffe, J. and R. N. Stavins, 2010, "Linkage of Tradable Permit Systems in International Climate Policy Architecture," in *Post-Kyoto International Climate Policy: Implementing Architectures for Agreement*, edited by J. E. Aldy and R. N. Stavins, 119–150. New York: Cambridge University Press.

Jiang, K., 2008, "Opportunities for Developing Country Participation in an International Climate Change Policy Regime," discussion paper 08–26. Cambridge, Mass.: Harvard Project on Climate Agreements.

Karp, L. and J. Zhao, 2010, "Kyoto's Successor," in *Post-Kyoto International Climate Policy: Implementing Architectures for Agreement*, edited by J. E. Aldy and R. N. Stavins, 530–562. New York: Cambridge University Press.

Keeler, A. and A. Thompson, 2010, "Resource Transfers to Developing Countries: Improving and Expanding Greenhouse Gas Offsets," in *Post-Kyoto International Climate Policy: Implementing Architectures for Agreement*, edited by J. E. Aldy and R. N. Stavins, 439–468. New York: Cambridge University Press.

Keohane, R. and K. Raustiala, 2010, "Toward a Post-Kyoto Climate Change Architecture: A Political Analysis," in *Post-Kyoto International Climate Policy: Implementing Architectures for Agreement*, edited by J. E. Aldy and R. N. Stavins, 372–402. New York: Cambridge University Press.

McKibbin, W. J., A. Morris, and P. J. Wilcoxen, 2010, "Expecting the Unexpected: Macroeconomic Volatility and Climate Policy," in *Post-Kyoto International Climate Policy: Implementing Architectures for Agreement*, edited by J. E. Aldy and R. N. Stavins, 857–888. New York: Cambridge University Press.

McKibbin, W. J. and P. J. Wilcoxen, 2007, "A Credible Foundation for Long-Term International Cooperation on Climate Change," in *Architectures for Agreement: Addressing Global Climate Change in the Post-Kyoto World,* edited by J. E. Aldy and R. N. Stavins, 185–208. New York: Cambridge University Press.

Michaelowa, A., 2007, "Graduation and Deepening," in *Architectures for Agreement: Addressing Global Climate Change in the Post-Kyoto World,* edited by J. E. Aldy and R. N. Stavins, 81–104. New York: Cambridge University Press.

Newell, R., 2010, "International Climate Technology Strategies," in *Post-Kyoto International Climate Policy: Implementing Architectures for Agreement*, edited by J. E. Aldy and R. N. Stavins, 403–438. New York: Cambridge University Press.

Pan, Y., 2007, *Thoughts on Environmental Issues*, Beijing: China Environmental Culture Promotion Association.

Pizer, W. A., 2007. "Practical Global Climate Policy," in *Architectures for Agreement: Addressing Global Climate Change in the Post-Kyoto World,* edited by J. E. Aldy and R. N. Stavins, 280–314. New York: Cambridge University Press.

Plantinga, A. and K. Richards, 2010, "International Forest Carbon Sequestration in a Post-Kyoto Agreement," in *Post-Kyoto International Climate Policy: Implementing Architectures for Agreement*, edited by J. E. Aldy and R. N. Stavins, 682–714. New York: Cambridge University Press.

Posner, E. and C. Sunstein, 2010, "Justice and Climate Change," in *Post-Kyoto International Climate Policy: Implementing Architectures for Agreement*, edited by J. E. Aldy and R. N. Stavins, 343–371. New York: Cambridge University Press.

Sawa, A., 2010, "A Sectoral Approach as an Option for a Post-Kyoto Framework," in *Post-Kyoto International Climate Policy: Implementing Architectures for Agreement*, edited by J. E. Aldy and R. N. Stavins, 201–239. New York: Cambridge University Press.

Schmalensee, R., 2010, "Epilogue: Implementing Architectures for Agreement," in *Post-Kyoto International Climate Policy: Implementing Architectures for Agreement*, edited by J. E. Aldy and R. N. Stavins, 889–898. New York: Cambridge University Press.

Somanathan, E., 2010, "What Do We Expect from an International Climate Agreement? A Low-Income Country Perspective," in *Post-Kyoto International Climate Policy: Implementing Architectures for Agreement*, edited by J. E. Aldy and R. N. Stavins, 599–617. New York: Cambridge University Press.

Teng, F., W. Chen, and J. He, 2010, "Possible Development of a Technology Clean Development Mechanism in a Post-2012 Regime," in *Post-Kyoto International Climate Policy: Implementing Architectures for Agreement*, edited by J. E. Aldy and R. N. Stavins, 469–492. New York: Cambridge University Press.

Victor, D. G., 2007, "Fragmented Carbon Markets and Reluctant Nations: Implications for the Design of Effective Architectures," in *Architectures for Agreement: Addressing Global Climate Change in the Post-Kyoto World*, edited by J. E. Aldy and R. N. Stavins, 133–160. New York: Cambridge University Press.

——, 2010, "Climate Accession Deals for Taming Growth of Greenhouse Gases in Developing Countries," in *Post-Kyoto International Climate Policy: Implementing Architectures for Agreement*, edited by J. E. Aldy and R. N. Stavins, 618–648. New York: Cambridge University Press.

Wirth, T., 2010, "Foreword," in *Post-Kyoto International Climate Policy: Implementing Architectures for Agreement*, edited by J. E. Aldy and R. N. Stavins, xxxiii–xxxviii. New York: Cambridge University Press.

4

Urbanizing the Challenges of Global Governance

Introduction

The City Level in Governance Challenges: Enabling Protection Without Protectionism

Opening up existing formal governance frames to the city level carries significant implications. It can help overcome the narrow nationalisms of interstate negotiated agreements. Large, complex cities share far more with other cities across the world in terms of challenges and the resources they need than they share with their national states and that national states share with each other. Cities share a specific position in a multiscalar global governance system. The ongoing elaboration of the European Union has brought this to the fore, notably in the need for subsidiarity regimes that go from the European to the local level. Given this transnational affinity among cities when it comes to challenges and needed resources, bringing the city level into global regimes might be one of the most effective ways of achieving protection without national protectionism.

If we are to open up macrolevel regimes to this subnational scale, it becomes critical to recognize the specific and specialized difference of the local level. Three features stand out in this regard.

First is that the city level makes possible the implementation and application of forms of scientific knowledge and technological capacities that are not practical at a national level; this is partly because the city's multiple ecologies enable the mixing of diverse forms of knowledge and diverse technologies. In doing this, the city introduces a type of environmental governance option that takes a radically different approach from the common and preferred choice of an international carbon trading regime. The aim becomes addressing the carbon and nitrogen cycles in situ by implementing measures that reduce damage in a radical way. Saskia Sassen's chapter addresses these issues.

Second, introducing the city level into global governance regimes enables what Arthur Moll and Kristine Kern refer to as horizontal governance, encompassing regimes that can work alongside traditional vertical forms of governance. In their chapter, they examine diverse urban initiatives and show us that these initiatives have been an essential part of climate governance from the outset even if not a formal part of the global regime. Leading cities such as London, Stockholm, and New York have become global players, with far more ambitious goals than their national governments. They have developed comprehensive models to make cities carbon-free and climate-proof, thereby contributing to developing climate governance "from below." This makes visible three crucial challenges for multilevel climate governance: (1) the lack of institutional arrangements that guarantee that national climate policies are implemented at local levels (hierarchical climate governance); (2) the independent development of urban climate protection policies and the bypassing of nation-states (vertical climate governance); and (3) the emergence of horizontal coordination through the establishment of various forms of direct cooperation among cities (horizontal climate governance).

Third, opening up the global regime to the city level brings into the frame a range of troublesome developments that can be avoided at the very general global level. In their respective chapters, Tony Travers and Sophie Body-Gendrot explore city-level challenges such as immigration, racism, extreme forms of inequality, and a proliferation of new types of challenges faced by cities.

Travers sees incorporating cities into the traditional global governance paradigm as "a potential new sphere for research and policy within the field of global governance." He finds that city mayors and leaders are increasingly willing to join international organizations and to consider wider questions relating to the future development and evolution of metropolitan areas. City leaders have had to confront the direct and indirect impacts of global conflict, the movement of people, and the management of immigrant communities originating in many different countries. Further, he finds that international politics has begun to create a demand for urban solutions.

Body-Gendrot shows us how conflict is now wired into urban space itself. The reasons are numerous: Extreme inequalities generate the resentment of those confined to the less hospitable urban areas at a time when information reaches the most distant points of the world and makes residents aware of their fate; the fascination and rejection such cities provoke among radical activists such as in the Mumbai terrorist attacks where luxury hotels, among other targets, were hit; the diversity of people leaving and entering these urban spaces, most ready to compete for survival. One effect is that policing and maintaining order become central functions in global cities, a focus that is not helpful in addressing the governance challenges confronting these cities. As a member of the National Council for Professional Standards in Security (known as CNDS, Commission Nationale de Déontologie de la Sécurité) in France, Body-Gendrot receives a large number of complaints from young people regarding this dominance of order maintenance—police harassment, humiliating stops and searches in the gray areas where witnesses will not talk, and powerlessness when it comes to seeking fair treatment and judgments. Body-Gendrot explores what it might take to reorder the priorities of urban government toward major challenges and away from this order maintenance rationale.

We can organize the urbanizing of the various challenges we confront along three vectors:

Global Warming, Energy, and Water Insecurity

These and other environmental challenges are going to make cities frontline spaces. These challenges will tend to remain more diffuse for nationstates and for the state itself. One key reason is the more acute and direct dependence of everyday life in cities on massive infrastructures and on institutional-level supports for most people—apartment buildings, hospitals, vast sewage systems, water purification systems, vast underground transport systems, whole electric grids dependent on computerized management vulnerable to breakdowns. We already know that a rise in water levels will flood some of the most densely populated cities in the world.

The urgency of some of these challenges goes well beyond lengthy nego-tiations and multiple international meetings, still the most common form of engagement at the level of national politics and especially international politics. When global warming hits cities, it will hit hard, and preparedness will be critical. The new kinds of crises and the ensuing violence will be particularly felt in cities. A major simulation by NASA found that, by the fifth day of a breakdown in the computerized systems that manage the elec-tric grid, a major city such as New York would be in an extreme condition and basically unmanageable through conventional instruments.

These challenges are emergent, but before we know it they will become concrete and threatening in cities. This contrasts with possibly slower tra-jectories at the national level. In this sense, cities are in the frontline and will have to act on global warming whether national states sign on to in-ternational treaties or not. Because of this, many cities have had to develop capabilities to handle such challenges. The air quality emergency in cities such as Tokyo and Los Angeles as early as the 1980s is one example: These cities could not wait until an agreement such as Kyoto might appear, nor could they wait until national governments passed mandatory laws (i.e., for car fuel efficiency and zero emissions). With or without an interna-tional treaty or a national law, they had to address air quality urgently. And they did.

Asymmetric Wars

When national states go to war in the name of national security, major cities are likely to become a key frontline space in today's prevalent type of war. In the past, large open fields or oceans were the frontline spaces needed by large armies to engage and fight. Under these condi-tions, doing war in the name of national security becomes the making of urban insecurity. We can see this today with the so-called War on Terror, whereby the invasion of Iraq became an urban war theater. But we also see the negative impacts of this war in the case of cities that are not even part of the immediate war theater—the bombings in Madrid, London, Casablanca, Bali, Mumbai, Lahore, and so many others. The traditional security paradigm based on national state security fails to accommodate this triangulation. What may be good for the protection of the national state apparatus may go at a high or increasingly higher price to major cities and their people.

Urban Violence

Cities also enter the domain of global governance challenges as a site for the enactment of new forms of violence resulting from various crises. We can foresee a variety of forms of violence that are likely to escape the macrolevel normative propositions of good governance. For instance, São Paulo and Rio have seen forms of gang and police violence in the early 2000s that point to a much larger breakdown than the typically invoked fact of inadequate policing. We could say the same about the failures of the powerful U.S. forces in Baghdad. To explain this simply as anarchy is inadequate. Further, immigration and new types of environmental refugees are one particularly acute instance of urban challenges that will require new understandings of the civic.

These and other challenges examined in this section resonate with questions addressed in other parts of this book. As the editors posit in the introduction to part 2:

> In the past, the most important external security threat was considered an attack by a foreign state. That threat has all but disappeared since the end of the Cold War. Now the sources of insecurity are usually identified as a range of global risks. Some have to do with potential or actual violence: terrorism, war and counter insurgency, ethnic cleansing, the spread of weapons of mass destruction, massive human rights violence, and organized crime.

In the introduction to part 5, the editors write that

> An active global or international civil society has insistently drawn the world's attention to such issues as global poverty, climate change, disease, and human rights violations. New forms of identity politics around religion or ethnicity are increasingly transnational. Yet this new type of informal politics has no institutional counterpart and no address to which demands can be directed.

This urbanizing of what we have traditionally considered national or international challenges is part of a larger disassembling of the two traditional all-encompassing formats, the nation-state and the interstate system. As some of the chapters in this book signal, there is growing recognition of the multiscalar structures at work in many of our global governance challenges. This opens up possibilities and opportunities for the local level to become part of the larger governance framing of diverse issues.

9

A Focus on Cities Takes Us Beyond Existing Governance Frameworks

SASKIA SASSEN

Introduction

Incorporating the urban scale into global-level environmental governance framings can take us beyond the limitations and distortions of a carbon trading regime. This in turn takes us beyond the kinds of nationalisms that carbon trading brings into negotiations. Among the key properties that distinguish cities as a site for environmental policymaking, and thereby as a source of policy innovations, are their multiple scales and diverse socio-physical ecologies. I want to argue that these two features should be conceived of as urban capabilities for addressing the environmental challenge. A key obstacle to this potential is that cities tend to be excluded from current practice and environmental governance discourse: Cities are flattened into one scale—the "local," the bottom of the institutional hierarchy that runs through the national state.

Mobilizing these scalar and ecological urban capabilities would enable more complex applications of mixes of policy and scientific knowledge. Further, recognizing the city as a multiscalar and multiecological system is critical for developing more sophisticated types of policies and anchors for policy implementation. The biosphere shows us that what might be negative at one scale, can become positive at another scale: When we flatten the city into the "local" level we miss these possibilities. Finally, making the application of scientific knowledge more central to the governance discussion counteracts the excessive weight of markets (i.e., carbon trading) as a means to address the environmental crisis. This counteracting matters because misplaced protectionisms of the "right" of countries to pollute is not going to help much in addressing the larger environmental crisis.

The articulation between cities and international regimes can generate a novel type of governance vector: a global regime centered in cities that promotes the development of new kinds of urban capacities regardless of (sovereign) country. Cities are de facto components of the global environmental governance regime, though they are not so de jure. Neither their weight in environmental damage production nor their specific capacities to reduce this damage have been factored into the formal regime. Incorporating this dual role of cities into the global regime would make a major difference in the reduction of environmental damage. Further, the mechanisms for achieving this difference would be drastically different from those of carbon trading, though they could coexist with the latter: The focus here is particularly on the potential use of scientific knowledge to detect biospheric capabilities we should use to replace chemicals we now make in factories.

This chapter is an exploration of these possibilities.

The Multiple Articulations of Cities and the Biosphere

The massive processes of urbanization under way today are inevitably at the center of the environmental future. It is through cities and vast urban agglomerations that mankind is increasingly present in the planet and through which it mediates its relationship to the various stocks and flows of the environment. The urban hinterland, once primarily a confined geographic zone, is today a global hinterland. With the expansion of the global economy, a growing number of countries and firms have raised our collective capacity to annex growing portions of the world to support a limited number of industries, places, and people.

A key starting point in the larger project (Sassen 2009; Sassen and Dotan 2011) on which this chapter is based has to do with recognizing the multiple articulations cities have with the biosphere. Today these articulations are mostly negative—they damage the environment and produce ruptures in biospheric cycles that are meant to be continuous. The challenge is how to make these articulations positive. In contrast, today's more common policy approach is to focus on the damage and on what are basically minor mitigations of that damage; this is fine but not enough. Particular systemic properties of cities can enable a switch in the valence of those articulations, from negative to positive.

The substantive rationale for this project is that we need a better understanding of the role of cities, because existing theories about environmental sustainability and global environmental governance do not accommodate cities in a productive way. Cities are reduced to the local level and to a source of damage. My effort goes in the opposite direction: to work with what is there at its most variable and complex. This also means going beyond the notion that the only way for cities to contribute to sustainability is mitigation and adaptation or to start from scratch. Mitigation and adaptation are not enough to address environmental damage. And most cities cannot start from scratch. Thus for most countries, Abu Dhabi's Masdar project of a fully self-sustained city is not a model because it is far too expensive and accommodates only a small population; it should be seen as a laboratory experiment that shows us what is possible, even if realistically it cannot be the solution for most of our existing cities. Thus it becomes urgent to recognize that one path into making cities part of the solution is to work from what is there but with the aim of changing the negative valence of current articulations with the biosphere.

The larger project has focused especially on the multiscalar and ecological properties of cities; these mimic those of the biosphere thereby enabling a notion of bridging between these two parallel worlds. But once cities reach a certain size (i.e., very large cities), cities become "unbiological" consumers of the biosphere (Bettencourt et al. 2007; Bettencourt and West 2010; Environment and Urbanization 2007; Sonnenfeld and Mol 2011) and thus need to be conceived of as representing a diverse logic from that of the biosphere. In other words, the social, legal, and economic characteristics of cities need to be factored into this bridging with the biosphere. Scientific and technological types of knowledge are critical to this bridging, especially for amplifying the capacities of the biosphere so as to compensate for the "unbiological" consuming of the biosphere. But implementation of that scientific and technological knowledge will, in turn, require significant changes in the social, legal, and economic modus operandi of cities.

One assumption in the larger project is that the scale of the city can enable these transformations in more direct ways than can the scale of nation-states. This is partly because cities can avoid the nationalisms so present in the interstate debates about environmental sustainability. The fact is that cities across the world are learning from each other and implementing a range of similar innovations. This points to an emergent de facto cross-border, intercity geography for addressing environmental sustainability that can bypass much of the, often fruitless, debate around international carbon trading. Cities have implemented far more innovations than national governments, partly enabled by global urban networks for cross-border collaboration (Toly 2008). These types of interventions are beginning to reorient at least some of the articulations between cities and the biosphere. It is critical to avoid flattening the city into one singular scale and system, as is typical today, and to develop and bring to the fore the multiscalar and ecological properties of cities.

A major obstacle to this type of intervention is the absence of recognition of the urban level in most international agreements and documents aimed at protecting the environment.

The Gaping Hole in the Current Climate Change Governance Framework

Neither the Kyoto Protocol (KP) nor the United Nations Framework Convention on Climate Change (UNFCCC) contain specific references to local government or city-level actions to meet the Protocol commitments. There are just a few references to local-level involvement; for example, Article 10 in the KP recognizes that regional programs may be relevant to improve the quality of local emission factors. The latest UN Climate Conference (COP15) did not advance matters much, even though the addition of a Local Government Climate Change initiative did introduce some local issues in some of the debates and briefings.

Even though neither the KP nor UNFCCC consider any role for cities or local governments, they have established and built up financial and fiscal incentives, local knowledge and education, and other municipal frameworks for action through the practical obligations and opportunities that municipal-level governments encounter. Based on their legal responsibility and jurisdiction, local governments have developed targets and regulations; in this work, they have tended to go beyond national and state jurisdictional obligations.[1] In view of the failure to recognize cities at the international climate negotiations, the Local Government Climate Roadmap (a consortium of global municipal partnerships) has focused on this failure from 2007 onwards. One basic premise in this effort is that including the local government level would ensure that the full chain of governance, from national to local, would be involved in the implementation of a climate agreement.

Further and very illuminating as to a specific urban structural condition, some of these local initiatives go back to the 1980s and 1990s when major cities, notably Los Angeles and Tokyo, implemented clean air ordinances, not because their leaderships were particularly enlightened but because they had to for public health reasons. The global initiative "Cities for Climate Protection," developed by the International Council for Local Environmental Initiative's (ICLEI) Local Governments for Sustainability network, has been active as far back as 1993; these were mostly result-based, quantified, and concrete local climate actions, launched long before the Convention and KP came into force.[2] Local governments held Municipal Leadership Summits in 1993, 1995, 1997, and 2005, parallel to the official Conference of Parties (COP) meetings of national governments. Thereby the Local Government and Municipal Authority Constituency (LGMA) has built upon its role as one of the first NGO constituencies acting as an observer to the official international climate negotiations process (UNFCCC).[3]

These interactions have led to an increasing recognition of a role for local governments and authorities, particularly regarding discussions on reducing emissions from deforestation and forest degradation in developing countries (REDD) and on the Nairobi work program (REDD Web Platform; UNFCCC) on adaptation within the new and emerging concepts of the international climate negotiations. There is by now a rather extensive set of studies showing that cities and metro regions can make a large difference in reducing global environmental damage, focused mostly on greenhouse gas (GHG) emissions. But the international level, whether the Kyoto Protocol or the post-2012 UNFCCC negotiations, fails formally when it comes to recognizing this potential, nor is this potential built into draft agreements (Arikan 2009). The discourse on mitigation and adaptation needs to be localized, including in its international financing options. This would involve both a bottom-up—information from local level—and a top-down understanding of how existing protocols and post-2012 agreements integrate cities.

But ultimately, I will argue, there is a need, and cities make this need visible and urgent, to go well beyond these governance frameworks. We cannot simply redistribute carbon emissions, nor are mitigation and adaptation directives enough. We need to bring in the knowledge that diverse natural sciences have accumulated, including practical applications, to address the major environmental challenges.

At the level of the city, using this knowledge is a far more specific and domain-interactive effort than at the level of national policy. Further, it will entail an internationalism derived from the many different countries that are leaders in these scientific discoveries and innovations. But this will be an internationalism that runs through thick local spaces, each with their own political and social cultures for implementing change. Finally, as I will argue, capturing the complexity of cities in their multiscalar and multiecological composition will allow for many more vectors for implementation than just about any other level, whether national, international, or suburban, such as the neighborhood. This should, in turn, allow us to go well beyond adaptation and mitigation as currently understood.

The Urbanizing of Global Governance Challenges

Many of today's major global governance challenges become tangible, urgent, and practical in cities worldwide. Urban leaders and activists have had to deal with many issues long before national governments and interstate treaties addressed them. Cities are sites where these challenges can be studied empirically and where policy design and implementation often is more feasible than at the national level. Among these global governance challenges are those concerning the environment; human insecurity, including the spread of violence against people of all ages and a proliferation of racisms; and the sharp rise in economic forms of violence. Cities also constitute a frontier space for new types of environmentally sustainable energy sources, construction processes, and infrastructures. Finally, cities are critical for emerging intercity networks that involve a broad range of actors (NGOs, formal urban governments, informal activists, global firms, and immigrants) that potentially could function as a political infrastructure with which to address some of these global governance challenges.

Cities also enter the global governance picture as sites for the enactment of new forms of violence resulting from various crises. In the dense and conflictive spaces of cities, we foresee a variety of forms of violence that are likely to escape the macrolevel norms of good governance. For instance, drug gang violence in São Paulo and Rio de Janeiro point to a much larger challenge than inadequate local policing. So do the failures of the powerful U.S. forces in Baghdad to institute order. To explain this away as acute anarchy is inadequate and too facile. It will take much effort to maintain somewhat civilized environments in cities. In discussing global governance questions, one challenge is to push macrolevel frames to account for, and factor in, the types of stress that arise from violence and insecurity in dense spaces in everyday life—the type of issue that global governance discourse and its norms do not quite capture. Yet it is critical that such everyday conditions be incorporated into the global governance framing, because some of these may eventually feed into micro- and macrostyle armed conflicts, which will not solve the matter but make it worse.

More than nation-states, cities will be forced into the frontlines by global warming, energy and water insecurity, and other environmental challenges (Reuveny 2008; Dietz, Rosa, and York 2009; Warner et al. 2009). The new kinds of crises and, possibly, ensuing violence will be felt particularly in cities because of the often extreme dependence of cities on complex systems. City life depends on massive infrastructures (electricity for elevators and abundant public transport) and institutional support (e.g., hospitals, water purifying plants). Apartment buildings, hospitals, vast sewage systems, vast underground transport systems, entire electric grids dependent on computerized management—all are vulnerable to breakdown. In a major simulation by NASA of a breakdown in the computerized systems that manage the electrical grid of a major city, it was discovered that the population would be in a fairly desperate situation by the fifth day. We already know that a rise in water levels will flood some of the densest areas in the world. When these realities hit cities, they will hit hard, and preparedness will be critical. These realities are overtaking the abstract norm-oriented arguments of global governance debates that consist largely of future-oriented "oughts"—what we ought to do.

These challenges are emergent, but before we know it they will become tangible and threatening in cities. This contrasts with possibly slower trajectories at the national level. In this sense, cities are in the frontline and will have to react to global warming, whether or not national states sign on to international treaties. The leadership of cities is quite aware of this.

Can We Bridge the Ecologies of Cities and the Biosphere?

The enormously distinctive presence that is urbanization is changing a growing range of nature's ecologies, from the climate to species diversity and ocean purity. It is creating new environmental conditions—heat islands, ozone holes, desertification, and water pollution. We have entered a new phase. For the first time, mankind is the major consumer in all the significant ecosystems, and urbanization has been a major instrument. There is now a set of global ecological conditions that have never been seen before. Major cities have become distinct socioecological systems with a planetary reach. Cities have a pronounced effect on traditional rural economies and their long-standing cultural adaptation to biological diversity. Rural populations have become consumers of products produced in the industrial economy, which is much less sensitive to biological diversity. The rural condition has evolved into a new system of social relationships, one that does not work with biodiversity. These developments signal that the urban condition is a major factor in any environmental future. It all amounts to a radical transformation in the relationship between mankind and the rest of the planet.

But is it urbanization per se or the particular types of urban systems and industrial processes that we have instituted? That is to say, is it the urban format marked by agglomeration and density dynamics or what we have historically and collectively produced partly through processes of path-dependence that kept eliminating options as we proceeded? Are these global ecological conditions the results of urban agglomeration and density or are they the results of the specific types of urban systems that we have developed to handle transport, waste disposal, building, heating and cooling, food provision, and the industrial processes by which we extract, grow, make, package, distribute, and dispose of the foods, services, and materials that we use?

It is, doubtless, the latter—the specific urban systems that we have made. Among the outstanding features that are evident when one examines a range of today's major cities are the pronounced differences in environmental sustainability. These differences result from diverse government policies, economic bases, patterns of daily life, and so on. In addition to these differences, there are a few foundational elements that now increasingly dominate our way of doing things. One of them is the fact that the entire energy and material flux coursing through the human economy returns in altered form as pollution and waste to the ecosphere. The rupture at the heart of this set of flows is *made* and can, thus, be unmade—and some cities are working on it. This rupture is present in just about all economic sectors, from urban to nonurban. However, it is in cities where it has its most complex interactions and cumulative effects. This makes cities a source of most of the environmental damage, and of some of the most intractable conditions that feed the damage. Nevertheless, it is also the complexity of cities that is part of the solution.[4]

It is now imperative to make cities and urbanization part of the solution. We need to use and build upon those features of cities that can reorient the material and organizational ecologies of cities to positive interactions with nature's ecologies. These interactions, and the diversity of domains that they cover, are themselves an emergent socioecological system that bridges the city's and nature's ecologies. Part of the effort is needed to maximize the probability of positive environmental outcomes. Specific features of cities that help in this effort are economies of scale, density, and the associated potential for greater efficiency in resource use as well as important but often neglected dense communication networks that can serve as facilitators to institute environmentally sound practices in cities. More theoretically, one can say that insofar as cities are constituted through various processes that produce space, time, place, and nature, they also contain the transformative possibilities embedded in these same processes. For example, the temporal dimension becomes critical in environmentally sound initiatives. Thus, ecological economics enables us to recognize that what is inefficient or value-losing, according to market criteria with short temporal evaluation frames, can be positive and value-adding, using environment-driven criteria.[5]

The Complexity and Global Projection of Cities

As has been well-documented, cities have long been sites for innovation and for developing and instituting complex physical and organizational systems. It is within the complexity of the city that we must find the solutions to much environmental damage and the formulas for reconfiguring the socioecological systems that constitute urbanization. Cities contain the networks and information loops that may facilitate communicating, informing, and persuading households, governments, and firms to support and participate in environmentally sensitive programs and in radically transformative institution building.

Urban systems also entail systems of social relationships that support the current configuration.[6] Aside from adoption of practices such as waste recycling it will take a change in these systems of social relationships themselves to achieve greater environmental sensitivity and efficiency. For instance, a crucial issue is the massive investment around the world promoting large projects that damage the environment. Deforestation and construction of large dams are perhaps among the best known problems. The scale and the increasingly global and private character of these investments suggest that citizens, governments, and NGOs lack the power to alter these investment patterns. However, there are structural platforms for acting and for contesting these powerful corporate actors (Sassen 2005). The geography of economic globalization is strategic rather than all encompassing, and this is especially true in the managing, coordinating, servicing, and financing of global economic operations. The fact that it is strategic is significant for a discussion of the possibilities of regulating and governing the global economy. There are sites in this strategic geography, such as the network of global cities, where the density of economic transactions and top-level management functions come together to form a strategic geography of decision-making. We can see this also as a strategic geography for demanding accountability for environmental damage. It is precisely because the global economic system is characterized by an enormous concentration of power in a finite number of large, multinational corporations and global financial markets that makes for concentrated (rather than widely dispersed) sites for accountability and changing investment criteria. Engaging the headquarters is a very different type of action than engaging the thousands of mines and factories and the millions of service outlets of such global firms. This engagement is facilitated today by the recognition of an environmental crisis by consumers, politicians, and the media. Certainly, it leaves out millions of small, local firms that are responsible for much of the environmental damage. However, they are more likely to be controllable by means of national regulations and local activism.

A crucial issue raised by the foregoing is the question of the scale at which damage is produced and intervention or change should occur. This may, in turn, differ from the levels and sites for responsibility and for accountability. The city is, in this regard, an enormously complex entity. Cities are multiscalar systems where many of the environmental dynamics that concern us are constituted and that, in turn, constitute what we call the city. It is in the cities where different policy levels, from the supra- to the subnational, are implemented. Further, specific networks of mostly global cities also constitute a key component of the global scale and, hence, can be thought of as a network of sites for accountability of global economic actors.

Urban complexity and diversity are further augmented by the fact that urban sustainability requires engaging the legal systems and profit logics that underlie and enable many of the environmentally damaging aspects of our societies (Sassen 2008, chapters 4 and 5). The question of urban sustainability cannot be reduced to modest interventions that leave these major systems untouched. The actual features of these systems vary across countries and across the North–South divide. Although in some of the other environmental domains it is possible to confine the discussion of the subject to scientific knowledge, this is not the case when dealing with cities. Nonscientific elements are a crucial part of the picture. Questions of power, poverty, and inequality and of ideology and cultural preferences are all part of the question and the answer. One major dynamic of the current era is globalization and the spread of markets to more and more institutional realms. Questions of policy and proactive engagement possibilities have become a critical dimension of treatments of urban sustainability, whether they involve asking people to support garbage recycling or demanding accountability from major global corporations that are known to have environmentally damaging production processes.

Toward a Multiscalar Ecological Urban Analysis

City-related ecological conditions operate on a diversity of geographic scales. Importantly cities incorporate a range of scales on which a given ecological condition functions and, in that sense, cities make visible the fact itself of scaling. Further, cities make the multiscalar properties of ecological systems present and recognizable to its residents. This urban capacity to make visible should be developed and strengthened as it will become increasingly critical for policy matters not only of cities but also at regional, national, and global levels. For the majority of those who write about environmental regulation in, and of, cities, the strategic scale is the local (see, for example, Habitat II, Local Agenda 21). Others have long argued that the ecological regulation of cities can no longer be separated from wider questions of global governance (Low 2000). This is also a long-standing position in general, nonurban analyses of the economy and the environment (Etsy and Ivanova 2005).

Beyond regulation, the city is a key scale for implementing a broad range of environmentally sound policies and a site for struggles over the environmental quality of life for different socioeconomic classes (Satterthwaite et al. 2007; Van Veenhuizen and Danso 2007; Redclift 2009). Air, noise, and water pollution can all be partly addressed inside the city, even when the policies involved may originate at the national or regional level. Indeed, thousands of cities worldwide have initiated their own de facto environmental policies to the point of contravening national law, not because of idealism but because they have been compelled to, as national governments are far more removed from the immediate catastrophic potentials of poisoned air and floods and have been slow to act.

The acuteness of environmental challenges at the urban level has been further sharpened by the current phase of economic globalization, which puts direct pressures on cities. One example of these pressures is the global corporate demand for the extreme type of built environment epitomized by Dubai. The other side of this is the sharply increased demand for inputs, transport, and infrastructure for mobility—the enormous demand for wood, cement, nonrenewable energy, air transport, trucking, shipping, and so on. A second element that the current global corporate economy has brought is the World Trade Organization's subordination of environmental standards to what are presented as "requisites" for "free" global trade and proprietary "rights" (Gupta 2004; Mgbeogi 2006). Finally, privatization and deregulation reduce the role of government, especially at the national level, and hence weaken its mandatory powers over environmental standards.

The city becomes a strategic space for the direct and brutal confrontation between forces that are enormously destructive *to* the environment and increasingly acute needs *for* environmental viability.[7] Much of what we keep describing as global environmental challenges becomes tangible and urgent in cities. It is likely that international and national standards will need to be implemented and enforced at the urban scale.[8] There are limits to the urban scale, especially in the Global South where local governments have limited funds. However, it is one of the scales at which many specific goals can be achieved. Local authorities are in a strong position to pursue the goals of sustainable development as direct or indirect providers of services, as regulators, leaders, and partners, and as mobilizers of community resources.[9] Each urban combination of elements is unique, as is its mode of insertion within local and regional ecosystems. From this specificity comes place-based knowledge that can be scaled up and that can contribute to the understanding of global conditions. The case of ozone holes illustrates this scale-up. The damage is produced at the microlevel of cars, households, factories, and buildings, but its full impact becomes visible and measurable only over the poles, where there are no cars and buildings.

A debate that gathered heat, beginning in the 1990s and remaining unresolved, pits the global against the local or vice versa as the most strategic scale for action. Redclift (1996) argued that we cannot manage the environment at the global level. Global problems are caused by the aggregation of production and consumption, much of which is concentrated within the world's urban centers. For Redclift, we first need to achieve sustainability at the local level. He argues that the flurry of international agreements and agencies are international structures for managing the environment that bear little or no relationship to the processes through which the environment is being transformed. Not everyone agrees. Thus Satterthwaite has long argued that we need global responsibilities but cannot have such without international agreements (Satterthwaite 1999). Low (2000; see also Low and Gleeson 2001) adds that we have a global system of corporate relationships in which city administrations are increasingly taking part. This complex cross-border system is increasingly responsible for the health and destruction of the planet. Today's processes of development bring into focus the question of environmental justice at the global level, a question that, if asked, would have been heard at the national level in the early industrial era.

I make two observations here. One is that what we refer to or think of as the local level may actually entail more than one scale. For instance, the operations of a mining or manufacturing multinational corporation involve multiple localities scattered around the globe. Yet these localities are integrated at some higher organizational level into what then reemerges as a global scale of operations. Each locally produced set of damages will require much clean up and the establishment of preventive measures. However, the global organizational structure of the corporation involved also needs to be engaged. Along these same lines, the focus on individual cities promoted by notions of intercity competition in a global corporate economy has kept analysts and political leaders from understanding the extent to which the global economy needs networks of cities, rather than just one perfect global city. Hence, specific networks of cities are natural platforms for cross-border city-alliances that can confront the demands of global firms. One key benefit of international agreements for cities is in preventing some countries and cities from taking advantage of others that are instituting environmentally sound policies. Implementing such policies is likely to raise costs, at least for the short term, thereby possibly reducing the "competitiveness" of such cities and countries, even if it is likely to enhance their competitiveness in the long term. Cities that succeed in instituting such policies should not bear the expense incurred by the lack of such policies in other cities, whether at the national or international level. This will, at times, require policies that restrain the transfer of environmental costs to other locations.[10]

The second observation is that an enormous share of the attention devoted to urban sustainability in the literature has been on how people as consumers and household-level actors damage the environment. When measuring cities, inevitably individuals and households are by far the most numerous units of analysis. Yet, there clearly are shortcomings in this focus. In matters of policy, it leads to an emphasis on household recycling activities without addressing the fundamental issue of how an economic system prices modes of production that are not environmentally sound. An "urban" focus limited to individuals and households is problematic in that it can easily leave out global economic and ecological systems that are deeply involved, yet cannot be addressed at the level of households or many individual firms. For instance, those who insist that greenhouse gas emissions will have to be controlled at the local level are, in many ways, right. However, these emissions will also have to be addressed at the broader macro levels of our economic systems. Further, some recent innovations suggest the possibility of planetary interventions though multiple local initiatives.

One matter that I have researched is a range of discoveries in biological laboratories that would allow us to use biospheric capacities to do what we now do with chemicals made in factories (Sassen and Dotan 2011; Sassen 2013). For instance, a newly developed "paint" that has been mixed with bacteria that can live in concrete and deposit a kind of calcium helps seal the surfaces of buildings. This diminishes green gas emissions and purifies the air around the building.[11] This simple technology may be used for all concrete buildings, whether they are located in modest neighborhoods or the business districts of global cities. It is just one example of how a global scale can be constituted through a vast number of local sites, all of which are using the same mix of scientific knowledge and technology.

These diverse questions can be analytically conceived of as questions of scale. Scaling is one way of handling what are now often seen as either/or conditions: local versus global, markets versus nonmarket mechanisms, green versus brown environmentalism. I have found some of the analytic work on scaling conducted by ecologists helpful for conceptualizing the city in the context of environmental sustainability, particularly the question of bridging between the biosphere and the city. Of particular relevance is the notion that complex systems are multiscalar systems, as opposed to multilevel systems, and that the complexity resides precisely in the relationships among scales. Understanding how tensions among scales might be operating in the context of the city can strengthen the analysis of environmental damages associated with urbanization and the ways in which cities as complex systems also contain the elements for solutions. One of the reasons this may be helpful is that we are still struggling to understand and situate various types of environmental dynamics in the context of cities; current environmental policy may be missing the best scale at which to use the city for a range of policy implementation. There is greater understanding of what needs to be done when it comes to remedial policy and clean-up.

Research has raised a set of specific issues concerning ecological systems that point to possibly fruitful analytic strategies to understand cities and urbanization processes with regard to environmental conditions and policy.

However, understanding the city as a broader system poses enormous difficulties precisely because of the multiple scales that comprise the city— as a system of distributed capabilities and as a political-economic and jurisdictional-administrative system. For instance, the individual household, firm, or government office can recycle waste but cannot address effectively the broader issue of excess consumption of scarce resources. An international agreement can call for global-level measures to reduce greenhouse emissions but depends on individual countries, individual cities, and individual households and firms to implement many of the necessary steps. A national government can mandate environmental standards, but the specifics of implementation may depend partly on the character of a country's systems of economic power and of wealth production. A key analytic step is to decide which of the many scales of ecological, social, and economic processes is appropriate for addressing a specific environmental condition, whether negative or positive, and to design a specific action or response. Another analytic step is to factor in the temporal scales or frames of various urban conditions and dynamics; for instance, the cycles of the built environment are not the same as those of the economy, nor does the life of infrastructures correspond to the time frames of more and more investment instruments. The combination of these two analytic steps helps to deconstruct a given concrete urban situation and locate it in a broader grid of spatial, temporal, and administrative scales.

The connection between spatial and temporal scales evident in the biosphere may prove useful analytically to approach some of these questions in the case of cities. In the biosphere, it is clear that what may be negative in a small spatial scale or a short time frame can become positive in a larger scale or longer time frame. For a given set of environmental disturbances in a city, diverse spatiotemporal scales may produce (or make visible) different responses. Using an illustration from ecology, we can say that individual forest plots may come and go, but the forest cover of a region can remain relatively constant overall. This raises a question as to whether a city needs to be conceived as a multiscalar system (rather than a collection of buildings, infrastructures, and population groups) in order to ensure a proper understanding of the character of the risk and how to address it; conceivably what is experienced as negative and hence deserving of an all-out deployment of resources to solve it, may turn out to be the equivalent of the forest plot, and in the long run have the effect of strengthening the overall forest (i.e., the city's overall capacity to deal with environmental damage). One research finding of ecologists in this domain is that movement across scales brings about change, which is the dominant process. It is not only a question of larger or smaller but that the phenomenon itself changes. Unstable systems come to be seen as stable; bottom-up control can turn into top-down control; and competition becomes less important. This mobile valence invites us to think of cities as containing solutions to types of environmental damage we now reduce to an "absolute" (i.e., absolute evil, absolutely destructive—with the city as a whole often seen as one such instance). What are the scales at which we can understand the city as contributing solutions to the environmental crisis?

An important issue raised by scaling in ecological research is the frequent confusion between levels and scales. What is sometimes described as a change of scales may merely be a change of level. A change of scale results in new interactions and relationships, often a different organization. Level, on the other hand, is a relative position in a hierarchically organized system. Thus, a change in levels entails a change in a quantity or size rather than the formation of a different entity. A level of organization is not a scale, even if it can have scale or be at a scale. Scale and level are two different dimensions.

Thus thinking of the city as multiscalar entails recovering, for instance, that an urban feature such as density actually alters the nature of an event or condition—it is not more of the same. The individual occurrence is distinct from the aggregate outcome. It is not merely a sum of individual occurrences (i.e., a greater quantity of occurrences). It is a different event. The city contains both and, in that regard, can be understood as instigating a broad range of environmental damage that may involve very different scales and origins. CO_2 emissions produced by the microscale of vehicles and coal burning by individual households can scale up and become massive air pollution covering the entire city with effects that transcend CO_2 emission per se. Air- and waterborne microbes materialize as diseases at the scale of the household and the individual body. But they become epidemics that thrive on the multiplier effects of urban density and are capable of destabilizing the operations of firms whose machines have no intrinsic susceptibility to the disease. A second way in which the city is multiscalar is in the geography of the environmental damages it produces. Some of the damage is atmospheric and becomes planetary, therewith transcending the city. And some of it is internal to the built environment of the city; this might be the case with sewage or disease, whereas some of it, such as deforestation, is in distant locations around the globe.

A third way in which the city can be seen as multiscalar is that its demand for resources can entail a geography of extraction and processing that spans the globe, although it does so in the form of a collection of confined individual sites distributed worldwide. This worldwide geography of extraction materializes in particular and specific forms (e.g., furniture, jewelry, machinery, and fuel) inside the city. The city is one moment—a strategic moment—in this global geography of extraction, and it differs from that geography itself. A fourth way in which the city is multiscalar is that it houses a variety of policy levels. It is one of the key sites where a very broad range of policies—supranational, national, regional, and local—materialize in specific procedures, regulations, penalties, forms of compliance, and types of violations. These specific outcomes differ from the actual policies—in terms of the design of these policies and the specifics of implementation at other scales of government.

Conclusion

Bringing the city level into larger governance regimes is not without its complications. Among the subjects examined in this chapter, let me emphasize two I consider strategic. One is the use of science and technology in ways that would mobilize urban capabilities to transform what are now negative articulations between cities and the biosphere into positive ones. This means making full use of the complexity of cities, notably their multiscalar and ecological features. I do not think we are close to such a full use, but there is the beginning of a mobilizing in this direction. This should enable urban experts and scientists to connect on far more processes than they do now.

The second strategic element concerns the city as a social and power system—with laws, extreme inequalities, and vast concentrations of power. Implementing environmental measures that go beyond current modest mitigation and adaptation efforts will require engaging the legal systems and profit logics that underlie and enable many of the environmentally damaging aspects of our societies. Any advance toward environmental sustainability is necessarily implicated in these systems and logics. To this we need to add that the actual features of these systems vary across countries and across the North–South divide. Although in some domains concerned with the environmental question, such as national states, it might be possible to confine the analysis to scientific knowledge this is not the case when dealing with cities.

And yet we must try. A focus on cities makes visible the limitations of existing climate governance framings. It would make every major city, regardless of country, a complex space for the implementation of processes that actually cut environmental damage rather than shifting it around as is the case with the carbon trading proposals. Using science and technology to reverse the negative articulations of cities with the biosphere would help make cities a strategic ground for active reductions of environmental damage. These types of efforts might well, and partly already do, bypass the intergovernmental debate on carbon trading and the protectionism of a country's "right" to pollute more than is allowed by the carbon trading regime.

Making "urban ground" a key component of a multisited global regime would operate on a practical rather than formal vector: The fact that cities tend to be ahead of their national governments in addressing environmental issues, and the fact that this is not the result of "good politics" but rather of practical and often urgent needs.

Notes

1. See, for instance, the *Global Status Report on Local Renewable Energy Policies*, Institute for Sustainable Energy Policies. Tokyo (http://www.ren21.net/Portals/97/documents/Publications/REN21_Local_Renewables_Policies_2011.pdf), accessed 13 October 2012.

2. See, for instance, the ICLEI Climate Program at www.iclei.org/index.

3. The UNFCCC is focussed on a successor to the climate protection agreement following 2012, also known as the post-Kyoto or post-2012 agreement.

4. That it is not urbanization per se that is damaging, but the mode of urbanization, also is signaled by the adoption of environmentally harmful production

processes by pre-modern rural societies. Until recently, these had environmentally sustainable economic practices, such as crop rotation and foregoing the use of chemicals to fertilize and control insects. Further, our extreme capitalism has made the rural poor, especially in the Global South, so poor that for the first time, many now are also engaging in environmentally destructive practices, notably practices that lead to desertification.

5. One key component here is ecological economics. For some of the foundational concepts and logics of ecological economics, see Daly (1977), Daly and Farley (2003), Gund Institute (2009), Rees (2006), Schulze (1994), and Porter et al. (2009).

6. See, for instance, Sassen (2001, 2005), Satterthwaite et al. (2007), Girardet (2008), Beddoe et al. (2009), and Morello-Frosch et al. (2009).

7. This is a broad subject. For studies that engage a range of aspects, see Rees (1992), Sassen (2001, 2005, 2009), Satterthwaite et al. (2007), Girardet (2008), Mol and Sonnenfeld (2000, 2011), Beddoe et al. (2009), and Morello-Frosch et al. (2009).

8. Some kinds of international agreements are crucial. Examples include agreements that set enforceable limits on each national society's consumption of scarce resources and their use of the rest of the world as a global sink for their wastes. Other agreements I find to be problematic, notably that concerning the market for carbon trading. The latter contain negative incentives. Firms need not change their practices insofar as they can pay others to take on their pollution. Overall there is a good chance of no absolute reduction in pollution.

9. For instance, instituting a sustainable consumption logic can be aided by zoning and subdivision regulations, building codes, planning for transport, water and waste, recreation and urban expansion, local revenue raising (environmental taxes, charges, levies), and by introducing environmental considerations when preparing budgets, purchasing, contracting, and bidding (see Satterthwaite's and other researchers' work on the International Institute for Environment and Development [IIED] Web site (http://www.iiep.unesco.org/) for one of the most detailed and global data sets on these issues.

10. For instance, the vast fires to clear large tracts of the Indonesian forests in order to develop commercial agriculture (in this case, palm oil plantations geared to the world market) have regularly produced thick smoke carpets over Singapore, a city-state that has implemented very stringent air pollution controls often at high taxation expense to its inhabitants and firms.

11. Bacteria residing within concrete structures seal cracks and reduce the permeability of concrete surfaces by depositing dense layers of calcium carbonate and other minerals. Our buildings would thus more closely model the self-sustaining homeostatic physical structures found in nature (Jonkers 2007). This is particularly significant in the current period because (a) buildings are the largest single source of greenhouse gas emissions and (b) it would create employment, mobilize citizens in their neighborhoods, and allow local governments to get involved by initial small subsidies, especially in modest neighborhoods. An experimental technology with a similar capacity to be deployed "globally at the local level" is the so-called carbon negative cement (see www.novacem.com/docs/novacem_press_release_6_aug_2009.pdf). There are many other such uses of nature's capacity to address the environmental challenge in cities, although

none as globally present as the challenge of greening buildings. Some of these were developed a decade ago. For instance, bioreactors (essentially, controlled ponds) that combine bacteria and algae can clean nitrate-contaminated water as gaseous nitrogen (N_2) can be recycled into the atmosphere (Garcia et al. 2000).

References

Arikan, Y., 2009, *Local Climate Mitigation Action: From a Voluntary Initiative to a Global Mainstream Commitment*, Boston: ICLEI.

Beddoe, R., R. Costanza, J. Farley, et al., 2009, "Overcoming Systemic Roadblocks to Sustainability: The Evolutionary Redesign of Worldviews, Institutions, and Technologies," *PNAS, 106*(8):2483–2489.

Bettencourt, L., J. Lobo, D. Helbing, et al., 2007, "Growth, Innovation, Scaling, and the Pace of Life in Cities," *PNAS, 104*:7301–7306.

Bettencourt, L. and G. West, 2010, "A Unified Theory of Urban Living," *Nature, 467*:7318.

Daly, H. E., 1977, *Steady-State Economics: The Economics of Biophysical Equilibrium and Moral Growth*, San Francisco: W. H. Freeman.

Daly, H. E. and J. Farley, 2003, *Ecological Economics: Principles and Applications*, Washington, D.C.: Island.

Dietz, T., E. A. Rosa, and R. York, 2009, "Environmentally Efficient Well-Being: Rethinking Sustainability as the Relationship Between Human Well-Being and Environmental Impacts," *Human Ecology Review, 16*(1):114–123.

Environment and Urbanization, 2007, *Special Issue: Reducing the Risk to Cities from Disasters and Climate Change, 19*(1), Sage Publications, available at http://eau.sagepub.com/content/vol19/issue1. (accessed October 14, 2012).

Etsy, D. C. and M. Ivanova, 2005, "Globalisation and Environmental Protection: A Global Governance Perspective," in *A Handbook of Globalisation and Environmental Policy: National Government Interventions in a Global Arena*, edited by F. Wijen, et al., 541–580. Cheltenham, UK: Edward Elgar.

Garcia, J., R. Mujeriego, and M. Hernández-Mariné, 2000, "High Rate Algal Pond Operating Strategies for Urban Wastewater Nitrogen Removal," *Journal of Applied Phycology, 12*:331–339.

Girardet, H., 2008, *Cities People Planet: Urban Development and Climate Change,* 2nd ed. Amsterdam: John Wiley.

Gund Institute for Ecological Economics, University of Vermont, 2009, available at http://www.uvm.edu/giee. (accessed October 14, 2012).

Gupta, A. K., 2004, *WIPO-UNEP Study on the Role of Intellectual Property Rights in the Sharing of Benefits Arising From the Use of Biological Resources and Associated Traditional Knowledge*, Geneva: World Intellectual Property Organization and United Nations Environmental Programme.

Habitat II: UN-Habitat., 2003, "The Habitat Agenda Goals and Principles, Commitments and the Global Plan of Action," UN-Habitat, available at http://www.unhabitat.org/downloads/docs/1176_6455_The_Habitat_Agenda.pdf, (accessed October 14, 2012).

ICLEI: Local Governments for Sustainability, 2011, "Local Solutions to Global Challenges," available at www.iclei.org/fileadmin/user_upload/documents/Global/About_ICLEI/ brochures/ICLEI-intro-2009.pdf (accessed July 11, 2011).

Jonkers, H. M., 2007, "Self-Healing Concrete: A Biological Approach" in *Self-Healing Materials: An Alternative Approach to 20 Centuries of Materials*, edited by S. van der Zwaag, 195–204. Dordrecht, The Netherlands: Springer.

Local Agenda 21: United Nations Programme of Action, 2009, "Agenda 21," Earth Summit: Rio De Janiero, available at http://www.un.org/esa/dsd/agenda21/index.shtml, (accessed October 14, 2012).

Low, N. P., ed. 2000, *Global Ethics and Environment*, New York: Routledge.

Low, N. P. and B. Gleeson, eds., 2001, *Governing for the Environment: Global Problems, Ethics and Democracy*, Basingstroke, UK: Palgrave.

Mgbeogi, I., 2006, *Biopiracy: Patents, Plants, and Indigenous Knowledge*, Vancouver: University of British Columbia.

Mol, A. P. J., and D. A. Sonnenfeld, 2000, *Ecological Modernisation Around the World: Perspectives and Critical Debates*, New York: Routledge.

Morello-Frosch, R., M. Pastor, J. Sadd, and S. B. Shonkoff, 2009, *The Climate Gap: Inequalities in How Climate Change Hurts Americans & How to Close the Gap*, Los Angeles: USC Program for Environmental and Regional Equity. Retrieved from http://college.usc.edu/geography/ESPE/documents/The_Climate_Gap_Full_Report_FINAL.pdf, (accessed October 14, 2012).

Porter, J., R. Costanza, H. Sandhu, et al., 2009, "The Value of Producing Food, Energy, and Ecosystem Services Within an Agro-Ecosystem," *Ambio, 38*(4):186–193.

Redclift, M., 1996, *Wasted: Counting the Costs of Global Consumption*, London: Earthscan.

———, 2009, "The Environment and Carbon Dependence: Landscapes of Sustainability and Materiality," *Current Sociology, 57*(3):369–387.

REDD Web Platform, United Nations Framework Convention on Climate Change, available at http://unfccc.int/methods_science/redd/items/4531.php, (accessed October 14, 2012).

Rees, W. E., 1992, "Ecological Footprints and Appropriated Carrying Capacity: What Urban Economics Leaves Out," *Environment and Urbanization, 4*(2):121–130.

———, 2006, "Ecological Footprints and Bio-Capacity: Essential Elements in Sustainability Assessment," in *Renewables-Based Technology: Sustainability Assessment*, edited by J. Dewulf and H. Van Langenhove, 143–158. Chichester, UK: John Wiley.

Reuveny, R., 2008, "Ecomigration and Violent Conflict: Case Studies and Public Policy Implications," *Human Ecology, 36*:1–13.

Sassen, S., 2001, *The Global City*, 2nd ed., Princeton, N.J.: Princeton University Press.

———, 2005, "The Ecology of Global Economic Power: Changing Investment Practices to Promote Environmental Sustainability," *Journal of International Affairs, 58*(2): 11–33.

———, 2008, *Territory, Authority, Rights: From Medieval to Global Assemblages*, Princeton, N.J.: Princeton University Press.

———, 2013, "Bringing Laboratory Findings into Environmental Policy," (Columbia University, on file with author).

Sassen, S., ed. 2009, "Human Settlement and the Environment," in *EOLSS Encyclopedia of the Environment*, vol 14. Oxford: EOLSS and UNESCO.

Sassen, S. and N. Dotan, 2011, "Delegating, Not Returning, to the Biosphere: How to Use the Multi-Scalar and Ecological Properties of Cities," *Global Environmental Change*, 21(3):823–834.

Satterthwaite, D., 1999, "Sustainable Cities or Cities That Contribute to Sustainable Development?" *The Earthscan Reader in Sustainable Cities*, edited by D. Satterthwaite, 80–107. London: Earthscan.

Satterthwaite, D., S. Huq, H. Reid, et al., 2007, "Adapting to Climate Change in Urban Areas: The Possibilities and Constraints in Low- and Middle-Income Nations," Human Settlements Discussion Paper Series, London: IIED, available at www.iied.org/pubs/pdfs/10549IIED.pdf.

Schulze, P. C., 1994, "Cost-Benefit Analyses and Environmental Policy," *Ecological Economics*, 9(3):197–199.

Sonnenfeld, D. A. and A. P. J. Mol, 2011, "Social Theory and the Environment in the New World (dis)Order," *Global Environmental Change*, 21(3):771–775.

Toly, N. J., 2008, "Transnational Municipal Networks in Climate Politics: From Global Governance to Global Politics," *Globalizations*, 5(3):341–356.

United Nations Framework Convention on Climate Change, available at http://unfccc.int/2860.php, (accessed October 14, 2012).

Van Veenhuizen, R. and G. Danso, 2007, *Profitability and Sustainability of Urban and Peri-Urban Agriculture*, Rome: Food and Agriculture Organization of the United Nations, available at http://www.ruaf.org/node/2295), (accessed October 14, 2012).

Warner K., C. Erhart, A. de Sherbinin, et al., 2009, *In Search of Shelter: Mapping the Effects of Climate Change on Human Migration and Displacement*, CARE International, available at http://www.ciesin.columbia.edu/documents/clim-migr-report-june09_final.pdf, (accessed October 14, 2012).

10

Violence in the City: Challenges of Global Governance*

SOPHIE BODY-GENDROT

What is new in our civilization is not the solutions, what is new is that the questions we are confronting were not confronted before. It is not the responses but the formulation of the questions which matter.

paul valéry, *REFLECTIONS ON THE WORLD TODAY*

Introduction

Lack of safety, insecurity, and violence raise complex challenges that cities need to address as part of the pursuit of environmental sustainability. Large cities have long evinced a general inability to anticipate what may happen: accidents, catastrophes, or collective violence (Virilio 2002). But if we are to make cities key spaces for advancing an environmental agenda, then urban violence in its many manifestations becomes urgent.

This chapter examines this issue and situates it as part of the groundwork for the environmental process. Several questions organize the chapter. How are global cities doing in this respect? What resources do they have to deal with major risks and threats, in current times of global uncertainty? How do they transmit a sense of order and protection to their residents and to a variety of visitors, as well as to the hypermobile actors on whom they increasingly depend? Can and should order be coproduced by institutions, by private entrepreneurs, and by citizens in a well-designed form of urban governance? If so, at what scale and in what shape should this coproduction

---

*This chapter builds on Body-Gendrot (2012).

take? What coordination of actions should be favored and at what level of decision-making? How comprehensive should it be?

Unsafe Cities

The tragedy of 9/11 supports the idea that the city is the repository of accidents that it provokes or enables (e.g., riots) as a symbolic site for producing global changes and representing wealth. Vast resources are thus spent on catastrophe preparedness, on risks, and on imagining the worst scenarios and their consequences for cities. And yet, the expected always occurs as a surprise.

When we reflect on safety/insecurity, order/disorder, and urban violence/conflicts—all of which are formidable challenges to cities—we can identify urban capacities that enable cities to respond. These signal that cities are resilient and that they complement—and sometimes bypass—states in securing their spaces and their residents. As sites where top-down measures regarding security are implemented and sometimes designed, cities mobilize very different scales and sectors. They even can reach out to supranational levels (for instance, the European Community or the International Court of Justice) in order to protect their populations and their very essence. With their density and diversity, they display an accumulated knowledge for alleviating conflicts and unrest, healing wounds, solving antagonisms, and restoring public tranquility after disruptive events. Finally and paradoxically, by allowing empowered citizens to express their claims and discontent in the very space that unites them, cities perform a catalyst function and are a motor of democratic life. These are indications that the capacities of resistance of civil society should not be downplayed.

Traumatic events may rapidly transform a society. Respect for cultural diversity had been a deeply rooted tradition in Dutch society for many years, yet the murder of Theo Van Gogh by a radical Muslim, Mohammed Bouyeri, in Amsterdam in 2004 shook the country's "culture of control" and its norms. Discourse on immigration, integration, and crime changed radically. The traumatic event shattered residents' belief in multiculturalism and in cultural diversity. Negative stereotypes of Muslims, previously taboo, were openly expressed.

This section examines various types of security challenges faced by cities. The central question here is whether people are adaptable enough to get on with their lives under almost any threat, or if certain kinds of threats deeply unsettle urban populations.

A first threat faced by cities is that of terrorism, particularly that of homegrown terrorism associated with young, male, single suicide bombers. Although terrorist attacks present a potentially lethal threat, many people are able to make sense of this threat. According to their testimonies, people are aware of what terrorist violence can do and why certain targets are chosen, and they can handle their fears and rationalize such occurrences. Accordingly, they do not necessarily change their modes of living in response to this threat.

A second type of urban threat, crime, takes on a more complex character due to its repetitive, eroding character and to the insufficient protection provided by law enforcement to poor residents living in marginal neighborhoods. Victimization surveys reveal that fear of crime varies according to gender, age, social class, the consumption of television, and the neighborhood where one lives. As such, it would be hazardous to make overly general statements about this threat. Yet, by contrast with a middle class *concern* for insecurity, *fear of crime* (also referred to as a "feeling of insecurity" in some countries) is acute in neighborhoods where drug dealers operate visibly in public spaces, where rumors contaminate daily conversations, and where people experience a loss of control over local norms and values (Furstenberg 1971). Fear of downward mobility or feelings of powerlessness due to public and private neglect in these neighborhoods may exacerbate anxieties. These anxieties, in turn, may be projected onto fears of the "unsafe city" or of dangerous "others." Whatever the cause, however, as Thomas (1928) observes, if men define their situations as real, they are real in their consequences. To this, Sampson (2009) adds that if a person believes some behaviors to be a problem in society, he or she will "see" them more: "believing is seeing."

The political impact of perceptions of threat is strong. The interplay between structure and perception drives action and, as seen in northern and southern global cities, results in demands for "zero-risk societies." Such attitudes lead households into lockdown strategies. Disorder threatens the trust needed for social interaction and innovation, and it takes advantage of distended mechanisms of social control (Wikström 2009; Sampson 2012). When too many windows are broken and left unrepaired, fearful people may decide to lock themselves in (as in gated communities), while pressuring authorities to lock others out (massively, in prisons). In Europe, where punitive populism is not as strong as it is in the United States, these "trends of exile and exclusion," according to Simon (2007), are just starting to emerge. Yet not all European societies are experiencing this trend; judges are not elected, justice is less procedural and professionalized, and it is less insulated from real people. Many cultural and historical factors make a difference.

Overall, European societies are run less by the politicization of fear than by the exercise of security measures (Baker 2010; Body-Gendrot et al. 2013).

A third type of threat, civil unrest, always comes as an unanticipated happening, despite its long history in Western cities. Two European societies in particular, France and the United Kingdom, have experienced recurrent urban unrest, social insurgency, confrontations, and protest. Such violent happenings become modes in which mostly young men express their emotions and make their claims. They introduce a rupture in the life of the city.

"Riots": A Word Too Much?

In describing various instances of urban civil unrest, the media uses blanket terms such as disorder, riots, disturbances, unrest, rebellion, confrontation, uprising, and others, which suggest that all such events are alike. (For another example, think of the currently undifferentiated use of "al-Qaeda"). Words have the power to make everything look alike (Body-Gendrot 2008). They blend and conflate phenomena that are in fact distinct from one country, one city, one month, one year to another. What they have in common in this case is the evocation of an unbearable threat to the social order.

In the French case, during the 2005 riots, the foreign media emphasized the ethnicity of the rioters: the *clash of civilizations*, the fury of Muslims of North-African descent, a Jihad-led revolt, the role of *French-Arabs*, of *French-Africans*, and of imams. By contrast, the French media, influenced by "a culture of excuse," focused on the structural causes of these events: the lack of hopes and dreams among marginalized young men in derelict areas and the consequences of globalization for post-Fordist, decaying, working-class areas. Many French commentators blamed a society that produces exclusions and excused the youths taking part in the events, whom they perceived as victims of global/local mutations and the resulting economic mismatch. When upheavals took place in London and in other British cities in August 2011, observers did not label these events as "race riots," as they had done for decades in describing similar incidents. Instead the looting frenzy was variously explained as the consequence of the deprivations of poverty, the result of austerity policies that generated rapid cuts in social services, or a product of the malaise of a young, deprived generation that was acting out, looting, vandalizing, and expressing its frustrations (Singh et al. 2011).

There are many reasons why the term "race riot" does not adequately describe these segmented forms of urban violence. As suggested by Tilly

(2003:18) the term "riot" expresses a political judgment rather than an ana lytic distinction. For Hobsbawn (1959), riots are a prelude to a negotiation and thus imply a political awareness. This can be seen, for instance, in the case of French unionized fishermen, who walked with poise to regional parliaments or préfectures in order to deliberately ransack and vandalize them, before walking back calmly to a press conference.

Both Tilly and Hobsbawn hint at rioters' political consciousness. In the 751 French problem areas, also called "sensitive urban zones" (ZUS), thirty to forty different groups of "new French"—some recent migrants to France, others second- or third-generation immigrants—live together, side by side with poor, old stock French families in massive housing projects hastily built in the 1960s. The residents of such sites are marked by a stigma, making many feel different and embarassed to give their postal address. Lacking channels to express their frustrations, many residents of these areas feel too disenfranchised to vote in elections, even to express a protest vote (abstention rates are the highest in these peripheries). The young people of Clichy-sous-Bois who expressed their anger and uttered the cry "Dead for nothing" in 2005 did not mobilize as Muslims or French Arabs. (Between 5 percent and 10 percent of Muslims in France practice their religion regularly, as other youths. According to official statistics, only 4.5 percent of Roman Catholics attend mass every week [Wihtold de Wenden 2006]). Neither was what took place in Clichy-sous-Bois a jihad-led mobilization: Al-Qaeda has little interest in events located in marginalized areas or in mobilizing youths who have frequently failed in school.

In Britain in August 2011, young people were upset by the shooting of Mark Duggan in Tottenham, also a "death for nothing." But, as in France, outrage was caused by deeper motivations: exclusion, discrimination, poverty, disrespect, and other issues that mobilized identities, differences, modes of belonging, and experiences of deprivation (Body-Gendrot 2013). As Sassen (2011) remarks, "These conditions were far more significant in provoking the riots than the unwarranted killing of a young man by the police." The unemployment rate for people under age 25 in the United Kingdom stood at 22.2 percent, versus the overall unemployment rate of 8.4 percent nationally in November 2011. In France, the rates were similar: 21.7 percent and 10.0 percent, respectively (Gatinois 2012).

Specific urban contexts (and the rationales triggering events) and structural causes interplay in varying ways, according to particular places, times, and local cultures. Not every death of a young person after an encounter with the police causes civil unrest, and not every derelict area is a springboard for violent reactions. Local contexts have accumulated (or lost) social capital and, in some of them, reservoirs of grievances characterize a history and geography of resentment. Single male youths—once again, a deceptively general word—living in problem areas are diverse: Some are still in high school, some have regular jobs, while others are jobless (Bourdieu 1984). Their ages range from the teens to the twenties. Their attitudes vary according to their origin; their socialization by their families, schools, and neighborhoods; and their own experiences of inclusion/exclusion. Yet in specific circumstances, such as a publicized death, generational bonds may draw them together (Bourdieu 1984).

As vectors of unrest, many young people are stimulated by the potential media attention they can get from resorting to urban violence. For these young people, the goal is not revolution but attention and the visibility it brings. The media bring the capacity to connect the local and the global. As one young man explained to a journalist during the French urban unrest in 2005, "We are perfectly aware that there won't be one TV cameraman left when all becomes quiet again. We won't exist anymore" (Body-Gendrot 2008:269).

Although the circumstances are particular, the sentiments of this statement are not novel. After the 1965 riots in Watts, a young, unemployed black person who had participated told civil rights activist Bayard Rustin that they had "won" (Rustin 1966:30). When Bayard objected, citing the casualties and the destruction of the area, the young man replied, "We won because we made the whole world pay attention to us. The police chief never came here before; the mayor always stayed uptown. We made them come."

Similar statements were heard from young people with no hopes and no dreams following the unrest in the United Kingdom in August 2011. The media—and, as in the British case, the social media—act as a magnifying glass, amplifying isolated incidents. It sends flash messages, rewards negative heroes, and weaves a narrative via similar words and images, making sense out of fragmented acts and creating a movement "à distance" (Balibar 2007).

For the most part, instances of urban disorder do not lead to further social integration via their transformation into larger conflicts. They are flashpoints ignited by perceptions of police abuse against a complex and ambivalent "us." This "us" hides an enigmatic collective identity, one that reveals the difficult adjustments that the children and grandchildren of poor, frequently migrant, working-class populations often face in Western cities. Such difficulties are exacerbated by new austerity policies that negatively impact their living conditions. In 2004, the year before unrest broke out in Clichy-sous-Bois, the rate of unemployment had reached 23.5 percent (compared with 16 percent in 1993) and 31 percent among youths under age 25. Dependent families made up 67.4 percent of the population, and 46.6 percent of households were under the poverty threshold. One-third of the residents were nonnational immigrants and, among them, 60 percent were jobless (Kokoreff 2006:166). Rather than getting better, the social situation was deteriorating.

Following the unrest in London in 2011, 90 percent of the 2,000 people brought to the courts were male, 74 percent were aged 24 or younger, 46 percent were black, 42 percent white, and 7 percent Asian. Almost half of the juveniles involved came from homes in the lowest 10 percent of income levels, substantiating a theory of relative deprivation. In the northern industrial cities of the United Kingdom in 2001, in former East Germany *länder*, and in the Scandinavian countries, white youths on the Far Right have fought immigrants' children in horizontal clashes without explicit reference to a dominant order. By contrast, in the case of the French *banlieues*, the police—a symbol of the state and of mainstream society— were confronted with the rage of marginalized young men. The more politicized among these young men wanted recognition of the unfairness of their humiliating living conditions. "Violence? It is to be twenty, with no job and the police on your back," someone wrote in 1981 at Les Minguettes. Enacted in short, intense, damaging actions, such rebellions carry expectations: "Being part of" is indeed a generalized claim.

The multiple problems leading to instances of urban violence identified by researchers—unemployment, social integration, identity, citizenship, disempowerment, disenfranchisement, and others—crystallize in isolated and segregated spaces. Sometimes these instances of urban violence spill over into more affluent areas of the city, as they did in Oxford Circus in London in 2011. In either instance, they articulate multidimensional grievances. What is frequently overlooked, however, is how local agency and places become articulated through myriad channels with the global scale.

New "Order" Regimes

In the regime of order that distinguishes Western cities post-9/11, governments will not tolerate lasting expressions of disorder. Disorder is perceived by the majority of people as evidence of institutional weakness, a narrative easily reinforced by populist demagogues at election times and which may be reflected in financial and business disinvestment and/or the exodus of visitors, tourists, and students. States are committed to ensuring security through their legitimate monopoly on violence or force. Yet their repressive modes of intervention may also be questioned.

In Europe, three overlapping strategies of "order" have been launched by states (Body-Gendrot 2010). The first of these aims at securing space without focusing on any specific groups. This strategy is used, for instance, in airport inspections and army patrols in railway stations and in other crowded places, such as in the French Vigipirate system. These spaces contain diverse groups of people, and everyone is subject to similar treatment. This approach to securing order is usually symbolic, except when police forces intervene to repress outbreaks of disorder in the public space. In such instances, they need to act efficiently rather than just symbolically to end disorder. The nature and methods of such "efficient" actions are sometimes questioned.

The second strategy involves legitimizing the identification, surveillance, and repression of particular individuals and groups perceived as threats to the urban order. Muslim fundamentalists are especially targeted in European cities but so are Roma, Basque, or other nationalist groups. Some countries such as France act silently on risks of terrorism via the savoir faire of intelligence services and of specialized investigating judges. Since 1995, no terrorist attack has occurred in the country. In 2010 alone, ninety-four radical fundamentalists were arrested, joining between 100 and 200 fundamentalists currently detained in French prisons (Hecker 2012; Le Bars 2012). Extracting information from terrorist networks is a complex task. A small group of people may accumulate hundreds of different identities, thousands of SIM cards, and so on. In some cities, for instance in New York, powerful transnational surveillance networks allow the local police to gather information daily on problems occurring in other countries. Physically, a metropolis houses a variety of supranational, national, regional, and local bodies charged with ensuring order, each concerned with specific procedures, regulations, penalties, forms of compliance, and types of violations.

In Toulouse, in March 2012, the Mohamed Merah case raised questions about dysfunctions in the centralized Directorate of Domestic Intelligence (DCRI), a merger of intelligence services and national police. How did the lone murderer of seven unarmed people—three soldiers, three children, and a rabbi—who had made several trips to the Afghan-Pakistani border, connected to Salafist Web sites, and detained an arsenal of weapons in his home slip through their surveillance? Does the national DCRI service pay enough attention and respect to its local branches? Does it grant them enough resources and information? The French, it seems, have one-tenth of the resources of Americans for any given case. Such questions are more frequently raised in poorly coordinated federal systems, yet in Toulouse, local prosecutors seemed to be unaware of Merah, who had lived in the same place for two years under his real name (Erlanger 2012; Heisbourg 2012; Vadillo 2012).

The British government, meanwhile, engages—or at least claims to engage—citizens, local communities, institutions, and firms in the "coproduction" of security. According to former British Prime Minister Gordon Brown (2006), such a partnership is required to tackle the "root evils" that risk driving people, particularly vulnerable young people, into the hands of violent extremists (Kackman 2005). This strategy, very different from the French one, is dangerous for a democracy. It leaves targeted groups very vulnerable to discrimination, and it encourages a culture of suspicion that is detrimental to the essence of cities, which are founded on commonalities, trust, diversity, and an architecture of sympathy. Security measures frequently cause more fear than they alleviate.

Space is a decisive element in strategies for maintaining order. Statistics on stops in neighborhoods are sometimes more revealing than those on the race or ethnicity of individuals stopped. Through punctual and unexpected interactions, the police are an institution of domination. They distribute definitive and temporary status to their "clients" via their own culture. If these clients do not behave as expected according to the place where they are, they may be stopped and searched, less for what they do than for who they are. However, if the territory is their own and they are not known offenders, the French police are unlikely to target them. There are too many bodies of control and too many amateur cameras discouraging the police from acting inappropriately in close-knit neighborhoods (Jobard 2003).

As a member of the National Police Complaints Authority in France—the former national civilian review board for law enforcers—I heard young people complaining of police harassment, of humiliating stops and searches in the gray areas where witnesses will not talk, of their powerlessness when it comes to getting fair treatment, and of judges' disregard for their constitutional rights. The confrontational, adversarial identities that young people develop very early ensure that most encounters with institutions are marked by distrust. Distrust of the national police cannot just be explained by a strong ethnic bias in the system but rather by the daily experiences of hostile contacts with a police force required by conservative elites to multiply "the stops and searches" and instill social discipline into young people. Top-down injunctions transform some marginalized urban zones into tinderboxes, where continuous surveillance is exerted at a heavy cost. Policemen are turned into the wardens of order. Their presence raises expectations disproportionate to the resources and training that they have received.

A third strategy for maintaining order perceives security as a "thick" public good, not reducible to the activities of the state but instead relying on prevention, citizenship, and social cohesion (Loader and Walker 2006). Cities, the targets of external and internal enemies, appear as the major actors in this strategy, because they have so much to lose from instances of disorder.

The Challenges of Global Changes for Metropolises

In assessing urban capacities for ensuring order, cities' resources are frequently overlooked. However, at least four approaches demonstrate the power of urban capacities: innovation and implementation; connection to other scales; prevention and conflict-solving; and empowerment.

First, very large cities often take the lead in securing their space and their populations. This approach is more easily performed in decentralized systems where mayors can appoint their police chiefs and where the police are local. The example that comes to mind is that of New York City. The spectacular crime decline of 82 percent over nine years in New York is obviously not due just to the strategy, methods, and resources of the police force; yet the decline represents twice that of the national average, and it says something specific about New York (Zimring 2012). Just as modes of punishment reveal something about the culture of a civilization, the culture of a city is reflected in its methods of policing. By becoming more professionalized and obtaining better tools, the New York Police Department gained self-confidence, an intelligence-driven method for maintaining order, and the budget needed to mobilize adequate resources post-9/11. Putting the city back in order and cleaning up the streets strengthened this counterterrorist approach. The control of crime became more global because the threats facing New York are global (Body-Gendrot 2012:75). In all large cities, implementing security measures requires mobilizing different scales and sectors, forming partnerships among and activating a large diversity of overlapping agencies. New York City has such "costly" savoir faire. Abuses relating to ethnic and racial profiling regularly have the police institution accused and sent to court by organized interest groups.

In cities aiming at inclusion, policing is better carried out by "consent." As Sir Richard Mayne, one of the first two commissioners of the Metropolitan Police Force in London, advocated in 1829:

> The primary object of an efficient police is the prevention of crime: the next that of detection and punishment of offenders if crime is committed. To these ends, all the efforts of police must be directed. The protection of life and property, the preservation of public tranquility, and the absence of crime, will alone prove whether those efforts have been successful and whether the objects for which the police were appointed have been attained.

Coproducing public tranquility is a goal pursued in many northern European cities. To use Jane Jacobs' more contemporary phrasing: "The public peace on our streets is primarily kept by an intricate, almost unconscious network of voluntary controls and standards among the people themselves, cooperating with community policemen" (Jacobs 1961). A strategy launched by former London Metropolitan Police Commissioner Ian Blair focused on a "reassuring police," in which small teams of policemen walked in pairs through 630 wards across the city. Their task was to get closer to the communities, find out what residents wanted, and be present to reassure them, like the bobbies of the old days.

Most mayors are reluctant to resort to measures that might generate antagonism among residents, themselves ambivalent on many issues. In the United States, local police chiefs do not want to alienate substantial segments of their community or lose information about the incidence of a crime or the identification of criminals by sharing sensitive information with the FBI. "The police chief whose only desire is to ensure local peace will be prone to give the Feds too little help, not too much" (Richman 2006:38). It is indeed only by cooperating with Muslim communities and especially with women and moderate youths in those communities that important information may begin to trickle upwards. Local law enforcers then need to display an "entrenched realism" and trust their know-how. In this perspective, both intelligence-based counterterrorism and ward policing rely on the police having knowledge of cities and of their social environments. This point is illustrated by the restraint with which a lot of policemen, educators, public housing managers, and other social actors work collectively to restore order in their localities following instances of disorder.

Second, global (or globally aspiring) cities are in a prominent position to exert functions of command, control, and planning. As their assets grow at a very fast pace in an unstable environment, they jealously safeguard their power via various linkages. Sassen (2006) points out that new, distinct assemblages of territorial insertions, authority, and national rights are emerging in specialized and highly singular fields, allowing multiple and often novel transactions for various uses. In using the term "city," one refers not to a static bounded space but to new boundaries and shifts in the frontiers of numerous places and institutions.

In Europe, via myriad assembled networks and overlapping organizations, city mayors are able to reach out to supranational levels. The European Forum on Urban Security is a case in point. It organizes regular conventions where mayors from various countries meet and exchange ideas, expressing claims and demands that then trickle down and spread like rhizomes at other levels. Cities are indeed hubs for many actions and innovations symptomatic of "newness." Urbact is another European Territorial Cooperation program, among many, offering transnational exchanges between communities and methodological support and focusing on burning issues such as the empowerment of young people or the integration of Roma populations into local services.

Third, cities' long experience with density and diversity enables potentially antagonistic groups to live side by side without major conflicts. Riots or the takeover of a city by a cartel of gangs, as in Sao Paulo, or by the mafia and camorra as in Southern Italy remain unusual. Most of the time, it is in mayors' interest to strengthen prevention, trust, and, thus, safety by emphasizing consensus and commonalities. After tragedies, it is in their interest to multiply symbolic actions such as silent marches or cleaning streets and repairing damaged buildings in order to heal grieved residents and mobilize communities into civic action. It follows from such preventative measures, conflict-solving, and healing capacities that more secure, yet heterogeneous, populations are enabled to bond, bridge, and "get by" within the city and beyond, and to thereby live safely together.

Cities' capacity for empowerment is certainly an asset. Instances of disorder that hit cities are both events and opportunities. They often highlight issues that are being ignored in public discourse such as situations of injustice and people's emotions (Body-Gendrot 2012:162). They may not make the headlines but they make a difference; they form a connection between the global and the local. Disturbances give globalization its confrontational dimension, without immediately resorting to political claims. They point to democracies' social failures. Using public space as a strategic site, they organize a drama and signal that disjunctive democracies go too far in their excess. Inequality is a powerful social divider, but in these circumstances it is a social unifier. If elites do not pay attention to the have-nots, they cannot ignore their violent transgressions as primary forms of revolt. This is all the more so if, as in Britain, this revolt is predatory and consumerist.

Cities provide both the material support and the symbolic stake that disorders and protest need. In troubled times, in Tunis, Cairo, Tripoli, Tel Aviv, Athens, Madrid, and in cities across Latin and North America, citizens have collectively measured their strength and made peaceful claims via the convergence that cities allow in their public spaces. Consequently, there may be a correlation among macroeconomic developments, rising inequalities, elites' loss of legitimacy, and the dialectics of order and disorder embodied by civil unrest (Body-Gendrot 2013).

On a more peaceful note, new visions of public space can help a city find its own order and specific life again. For instance, redesigning mixed-use buildings, such as sports centers, plazas, parks, and open markets, serves such a purpose for those who work, relax, and live in the city. Residents become proud of well-designed public spaces, which contribute to their feeling of collective belonging. An example of this is Chapultepec Park in Mexico City, which was partly financed by the million-plus residents who each gave one peso for the renovation of this large public space. Parks provide a means to coalesce a great variety of visitors at the same time and in the same space. Their designers often aim for social cohesion that transcends class divisions and relies on the universal needs for peace, entertainment, and recreation within cities. Signals of tranquility and the absence of fear abound. Microcontrol systems are at work: Security guards make sure that the processes necessary for smooth movements are respected. They act invisibly. They interpret situations and make sense of them. In so doing, they represent an alternative to CCTVs and high-end surveillance technologies (Body-Gendrot 2012:173). The same could be said of the cultural events that draw very diverse crowds at the periphery of large cities of the global south, based on trust in the local organizers' savoir faire.

An intriguing example comes from Johannesburg, South Africa, a city with a very high homicide rate. The legacy of a brutal apartheid regime and the fear of crime have been instrumentalized by affluent groups in order to justify territorial separation, leaving the residents of townships and squatters very vulnerable and deprived. Self-help and privatization seem to be the preferred options in this city (Murray 2011). But when the state grants too little public protection to large numbers of its residents, it is a catastrophe. Struggles over rights occur daily and conflicts abound. In several judicial cases, the right to stay "alive" has won over the right to "security" invoked by those who live in exile behind their high walls refusing to pay taxes for the safety of others (Lazarus and Goold 2007).

Conclusion

Why should cities be on the frontlines of promoting change? For one thing, they have a lot to lose from fear and from unexpected attacks. Cities have an accumulated knowledge that allows them to open up new capacities on issues such as security. They have the resources to confront threats and to alleviate the erosion of solidarity. It takes time, patience, imagination, skills, and resources to bring areas back to life and enable diverse people to live together in acceptance of their differences. It does happen. Inclusive, unexpected spaces send out powerful messages. Each "solution" for change reveals a mixture of various imaginations, voices, expertise, trust, and political will. Specific demands from a population can lead to better governance and to partnerships between city residents and various agencies. Trust between citizens and more or less visible "alchemists" may give each user (resident, commuter, investor) the sense of belonging to a shared urban space, which can become synonymous with public tranquility. The continuous concentration of diverse people in dense cities sends a clear message of resilience, of trust in institutions' efficacy, and in their own civic capacities.

The question that comes to mind here concerns the exceptional character of urban innovations: How often can large-scale or small-scale experiments be launched with success? And why? And should they be duplicated? How can trust and consent to change be expected in times of high uncertainty? Cities need to find the capacity to enlighten the masses and, rather than looking for allies in intolerant groups, they have to organize forums at all levels where people can talk about their fears, discuss racism and xenophobia, and be taught how to deconstruct and handle their fears collectively.

Any theory that addresses how cities cope with forms of insecurity generated by global phenomena calls for an interdisciplinarity that embraces spaces of multiplicity (Beauregard 2011:189). A city is indeed "a spatial location, a political entity, an administrative unit, a place of work and play, a collection of dreams and of nightmares, a mesh of social relations, an agglomeration of economic activity" (Hubbard 2006:1). Civil societies' capacities of resistance should not be downplayed. People are not at the mercy of global forces beyond their control. They can act. Although eliminating inequality is not within cities' grasp, it remains in their power to choose measures and policies at various scales that will alleviate some of its effects and make a difference.

References

Baker, A., 2010, "Governing Through Crime: The Case of the European Union," *European Journal of Criminology*, 7(3):187–213.

Balibar, E., 2007, "Uprisings in the Banlieues," *Constellations*, 14(1), 47–71.

Beauregard, Robert, 2011, "Radical Uniqueness and the Flight from Theory," in *The City Revisited. Urban Theory from Chicago, Los Angeles, New York*, edited by D. R. Judd and D. Simpson, 186–202. Minneapolis: University of Minnesota Press.

Body-Gendrot, S., 2008, "Urban Violence in France: Anything New ?" In *Governance of Security in the Netherlands and Belgium*, edited by L. Cachet, 263–280. Den Haag, Netherlands: Boom Legal.

———, 2010, "European Policies of Social Control Post 9/11," *Social Research*, 77(1):181–204.

———, 2012, *Globalization, Fear and Insecurity. The Challenges for Cities North and South*. Basingstoke, UK: Palgrave Macmillan.

———, 2013, "Urban Violence in France and Britain: Comparing Paris (2005) and London (2011)," *Policing and Society* (forthcoming).

Body-Gendrot S., et al. (eds.), 2013, "Introduction," in *Routledge Handbook of European Criminology*, Oxford: Routledge.

Bourdieu, P., 1984, "La jeunesse n'est qu'un mot," in *Questions de sociologie*, Paris: Minuit.

Brown, G., 2006, Speech at the Royal United Services Institute, London, Feb. 13.

Erlanger, S., 2012, "French-U.S. Anti-Terrorism Divide," *International Herald Tribune*, April 2.

Furstenberg, F., 1971, "Public Reaction to Crime in the Streets," *American Scholar*, 40:601–610.

Gatinois, C., 2012, "En Europe, le chômage des jeunes explose," *Le Monde*, April 14.

Hecker, M., 2012, *Intifada Française?*, Paris: Ellipses.

Heisbourg, F., 2012, "Une commission d'enquête s'impose," *Le Monde*, March 30.

Hobsbawn, E., 1959, *Primitive Rebels*, Manchester, UK: Manchester University Press.

Hubbard, P. 2006, *City*, London: Routledge.

Jacobs, J., 1961, *The Life and Death of American Cities*, Hardmondsworth, UK: Penguin.

Jobard, F., 2003, "Research Note: Counting Violence Committed by the Police: Raw Facts and Narratives," *Policing and Society*, 13(4):423–428.

Kackman, M., 2005, *Citizen Spy: Television, Espionage and Cold War Culture*, Minneapolis: University of Minnesota Press.

Kokoreff, M., 2006, "Le sens des émeutes de l'automne 2005," *Regards sur l'actualité*, 319:15–26.

——, 2008, *Sociologie des émeutes*, 149–150. Paris: Payot.

Lazarus, L. and B. Goold, eds., 2007, *Security and Human Rights*, Oxford, UK: Hart.

Le Bars, S., 2012, "L'administration estime entre 100 et 200 le nombre de radicaux islamistes en prison," *Le Monde*, March 24.

Loader, I. and N. Walker, 2006, "Necessary Virtues: The Legitimate Place of the State in the Production of Security," in *Democracy, Society and the Governance of Security*, edited by J. Wood and B. Dupont, 165–195. Cambridge, Mass.: Cambridge University Press.

Murray, M., 2011, *City of Extremes. The Spatial Politics of Johannesburg*, Durham, NC: Duke University.

Richman, D., 2006, "The Past, Present, and Future of Violent Crime Federalism," *Crime and Justice: A Review of Research*, 34:377–439.

Rustin, B., 1966, "The Watts 'Manifesto' and the McCone Report," *Commentary*, 41:33–34.

Sampson, R., 2009, "Analytic Approaches to Disorder," *British Journal of Sociology*, 60(1):1–32.

——, 2012, *Great American City. Chicago and The Enduring Neighborhood Effect*, Chicago: Chicago University Press.

Sassen, S., 2006, *Territory-Authority-Rights*, Princeton: Princeton University Press.

——, 2011, "Why Riot Now?," *The Daily Beast*, August 15.

Simon, J., 2007, *Governing Through Crime*, Chicago: Chicago University Press.

Singh, D., S. Marcus, H. Rabbats, and M. Sherlock, 2011, *5 Days in August. An Interim Report on the 2011 English Riots*, London: Riots, Communities and Victims Panel.

Thomas, W., 1928, *The Child in America*, New York: Knopf.

Tilly, C., 2003, *The Politics of Collective Violence*, Cambridge, UK: Cambridge University Press.

Vadillo, F., 2012, "Une opération policière trop politisée," *Le Monde*, March 30.

Valery, P., 1948 [1931], *Reflections on the World Today*, New York: Pantheon.

Virilio, P., 2002, *Ce qui arrive*, Paris: Actes Sud, Fondation Cartier.

Wihtold de Wenden, C., 2006, "L'intégration des populations musulmanes en France: Trente ans d'évolution," In *Histoire de l'islam et des musulmans en France*, edited by M. Arkoun. Paris: Albin Michel.

Wikström, P. O., 2009, "Questions of Perception and Reality," *British Journal of Sociology*, 60(1):59–63.

Zimring, F., 2012, *The City That Became Safe: New York and the Future of Crime Control*, Berkeley: University of California Press.

11

Cities and Conflict Resolution

TONY TRAVERS

Introduction

This chapter represents first thoughts about a potential new sphere for research and policy within the field of global governance. The ideas included are an attempt to stimulate a discussion and debate about the way cities may be able to play a role in the evolution of good government across international boundaries.

Global governance has traditionally been concerned with the activities of nation-states and with the international organizations that have been created to provide laws, regulation, oversight, and intervention in relation to people, their rights, and their protections. Research and practice have concentrated on key players and institutions within diplomacy and on representative institutions. The complexity of international relations and the evolution of conflict resolution studies have ensured that efforts in this field have generally focused on national and international players.

Elsewhere, experts have undertaken significant research into cities and into urbanism, embracing social, cultural, and economic issues in relation to major urban agglomerations. A number of leading commentators have written about the importance of cities as the location of transnational impacts and consequences. But there has, arguably, been less interest in the potential for cities and their leaders to assume a more active role in the problems of conflict resolution.

City governments themselves have, to a limited extent, taken initiatives in relation to peace and international security. For example, in 1982, at the second United Nations Special Session on Disarmament held at UN headquarters in New York, the then-mayor of Hiroshima proposed a new program to promote a consistent approach among major cities in relation to nuclear weapons. This proposal offered cities an opportunity to work outside national borders and to press for the abolition of nuclear arms.

Subsequently, the mayors of Hiroshima and Nagasaki encouraged mayors around the world to support their initiative. In 1990, the Mayors' Conference was officially registered as a UN non-governmental organization (NGO). Mayors for Peace consists of cities around the world that have formally expressed support for the program announced in 1982. In early 2011, membership stood at 4,467 cities in 150 countries and regions. The grouping is important, though largely symbolic.

There is a modest literature on the role of cities in promoting advances in global governance and civil society. Articles with titles such as "Transnational Municipal Networks in Climate Politics: From Global Governance to Global Politics" and "Local Governments as Foreign Policy Actors and Global Cities Network Makers: The Cases of Barcelona and Porto Alegre" provide clues as to the reach of the authors concerned (Toly 2008:341–356; Salomon 2009). Many of the research centers and academics concerned with global governance issues are involved in issues that are also the concerns of progressive municipal administrations and that can then be aggregated into something that is itself globalized. Put simply, the local can become the global. Academics can then analyze and describe it.

There is clearly space for fruitful interdisciplinary collaboration about the idea that the world's larger cities might play a role in the development of improved thinking in relation to the resolution of conflict. With such an objective in mind, this chapter addresses a number of key questions:

- Are cities already, in a geographical sense, the places where global conflicts are confronted and, on occasion, mediated?
- Do cities provide an anonymous place to live for people seeking to escape persecution and human rights violations in their home country?
- How do major cities use their systems of government to resolve conflicts that have an international dimension?
- Are there implications to be drawn from the governance and management of cities that have wider application?
- Could city leaders expand their role, possibly jointly, to provide more general leadership on key issues of importance to global governance?

Cities as Mediators of Global Conflicts

To take these questions in turn: first, are cities already, in a geographical sense, the places where global conflicts are confronted and, on occasion, mediated?

The answer to this question is surely "yes." Many of the metropolitan centers that Saskia Sassen (2001) has called "global cities" are places where millions of people move in and out from countries all over the world. Their characteristics include being poles of activity—such as international business decision-making, political power, immigration, and transport.

Political and social elites are generally present in major cities. However, as Sassen and others have noted, these places often also include large sections of the population that are seriously disadvantaged. The gap between wealth and poverty is often very great, as are differences based on race, migration status, and ethnic background. If the cities are to succeed, they need to find ways of resolving these differences. Proximity demands that problems cannot be wholly ignored.

Thus, even in divided cities, efforts must be made by their leaders to ensure that different groups can live side by side in reasonable harmony. The consequences of failure would be permanent social disruption, riot, and disorder. Within many of the world's larger developed cities there are substantial differences between rich and poor, among ethnic and religious groups of various kinds, and even among a city's geographical divisions.

New York, for example, has long been the gateway for successive waves of migrants who settle together within its boundaries (Foner 2000). London has, within the past decade or so, accepted a million new overseas-born citizens (Howes and Finnela 2003). In sections of the city, people who would not live easily together back at home do so in the suburban streets. Thus, for example, Greek Cypriots, Turks, and Kurds live together on the Hackney/Haringey border around Green Lanes. In sections of New York and London, people from very different and sometimes antagonistic backgrounds can coexist.

Perhaps this is stating an obvious fact about major cities and their neighborhoods, but this obvious fact has wide implications for global governance. A number of people are forced by conflict or by poverty to move to a foreign country and city, although others voluntarily move from city to city. Regardless of the motivation for their movement, there is something encouraging about their capacity to live side by side, generally without difficulty, in the major cities where they choose to locate. At the very least, it suggests there is nothing inevitable about conflict.

Moreover, there is a tradition among new migrants of sending money back to their home country, thus providing additional resources targeted at the household sector of the economy (Ratha 2005). This is probably as effective a form of development aid as the official ones that are rather more familiar. Migrants, often congregated in and around major cities, are providing help for poorer communities in other parts of the world.

Then-mayor of London, Ken Livingstone, speaking in 2005, stated:

> Too often we take this work [fighting global poverty] for granted. . . . In fact, London out of all the UK cities plays a key but often underrated role in international development through its strong connections with many overseas countries and particularly those touched by recent disasters. In addition to the generosity of all Londoners to recent relief efforts, we know that Londoners make a significant contribution to developing countries through both the money sent home to family members and through the visits and ongoing contact with these countries (Livingstone 2005).

Cities, Anonymity, and Human Rights

This willingness of migrants to send remittances home leads to a second question: Do cities provide an anonymous place to live for people seeking to escape persecution and human rights violations in their home country? Of course, people who become asylum seekers must deal with national laws about cross-boundary travel and settlement. Cities do not have the power to decide to take people from other countries who might wish to migrate to a place of safety.

However, cities do offer the cloak of anonymity and the possibility that an individual or group can "disappear." Kenneth Jackson, editor of *The Encyclopedia of New York City* (1995), has made this point about the role of cities for people of all kinds (including from within their own country) who wish to escape to a new place to live their own life on their own terms.

In short, although cities may be hard places to survive in for many reasons, they have the advantage of being places within which it is easy to become invisible. But this is a somewhat negative reason for seeing such places as having advantages for those fleeing persecution. More positively, global cities provide support networks, advice, homes, jobs, and public services for asylum seekers and other people in similar circumstances.

Major cities such as New York, London, Toronto, and Johannesburg have associations for immigrants and have powerful networks of NGOs devoted to representing asylum seekers, migrants, and others. Even more importantly, because there are already groups of settled people from many different countries, there will be networks with which people can make contact. These contacts then lead to the possibility of homes and jobs. However rudimentary and informal such institutions may be, they will be better placed—and more humane, for those fleeing persecution, than anything provided by national governments or agencies.

The kind of professionals working in healthcare, social services, and other public provision in cities will be used to dealing with people from many different countries. Services have developed in London to assist those coping with trauma in the aftermath of experiences in countries damaged by civil wars, violence, and worse. Healthcare has adapted to meet the needs of people with rare illnesses and particular injuries. Moreover, liberal practitioners are clearly willing to provide assistance to people who do not qualify for public services or who cannot afford them.

It is possible to argue that major cities, partly because of their massive agglomerations of expertise but also because they include professionals who have interests and sympathies that extend beyond national boundaries, are likely to be conducive to sympathy and care for the oppressed and for new migrants. This is not to say that smaller cities or rural areas do not include such people but to suggest that the kind of liberals that congregate in large metropolitan areas will be both more numerous and more concerned with the interests of globally mobile populations.

Cities and the Resolution of International Conflict

A third key issue is this: How do major cities use their systems of government to resolve conflicts that have an international dimension? This issue is linked to the first one addressed here and concerns the way in which city leaderships use their policies and instruments to encourage people of many different nationalities with very different interests to live together in reasonable harmony.

Experienced global/international cities adopt a number of policies designed to secure good community relations. In attempting to improve relations among different groups of city residents, civic leaders—at their best—offer potential implications for global governance on a wider scale.

Mayors, leaders, and other officials must recognize the importance of distinct identities while encouraging mixing and socializing. Segregation, though common, needs to be linked to policies that explain differences in cultures and religions.

Effective leaders of divided cities such as pre-1989 Berlin or Jerusalem have had to adopt special policies and approaches to government so as to sustain their cities and to encourage reconciliation. Willy Brandt famously ran West Berlin during periods of high international tension during the Cold War, ensuring it remained independent and free. Teddy Kollek, elected six times as mayor of Jerusalem, encouraged religious toleration and attempted bridge-building among the different communities within his city. International conflicts and tensions can create profound demands on city governments.

Cities must also provide services that recognize the disparate nature of their populations, including language translation services, school catering that recognizes religious differences, tolerance of traditional forms of dress, and a range of other culturally sensitive behaviors. Such objectives need to be achieved in ways that are explained to the existing population. The benefits of new communities, though obvious to some—generally more affluent— parts of a city's population, often make less sense to the less affluent.

Indeed, it is city governments that almost always need to provide the local facilities and political management that is needed when significant groups of migrants arrive in a country. Border policies are in the hands of national governments, although the consequences of changes in border policy will require cities to cope with the resource and political costs associated with settling new overseas residents.

New migrants can put significant pressures on housing, health services, and schools. National governments rarely acknowledge the full impact of such demands, which then requires a complex management process in neighborhoods and communities. In most major global cities, the municipal government adopts such policies with enthusiasm. As will be explained here, modern city leaders see such behavior as an element in their city's "open" image.

From time to time, city governments also face tensions between ethnic and religious groups despite policy initiatives to avoid such problems. Inevitably, particularly visible or weak groups may face racism, religious intolerance, and/or discrimination. If these issues are not effectively tackled, civil disorder is an almost inevitable consequence. Periodically New York, London, Paris, and many other cities face rioting and serious breakdowns in community relations. But because of the densely packed nature of the city, spillover effects are inevitable. Unaffected neighborhoods feel threatened. City governments have to act. Sometimes politicians initiate aggressive "law and order" regimes in an attempt to impose order. Often leaders try mediation. Even where "hard" solutions are attempted, softer ones must follow if the problem is to be solved. The reality of daily life in cities of 5 or 10 million people (or more) is that unresolved differences between groups will erupt again and again. Quelling a riot will have to be followed up with regeneration programs, improved housing, and colleges.

Major metropolitan areas cannot, therefore, allow intercommunal conflicts to remain unresolved for very long. Or, if solutions are difficult, it is harder to avoid the need for continuous efforts to find solutions. Issues such as the gap between rich and poor are more easily understood in cities and will therefore be more likely to generate government action.

Wider Applications of City Governance

The fourth issue addressed here links to the third: Are there implications to be drawn from the governance and management of cities that have wider applications? The material presented here suggests that there are such implications. Indeed, the way city leaders "brand" their cities and present them to the world is of significant relevance to global governance debates.

New York, London, Paris, Toronto, and other global cities have developed an almost clichéd narrative. Mayors and other leaders describe them as "world" cities with "cosmopolitan" populations and "open" attitudes to the world. Airports are judged by the number of key centers that can be reached via direct flights. Internet traffic between London and New York is greater than between any other two places on earth. Toronto has a population that is more foreign-born than even New York. The best Indian restaurants are in London, though this is disputed by Birmingham. Paris has long been the refuge of the persecuted. Even persecutors will find their way to the anonymity of the global cities.

Crucially, these cities are proud to see themselves as open to the world, as places of intersection between the rich and poor, as being progressive and tolerant of difference. The word "London" has a different meaning than the word "Britain." "New York" is certainly not the same as "America." It is in these differences of meaning that it is possible to see how certain kinds of cities are likely to have a progressive influence on global politics and on government.

National politicians in most countries tend to denigrate major cities for being the home of the overprogressive and the overcreative, but they are unlikely to be unaware of the global visibility these same cities give their country. The media, the arts, and other forms of soft diplomacy convey images of New York, London, Paris, and other global centers that, whether good or bad, are inevitably glamorous. Tourism numbers alone show the importance of world cities for their countries. This glamor, in turn, has the effect of strengthening the propagation of "progressive" leadership ideas.

Major cities are often heavily influenced by liberals and progressives. Even when a conservative politician is elected to lead a major international city, he or she is unlikely to be able to adopt the median politics of the country in relation to migration, race, religious tolerance, lifestyle, and so on. The complexity and density of such cities, coupled with the self-image of their affluent and transient inhabitants, tend to demand a greater acceptance of differences than more settled, rural, and suburban places. Super-rich cities such as London, New York, and Paris are thus willing to elect left-of-center mayors, at least part of the time. Such leaders generally embrace pro-employment "growth coalition" policies to foster international, market-driven, economic success (Molotch 1976:309–332).

Expanding the Role of City Leaders

Finally there is the issue of whether city leaders could expand their role, possibly jointly, to provide more general leadership on key issues of importance to global governance. Here, the answer is clear: They already do so. Monica Salomon, writing about the possible rise in cities' global governance, has recently written:

> The local government of Barcelona, host of United Cities and Local Governments (the recently created world association of cities) has been one of the main promoters of the political articulation of cities at a global level and has been also a successful propagator of its own model of urban management, mainly to Latin American cities. Porto Alegre, also an active network maker, is widely known through the diffusion of its "participative budget" (a mechanism of municipal resource allocation based on wide participation of civil society representatives) all over the world, including some municipalities of the North (2009).

Cities have led national governments in relation to the environment. The C40 Large Cities Climate Leadership Group is a prime example of how city leaders can overtake national governments in an attempt to provide solutions to complex policy problems. Perhaps because environmental challenges are so visible in metropolitan areas, but also because of the generally progressive nature of their leaders (and thus, to some extent their voters), global cities have been able to take a stance on carbon emissions and other environmental issues well in advance of national governments.

Conclusion

Looking ahead, it is interesting to consider how cities might more self-consciously move in the direction of strengthening conflict resolution within the terms of the debate about global governance. A degree of corporate self-awareness on the part of municipal governments would be a good start. Despite a greater willingness to travel to other cities and to consider wider urban issues, city leaders inevitably have to spend most of their time and effort dealing with neighborhood and infrastructure problems. Global issues have generally been of secondary importance to them. The environment is a rare exception because of its visible global-to-local impact.

City mayors and leaders are, however, increasingly willing to join international organizations and to consider wider questions relating to the future development and evolution of metropolitan areas. Cities have generally been thought to present particular challenges such as the need to build basic infrastructure and to operate services such as transport and policing. But increasingly city leaders have been forced to confront the direct and indirect impacts of global conflict, the movement of people, and the management of communities from many different countries. International politics has begun to create a demand for urban solutions.

The main challenges likely to face cities in relation to conflict resolution in the years ahead include the following.

Continuing Cross-Border Migration to Megacities

There is little evidence that recent trends toward increased levels of international migration are likely to reverse in the near future. Large numbers of people will move across borders, often to large cities. Many of these migrants will be fleeing persecution and/or conflict. The way in which recipient cities handle these incomers will have potential impacts on intercommunal relationships within cities and beyond them. Traditionally, megacities have been willing and able to handle significant migration, though there is generally a complex period of adjustment as new populations settle in.

Provision of Services for Newly Arrived Migrants

Many migrants, notably those fleeing conflict or persecution, have particular service needs. Although some of this provision can be made available by civil society institutions, it is inevitable that city governments will be required to identify needs and to deliver services. In European cities, there is often a legal requirement that needs-based provisions be made available to all residents. The development and application of human rights legislation has extended the demand for fair treatment for all people living within many countries.

Possibilities of Joint Action in Relation to Relevant Policy Issues

The world's major cities often have charismatic leaders who have a significant national and international profile. In recent years, mayors or governors from cities such as Bogota, Toronto, Barcelona, Los Angeles, and Berlin have been seen as taking a visible role beyond their own city. In part, this is a recognition of the promotional importance of city mayors. But it is also evidence of a developing community of mayors coming together at international conferences and seminars to debate more general policy challenges.[1]

Climate change, migration, economic development, and the management of complexity are among the issues that city leaders have been most likely to discuss. Although cities can be seen to some extent as being in competition, they are also collaborative: Megacities often have more in common with each other than with other places within their own country.

Stimulation of Research into Possible Roles

Global governance researchers may need to work with city government practitioners to distill a number of key issues and policies in situations where urban leaders have important expertise that could be transferred to the national or global spheres. Conflict resolution is an area of policy where there may be significant experience at the city level from which national, regional, and international institutions might be able to learn.

To this end, researchers may wish to provide city leaders with an agenda for action on the international level. The issues considered in this chapter provide a number of possible spheres of activity. Major cities often have international bureaus and overseas representation. Working with these externally focused officials and also with the mayors' offices, it would be possible to make the case for greater city-level involvement in international and global policy.

But there are other challenges metropolitan areas must increasingly tackle. In the twenty-first century, the growth of new economic zones across the world will create many more megacities. In China, India, and Latin America, cities of more than 8 million people (i.e., the current population of London and of New York) are rapidly increasing in number. Indeed, it is likely that some rapidly growing cities will sprawl so much that conventional definitions of a "city" will hardly be relevant. City populations of between 10 and 20 million are likely to proliferate.

Most mayors and leaders have to devote much of their time to "fighting fires" within their cities: Transport failures, strikes, fear of crime, and scandals are the issues that dominate city hall press conferences. The day-to-day pressure on city administrations is profound, largely because of the compound nature of the problems created by many millions of people living together in a relatively small space. Ensuring people can get to and from work every day is a massive logistical effort. Rapid population and economic growth will intensify the need to provide basic infrastructure and services.

City mayors and leaders have already tackled "local" problems that are, in fact, "global." That they have done so without understanding the full extent of their success suggests that it would be possible to go far further. As nations and regions become increasingly aware of their interdependence, this may be an appropriate time to promote extending the role of cities in conflict resolution. Global problems almost always have locally initiated solutions.

CITIES AND CONFLICT RESOLUTION   287

Note

1. For example, the Urban Age series of conferences organized by the London School of Economics has explicitly sought to bring together city leaders in a number of megacities. See www.urban-age.net.

References

Foner, N., 2000, *From Ellis Island to JFK: New York's Two Great Waves of Immigration*, New Haven: Yale University Press.

Howes, E. and G. Finella, 2003, "2001 Census: Ethnic Groups in London and Other Districts," *DMAG Briefing*. London: Greater London Authority Data Management and Analysis Group.

Jackson, K., 1995, *The Encyclopedia of New York City*, New Haven: Yale University Press.

Livingstone, K., 2005, speaking at City Hall, London, March 8, available at www.london.gov.uk/media/press_releases_mayoral/london-key-uks-international-development-programme-says-mayor (accessed November 2, 2012).

Molotch, H., 1976, "The City as a Growth Machine: Toward a Political Economy of Place," *The American Journal of Sociology*, 82(2):309–332.

Ratha, D., 2005, "Remittances: A Lifeline for Development," *Finance & Development: A Quarterly Magazine of the IMF*, 42(4), available at http://www.imf.org/external/pubs/ft/fandd/2005/12/basics.htm (accessed November 2, 2012).

Salomon, M., 2009, "Local Governments as Foreign Policy Actors and Global Cities Network-Makers: The Cases of Barcelona and Porto Alegre," chapter presented at the ISA's 49th Annual Convention, *Bridging Multiple Divides*, San Francisco, CA. Available at www.allacademic.com/meta/p252346_index.html.

Sassen, S., 2001, *The Global City: New York, London, Tokyo*, Princeton: Princeton University Press.

Toly, N., 2008, "Transnational Municipal Networks in Climate Politics: From Global Governance to Global Politics," *Globalisations*, 5(3):341–356.

12

Cities and Global Climate Governance: From Passive Implementers to Active Co-Decision-Makers

KRISTINE KERN AND ARTHUR P.J. MOL

Introduction

Cities have emerged as important actors within multilevel arrangements that govern climate change. Global climate change affects local governments in three different ways. First, a high and increasing proportion of greenhouse gas (GHG) emissions is generated in metropolitan areas (Stern 2006; International Energy Agency 2008), and the world's biggest cities such as London, Tokyo, and Beijing generate more GHG emissions than small countries. Second, the effects of global climate change have direct impacts on metropolitan regions and, although the vulnerabilities of both ecosystems and social systems vary considerably, cities need to adapt to the changing situation. Third, metropolitan regions are also places where social and technological innovations are generated that help in the reduction of GHG emissions and the adaptation to new challenges (Florida 2003).

Because climate change is a complex global problem that requires action at local and regional levels, urban climate governance has become highly internationalized. Although many large cities have become global players and even medium-sized cities now have an office for foreign relations, all cities are strongly affected not only by global climate change but also by national, European, and international climate change policies

(Monni and Raes 2008). Therefore, it can be assumed that both global climate change and global climate governance alter local practices and policies and vice versa.

In many countries around the world, climate mitigation and adaptation policies are high on the political agenda. Although it is generally acknowledged that climate change is a global problem that requires local action, existing research on climate governance has started from a top-down rather than from a bottom-up perspective and has concentrated mainly on international, European, and national climate change policies (Harris 2007; Pettenger 2007; PEER 2009; Harrison and Sundstrom 2010; Jordan et al. 2010; Oberthür and Pallemaerts 2010; Rabe 2010). In recent years, however, research on urban climate governance has emerged as a new and promising research area (Bulkeley 2010).

The scope of urban climate governance studies was limited until recently: Scholars had focused primarily on local mitigation activities and concentrated on individual or on only a very limited number of cities in individual Organization for Economic Cooperation and Development (OECD) countries (see, for example, Betsill 2001; Bulkeley and Kern 2006; Granberg and Elander 2007; Lundqvist and Borgstede 2007). Although a general shift toward (1) studies on adaptation (Lindseth 2005; Storbjörk 2007; Zahran et al. 2008; Van den Berg, et al. 2010) and (2) cities in low- and middle-income countries (Bicknell et al. 2009) can be observed, research on vertical and horizontal coordination and integration of climate governance systems is still underdeveloped (Gupta 2007; Bommel and Kuindersma 2008; Monni and Raes 2008; Beck et al. 2009; Corfee-Morlot et al. 2009; Kern and Bulkeley 2009; Bouteligier 2011; Kern, 2013).

Thus, the following sections concentrate on an analysis of the role cities play for climate governance in multilevel governance systems. The concept of multilevel governance was originally developed to describe the relations between EU institutions and subnational governments (Marks and Hooghe 2004) but can be used also to analyze the relations among levels of government within nation-states and beyond the EU (Bache and Flinders 2004; Bache 2008). From a multilevel governance perspective, the development of urban climate governance is situated "at the interface of horizontal networked forms of authority and vertical divisions of responsibilities among different parts of the state" (Bulkeley 2010:237).

The chapter starts with the general question of how the complexities, uncertainties, and ambiguities of global climate change can be governed by dynamic multilevel systems and then analyzes three crucial challenges for the establishment of climate governance systems in which cities play a prominent role (Kern, 2013): (1) a lack of institutional arrangements that guarantee that international, EU, and national climate change policies are actually implemented in cities (hierarchical climate governance); (2) the independent development of urban climate protection policies and the vertical coordination with other parts of climate governance systems (vertical climate governance); and (3) the emergence of horizontal coordination of climate change policy below the nation-state through the establishment of national and transnational city networks (horizontal climate governance). Conclusions are drawn in the final section of this chapter.

Hierarchical Climate Governance

The first challenge for city involvement in climate governance is caused by the fact that the debate on climate change was, at least initially, dominated by (inter)national actors who framed climate change as a global problem. The urban dimension of climate governance was largely neglected because climate governance was dominated by the traditional perspective of international relations; that is, it was assumed that political legitimacy and sovereignty in addressing climate change is exercised only by nation-states. Or to put it in the words of Ulrich Beck (2005): Climate governance was caught in the nation-state container. Recent debates suggest, however, that the crucial role that subnational governments play in climate policy has been acknowledged now by scientists and policymakers alike. According to the Intergovernmental Panel on Climate Change (IPCC), most adaptation and mitigation actions tend to be implemented at regional and local scales (IPCC 2007).

Hierarchical climate governance implies that compliance with international agreements depends on national programs and their implementation, which in turn depends on state-local relations (table 12.1). In a hierarchically coordinated system, top-down governance prevails and urban policies are primarily determined by a nation-state that aims to harmonize subnational policies. Instead of acting on their own initiative, local governments are regarded as policytakers that implement national programs. This may, of course, lead to implementation deficits and limited effectiveness. Legitimacy is primarily limited to decision-making at the national level.

Hierarchical climate governance generates a need to establish appropriate institutional arrangements and tools to reach national goals, for example, by introducing mandates, developing guidelines for local

Table 12.1
Types of Climate Governance in Multilevel Systems

	Hierarchical Climate Governance	Vertical Climate Governance	Horizontal Climate Governance
Main role of cities and regions	Implementing international, EU, and national legislation	Lobbying and by-passing nation-states	City networking
Levels involved	International, EU, national	International, EU, cities/regions	Cities/regions
Dynamic between levels	Top-down	Top-down and bottom-up	Horizontal
International/ EU–local relations	Indirect relations: nation-states as "gatekeepers"	Direct relations: lobbying, consultation, and agreements (EU Covenant of Mayors)	International and EU institutions not directly involved (except as facilitator; funding)
State–local relations	Hierarchical local authorities as part of nation-states	Paradiplomacy; state–local relations loosen	Paradiplomacy; state–local relations loosen
Differences between local authorities	All local authorities affected differences along national and regional lines	Pioneers dominate associations and networks (C40, CCP, Climate Alliance, Energy Cities)	Pioneers dominate associations and networks (CCP, Climate Alliance, Energy Cities)

governments to report on their climate protection programs, or finding other forms to assess the performance of urban climate governance systematically and regularly. Although many high-income countries developed national action plans at a relatively early stage, such mandatory instruments for the implementation of national, EU, and international mitigation and adaptation policies are still missing in most countries. Hierarchical climate governance requires a highly centralized and interventionist state. It may be assumed that national governments in centralized states are better able to steer urban climate governance than governments in countries in which cities and regions enjoy a high degree of autonomy.

The UK is a typical example of a centralized state. Despite the devolution reforms of Tony Blair's New Labour government and the establishment of relatively independent regions, state–local relations remained highly centralized. In contrast to countries in which municipalities are relatively independent, in the UK, planning has been traditionally characterized by a strongly hierarchical relationship between local authorities and the national government. Local government can act only within the boundaries set by the UK Parliament. This relationship can ensure that local decision-makers fulfill national demands (John and Copus 2011:30).

At the national level, the UK has successfully launched many innovative climate policies, including ambitious reduction targets that supersede the targets set for the UK under the EU burden-sharing (1997/1998) and effort-sharing (2008) agreements. In 2000, the UK government set a domestic goal for reducing CO_2 emissions to 20 percent below 1990 levels by 2010. The government also set a target that required that 10 percent of the UK's electricity come from renewable sources by 2010 (DEFRA 2006). In 2008, the UK government passed the Climate Change Act, which included a legally binding, long-term framework for reducing GHG emissions through domestic and international action, to at least 80 percent below 1990 levels by 2050 and to at least 34 percent below 1990 levels by 2018–2022 (DECC 2009:30).

These ambitious goals had consequences for local authorities because the UK government used its authority to set mandatory requirements for local climate change policy. In 2008, the government included climate-policy indicators in the local government performance framework. In England, this assessment of local authorities encompassed three obligatory performance indicators—(1) CO_2 emission reductions from local authority operations; (2) per capita reductions in CO_2 emissions in the local authority area; and (3) adaptation to climate change—as part of a set of 198 national performance indicators for local authorities. These indicators were relevant for the Local Area Agreements (performance agreements for local authorities that are negotiated with the central government). Two-thirds of these agreements contained, for example, targets concerning the per capita emissions in cities (DECC 2009:55; Fudge and Peters 2009).

This example from the UK shows that hierarchical governance is facilitated when state-local relations are organized in a predominantly hierarchical manner. However, among those countries that have committed themselves to emission reduction targets under the Kyoto Protocol (Annex 1 countries), the degree of centralization and local autonomy varies considerably. Unlike the situation in the UK, most Annex I countries have chosen different strategies and tools to influence subnational climate governance because in most countries local authorities enjoy a higher degree of autonomy and independence from the national government than do local authorities in the UK.

In such less centralized states with more local autonomy, state-local relations are more cooperative, and the national government is in a considerably weaker position with regard to the implementation of climate change policy at the local level. This may explain why the Dutch approach, for example, differs considerably from its British counterpart. In the Netherlands, the implementation of national climate policy at the local level is based primarily on a covenant. The Dutch "Klimaatcovenant" is a soft-law, multilevel arrangement involving municipalities, provinces, and several national ministries. Moreover, urban governance in federal states—such as Germany, Canada, Australia, and the United States—depends primarily on the federal states and provinces and the relationship between this additional layer of regional governments and their municipalities (Lutsey and Sperling 2008; Betsill and Rabe 2009). As urban climate action tends to remain a voluntary task in federal systems, national initiatives are dominated by forms of voluntary climate governance (facilitating, enabling, stimulation, motivating, etc.). If hierarchical governance is not an option, voluntary benchmarking, for example, may help to generate more action on the ground. Competitions, awards, and rankings may be used to recognize and reward the best-performing local authorities. The limits of hierarchical climate governance point to the fact that polycentric systems have considerable advantages and "that simply recommending a single governance unit to solve global collective-action problems—because of global impacts—needs to be seriously rethought" (Ostrom 2010:552).

Vertical Climate Governance

Hence, in order to develop effective climate governance in multilevel systems, the top-down perspective of hierarchical climate governance needs to be complemented by a bottom-up perspective (Bommel and Kuindersma 2008). Although cities "are embedded in regional and national webs of rules, resources, and patterns of coordination, these webs do not prevent them from pursuing their interests within global arenas" (Peters and Pierre 2004:79). In vertical climate governance, local authorities develop their own initiatives and try to influence national and even global climate governance. Vertical climate governance is characterized by interdependency among governments at different levels, shared competencies, and joint decision-making. Cities may not only develop their own initiatives but may even bypass their national governments and become active in European and international policy arenas (Kaiser 2005) (table 12.1).

The main challenge here is that national climate change policy is not implemented in a domestic institutional vacuum but needs to be coordinated and integrated with diverse and fragmented subnational approaches. In many countries with ambitious national programs in place, the independent climate change policies of cities have been an essential part of climate governance from the outset. Initiatives in the leading cities have started simultaneously or even earlier than national initiatives. Furthermore, cities have developed more ambitious goals than the goals pursued by their national governments. This includes, for example, London's Climate Change Action Plan (2007) calling for a 60 percent reduction of GHG emissions from 1990 to 2025; New York's "A Greener, Greater New York" campaign (2007) calling for a 30 percent reduction from 2005 to 2030; and Tokyo's Climate Change Strategy (2007) calling for a 25 percent reduction from 2000 to 2020 (Corfee-Morlot et al. 2009:30).

Moreover, in the early 1990s, many cities joined the newly founded transnational city networks in the area of climate change policy. The formation of transnational city networks is indicative of diminishing national sovereignty and of the emergence of transnational spaces. In Europe, three such networks were founded in the early 1990s: the Climate Alliance, the Cities for Climate Protection campaign, and Energy Cities.[1] A more recent development is the founding of the C40 Cities Climate Leadership Group in 2005, a cooperative initiative among forty large cities (such as London, Beijing, Delhi, and Lagos) and the Clinton Climate Initiative. The most prominent national city network is the U.S. Mayors Climate Protection Agreement that was founded in 2005 and has been signed by more than 1,000 cities in the United States. Membership in such networks is decisive for the commitment of cities to climate protection measures. Joining the Climate Alliance meant a voluntary commitment to very ambitious goals, namely, reducing CO_2 emissions by 50 percent ultimately in 2030 compared with 1990 levels. Accordingly, many cities developed climate change strategies, action plans, policies, and measures.

Such networks share specific structural and functional similarities. The general goals of these networks are almost identical. The networks seek voluntary commitments from municipalities for the reduction of GHG emissions; they try to enhance local capacities for addressing climate change; they represent the interests of their constituents at national, European, and international levels; and they promote the exchange of experiences and transfer of knowledge among their member cities. Like most transnational city networks, climate change networks have developed forms of internal and external governance in order to operate efficiently within a multilevel governance context (Kern 2001; Kern and Bulkeley 2009). Unlike the more traditional associations, these networks were transnational organizations from the outset, based exclusively on direct membership.

Empirical evidence from the three leading countries in climate change policy in Europe—Sweden, the UK, and Germany, according to Germanwatch (2012)—suggests that the simultaneous development of national and subnational approaches may improve the performance of national climate governance systems. All three countries show a combination of internationally acknowledged best practices generated by city pioneers and far-reaching national initiatives.

The transnational activities of cities can take different forms. The external relations of cities are based on (1) direct lobbying at international and European levels; (2) financial incentives such as funds provided by the EU through a variety of programs; and (3) direct consultation and collaborative efforts in an international setting (including monitoring and benchmarking of the participating cities' performance). We will briefly elaborate on these three forms.

First, hierarchical climate governance differs from vertical climate governance in assuming, at least implicitly, that subnational authorities do not become active beyond the nation-state and do not lobby European and international institutions. Instead, their lobbying activities are regarded as restricted to the national policy arenas. When cities develop their own initiatives and try to influence international decisions directly, they change from being policy-takers to policy-makers. Many cities and regions no longer view globalization as a restriction but as a new opportunity because institutionalized forms of networking enable cities to actively pursue multilevel strategies (Goldsmith 2003:124; Kassim 2005:307). For example, several city networks (International Council for Local Environmental Initiatives [ICLEI], United Cities and Local Governments, Metropolis, World Mayors Council on Climate Change, and C40 Climate Leadership Group) launched in 2007 the World Mayors and Local Governments Climate Protection Agreement and the Local Government Climate Roadmap at the United Nations Climate Change Conference in Bali (Conference of Parties [COP] 13). The Local Government Climate Roadmap process was adapted to the timetable of the UN conferences. The consortium of several transnational networks used the momentum leading to the Copenhagen and Cancun conferences (COP 14 and 15) to demand and claim more recognition of the role of cities in (negotiations toward) a post-2012 climate agreement.

Second, funding has become an important driver for vertical climate governance. In contrast to the main areas of EU regional policy, many EU climate programs do not necessarily require the involvement of the member states. In the areas of energy and climate policy, we find a variety of programs that provide a basis for the establishment of direct relations between the EU and subnational authorities. This includes initiatives such as the EU's Intelligent Energy Europe (IEE) program, which seeks to bridge the gap between EU policies and their implementation at the subnational level. IEE-funded projects include the establishment of local and regional energy agencies, the ManagEnergy initiative, and the Sustainable Energy Europe Campaign. Such initiatives and programs contribute to the achievement of EU energy and climate policy goals and targets in the fields of renewable energy, energy efficiency, and alternative fuels by identifying solutions on a municipal or regional scale and by involving a wide variety of actors, including local and regional authorities, regional energy agencies, universities, and businesses. The EU's regional policy underwent fundamental changes in entering the new funding period (2007 to 2013). For this period, the EU is funding projects in the areas of renewable energies, energy efficiency, and energy management measures to the tune of EUR 9 billion. In addition, the setting up of local and regional energy agencies is cofunded under the IEE program.

Third, we also find direct forms of cooperation between cities and the EU. With the support of the Committee of the Regions and the EU Parliament, the European Commission initiated the Covenant of Mayors in January 2008. This initiative aims to bring together the mayors of Europe's pioneering cities to improve urban energy efficiency and to promote cleaner energy production. It includes a formal commitment by the cities to reduce their CO_2 emissions by more than 20 percent by 2020. The scheme is based on a voluntary agreement but goes beyond mere facilitation of local initiatives because it includes a funding scheme. The European Commission funds the Covenant of Mayors indirectly through the IEE program, using the European Investment Bank as an intermediary institution. The local authorities have to prepare a baseline emissions directory, present a sustainable energy action plan, and provide regular implementation reports, while the European Commission sets up a "benchmark for excellence" mechanism. Benchmarks of excellence are initiatives and programs that represent a worldwide model of successful implementation of sustainable energy development concepts in urban settings.

By March 2012, more than 3,700 cities and towns throughout Europe, including many capital cities (such as London, Paris, Madrid, Amsterdam, and Stockholm) had joined this initiative. Although signatories come from more than forty countries, the Covenant is particularly prominent in Italy and Spain, where about 75 percent of the member cities are located. Apart from cities, about 170 regional governments (most of them also located in France and Spain), associations of local governments, and city networks have joined the Covenant of Mayors. The Covenant of Mayors Office (COMO) facilitates monitoring, networking, and promotion. It is managed by a consortium of local and regional authorities' networks, and led by Energy Cities.

When national governments relinquish their gatekeeper position, which allows subnational authorities to bypass the nation-state and develop their own foreign policy, the reality becomes more complex than a hierarchical climate governance model would suggest. These new opportunities have given rise to new strategies, and many regions and cities now search actively for direct access to international institutions. Institutionalized forms of networking enable cities to pursue multilevel strategies. This development can be regarded as an expression of paradiplomacy, meaning that cities represent their interests independently from national governments. However, subnational mobilization is uneven across countries. Differences across local authorities exist along national lines but also among cities within the same country. Cities that become active at the international level share an entrepreneurial spirit and the desire to shape (climate) policy at the international level (Kassim 2005). The international profile of pioneering cities also reflects on their ambition to become internationally known as pioneers in climate change policy (Gustavsson et al. 2009:71). These city pioneers have joined transnational networks, participate in EU and international initiatives such as the Covenant of Majors, are highly committed to reducing GHG emissions, and are eager to learn from their peers in other countries (Kern 2013). Moreover, recent developments at international and European levels show that city networks pursue new strategies. Vertical climate governance appears to lead to the emergence of new forms of cooperation, not only between cities and higher levels of government but also among city networks. These specialized national and transnational networks are important not only for vertical but also for horizontal climate governance.

Horizontal Climate Governance

Transnational city networks do not limit their activities to the aggregation and representation of their members' interests and have become active cogovernors at European and international levels (table 12.1). They also stimulate the exchange of knowledge, the spread of best practices among cities, and the joint development of solutions for common problems. Horizontal climate governance requires institutionalized forms of cooperation among cities because such arrangements can be used by local actors as platforms for transnational networking and learning. The ties between local authorities, which are developed on a strictly voluntary basis, can be either bilateral or multilateral. Such ties foster horizontal climate governance because they are used by local actors as tools for transnational networking, exchange of experience, and learning from best practices. In recent years, horizontal climate governance has gained in importance and currently provides additional opportunities for local actors.

Three types of horizontal climate governance can be identified: (1) bilateral twinning; (2) transnational networking; and (3) project networking. Bilateral twinning has a long tradition, in the form of direct cooperation between cities. Local foreign policy is by no means restricted to membership of transnational networks such as the C40 network but also as direct relations between cities. The idea of twin city partnerships developed after World War I but came to fruition only after World War II. Traditionally city twinning has been restricted to a cultural mission, but such institutionalized direct relations now also serve as a basis for the transfer of climate change policy. The second type of horizontal climate governance, the establishment of transnational city networks, aims to facilitate the exchange of experiences and the transfer of best practices. Apart from lobbying, which was discussed in the previous section, facilitating best-practice transfer and organizing the exchange of experiences among members form important parts of the mission of transnational city networks such as the Climate Alliance (Keiner and Kim 2008; Toly 2008; Kern and Bulkeley 2009). Transnational city networks have fostered horizontal urban climate governance because local actors use such networks for transnational learning. Finally, cities become involved in short-term project networks that differ considerably from city twinning and transnational city networks in that the latter are long-term relationships. Formal-legal and long-term relationships between municipalities are being increasingly superseded by institutional arrangements of limited duration.

Project networks can, but do not necessarily, overlap with city twinning and transnational networks. Long-term relationships can be used to stabilize short-term projects, and short-term project networks can concretize transnational networks. An established network of sister cities and membership of a transnational city network such as Energy Cities provide excellent bases for finding city partners if required for a project application. Cooperative projects involving cities from different countries create transnational spaces beyond nation-states. Membership in transnational networks pays off for most cities because transnational city networks initiate and even manage such cooperative projects.

Although best-practice transfer has become an overall catchword and is often depicted as a solution if harmonization is not possible, the transfer of best practice faces several challenges. Although pioneer cities are usually involved in national and transnational networks and improve their urban climate performance by learning from their peers at home and abroad, there is no guarantee that best practices are eventually taken up by the laggards (Kern and Bulkeley 2009). This may be caused, first, by a lack of capacities on the side of the potential adopters, in particular the smaller cities and towns. Second, there is also evidence that the diffusion of climate policies is not always a self-sustaining process, even if successful models and sufficient capacity exist. Nonadoption of best practices may be a rational strategy, in particular for powerful and dominant players. Third, general studies on policy transfer and policy diffusion show that the transfer of best practices depends on the specific context; that is, even successful innovations may not diffuse rapidly because local experiments cannot be transferred to other contexts. Although local governments are in a far better position for policy transfer than their national counterparts because local governments can choose from a much greater variety of best-practice cases, the lack of transfer of best practices appears to be a serious problem for the design of multilevel climate governance.

Although London, Munich, and New York may be internationally acknowledged and acclaimed leaders in urban climate change governance, other cities in the United Kingdom, Germany, and the United States are not. Even in the leading countries we find a split between the city frontrunners and the subnational authorities that lag behind; (adaptive) capacities of local authorities not only vary considerably, it also appears that the development of such capacities is path-dependent. Cities that have a proven record in environmental policy and in sustainable development tend to become pioneers in climate change policies as well (Kern et al. 2005;

Kern et al. 2007). Thus it does not come as a surprise to learn that inno
vative new approaches to climate protection, such as the combination of
mitigation and adaptation strategies, have been initiated by the most active metroregions. Traditional policy tools, such as subsidies, cannot solve
this problem of divergence among cities. Existing differences may become
even more pronounced if the pioneers strengthen their capacities due to
national funding and international benchmarking, while the "rest of the
pack" lacks the capacity to apply for additional resources and the motivation to catch up.

Conclusion

This chapter's analysis has demonstrated that three dimensions of urban
climate governance have to be distinguished: (1) hierarchical climate
governance, which is restricted to cities implementing international, EU,
and national climate change policy; (2) vertical climate governance, in
which cities start to influence international and EU climate governance
directly; and (3) horizontal climate governance where cities cooperate
directly in developing and implementing climate change policy through
the establishment of transnational city networks, twinnings, and project
networks (Kern 2013). Through these three modes cities are increasingly
becoming vital elements and active actors in multilevel climate governance systems, although not all cities participate to the same extent.
Multilevel climate change governance requires integrated approaches
and institutional innovations to cope with the fragmented landscape of
climate governance through the vertical and horizontal integration of
climate governance systems. Hierarchical, vertical, and horizontal climate governance arrangements contribute to such integration and innovation. Such arrangements face a dual challenge because they must
cope not only with the complexity of climate change and the uncertainty
of its impacts but also with the spatiotemporal disparities of subnational
climate policy.

While hierarchical climate governance neglects bottom-up initiatives,
vertical and horizontal climate governance combines bottom-up initiatives
with the initiatives started by international organizations and national governments. These latter two modes exemplify the fact that the opportunities
for cities to gain access to climate change decision-making have improved
considerably over time. The establishment and stabilization of various

transnational city networks in the area of urban climate change policy mean that traditional forms of hierarchical climate governance, which restricts local authorities to only the implementation of national legislation, have been supplemented by alternative forms of climate governance where cities take an active stance. Today, the international system and, in particular, the European Union provide an opportunity structure in the area of climate change policy that allows cities and their representatives to gain access to decision-making in international and EU institutions (such as the European Commission).

However, city transnational networking in the area of climate change policy still appears to be the privilege of relatively few pioneering cities, which have the capacities and the entrepreneurship to initiate such activities. Transnational city networks such as the CCP Campaign are still networks of pioneers and for pioneers (Kern and Bulkeley 2009). Differences between cities exist and will most likely persist, even within countries. Some cities become Europeanized or even globalized and join the Covenant of Mayors, while others stay bound by regional and national ties. As pioneering cities can be found in all member states, a cluster of truly globalized cities is slowly emerging. Although the development and implementation of active climate change strategies are limited to a restricted cluster of cities, this may change over time if globalized cities become models and influence the climate change policy of less globalized cities. This is of course far from an inevitable evolutionary process, but globalization does provide cities with new opportunities because urban centers are "becoming arenas of globalization, rather than passive victims of global forces" (Gustavsson et al. 2009:59). Whether cities use and seize these opportunities depends mainly on each city's competences and authority to regulate climate-relevant issue areas, its commitment and entrepreneurship to fight global climate change, and its capacity to do so (Kern and Alber 2008). Pioneering cities in the area of climate change policy like London, Barcelona, Stockholm, and Munich are far more globalized and globally networked than small towns in rural areas; but even such towns can participate in international projects, join transnational city networks, and stimulate climate policy through city twinning. Nevertheless, for most cities, climate governance is, and will remain, mainly about the implementation of national and international climate policy. For the pioneers, vertical and horizontal climate governance offers manifold opportunities. As often these pioneers are powerful metropolises, they can make a difference by boosting global climate change governance.

Note

1. With more than 1,300 full members in sixteen European countries, the Climate Alliance, whose headquarters are located in Frankfurt am Main, is by far the largest of these networks. Cities for Climate Protection has around 170 member cities in nineteen European countries. It is an ICLEI initiative—a global transnational city network of "Local Governments for Sustainability" whose European headquarters are in Freiburg (Germany). Energy Cities has around 200 individual members in twenty-six European countries and its headquarters are located in Besançon (France). (All figures as of January 2011.)

References

Bache, I., 2008, *Europeanization and Multi-level Governance: Cohesion Policy in the European Union and Britain,* Lanham/Plymouth, UK: Rowman/Littlefield.

Bache, I. and M. Flinders, eds., 2004, *Multi-level Governance,* Oxford, UK: Oxford University Press.

Beck, S., C. Kuhlicke, and C. Görg, 2009, *Climate Policy Integration, Coherence, and Governance in Germany,* Leipzig: UFZ.

Beck, U., 2005, *Power in the Global Age. A New Global Political Economy,* Cambridge, UK: Polity.

Betsill, M., 2001, "Mitigating Climate Change in U.S. Cities: Opportunities and Obstacles," *Local Environment,* 6(4):393–406.

Betsill, M. M. and B. G. Rabe, 2009, "Climate Change and Multi-Level Governance: The Emerging State and Local Roles," in *Towards Sustainable Communities,* 2nd ed., edited by D. A. Mazmanian and M. E. Kraft, 201–226. Cambridge, Mass.: MIT.

Bicknell, J., D. Dodman, and D. Satterthwaite, 2009, *Adapting Cities to Climate Change. Understanding and Addressing the Development Challenge,* London: Earthscan.

Bommel, S. van and W. Kuindersma, 2008, *Policy Integration, Coherence, and Governance in Dutch Climate Policy,* Wageningen: Alterra.

Bouteligier, S., 2011, "Cities and Global Environmental NGOs: Emerging Transnational Urban Networks?" In *Cities and Global Governance,* edited by M. Amen, N. J. Toly, P. McCarney, and K. Segbers, 151–175. Surrey, UK: Ashgate.

Bulkeley, H., 2010, "Cities and the Governing of Climate Change," *Annual Review of Environment and Resources,* 35:229–253.

Bulkeley, H. and K. Kern, 2006, "Local Government and the Governing of Climate Change in Germany and the UK," *Urban Studies,* 43(12):2237–2259.

Corfee-Morlot, J., L. Kamal-Chaoui, M. Donovan, I. Cochran, A. Robert, and P. J. Teasdale, 2009, *Cities, Climate Change, and Multilevel Governance,* OECD Environmental Working Paper No. 14.

Department for Environment, Food, and Rural Affairs (DEFRA), 2006, *Tomorrow's Climate—Today's Challenge,* the United Kingdom's Report on Demonstrable Progress under the Kyoto Protocol.

Department of Energy and Climate Change (DECC), 2009, *The UK's Fifth National Communication under the United Nations Framework Convention on Climate Change*, London: DECC.

Florida, R., 2003, *The Rise of the Creative Class*, New York: Basic.

Fudge, S. and M. Peters, 2009, "Motivating Carbon Reduction in the UK: The Role of Local Government as an Agent of Social Change," *Journal of Integrative Environmental Sciences*, 6(2):103–120.

Germanwatch, 2012, *The Climate Change Performance Index. Results 2012*, available at www.germanwatch.org/klima/ccpi.pdf (accessed October 5, 2012).

Goldsmith, M., 2003, "Variable Geometry, Multi-Level Governance: European Integration and Subnational Government in the New Millennium," in *The Politics of Europeanization*, edited by K. Featherstone and C. Radaelli, 112–133. Oxford: Oxford University Press.

Granberg, M. and I. Elander, 2007, "Local Governance and Climate Change: Reflections on the Swedish Experience," *Local Environment*, 12(5):537–548.

Gupta, J., 2007, "The Multi-level Governance Challenge of Climate Change," *Environmental Sciences* 4(3):31–137.

Gustavsson, E., I. Elander, and M. Lundmark, 2009, "Multilevel Governance, Networking Cities, and the Geography of Climate-Change Mitigation: Two Swedish Examples," *Environment and Planning C: Government and Policy*, 27(1):59–74.

Harris, P., ed. 2007, *Europe and Global Climate Change: Politics, Foreign Policy and Regional Cooperation*, Cheltenham/Northampton, UK: Edward Elgar.

Harrison, K. and L. Sundstrom, eds., 2010, *Global Commons, Domestic Decisions: The Comparative Politics of Climate Change*, Cambridge, Mass.: MIT.

Intergovernmental Panel on Climate Change (IPCC), 2007, Fourth Assessment Report: Climate Change 2007, Cambridge, UK: Cambridge University Press

International Energy Agency, 2008, *World Energy Outlook*, Paris: IEA.

John, P. and C. Copus, 2011, "The United Kingdom: Is There Really an Anglo Model?" In *Local and Regional Democracy in Europe*, edited by J. Loughlin, F. Hendriks, and A. Lidström, 27–48. Oxford: Oxford University Press.

Jordan, A., D. Huitema, H. Van Aselt, T. Rayner, and F. Berkhout, eds., 2010, *Climate Change Policy in the EuropeanUnion. Confronting the Dilemmas of Mitgation and Adaptation*, Cambridge: Cambridge University Press.

Kaiser, R., 2005, "Local Governments and the European Union," in *Handbook of Public Administration and Policy in the European Union*, edited by P. van der Hoek, 367–379. London: Taylor & Francis.

Kassim, H., 2005, "The Europeanization of Member State Institutions," in *The Member States of the European Union*, edited by S. Bulmer and C. Lequesne, 285–316. Oxford: Oxford University Press.

Keiner, M. and A. Kim, 2008, "Transnational City Networks for Sustainability," *European Planning Studies*, 15(10):1369–1395.

Kern, K., 2001, "Transnationale Städtenetzwerke in Europa," in *Empirische Policy- und Verwaltungsforschung. Lokale, nationale und internationale Perspektiven*, edited by E. Schröter, 95–116. Opladen: Leske and Budrich.

Kern, K., 2013, "Climate Governance in the EU Multi-level System: The Role of Cities," in *Beyond Bottom Up and Top Down: Multilevel Environmental Governance Today in Europe and North America,* edited by J. Meadowcroft and I. Weibust, Cheltenham, UK: Edward Elgar (forthcoming).

Kern, K. and G. Alber, 2008, "Governing Climate Change in Cities: Modes of Urban Climate Governance in Multi-level Systems," Proceedings of the OECD conference on Competitive Cities and Climate Change, Paris.

Kern, K. and H. Bulkeley, 2009, "Cities, Europeanization, and Multi-Level Governance: Governing Climate Change Through Transnational Municipal Networks," *Journal of Common Market Studies,* 47(2):309–332.

Kern, K., C. Koll, and M. Schophaus, 2007, "The Diffusion of Local Agenda 21 in Germany: Comparing the German Federal States," *Environmental Politics,* 16(4): 604–624.

Kern, K., S. Niederhafner, S. Rechlin, and J. Wagener, 2005, *Kommunaler Klimaschutz in Deutschland – Handlungsmöglichkeiten, Entwicklung und Perspektiven,* Wissenschaftszentrum Berlin, DP SP IV 2005-101, available at http://skylla.wz-berlin.de/pdf/2005/ivo5-101.pdf.

Lindseth, G., 2005, "Local Level Adaptation to Climate Change: Discursive Strategies in the Norwegian Context," *Journal of Environmental Policy and Planning,* 7(1):61–83.

Lundqvist, L. and C. Borgstede, 2007, "Whose Responsibility? Swedish Local Decision Makers and the Scale of Climate Change Abatement," *Urban Affairs Review,* 43(3):299–324.

Lutsey, N. and D. Sperling, 2008, "America's Bottom-up Climate Change Mitigation Policy," *Energy Policy,* 36:673–685.

Marks, G. and L. Hooghe, 2004, "Contrasting Visions of Multi-level Governance," in *Multi-level Governance,* edited by I. Bache and M. Flinders, 15–30. Oxford: Oxford University Press.

Monni, S. and F. Raes, 2008, Multi-Level Climate Policy: The Case of the European Union, Finland, and Helsinki, *Environmental Science and Policy,* 11:743–755.

Oberthür, S. and M. Pallemaerts, eds., 2010, *The New Climate Policies of the European Union. Internal Legislation and Climate Diplomacy,* Brussels: VUB.

Ostrom, E., 2010, "Polycentric Systems for Coping with Collective Action and Global Environmental Change," *Global Environmental Change,* 20:550–557.

Partnership for European Environment (PEER), 2009, *Europe Adapts to Climate Change: Comparing National Adaptation Strategies,* Helsinki: Finish Environment Institute.

Peters, G. and J. Pierre, 2004, "Multi-level Governance and Democracy: A Faustian Bargain?" in *Multi-Level Governance,* edited by I. Bache and M. Flinders, 75–89. Oxford: Oxford University Press.

Pettenger, M., ed. 2007, *The Social Construction of Climate Change,* Aldershot/Burlington, UK: Ashgate.

Rabe, B., ed. 2010, *Greenhouse Governance. Addressing Climate Change in America,* Washington, D.C.: Brookings.

Stern, N., 2006, *Stern Review on the Economics of Climate Change*, London: HM Treasury/ Cabinet Office.

Storbjörk, S., 2007, "Governing Climate Adaptation in the Local Arena: Challenges of Risk Management and Planning in Sweden," *Local Environment*, 12(5):457–469.

Toly, N., 2008, "Transnational Municipal Networks in Climate Politics: From Global Governance to Local Politics," *Globalizations*, 5:341–356.

Van den Berg, M., W. Lafferty, and F. Coenen, 2010, "Adaptation to Climate Change Induced Flooding in Dutch Municipalities," in *The Social and Behavioural Aspects of Climate Change. Linking Vulnerability, Adaptation and Mitigation,* edited by P. Martens and C. T. Chang, 130–156. Sheffield, UK: Greenleaf.

Zahran, S., H. Grover, S. D. Brody, and A. Vedlitz, 2008, "Risk, Stress, and Capacity: Explaining Metropolitan Commitment to Climate Protection," *Urban Affairs Review*, 43(4):447–474.

5

Global Governance

Introduction

The chapters in this final part are about the global democratic deficit. The fundamental problem is that politics and power are no longer congruent. On the one hand, procedural democratic processes are largely confined to the nation-state. But on the other hand, elected governments no longer have the same power to respond to the demands of the electorate as they once did; this is even true of a powerful country such as the United States. Power has moved beyond national borders. Many of the decisions that affect the everyday lives of citizens are no longer taken at national levels. Democracy has become hollowed out, an often bitter and personalistic struggle for national positions that have less and less to do with policy choices.

Politics has, of course, spilled over national borders. An active global or international civil society has insistently drawn the world's attention to such issues as global poverty, climate change, disease, and human rights violations. New forms of identity politics around religion or ethnicity are increasingly transnational. Yet this new type of informal politics has no institutional counterpart and no address to which demands can be directed. Global civil society helps to change the global discourse; it influences the milieu of ideas that are discussed on a global level, but it has no formal access to decision-making.

Previous chapters have set out an interrelated agenda for "civilizing" globalization—the content of a possible global covenant. This includes

- how to overcome global poverty, how to protect the poor and disadvantaged, while not protecting national borders;
- how to transform national security machines into human security capabilities that can implement a comprehensive law-based approach to the reduction of violence world wide;
- and how to address the global challenge of climate change and invest in the new low-carbon technologies that are a precondition not only for slowing global warming but also for a new productive phase of economic growth.

The fourth part of the book suggests that some of these challenges might be met at the level of cities. Cities are closer and more responsive to civil society than states. Social safety nets, climate change strategies, and improved rule of law and policing are beginning to be practiced in a number of cities, such as Chicago, London, Medellín in Colombia, and Porto Alegre in Brazil. Even so, this approach is highly uneven, and cities are no substitute for a framework of global governance.

The chapters in this part, however, demonstrate that existing global governance is actually extremely weak. To be sure, in the period since World War II and especially after the end of the Cold War, the network of global and regional institutions has become ever broader and denser. Indeed there has been a proliferation of organizations, agencies, agreements, treaties, and so on. But some of the big problems include the following:

- The global governance framework is still dominated by a few great powers. It is sometimes argued that this is necessary for effectiveness. But what type of effectiveness and who benefits? If global economic redistribution or a global response to climate change is to be achieved, does there not need to be more voice for the poor and excluded, those who are most vulnerable to disasters, including war?
- The global governance framework lacks formal representativeness and accountability mechanisms, not only to the majority of states but also to global civil society. Thus the institutions lack the necessary legitimacy to be able to provide public goods and to enforce agreements.

- The global governance framework is hugely fragmented. A growing number of agencies and organizations generally have overlapping competencies and yet important responsibilities fall through the gaps between them. Thus the system is characterized by gaps and duplication.

The problems of lack of accountability and fragmentation are explored in David Held and Kevin Young's chapter in all three domains touched on by this book—finance, the environment, and security.

Ngaire Woods suggests that ad hoc global institutions such as the G20 might be the answer. The G20 grouping goes beyond a club of advanced industrial countries to include the emerging markets and, even though some 175 countries are excluded (not to mention the campaigning groups often arraigned beyond the guarded fences), she suggests that responsiveness might be preferable to representativeness. But despite its early achievements in heading off the worst of the global financial crisis, it is not yet evident how much can be done as the organization gets institutionalized and bureaucratized like the many other global agencies. The general picture remains bleak.

One way forward suggested by José Antonio Ocampo is through regional organizations, and he cites the European Union as a relatively successful example. At present, the EU is in crisis, facing a wave of sovereign debt amongst its weaker members. The knee-jerk reaction has been neoliberal: more reductions in public spending, which may well worsen the problem in a spiral of beggar thy neighbor cuts. If the euro is to survive—and the members of the EU are keen that it should—then reforms will need to be undertaken along the lines proposed in this book. They would include the following ideas:

- A European fiscal mechanism that could guarantee a Europe-wide system of social protection. To achieve this, the EU would have to, at a minimum, double the EU budget (currently under 1 percent of the combined GDPs of member states) and to finance increased spending through taxes levied at a European level. This might include a carbon tax or a tax on short-term speculation, the so-called Tobin tax.
- A European program of investment in green infrastructure and the knowledge economy. This is needed to address climate change, lay the basis for a new sustainable model of development, and to bring the peoples of Europe together in the way that common investment in coal and steel did after World War II.

- An external policy based on human security At present, the EU is pioneering a new type of security policy based on civilian-military cooperation and on a commitment to human rights, but it remains tiny; despite its economic weight, the EU has failed so far to act as a global power.
- To achieve all this, we need to bring politics and power together. There would have to be a pan-European set of democratic processes to elect European officials. There is, of course, a European Parliament, but although it is increasing in power, it is elected on the basis of national constituencies. The best solution would be a single elected president of the European Council and the European Commission.

If all of this were undertaken, the EU could offer a model of a new type of institution designed to enable nation-states and peoples to cope with globalization.

Underlying the model is a fundamental change in ways of thinking. In place of the market fundamentalism of recent decades, there needs to be greater concern about the public sphere. This is not necessarily the state sphere; it is about public authorities at all levels (regional, global, national, and local) that take responsibility for the challenges of our world. This is where a progressive American administration should take the lead.

13

Rethinking Global Economic and Social Governance*

JOSÉ ANTONIO OCAMPO

Recent years have been characterized by growing frustration with globalization, reflecting unsatisfactory processes and outcomes in multiple areas. In the social area, disenchantment is the result of the uneven way the benefits of globalization have spread in developing and developed countries alike. In the economic area, high financial volatility and a broad regulatory deficit have resulted in a sequence of national and international financial crises and, most recently, in a global financial crisis unprecedented since the Great Depression. In the environmental area, no effective action has been taken so far to face the unprecedented challenges posed by climate change and the massive destruction of biodiversity. And this is certainly an incomplete list.

*This is a revised version of the paper presented at the Committee on Global Thought Conference, "A Manifesto for a New Global Covenant," in December 2008, and published in the *Journal of Globalization and Development* in 2010. It further develops ideas from my previous work and, in particular, draws from my experience during ten years working for the United Nations. The literature on the issues covered here is massive and so I only include specific references that complement the issues raised in the paper. I am grateful to Patrizio Civili, Michael Doyle, Eric Helleiner, Richard Jolly, and Inge Kaul for very useful comments to previous drafts of this chapter.

At the heart of the disappointment with current globalization is the deficit in governance. Indeed, the weakening of nation-states during the recent wave of globalization has not been substituted by new forms of governance of a regional or global character. Furthermore, the nation-state continues to be primarily responsible for the development of societies, but the effectiveness of its actions has been eroded by global processes. This erosion encompasses again a broad set of areas, from the capacity to strengthen social protection, to macroeconomic and financial stability, to environmental sustainability. This has, furthermore, come at a time when such processes have increased the demand for nation-states to respond to the unsatisfactory outcomes of globalization.

Divided into four parts, this chapter outlines a way to rethink global economic and social governance. ("Economic" is understood in a broad sense to include environmental sustainability.) The first part proposes a new typology of the objectives of international cooperation for development. The second analyzes the asymmetries of the global order and its implications for global cooperation for development. The third takes a look at principles and at challenges in designing new global governance structures. The last part briefly draws some conclusions.

The Objectives of International Cooperation

Three Essential Objectives of Global Cooperation for Development

There are many possible ways to define the scope of international cooperation, but the best is that provided by the three foundations upon which the United Nations is built: peace (to which security is usually added today), human rights, and development. I focus in this chapter on the latter, but it should be said at the onset that there are several interrelations among these three dimensions. The first is the link between development and peace. The second is that between development and economic, social, and cultural rights, which has been the focus of work on the rights approach to development shared by UN agencies and by many civil society organizations. The case for the United Nations to be at the peak of any global governance structure is based on its universality *and* the fact that it is the only organization that deals with these three dimensions of global cooperation. I will, nonetheless, overlook the first of these interrelations, which is central to the "human security" paradigm, but I will make some references to the second.

In this triad, "development" has two complementary meanings—a fact that is usually overlooked. The first relates to cooperation with *developing countries*. This is the agenda that has also been the subject of the "North–South" negotiations and is the major focus of attention of the G77, the major grouping of developing countries in the United Nations. The second meaning refers to the *development of societies* in industrial and developing countries alike. It is in this sense that the term has been used by most of the United Nations conferences and summits and by the World Commission on the Social Dimension of Globalization (2004) convened by the International Labour Organization (ILO), among others. Indeed, the agreements of the Copenhagen Social Summit or of the Beijing Summit on Women, to mention just a few (see a comprehensive list in table 13.1), apply to all countries. In either sense, development has, furthermore, a comprehensive character and should best be seen in terms of the concepts of "human" or "sustainable development," which encompasses in the latter case its economic, social, and environmental dimensions.

Table 13.1
Global Conferences and Summits

Children (1990)
Education for All (1990, 2000)
Least Developed Countries (1990, 2001)
Drug Problem (1990, 1998)
Food Security (1992, 1996)
Sustainable Development (1992, 2002)
Human Rights (1993, 2001)
Population and Development (1994)
Small Island Developing States (1994, 2005)
Natural Disaster Reduction (1994, 2005)
Women (1995, 2005)
Social Development (1995, 2005)
Human Settlements (1996, 2001)
Youth (1998)
Millennium Summit (2000, 2005)
HIV/AIDS (2001)
Financing for Development (2002, 2008)
Aging (2002)
Landlocked and Transit Developing Countries (2003)
Information Society (2003, 2005)

The growing literature on "global public goods" (Kaul, Grunberg, and Storm 1999; Kaul et al. 2003; International Task Force on Global Public Goods 2006; Barrett 2007) has underscored still another form of cooperation, which, as I will argue here, essentially deals with interdependence among nations. Therefore, global cooperation for development—or in terms of the preamble of the UN Charter, "employ[ing] international machinery for the promotion of the economic and social advancement of all people"—can be said to have three basic objectives:[1]

- *Managing interdependence*;
- *Furthering the development of societies*;
- Gradually *overcoming the asymmetries that characterize the world economic system*, which affect in particular the developing world.

The first of these objectives emphasizes the interdependence among nations. The other two reflect the two dimensions in which the concept of development is used in the global discourse. They also refer to equity, in its two dimensions: among *citizens* and among *nations*. But the second of these objectives goes beyond equity because it encompasses the recognition of social norms and standards, including some that should be considered an essential part of the "social contract," such as economic, social, and cultural rights and the "Fundamental Principles and Rights at Work" adopted by the ILO. Indeed, to the extent that it involves the extension of economic, social, and cultural rights, this objective of international cooperation may be thought of as a process of gradually building up global citizenship. In this chapter, I will use the concept of "global (or international) cooperation for development" to refer to the totality of these three objectives and thus avoid the use of the shorter term "development cooperation," which is generally meant to refer to the third of them. One particular advantage of the proposed typology is the clear recognition of the second objective of cooperation, which is central to the United Nations work but which has been generally ignored in most typologies of international cooperation for development.

Viewed in the light of this typology, the earliest historical forms of international cooperation were largely created to fulfill the first of these objectives, though few had the character of international organizations. The most common pattern was agreements among imperial powers and independent nations on issues of common interest, such as the free navigation of international rivers, interconnecting railroads, telegraph and mail systems, controlling communicable diseases, fostering scientific cooperation, and protecting patents and copyrights (Mangone 1954: chapter 3). Others involved the transformation of a practice of a dominant power into a global arrangement (as in the case of the gold standard). The few organizations that developed related to managing interdependence.[2]

A significant step forward in global cooperation came with the Treaty of Versailles, which created the League of Nations and the ILO. Although political cooperation was the main objective of the League, mutual support in the realm of development was also furthered by its creation. It enhanced cooperation in the first area (managing interdependence), including an expansion of international economic dialogue, by calling several international conferences on economic issues, which unfortunately largely failed.[3] Older forms of cooperation in the first field were enhanced by the League's Communications and Transit Authority, and Health Organization.

Equally important, the ILO and subsidiary bodies of the League of Nations—the aforementioned Health Organization as well as the International Commission on Intellectual Cooperation (the precursor of UNESCO)—created for the first time international cooperation in the second field (the development of societies). Indeed in this regard, the only important precedent had been the nineteenth-century efforts, led by Great Britain, to abolish the slave traffic and eradicate slavery more generally— which, interestingly, can also be seen as the first major, though only gradual, success of the influence of civil society on the international development agenda. The ILO helped to spread labor standards and to encourage social dialogue, and it was also an active participant in the global economic debates and conferences (Rodgers et al. 2009). Although the League's agencies had a limited amount of cooperation with nonindustrialized countries, the third form of cooperation was minimal prior to World War II (WWII). This is probably unsurprising, as most of the now-developing countries in Asia and Africa were European colonies at the time.

The full development of all forms of international cooperation for development only came, therefore, in the post-WWII period with the creation of the United Nations system, the Bretton Woods Institutions (BWIs), the General Agreement on Tariffs and Trade (GATT)—the only survivor of the failed International Trade Organization and most recently of the World Trade Organization (WTO)—the enhanced role given to the Bank of International Settlements, and several other mechanisms of cooperation. The second area of cooperation (development of societies) was considerably expanded on the basis of the United Nations and its network of specialized agencies, funds, and programs. A major step toward establishing the goal of the development of societies at the center of global cooperation was the Universal Declaration of Human Rights, which firmly incorporated the economic, social, and cultural rights into the human rights agenda. The Declaration borrowed from Franklin Delano Roosevelt's concept of "freedom from want," which had already been incorporated into the Preamble of the UN Charter when referring to the determination "to promote social progress and better standards of life *in larger freedom*" (emphasis added). In the academic realm, a firm formulation of the three dimensions of human rights (civil, political, and social) was provided soon after by T. H. Marshall (see Marshall 1992, which reproduces his 1950 piece), but the concept of economic and social rights had, of course, a long history behind it. This included, since the nineteenth century, mobilization of one of the major early manifestations of "global civil society": the sequence of socialist internationals.

The third realm of international cooperation for development (cooperation with developing countries) was closely tied to the process of decolonization and, interestingly, also to the birth of development economics. An important precedent was that the development issues were placed on the agenda of the Bretton Woods negotiations by the United States, which were inspired by the inter-American initiatives that materialized from Roosevelt's Good Neighbor Policy—political strategy he adopted to guarantee the support of Latin American countries during World War II (Helleiner 2009).[4] The major step forward was the novel concept of "development aid" (now generally referred to as official development assistance, ODA) triggered by U.S. President Harry Truman's Four Point Speech given at his inauguration in January 1949 and placed on the global agenda by the United Nations in the 1950s (Jolly et al. 2009:chapter 6). The UN played the initial lead in this new area of global cooperation for development in the early post-WWII period, but that leadership was effectively transferred to the World Bank in the 1980s, as part of the shift in conceptions of major industrial countries toward a market reform agenda. The United Nations kept, nonetheless, a central place in technical cooperation with developing countries and, in particular, as a forum for dialogue on issues of global concern. Given their stronger voice in the UN versus the BWIs, developing countries always continued to recognize the former as the preferred forum for dialogue. In the area of finance, bilateral aid quickly became dominant in terms of funding, complemented by the Multilateral Development Banks (MDBs)—the World Bank and the network of regional development banks.

One important feature of the post-WWII design of global cooperation for development was its decentralized character. This is in sharp contrast with the area of security, where United Nations' decisions and enforcement were centralized in the Security Council. Centralization was also a feature of decolonization and human rights. The decentralized character of economic and social cooperation in a sense mimicked how national governments are organized because economic, social, and environmental issues are handled by a multiplicity of organizations at the country level. What the post-WWII design lacked, however, was a strong mechanism of coordination to guarantee what in current terminology is called the "coherence" of the system. Weak coordination functions were assigned to the Economic and Social Council (ECOSOC), which historically exercised even these limited functions rather poorly (Rosenthal 2005, 2007). It faced, furthermore, the fact that the specialized agencies were created with their autonomous governance structures; that some of them (the BWIs) hardly ever considered themselves to be part of the UN system; and that still others were created outside that system (the WTO and Bank for International Settlements). This problem has been combined with weak accountability and, even more, weak enforcement mechanisms for international commitments. I return to these issues in the third part of this chapter.

The strong effort at international cooperation and institution-building in the area of development in the post-WWII period kept an "original sin": It inherited major features of the colonial structures that preceded it in terms of the voice and decision-making power given to different nations, and it did not correct the major international economic asymmetries that then plagued and continue to characterize the world economy. The North–South negotiations since the 1960s and the continued debate on "voice and participation" of developing countries in international economic decision-making are major reflections of this fact. The bipolar world may have had a positive effect on the voice of developing countries in the third area of cooperation, by in essence creating a competition between the Western industrial nations and the Soviet Union to attract developing countries to their camp. This had, nonetheless, limited effects, particularly due to the absence of the communist camp from the BWIs.

The end of the Cold War reversed this situation by effectively dismantling the debates on the New International Economic Order (NIEO) and further marginalizing the United Nations from decision-making in relation to international *economic* policy. These effects in the economic field were the opposite of those in the area of peace and human rights, where the end of the Cold War actually increased international cooperation—albeit in an unstable way, as became apparent during the 2003 Iraq war. The centrality of the UN was also recognized in the post–Cold War era in the rich sequence of UN conferences and summits (see table 13.1), which enhanced the second area of global cooperation for development (furthering the development of societies). In the economic field, the UN kept a role as a forum for dialogue. A remarkable case in this regard was the March 2002 International Conference on Financing for Development, held in Monterrey, Mexico. But, as Toye and Toye (2004:280) have argued, this role is riddled with what they call "a twin-track system" by which

> The UN General Assembly provides a world forum where economic ideas, interests, and policy proposals are presented, discussed, and negotiated. Its authority is and can continue to be, a moral authority. . . . Once the process of UN discussion and negotiation produces agreements, however, their implementation is delegated to executive agencies in which the countries that will foot most of the subsequent bills place their confidence (see also Jolly et al. 2009; Ocampo 2010b).

The Nature, Scope, and Limits of Cooperation

In relation to the first form of cooperation (managing interdependence), it should be underscored that in the existing literature the concept of "global public goods" has been understood in a broader sense than the traditional definition of welfare economics—goods that are nonexcludable and nonrival in consumption—to include goods and services that have high externalities but whose benefits can be privately appropriated, as well as global or regionally shared commons (which are rivals in consumption). In this broad sense, it includes, among others, human knowledge, cultural diversity, the fight against international pandemics, environmental sustainability, the regulation of the use of global and regional commons, rules that regulate international economic transactions, world macroeconomic and financial stability, and, of course, international peace and justice (which is not a subject of this chapter).

However, as Kaul and Mendoza (2003) have emphasized, at least as important to the technical features of consumption, which is the feature captured in the concept of "public goods" in welfare economics, is the fact that they are "social constructs"—that is, that society itself defines what is in the "public domain." If this is the case, it is better to emphasize that which is the specific feature of this form of international cooperation—managing *interdependence* among nations—and use the concept of "public goods" to refer to issues that are or should be in the "public domain." This is in fact the way the concept is used in other fields of social sciences, as well as in law and politics. I will therefore use the concept of "global (or international) public good" to refer to all the areas that are recognized to be of "global (or international) public interest."

In this typology, the second area of cooperation, "furthering the development of societies," should be understood, as already noted, as enhancing the different dimensions of development that have been subject to UN conferences and summits. The principles and international goals agreed in these meetings represent, in a deep sense, the United Nations Development Agenda (United Nations 2007) as well as the "social dimensions of globalization," to use the terminology of the World Commission on the Social Dimension of Globalization (2004) convened by the ILO—an agenda that goes beyond the Millennium Development Goals (MDGs), the subset of issues from that broader agenda that attracted large attention since the UN Millennium Summit (United Nations 2000).

The story of the impact of the United Nation Development Agenda that has derived from global conferences and summits on national and international politics is one that is yet to be told in a truly cogent way and one that it is generally ignored in the analysis and existing typologies of global economic governance. Jolly et al. (2009), which represents the concluding volume of the UN Intellectual History Project, have emphasized that UN ideas, analysis, and policy recommendations in the economic and social field have been among the UN's greatest achievements and have had much greater success than usually acknowledged. The series of global conferences and summits is an essential part of the UN contribution in this realm. The political relevance of the issues that these conferences have addressed—from gender equality, to social inclusion and sustainable development—and the "peoples' rights" they have been advancing in these domains, add up to a contribution to the development of societies that is unparalleled. The influence that they have had on the political debate, nationally and internationally, and on the leadership that they have enabled the UN to play in shaping the global agenda (not only for development but also for democracy) is probably unmatched by any other area of the work of the UN or other international organizations. The conferences and summits have also been exercises of consensus building among the community of nations and possibly the most successful exercises of coordination of the UN system.

They have further been success stories of the partnership between the UN and global civil society. These accomplishments are characterized, however, by unfulfilled potential for lack of appropriate accountability mechanisms, an issue to which I return on several occasions in this chapter.

A crucial difference between the first and second realms of international cooperation is that, whereas in the first case countries have been willing to transfer or, better, *share* national sovereignty in the international organizations when it involves the management of interdependence, the nation-state continues to be the indisputable institution responsible for the development of societies. International agreements in this area are therefore confined to the definition of global principles and plans of action in the context of UN conferences and summits and the decisions of the UN General Assembly and ECOSOC, which generally lack clear accountability mechanisms. Only Europe has built broader frameworks, both in the context of the European Union and, in human rights, of the Council of Europe. The European Social Charter, signed by members of the Council in 1961 and revised in 1996, provides the only international framework in which citizens can judicially demand the fulfillment of the social rights guaranteed by the Charter. Although the UN human rights machinery and other regional bodies have some provisions in this area, their judicial scope is generally limited to violations of civil and political rights. The major way international cooperation influences citizens is, therefore, through the national adoption of international conventions, as well as through the influence of international principles and UN cooperation in helping shape national debates in the whole array of areas covered by UN conferences and summits and then reflected in national rules and policymaking. Global civil society has played a crucial role, not only in shaping the global agenda for the development of societies but also in helping push for its implementation throughout the world. It has been, in this sense, a double ally of the United Nations.

The third objective of global cooperation for development (overcoming world economic asymmetries) implies that, just as the redistributive action by the state is essential at the national level to ensure equality of opportunity, national efforts can fully succeed at the global level only if they are complemented by international cooperation designed at gradually overcoming the basic asymmetries of the global order. An issue that this third dimension of cooperation shares with the second is the fact that economic development is also recognized as the domain of the nation-state. International cooperation is confined to the creation of the network of Multilateral

Development Banks (MDBs), official development assistance (ODA), and technical cooperation by the MDBs, UN agencies, and regional and national institutions, and to the (increasingly weaker) "special and differential treatment" granted to developing countries in trade treaties.

The lack of fulfillment of ODA goals that have been agreed to since the 1960s within the framework of the United Nations has been a major failure in this realm of cooperation. A broader framework could be the creation of explicit redistributive mechanisms at the global level, similar to those that exist at the national level or the coherence funds of the European Union but that are absent in other international economic negotiations.[5] So in the long run, and given the sharp inequalities that characterize the global order, the fulfillment of the second and third objectives of international cooperation for development should lead to the creation of a true "global social cohesion fund" along the European model.

Given the essential national responsibility for social and economic development, an important issue that the second and third forms of cooperation share is the possible conflict between the agreements aimed at managing interdependence and the autonomy or "policy space" that nation-states have to further their social and economic development. I return to this issue in the following sections.

What also should be emphasized is that all areas of global cooperation for development face two major problems. The first is the huge gap between the growing recognition of global public goods, in the broader sense of the term, and the weakness of the existing international structures—decision-making, financing, and management—that guarantee that they are adequately supplied (Kaul et al. 1999, 2003). The second is the very uneven progress of international cooperation: Whereas it has advanced significantly in certain areas, there continues to be significant deficits in others, and it is entirely absent in still others that continue to be regarded as the strict domain of the nation-state. These gaps are present in areas that have been the subject of global attention in recent years—climate change and global macroeconomic and financial stability—but also others where there is a significant level of interdependence but that continue to be regarded as areas for the unrestricted exercise of national sovereignty. Most important among the latter are the issues of international migration and tax cooperation. In the case of migration, although there is a significant level of international cooperation on issues related to refugees and human trafficking, there is at best only an incipient process of cooperation on economic migration. In the case of taxation, there is a framework for cooperation among OECD countries and within the European Union (with significant gaps, as reflected in European debates on the issue), and the Group of 20 (G20) put this issue at the center of its attention in 2008. However, there is still only a weak framework for dialogue among the broader international community around the Group of Experts of International Cooperation on Tax Matters that is a part of the ECOSOC machinery.

World Economic Asymmetries

The growing historical disparities in the levels of development among countries indicate that, although domestic economic, social, and institutional factors are obviously important, economic opportunities are significantly affected by the position that countries occupy within the global hierarchy. Convergence of income levels was the exception rather than the rule in the nineteenth and twentieth centuries, following a pattern of "divergence, big time" to quote Pritchett (1997) or "dual divergence" (Ocampo and Parra 2007) if we capture the fact that there has also been divergence within the developing world. We have been experiencing a convergence since the early twenty-first century, but it is too soon to say whether this is a stable trend. What past historical patterns imply is that rising up on this international ladder is a difficult task due to fundamental asymmetries of the international economy—that is, with the fact that the global economy is *not* a "level playing field."

These asymmetries are of three kinds (Ocampo and Martin 2003). Two of them refer to structural features of the world economy whereas a third refers to a missing policy regime. The global agenda is, of course, full of other asymmetries, particularly associated with the uneven distribution of decision-making power among nations—what I have called the "original sin" of post-WWII arrangements, but I concentrate here on structural asymmetries in the functioning of the world economy.

The first asymmetry is associated with *the greater macroeconomic vulnerability of developing countries to external shocks*, which has tended to increase with the tighter integration of the world economy. The nature of this vulnerability has been changing in recent decades. Although the transmission of external shocks through trade remains important, financial shocks have played the most prominent role in recent decades, revisiting patterns that have been observed in the past, especially during the boom and financial collapse of the 1920s and 1930s.

In this area, macroeconomic asymmetries are associated with the segmentation that characterizes world financial markets and with the fact that international currencies are the currencies of the industrial countries. This segmentation is reflected in the sharp procyclical character of capital flows to developing countries—which, as the recent crisis has shown, have even been a feature of capital flows to the European periphery. Furthermore, whereas macroeconomic (and monetary, more than fiscal) policy tends to be countercyclical in industrial countries, in developing countries procyclical macroeconomic policies have tended to reinforce the capital account cycle.[6] The dominant response of developing countries to overcome these patterns has been to accumulate massive amounts of foreign exchange reserves in recent decades to gain some room during crises, a pattern that has come to be called "self-insurance" or "self-protection" (Ocampo 2010a). However, although this has helped developing countries weather much better the recent global financial crisis, this pattern by itself has demonstrated the nature of the asymmetry because industrial countries do not face a similar demand to increase their reserves to undertake countercyclical macroeconomic policies.

The second asymmetry is derived from the *high concentration of technical progress in the developed countries*. The diffusion of technical progress from the source countries to the rest of the world remains "relatively slow and uneven" according to Raúl Prebisch's (1950) classic predicament. This reflects the high and even prohibitive costs of entry into the more dynamic technological activities, including the obstacles that developing countries face in technologically mature sectors, where opportunities for most of them may be largely confined to attracting multinationals that control the technology and global production and distribution networks. In turn, technology transfer is subject to the payment of innovation rents, which have been rising due to the generalization and strengthening of intellectual property rights. The combined effect of these factors explains why, at the global level, the productive structure has exhibited a concentration of technical progress in the industrialized countries, which also maintain their dominant role as the headquarters of large transnational enterprises (though facing now an increasing number of multinationals from large emerging economies).

The third asymmetry is associated with the *contrast between the high mobility of capital and the restrictions on the international movement of labor*, particularly of unskilled labor.[7] This asymmetry is a characteristic of the present phase of globalization because it was not manifested in the nineteenth and early twentieth centuries (a period characterized by large mobility of capital and labor) nor in the first twenty-five years following World War II (a period in which both factors exhibited very little mobility). As has been pointed out by Rodrik (1997), the asymmetries in the international mobility of the factors of production generate biases in the distribution of income in favor of the more mobile factors (capital and skilled labor) and against the less mobile factors (less skilled labor) and, in turn, affect relations between developed and developing countries in as much as the latter have a relative abundance of less skilled labor.

Because of the strong trend toward international inequality generated by international asymmetries, "leveling the playing field" by regulatory means can facilitate trade, investment, and financial flows worldwide but may enhance divergence in income levels. In short, attempts to apply the same measures to different situations may only serve to heighten existing inequalities.

Since the creation in 1964 of the United Nations Conference on Trade and Development (UNCTAD),[8] the need to correct the asymmetries that characterized and continue to characterize the world economic system has been explicitly recognized. The commitments concerning the flow of ODA and "special and differential treatment" for developing countries in trade issues were some of the partial though relatively frustrating results of this effort to build a new international economic order in the 1960s and 1970s. This vision has been radically eroded in the last decades and has been replaced by an alternative paradigm according to which the basic objective of international economic cooperation should be to ensure a uniform set of rules—a "level playing field"—that facilitates the efficient functioning of market forces.

It is important to underline that, contrary to this trend, an area of new sustainable development principles was agreed to at the outset of the 1990s, notably principle 7 of the Declaration of the Conference on the Environment and Development that took place in Rio de Janeiro in 1992 (commonly known as the Earth Summit), relative to "common but differentiated responsibilities" of developed and developing countries in the international order.

In the new vision of the international economic system that emphasizes the need for a level playing field, the essential gains for the developing countries lie in the eventual dismantling of protection of "sensitive" sectors in industrialized countries, guarantees that export sectors derive from an international trading system with clear and stable rules, and the design of preventive macroeconomic policies that serve as self-protection against international financial volatility. The correction of the international asymmetries is only confined to the recognition of international responsibility toward least developed countries, replicating at an international level the vision of social policy as a strategy that focuses state activities on the poorest segments of the population.

However, as already pointed out, the application of the same measures in very different situations may aggravate existing inequalities. Moreover, leveling the playing field implies restrictions on the developing countries that the industrial countries themselves never faced in previous phases of their history. This includes international standards of intellectual property protection taken from those countries that generate technology rather than standards followed by countries that copied technology, as well as limitations on policy options for promoting new productive sectors for either the domestic or the external markets (Chang 2002; Rodrik 2007). Thus, the concept of "common but differentiated responsibilities" of the Rio Declaration and the already classic principle of "special and differential treatment" incorporated in the agenda of international trade negotiations are more appropriate guidelines for building a more equitable global order than leveling of the playing field.

These considerations lay down the essential elements that should guide international economic reform vis-à-vis the developing countries. The first of these asymmetries suggests that the essential function of the international financial institutions, from the perspective of the developing countries, is to adopt a comprehensive approach to reduce the segmentation and volatility of developing countries' access to international financial markets and to provide them room to maneuver in order to adopt countercyclical macroeconomic policies. This requires, in particular, adequate official financing during crises to smooth the required adjustment in the face of "sudden stops" of private external financing. An additional function, which is equally essential, is to make resources available to countries and to economic agents that have limited access to credit in international capital markets.

With respect to the second asymmetry, the multilateral trading system must facilitate the smooth transfer to developing countries of the production of primary commodities, technologically mature manufacturing activities, and standardized services. It should, therefore, avoid erecting obstacles to such transfers through protection or through subsidies. Moreover, this system must also accelerate developing countries' access to technology and ensure their increasing participation in the generation of technology and in the production of goods and services with high technological content. To facilitate these processes, the trading system should give adequate room for the adoption of active domestic productive strategies in developing countries.

Lastly, to overcome the third asymmetry, labor migration must be fully included in the international agenda through a globally agreed framework for migration policies, complemented with regional and bilateral frameworks and, particularly, with a strict protection of human and labor rights of migrants. Moreover, such agreements must envisage complementary mechanisms to facilitate migration, such as the recognition of educational, professional, and labor credentials; the transferability of social security benefits; and a low cost for transferring remittances.

A "development-friendly"—or, perhaps, following the typology I propose in this chapter, a developing-country–friendly—international system should start by overcoming the basic asymmetries of the global system, but it cannot ignore the fact that the responsibility for development resides in the first instance with the countries themselves. This has been reiterated in numerous international declarations, particularly in the "Monterrey Consensus" adopted by United Nations Conference on Financing for Development (United Nations 2002). This principle also responds to an old postulate of development literature: that institutional development, the creation of mechanisms of social cohesion, and the accumulation of human capital and technological capacities ("knowledge capital") are essentially *endogenous* processes. To use a term coined by Latin American structuralism, in all of these cases development can only come "from within" (Sunkel 1993). There are no universal models and there is, therefore, vast scope for institutional learning and diversity and, as we will see in this chapter, for the exercise of democracy.

However, the previous analysis implies that such a developing-country–friendly international system must provide enough room for the adoption of the development strategies that developing countries consider adequate to their economic circumstances—"policy space"—to use the term that has become familiar in recent years. Such policy space is particularly critical in the design of policies and strategies in three areas: (1) macroeconomic policies that reduce external vulnerability and facilitate productive investment; (2) active productive development strategies that facilitate the process of structural change that is inherent to economic development; and (3) ambitious social policies designed toward increasing equity and guaranteeing social inclusion.

Global Governance Structures

The Long Road to Better Global Governance

In the absence of suitable institutions that guarantee the capacity of the global system to fulfill the essential objectives of international cooperation for development, globalization is proving to be a highly disintegrative force, both at the international and at the national levels. This places an enormous demand on governance at all levels. There is now a broad consensus as to the decisive role played by national strategies and governance in determining how successful a country will be in forming strong links with the international community. However, without a suitable international framework, the insufficient supply of global public goods (in the broad sense of the term) and the inequality-generating forces spawned by the international asymmetries will hinder national development.

In any case, the road to better global economic governance is long and rocky because the main features of the present globalization and the resulting distributive tensions reflect the political economy of the world today. Indeed, the imbalance of the current globalization agenda reflects the greater influence exerted by the more powerful states and by the large multinational firms. It is also the result of the disorganization of other actors, particularly developing countries, in international debates. This behavior is linked not only to the weakening of historical mechanisms of collective action of the developing countries (such as the Group of 77) but also to the "policy competition" that globalization itself has created: the incentive for each country to show its attractiveness to investors in an era of capital mobility and greater susceptibility to relocation of production. An opposite development has been the rise of coalitions of emerging economies, such as the BRICS (the association of Brazil, Russia, India, China, and South Africa), which have already felt their influence in some processes, such as the reform of the governance of the BWIs.[9]

This situation is also affected by an element of politics and political economy: the resistance of the majority of countries to share their economic sovereignty in international organizations. Under the strong market forces that characterize globalization, the resulting weakening of the policy space of nation-states, and the unilateral liberalization processes simultaneously undertaken by countries, regulations of markets have weakened worldwide. Many analysts see this as progress, but it is also a source of distortion and, as the recent global financial crisis reflects, of serious risk.

In addition, although open regionalism is one of the traits of the current globalization process, and it has led to integration efforts in many regions of the developing world (such as in Latin America, Southeast Asia, and, more recently, Africa), these efforts have not resulted so far in strong coalitions among developing countries. In fact, the EU aside, countries are not ready to share their sovereignty in regional organizations—and even in the EU, they do so only in a limited way.

These characteristics of politics and political economy have had important consequences for international reform. The most obvious is that efforts toward substantial reform will continue to be weak. Furthermore, they have prevented a more balanced negotiation process, thus undermining or even ignoring the interests of some actors. Hence, the asymmetries in global power relations and the high cost of establishing international coalitions to compensate for them have taken on greater importance.

An additional implication of this analysis is that no international architecture will be neutral in terms of the balance of power in international relations. In this regard, an international system that depends exclusively on a few global institutions will be less balanced than a system that relies also on regional organizations. The positions of countries lacking power at the international level will improve if they actively participate in such regional schemes, as they offer these countries levels of autonomy and mutual assistance that countries would otherwise not be able to obtain in isolation.

The absence of a strong drive toward institution building at the international level implies that the institutions thus far created at the national level will not exist at the global level or that they will only have limited functions, thus reinforcing or only partly correcting existing gaps in global cooperation for development. Given the likelihood of incomplete international arrangements, countries—and particularly developing countries—should continue to claim autonomy in areas of critical importance, particularly in defining strategies of economic and social development and in preserving adequate policy space to implement them.

Furthermore, national autonomy in these areas is the only system consistent with the promotion of democracy at the global level. The tensions generated by the liberalization of market forces in an incomplete governance structure have weakened nation-states. The current system has thus kept the complex task of sustaining social cohesion and economic development in the hands of nation-states, but at the same time it has constrained their room for maneuver. Moreover, the necessary space required by democracy to foster diversity has been reduced as a result of the homogeneity pushed by the "policy competition" engendered by globalization and, in the case of developing countries, by the strong weight of conditionality in international financial assistance.

In this sense, the absence of a true internationalization of politics is the major gap and indeed paradox of the current globalization process. The strengthening of democracy has been coupled with adverse distributive trends, but national political institutions have been given reduced space to manage the tensions between these two processes. On the other hand, there are incipient instances of active global citizenship that take place in the form of struggles by global civil society, which has had a long history of struggle for human rights, social equity, gender equality, protection of the environment, and, more recently, globalization of solidarity and cultural diversity. But even if they have been able to translate several of these principles into global commitments through the sequence of UN conferences and summits, their capacity to make them effective still depends on the ability of global civil society to influence national political processes.

The major implication of this is that it is necessary to create democratic spaces of a global character. However, this process will necessarily be slow and incomplete, as the only experience of its kind (the European Union) indicates. Therefore, as long as the nation-state remains the main space for the expression of political citizenry, the promotion of democracy as a universal value will only make sense if national processes of representation and participation are allowed to determine economic and social development strategies and to mediate the tensions created by globalization.

The support for these processes, the respect for diversity, and the formulation of norms that would facilitate it are essential for an international democratic order. This means, therefore, that *the international order should be strongly respectful of diversity*, obviously within the limits of interdependence. It also implies that an essential function of international organizations is to support national strategies that contribute to reducing, through political citizenry, the strong tensions that exist today between the principle of equality and the functioning of globalized markets.

It is convenient to recall, in this regard, that successful multilateralism under the original Bretton Woods arrangement was precisely based on a judicious mix of international rules and cooperation, which provided sufficient degrees of freedom for national authorities to pursue their macroeconomic policies aimed at full employment and growth, as well as, in the case of middle- and low-income countries, their development goals.

It was based on strong and effective national authorities, not on weak ones. In this light, the current mix of incomplete international arrangements and weakened national policy effectiveness must be seen as the most inappropriate of all possible mixes.

Five Major Challenges in Global Economic and Social Governance

A major implication of the foregoing analysis is that the effort at building strong institutions for a better global order should be based on a *dense network of world, regional, and national institutions*, rather than being limited to a few global international organizations. National (and, we could add, local) institutions are crucial here as they are the space for political citizenship. Action at the regional (and subregional) level plays, in turn, a critical role as a midway point between the global and national orders for four main reasons: (1) the complementarities between global and regional institutions in a heterogeneous international community; (2) the unequal size of the actors involved in global processes, which means that the voice of smaller countries will be better heard if expressed as a regional voice; (3) the greater sense of ownership of regional and subregional institutions; and (4) the fact that the scope for effective economic policy space has shifted in some areas (e.g., macroeconomic and regulatory policies) from the national arena to subregional or regional levels.

Thus a system that relies on networks of global and regional institutions is both more efficient and more balanced in terms of power relations. The international order should, therefore, offer ample room for the functioning of strong regional institutions respectful of a rules-based global order—in other words, a system of "open regionalism." Indeed, building a strong network of regional institutions may be the best way to gradually build a better international order.

The second major challenge in restructuring global governance, and one that is broadly recognized today, is the need to ensure *equitable participation of developing countries in global governance*—that is, to finally overcome the "original sin" of the governance structures created in the aftermath of World War II. The multipolar world that may be forming, in which some formerly developing countries become major powers, may be more conducive to this result than the bipolar or unipolar worlds that dominated the post-WWII period, but this is not guaranteed, as reflected in at least three different processes: (1) the hard and inconclusive debate on "voice and representation" of developing countries in international economic decision-making launched by the Monterrey Consensus, which has led to very limited advance so far in the IMF and the World Bank; (2) the continuous marginalization of the United Nations from global economic decision-making by major industrial countries, as reflected, for example, in the limited importance given to the follow-up of the Monterrey Conference or in the effective sidetracking of the United Nations in crucial areas of cooperation with developing countries (e.g., in the debate on aid effectiveness); and (3) the revealed preference by industrial countries for ad hoc "Gs" over which they can exercise greater influence (either the G7 or now possibly the G20) and perhaps even the preference of some major developing countries for such arrangements. This is reflected, particularly but not exclusively, in the decision at the September 2009 meeting by the leaders of the G20 to designate that body "the premier forum for our international economic cooperation" (G20, Preamble, paragraph 19).

The preference for "Gs" over global institutions reflects a third challenge: the *need to overcome the tension between inclusiveness and the legitimacy associated with it, on the one hand, and existing power structures, on the other.* The latter issue is sometimes expressed as the need for "effectiveness," but this is clearly a wrong way to pose it because national democratic processes indicate that inclusive institutions can be effective. At the international level, the United Nations could be equally effective as the BWIs—whose effectiveness has been subject, in any case, to much debate.

In this way, although Gs can play an important role in placing new issues on the agenda and in facilitating consensus, no structure of governance can generate legitimacy as long as decision-making processes are not inclusive and thus give adequate voice to industrial and developing countries, and to large and small countries. The governance system must therefore be based on *representative institutions,* not on ad hoc grouping of countries. For this reason, the United Nations should be the center of any global institutional structure, given its character as the most representative global institution—with the exception of the UN Security Council, which still reflects the inheritance of colonial arrangements and the bipolar world. It is no accident, therefore, that global conferences and summits have always taken place in the framework of the United Nations. But the lack of trust by major powers in the United Nations has led at the same time to the weak accountability for commitments made in these processes and to limiting the executing capacity of the United Nations system while reinforcing that of the institutions over which industrial countries have greater influence. To illustrate by drawing parallels to national processes, the United Nations is respected as a parliament, but its legal provisions are not meant to be binding nor are the most powerful countries willing to place a great deal of executive power in organizations that depend upon such a parliament.

There have been several attempts at resolving the tension between representation and power structures. In the BWIs, this has been solved by weighted vote and a constituency system. This mix is probably the best way to solve this tension because it allows the most powerful countries to sit at the table while guaranteeing the representation of all countries through their constituency. This obviously works well only if the system of weighted votes reflects current rather than past realities, a condition that the BWIs do not meet today. An alternative route to follow is that of the WTO, which operates on the principle of consensus. However, although formally built upon this principle, decision-making in this institution effectively works through "green rooms" that lack clear rules of representation and it includes a significant amount of arms twisting. It is built, therefore, on a system of formal democracy but operates as an informal oligarchy, to use Evans's (2003) characterization.

Any arrangement must therefore aim at the advantages of inclusiveness that the United Nations incarnates but should also reflect power structures. I return to this issue later in this chapter. It must be emphasized that any arrangement of this sort should meet additional requirements. It requires an effort by smaller countries to organize themselves within the framework of regional and subregional institutions. But it also requires appropriate rules of governance that guarantee a voice for and basic rights of smaller countries. This requires institutionalizing accountability and strengthening auditing functions carried out by institutions that enjoy credibility with all relevant actors, particularly by smaller countries. This approach should include special mechanisms for small countries to voice what they consider abuses by the staff of international institutions, mechanisms to institutionally correct such abuses, and, crucially, to limit the power of the countries having the most influence over international institutions. However, this is not necessarily to the detriment of larger countries because it will also lead to a greater commitment by smaller countries to the global institutional order. Large countries have, in any case, strong voice and influence on decision-making.

The fourth challenge, and that which has been a subject of broader debate, is the challenge of *coherence*, the major issue of attention in UN reform in recent years but also one of the central recommendations of the Commission of the Social Dimensions of Globalization (2004) and of proposals aimed at the creation of better mechanisms of international cooperation in the economic and social field through the creation of an Economic (or Economic and Social) Security Council (Commission on Global Governance 1995; Dervis 2005; Jolly et al. 2009).

The problems lie in different areas. Some of them are related to the institutional design by which the major multilateral financial and trade institutions are totally autonomous, regardless of whether they are formally specialized UN agencies (the BWIs) or not (WTO). To that feature, we should add the decentralized—and even fragmented—structure that characterized the design of the UN system since its conception in the aftermath of World War II. Existing mechanisms of coordination include the Chief Executive Board of the UN system (CEB). The CEB includes the BWIs and WTO and serves as an instrument of information sharing and of some coordination. However, despite its mandate, it lacks—as does its head, the UN Secretary-General—effective coordination powers. As pointed out in the first part of this chapter, the Economic and Social Council (ECOSOC) was also endowed by the UN Charter with some responsibilities to coordinate the UN funds and programs and specialized agencies. However, these powers are weakly exercised vis-à-vis the first group (except for the capacity to designate the boards) and almost entirely ignored in relation to the second. Although this lack of coordination may have introduced more pluralism in the international debate and policy advice on economic and social issues—which has been healthy in the era of market fundamentalism—it has also generated incoherence in the system.

These problems can only be solved by creating a true global economic and social governance mechanism. This is the reason behind the proposals to create an Economic and Social Security Council; by dropping the word "Security," it can perhaps be renamed Global Sustainable Development Council,[10] to emphasize that its scope should be the three dimensions of sustainable development: economic, social, and environmental. The legitimacy of this Council requires that it be attached to the United Nations. However, weighting voting and constituency formation is desirable to reflect existing power structures, a condition without which major countries will be unwilling to use that body for international economic decision-making. The Council would meet at the heads-of-state level once a year, during the meetings of the General Assembly. In this sense, it could be seen as an institutionalized G20, though its members may not be exactly the same and, in any case, most of them would represent the constituency that elects them to be members, not their own country. In this sense, the G20 should be seen as a very positive step to the extent that it represents a transition to a more legitimate body, but it can also become an obstacle to achieving this objective. A regular institutional structure would have to be put in place to guarantee that decision-making by heads of state is effective and, therefore, to establish regular links with the major organizations that are in charge of executing them.

The particular nature of the relations between this Council and the governing bodies of the BWIs and WTO must be subject to careful design. In this regard, the best way would be to think of it as governing the UN *system* and not the UN *Organization*, so that the Bretton Woods Institutions are clearly included and do not see themselves in the proposed arrangement as being *under* the UN but as being *part* of it. (As mentioned throughout this chapter, they are formally specialized agencies of the UN system but rarely recognize themselves as such.) A similar arrangement could be adopted in relation to the WTO, by formally including it in the UN system, since it is not part of it today. A proposal along these lines has been made by the Commission of Experts of the President of the UN General Assembly on Reforms of the International Monetary and Financial System (United Nations 2009:chapter 4), which suggested the creation of a Global Economic Coordination Council based on a constituency system, which would be served by five organizations: the United Nations, ILO, IMF, World Bank, and WTO.[11]

Such reform would obviously go beyond the current ECOSOC. But a reform of ECOSOC should continue along the lines that followed the 2005 UN Summit by establishing three strong functions: (1) a more effective and integrated follow-up to UN conferences and summits; (2) an effective coordination of the UN funds and programs and specialized agencies, as mandated by the UN Charter; and (3) a specific mandate to look at major gaps in the current global economic and social governance. Note that this reform is incremental, along the lines of the recommendations by Rosenthal (2005), but it is not inconsistent and could thus be parallel to the creation of the Global Sustainable Development Council (or the Global Economic Coordination Council). Indeed, because the current ECOSOC is a *system* made up of functional and regional commissions, which attract a large participation of civil society, it would be a great mistake to subsume the current ECOSOC under the proposed Global Council. The latter should rather aim specifically at the "coherence" of the global system, by effectively bringing the BWIs and WTO under the broader UN umbrella.

The final challenge is to design *effective systems of surveillance and accountability for international commitments*. The IMF and WTO have well-developed surveillance mechanisms, in which the commitments made by countries are subject to periodic review, through the Article IV consultations and the Trade Policy Reviews, respectively. The WTO also has a well-functioning dispute settlement mechanism. Indeed, trade and investment are the only cases in which there are formal dispute settlement mechanisms in place. In the case of investment, existing mechanisms include the World Bank's Multilateral Investment Guarantee Agency (MIGA) and the provisions included in bilateral and plurilateral free trade and in investment agreements. OECD has a peer review process. This form of accountability was also introduced when the UN Human Rights Commission was transformed into the Human Rights Council in 2006 and has been practiced by the African Union. However the commitments made by countries in the UN conferences and summits, including the commitments on ODA, have no surveillance or accountability mechanism of any sort, and the decisions of ECOSOC and its functional commissions have no binding power.

In terms of the typology developed in the first part of this chapter, there are some accountability and dispute mechanisms in place to manage some areas of interdependence, but even in this area accountability is limited, as reflected in the failure to meet the commitments made under the Kyoto Protocol or in the very weak influence that IMF Article IV consultations have on major industrial countries. In the second and third areas of cooperation (development of society and overcoming asymmetries of the global order), there are essentially no accountability mechanisms in place. The broad lack of accountability—and even further, enforceability—for international commitments represents, no doubt, one of the major deficiencies of current arrangements.

Stronger accountability mechanisms should, therefore, be put in place in all areas. In the case of UN conferences and summits, for example, the system could be based on compulsory national evaluations of the fulfillment of those commitments, which could be undertaken by countries themselves or by the UN agencies. National parliaments should play an essential role in the evaluations process, as well as organized civil society. A process of this type would contribute to creating a *national* culture of responsibility for meeting *international* objectives and commitments and adjusting domestic public policies accordingly. It would help, in short, to build strong political accountability for international commitments at the *national* level.

The political visibility and the mechanism designed to evaluate progress toward the MDGs represent major progress in this regard. It would be important to build on this experience and to create new and broader mechanisms that would eventually lead to an integrated evaluation covering the development goals agreed through UN conferences and summits as well as a covenant of economic, social, and cultural rights and of other internationally agreed social rights (e.g., ILO's Fundamental Principles and Rights at Work and the agreed rights of children, women, and ethnic groups, among others).

This process can be transformed into a system of peer reviews in relevant UN fora. This principle was accepted in the 2006 reform of ECOSOC, though only on a voluntary basis. ECOSOC and its system of functional commissions can play an active role in the review of how the commitments made have been met by member states. Obviously, the commitments made and the accountability mechanism designed must be commensurate with each country's level of development. Also, given the sharp inequalities that characterize the global order, this should be accompanied by ODA aimed at supporting the poorest countries in meeting agreed international goals. In the long run, as indicated earlier, this should be based on the design of a true "global social cohesion fund" along the European model.

Conclusions

This chapter proposes a new typology of global cooperation for development, based on three essential objectives: managing interdependence, furthering the development of societies, and gradually overcoming the asymmetries that characterize the world economic system. The lack of clear recognition of the second area of cooperation is seen as a basic deficiency of current typologies, which generally ignore it despite the central role it plays in the global agenda, notably in the sequence of the UN conferences and summits. The typology also recognized the dual meaning that the concept of "development" has, in the global discourse, to mean cooperation with developing countries and furthering certain norms and standards for societies in the developing and developed countries alike. Given this broader set of identified objectives, the chapter also proposes that the concept of "global public goods" be used in a broader sense than is typical of the existing literature, to focus on all objectives of global cooperation for development.

In relation to the third of these objectives, it also proposes a triad of major asymmetries in the structure of the global economy: the greater macroeconomic vulnerability of developing countries to external shocks, high concentration of technical progress in the developed countries, and the relatively slow and uneven process by which it is disseminated throughout the world, and the asymmetries generated by the contrast between the high mobility of capital and the restrictions on the international movement of labor. Given these asymmetries, it proposed that the concept of "leveling the playing field" through a uniform set of rules could enhance inequalities. It proposed, therefore, that the concept of "special but differentiated responsibilities" offers a much better framework for handling the special issues of developing countries in the global order.

Finally and in light of the revealed reluctance by nation-states to share national sovereignty through international organizations (even regional ones), the chapter presents a five-point agenda for improving global economic and social governance structures. This agenda includes: (1) a dense network of world, regional, and national institutions, rather than a system based on one or a few international organizations; (2) the need to ensure equitable participation of developing countries in global governance; (3) the need to overcome the tension between inclusiveness and the legitimacy associated with it, on the one hand, and existing power structures, on the other; it argues that this can only by guaranteed by the creation of a true global economic and social governance mechanism for the UN *system*, which includes the BWIs and should include the WTO, in which all countries participate based on a constituency system; (4) the challenge of "coherence" of a decentralized global governance structure in the economic and social field; and (5) effective systems of accountability for international commitments, based on highly visible national evaluations and international peer reviews to advance toward meeting such commitments.

Notes

1. I build here upon Ocampo and Martin (2003), but the terminology differs somewhat from my earlier work.

2. They included the International Telegraphic Union, later transformed into the Telecommunications Union (ITU), the General (now Universal) Postal Union (UPU), the United International Bureau for the Protection of Intellectual Property (now WIPO), the International Sanitary Bureau that led to Pan-American Health Organization (PAHO, now also regional office of the WHO for the Americas), and the Office International d'Hygènie Publique. The International Institute of Agriculture (the precursor of the Food and Agricultural Organization, or FAO) was also created in 1905 largely to share information on rural issues among its members.

3. The creation of the Bank for International Settlements in 1930 may be seen also as a step in that direction, though its initial focus was on how to facilitate German reparation payments imposed by the Treaty of Versailles. It became a major mechanism of cooperation among central banks, which included financing to countries facing payments problems (starting with Austria and Germany in the early 1930s). However, its major role as a mechanism of international cooperation came in the post-WWII period.

4. The initiatives included renegotiations of external debts, lending through the Export-Import Bank and the Inter-American Coffee Agreement, as well as an initiative to create an Inter-American Development Bank, which, however, only became a reality much later.

5. The free trade agreements between industrial and developing countries are important cases in this regard. See Bustillo and Ocampo (2004), where we contrast the lack of consideration of this issue in the now defunct Free Trade of the Americas negotiations with the arrangements in the European Union as well as in United States–Puerto Rican cooperation.

6. See Stiglitz et al. (2006). See also Kamisky et al. (2004), who call this feature of developing countries the "when-it-rains-it-pours syndrome."

7. See an extensive analysis of this issue in United Nations (2004).

8. See, for example, the first report of the Secretary-General of UNCTAD (Prebisch 1964).

9. We could add the rise of new groupings of developing countries that cross regions and are active in specific international negotiations, such as the G20 led by Brazil in WTO, and the coalition of Least Developed Countries (LDCs) and Small Island Developing States (SIDS).

10. Please note that this is a different proposal than that of creating a Council of Sustainable Development to replace the ECOSOC Commission with the same name that was proposed during the 2012 negotiations leading to Rio+20, and which would have a more limited scope.

11. See also Ocampo and Stiglitz (2011), who contrast the proposed Council with the G20.

References

Barrett, S., 2007, *Why Cooperate? The Incentive to Supply Global Public Goods*, New York: Oxford University Press.

Bustillo, I. and J. A. Ocampo, 2004, "Asymmetries and Cooperation in the FTAA," in *Integrating the Americas: FTAA and Beyond*, edited by A. Estevadeordal et al., 723–753. Cambridge, Mass.: The David Rockefeller Center Series on Latin American Studies, Harvard University.

Chang, H., 2002, *Kicking Away the Ladder: Development Strategy in Historical Perspective*, London: Anthem.

Commission on Global Governance, 1995, *Our Global Neighborhood*, New York: Oxford University Press.

Dervis, K., 2005, *A Better Globalization, Legitimacy, Governance and Reform*, Washington, D.C.: Brookings Institution Press for the Center for Global Development.

Evans, P., 2003, "Economic Governance Institutions in a Global, Political Economy: Implications for Developing Countries," in *Trade and Development: Directions for the 21st Century*, edited by J. Toye, 288–307. Cheltenham, UK: Edward Elgar.

Group of 20, G20, 2009, *Leaders' Statement, The Pittsburgh Summit*, September 24–25.

Helleiner, G. K., 2009, "The Development Mandate of International Institutions: Where Did it Come From?," *Studies in Comparative International Development*, 44:189–212.

International Task Force on Global Public Goods, 2006, "Meeting Global Challenges: International Cooperation and the National Interest," final report, Stockholm.

Jolly, R., L. Emmerij, and T. Weiss, 2009, *UN Ideas that Changed the World*, Bloomington and Indianapolis: Indiana University Press.

Kaminsky, G. L., C. M. Reinhart, and C. A. Végh, 2004, "When It Rains, It Pours: Procyclical Capital Flows and Macroeconomic Policies," *NBER Working Paper Series*, No. 10780, September.

Kaul, I., I. Grunberg, and M. Storm, eds., 1999, *Global Public Goods: International Cooperation in the 21st Century*, New York: Oxford University Press.

Kaul, I., P. Conceição, K. Le Goulven, and R. U. Mendoza, eds., 2003, *Providing Global Public Goods: Managing Globalization*, New York: Oxford University Press.

Kaul, I. and R. U. Mendoza, 2003, "Advancing the Concept of Global Public Goods," in *Providing Global Public Goods: Managing Globalization*, edited by I. Kaul, et al., 78–111. New York: Oxford University Press.

Mangone, G. J., 1954, *A Short History of International Organization*, New York: McGraw Hill.

Marshall, T. H., 1992, "Citizenship and Social Class," in *Citizenship and Social Class*, edited by T. H. Marshall and Tom Bottomore. London: Pluto.

Ocampo, J. A., 2010a, "Reforming the Global Reserve System," in *Time for a Visible Hand: Lessons from the 2008 World Financial Crisis*, edited by S. Griffith-Jones, J. Antonio Ocampo, and J. E. Stiglitz, 289–313. Oxford, UK: Oxford University Press.

———, 2010b, "The United Nations and Global Finance," in *Annual Review of United Nations Affairs 2009/2010*, Vol. 1, edited by J. Mueller and K. P. Sauvant, xxxi–xlv. New York: Oxford University Press.

Ocampo, J. A. and J. Martin, 2003, *Globalization and Development: A Latin American and Caribbean Perspective*, Palo Alto: Stanford University Press and ECLAC.

Ocampo, J. A. and M. Parra, 2007, "The Dual Divergence: Growth Successes and Collapses in the Developing World Since 1980," in *Economic Growth with Equity: Challenges for Latin America*, edited by R. French-Davis and J. L. Machinea, 61–92. Houndmills, Hampshire, UK: Palgrave Macmillan and ECLAC.

Ocampo, J. A. and J. E. Stiglitz, 2011, "From the G-20 to a Global Economic Coordination Council," *Journal of Globalization and Development*, 2(2): Article 9.

Prebisch, R., 1950, "Crecimiento, desequilibrio y disparidades: interpretación del proceso de desarrollo," in *Estudio Económico de América Latina 1949*, New York: United Nations.

———, 1964, *Nueva política comercial para el desarrollo*, Mexico: Fondo de Cultura Económica.

Pritchett, L., 1997, "Divergence, Big Time," *Journal of Economic Perspectives*, 2:3–18.

Rodgers, G., E. Lee, L. Swepston, and J. Van Daele, 2009, *The ILO and the Quest for Social Justice, 1919–2009*, Geneva: International Labor Office.

Rodrik, D., 1997, *Has Globalization Gone Too Far?*, Washington, D.C.: Institute for Internacional Economics (IIE).

———, 2007, *One Economics, Many Recipes: Globalization, Institutions, and Economic Growth*, Princeton: Princeton University Press.

Rosenthal, G., 2005, "The Economic and Social Council of the United Nations: An Issues Paper," New York: Friedrich Ebert Stiftung, Dialogue on Globalization, No. 15, February.

———, 2007, "The Economic and Social Council of the United Nations," in *The Oxford Handbook on the United Nations*, edited by T. G. Weiss and S. Daws, 136–148. New York: Oxford University Press.

Stiglitz, J. E., J. A. Ocampo, R. Spiegel, R. French-Davis, and D. Nayyar, 2006, *Stability with Growth: Macroeconomics, Liberalization, and Development*, New York: Oxford University Press.

Sunkel, O., ed., 1993, *Development from Within: Toward a new Neostructuralist Approach for Latin America*, Boulder: Lynne Rienner.

Toye, J. and R. Toye, 2004, *The UN and Global Political Economy: Trade, Finance, and Development*, Bloomington and Indianapolis: Indiana University Press.

United Nations, 2000, *The Millennium Declaration*, New York: General Assembly, Millennium Summit.

———, 2002, *The Monterrey Consensus*, International Conference on Financing for Development, Monterrey, México.

———, 2004, *World Economic and Social Survey 2004: International Migration*, New York.

———, 2007, *The United Nations Development Agenda: Development for All*, New York, ST/ESA/316.

———, 2009, *Report of the Commission of Experts of the President of the UN General Assembly on Reforms of the International Monetary and Financial System*, New York.

World Commission on the Social Dimension of Globalization, 2004, *A Fair Globalization: Creating Opportunities for All*, Geneva: International Labor Organization.

14

The G20 and Global Governance

NGAIRE WOODS

Introduction

The G20 leaders group seems a solution to global governance problems. Called to meet together in the wake of the collapse of Lehman Brothers in 2008, the group was able to convene rapidly. An agenda was quickly formulated. A work plan was announced. Averted were the excruciating slowness and dissent that characterize most international negotiations. This led some to herald the arrival of a new and better form of global governance (Helleiner and Pagliari 2009; Garrett 2010; Dewatripont, Freixas, and Portes 2011).

By 2010, the G20 leaders were still meeting regularly, but their initial momentum had slowed. Dissent marked the Toronto Summit in June 2010. Heroic efforts were made to find and express limited agreement in Seoul in November 2010. In one view, the waning of the G20 signaled the need to strengthen the organization, such as by institutionalizing its processes and developing a secretariat for it. France has already announced it would take this up during its presidency of the G20 in 2011 (Sarkozy 2010). A different, more critical view argues that the waning of the G20 is a good thing. They highlight that some 175 or so countries are not in the G20 and that it lacks legitimacy; global governance should take place through more traditional and representative forms of multilateral governance such as the United Nations (Payne 2010; Shorr and Wright 2010; Ocampo chapter 13, this volume).

Enthusiasts and critics of the G20 are united in their characterization of the leaders group as an incipient institution of global governance. This chapter presents a different view. First, I probe the origins of the G20 and use evidence from the earlier G20 finance minister's group to examine whether the G20 has broadened or narrowed agenda-setting in global governance. Second, I examine how the representativeness of the G20 might be expanded in an innovative way. Finally, I return to the question of whether the G20 needs to be more representative, arguing that a closer investigation of its role suggests it could be more responsive but need not necessarily be more representative.

The G20 and Global Governance: A Broadening or Narrowing of Inclusion?

The original G20 grouping was born of an attempt to make the governance of a previous financial crisis more inclusive. In 1997, a financial crisis began in Thailand and soon spilled over to become a regional and international crisis. The world's then "economic crisis committee"—the G7 finance ministers group—swung into action to coordinate the response of major industrialized economies. For at least two decades, the G7 finance ministers group had been playing this role, coordinating instructions to the IMF and others. But in 1997, the challenge they faced was more political in nature than they had ever faced before. East Asian countries were furious about the way in which the IMF (with the United States standing behind it) responded to the crisis (Blustein 2002). Japan proposed that the region should create its own Asian Monetary Fund (AMF). Commentators across the world wrote of the IMF having lost legitimacy.

In 1999, the G20 (as it would become known) was formed as a new "more inclusive and representative forum" for informal dialogue.[1] Non-G7 countries whose size or strategic importance gives them a particularly crucial role in the global economy were invited. South Korea and Indonesia (countries particularly aggrieved about the IMF's response to the crisis) were included. The exercise successfully headed off an Asian withdrawal from international negotiations led by North America and Europe.

In 2008, there was an even stronger argument for including emerging economies in negotiations to manage the crisis. Leaders of industrialized countries knew they needed collectively to stimulate domestic demand and not to use protectionism. Without the cooperation of China, India, Brazil, and others, the G7 countries would have been attempting to row against a tide that would have overwhelmed them. Media reactions to the G20 focused on its inclusiveness. For example, *The Jakarta Post* reported on April 3, 2009, "During the November 2008 Summit in Washington D.C., the leaders of advanced economies stood on an equal footing with their emerging nations' counterparts addressing the global economic and financial issues candidly." *Al Jazeera* reported on November 15, 2008, "We have seen for the first time under one roof . . . 20 of the key economic nations in the world. The crucial thing is that the emerging markets—the developing nations—are at the table as well."

Does a seat at the table actually give emerging economies a voice? Did creating a G20 alongside the G7 have any impact on decision-making, and how might this be ascertained? Two studies of the G20 probe this question (Martinez-Diaz and Woods 2009). In its early years, the G20 was a forum for consensus-building in crisis management. It forged consensus on a framework for debt restructuring (collective action clauses and voluntary standards) and on the need for IMF quota reform (Rubio-Marquez 2009). That said, an analysis of the outcomes of the G20 contrasted with those of the G7 reveals that there was little difference. During its early years, the formal statements of the G20 echoed those of the G7. Consensus-building may well have been a one-way street, with the G7 using the G20 to bind emerging economies into their own decisions.

The work of the G20 finance ministers' group became more distinctive over time with the group's positions and agenda diverging more noticeably from those of the G7 (Martinez-Diaz 2009). Equally, however, the group's agenda became less pressing. What lessons might we draw from this? The G20 was an early recognition of a shift in global economic power. After the East Asian crisis of 1997, its establishment was a vital political step to avoid an emerging economy withdrawal from international institutions led by North America and Europe. The G20 finance created a blueprint for a grouping through which to broaden participation. It may not have given emerging economies a voice in its early years, but it provided a powerful training ground for them to prepare for their participation in governance after 2008.

What has occurred in the G20 leader's group? Has the inclusion of emerging economies made a difference? There are two ways we can examine this: by analyzing and comparing the communiqués of the G8 (without emerging economies) and G20 and by examining outcomes on key issues.

By comparing G8 and G20 communiqués we can see that the G20 has become a more powerful group. There is a reversal of the previous trend cited with respect to the G7 and G20 finance ministers. Previously, G20 finance ministers seemed to be rubber-stamping G7 decisions or, as the years passed, debating broader issues. Now, the G8 leaders seem to be rubber-stamping G20 leaders' decisions, except where they debate broader issues. For example, much of the Chair's text from the 2009 G8 L'Aquila summit merely reaffirms commitments made by the G20 in London (Chair's Summary, L'Aquila 2009). The G8 communiqués of 2010 are mostly devoted to statements about foreign policy and security, including development (especially in sub-Saharan Africa), environmental sustainability, and international peace and security.

Are emerging economies within the G20 influencing outcomes? In substance, the G20 has addressed four sets of issues: (1) growth (including trade, fiscal and monetary stimulus, and exchange rates); (2) financial regulation; (3) development; and (4) institutional reform. The record of specific emerging economy influence is perhaps clearest in the latter.

On the issues of growth, the G20 is in disarray among industrialized countries, which makes the impact of emerging economies difficult to measure. There is disagreement between the United States and Europe over whether to promote stimulus or austerity, with Europeans pushing the latter since the eurozone crisis began in Greece in 2010. There is disagreement over exchange rates, most publicly between the United States and China, but all members are involved. And there is considerable ire among emerging economies over quantitative easing that pumps up the U.S. money supply, pushing down the value of the dollar, making yields on U.S. Treasury bonds less attractive, and thereby encouraging investors to speculate in emerging economies and other markets, increasing inflationary pressures and putting emerging economies under considerable additional strain. There is no agreement on these issues, although it is conceivable that without the emerging economies, the G7 might have called upon China to revalue its currency.

On financial regulation, the G20 created the Financial Stability Board and called on it and other organizations (including the IMF and the Basel Committee on Banking Supervision) to bring forward proposals to deal with capital adequacy, liquidity, international compensation standards, over-the-counter derivatives markets, systemically important financial institutions, and (further down the road) shadow banking. Progress has been slow, as the *Financial Times* reported on April 2 and 3, 2009. Members of the Basel Committee have subsequently reflected that the presence of China, India, and Brazil in the G20 has decreased backsliding that might have occurred as some G7 members encountered opposition to regulation by their powerful global financial sectors. That said, emerging economies have argued for a nationally differentiated approach rather than for a global regulator.

On development, emerging economies have left less of a mark on G20 decisions, in spite of South Korea's efforts, as Chair of the group in 2010, to push the issue to the top of the agenda and to bring a more specifically emerging economy focus to the fore.

On institutional reform, the G20 has continued a series of incremental changes to voting power that had already been underway in the IMF. The presence of emerging economies within the G20 has doubtless kept that process moving forward at a less than glacial pace. It has also provided a forum for emerging economies to coordinate their own positions and enable them to bargain harder for changes. This has been most obvious in the negotiations on new arrangements to borrow the credit-lines offered by a group of countries to the IMF thereby permitting it to lend more if necessary (and if the group of creditor countries agrees). In the aftermath of the eurozone crisis, emerging economies were reluctant to extend credit lines if they did not have a significant voice as to when the credit lines could be activated. After robust negotiations, China, Brazil, Russia, and India succeeded in pushing for an arrangement by which the four of them could collectively veto the activation of the credit lines (Woods 2010). Subsequently, a full governance reform package was negotiated but still awaits U.S. consent, without which it cannot come into force (IMF 2012).

Overall the inclusion of emerging economies has given some voice to them in shaping the response to the crisis and in shaping the ongoing reform of institutions that are making and implementing rules in the wake of the crisis. This suggests that expanding representation in the G20 could be worthwhile.

Might Representation in the G20 Be Expanded Innovatively?

Since its inception, the G20 has been criticized as insufficiently representative. At the Pittsburgh Summit in September 2009, when the G20 designated itself as "the premier forum for our international cooperation," annoyance was expressed by smaller emerging markets not in the G20 club, such as Thailand and Chile ("Cosmetic Surgery" 2009). A sensitivity about this issue led Canadian hosts in 2010 to invite a wider participation of non-G20 countries to the Toronto Summit, including Algeria, Colombia, Egypt, Ethiopia (NEPAD), Haiti, Jamaica, Malawi (African Union), the Netherlands, Nigeria, Senegal, Spain, and Vietnam (ASEAN).

Scholars have argued that the G20 lacks legitimacy due to its structure (or lack thereof) (Payne 2010; Shorr and Wright 2010). Simply put, it permits some 20 or so governments to make decisions that affect some 175 or so other countries and their governments. Furthermore, the argument runs, decisions are made without the input or information from other governments and without reporting back to non-G20 countries. By instructing international organizations (such as the IMF) to do things, the G20 informally bypasses the properly constituted decision-making process of that organization. These arguments are worth exploring. Let me start with what the G20 does (or not).

Some have proposed constituting a G20 along regional lines. The political problem lies in who would represent each region or subregion and how this might be achieved without appearing to most countries as a way of cementing the position of a regional hegemon. Using existing regional organizations to represent a full diversity of countries at the global level might overcome this. However, regional organizations acquire an agenda of their own and are perceived as too distant from governments. Rotating representation from a region or subregion around all of its members has the disadvantage of losing knowledge and information at each rotation.

An alternative is to use less formal representation of groups of countries to collate information and report on formal processes. One example is the IMF constituency structure. It may seem perverse to examine the IMF in this regard because the institution has long been perceived as inadequately representing developing countries and being inadequately responsive to them. However, buried within the workings of the IMF (which includes several features that inhibit adequate representation) is a system of representing groups of countries so as to ensure that their priorities, stakes, and views are heard by the governing body (executive board) of the institution.

The IMF has 185 members and is governed by an executive board comprising 24 directors, chaired by the managing director. The five largest members of the IMF (the United States, Japan, Germany, France, and the United Kingdom) each appoint their own director, although the G20 have agreed to shift to a system whereby all directors are elected. A further three members each also enjoy their own seat: China, Russia, and Saudi Arabia. All other members have gravitated into groupings or "constituencies" of countries that each elect a director to represent them. These constituencies vary in size. Although each country has an individual share of votes relative to its economic size, the constituency director wields the collective vote of all of his or her members.

Several lessons can be drawn from the workings of the IMF constituencies: I draw these from a study I completed in 2006 (with Domenico Lombardi). Several conditions emerged as important for ensuring the effective representation of countries in a constituency (Woods and Lombardi 2006).

The *accountability and transparency of representatives* (to those they represent) is vital. You cannot make all representatives equal, but you can try to make them equally accountable. The fact that the G20 publicizes its agenda, its work plans, and its proceedings is important. This kind of transparency took a long time coming in the IMF. Even now, within the IMF the fact that some directors are "appointed" and thereby directly accountable to their national governments, whereas others are "elected" and subsequently untouchable, magnifies differences in accountability. That said, the G20 has agreed to change this inequality in the next few years by electing all directors.

The *composition of constituencies* is a second key issue. IMF rules let individual countries decide which group they will belong to and be represented by (and change their minds). There are no binding rules about who is in which constituency. Countries can (and have) moved. For example, Indonesia first joined the constituency headed by Italy in the 1950s and then moved to one comprising the Islamic countries of North Africa and Malaysia, eventually also joined by Laos and Singapore. Subsequently in 1972, Indonesia formed a more geographically tidy constituency including Korea, the Philippines, and Vietnam. Another case is Australia, which joined the IMF in 1947 and formed a constituency with South Africa that eventually included various countries from southern Africa and the Pacific, including Lesotho, Swaziland, New Zealand, and Western Samoa. In 1972, African members began to move to other constituencies and Australia's constituency gained new Asian countries including Korea and the Philippines. Now this constituency accounts for fourteen countries spanning the whole Pacific region.

Balancing power within a constituency is vital. Within groups of countries in the IMF, three patterns emerge reflecting relative power and position within constituencies. Some groups are heavily dominated by one country that holds the chair and runs the constituency. Others tend to be led by an "inner circle" of countries. A third group is more egalitarian in their organization. To some degree, these differences reflect the distribution of voting power within each constituency. Some are clearly dominated by one country; others are relatively equal. What becomes apparent is that a representative is more likely to consult, report, and represent a wider set of interests than their own if their own position is at least balanced by a "runner-up" power within the group, if not by an egalitarianism across the group.

Procedures for consultation and report within each constituency are important and point to benefits of geographical proximity. We found that the most highly structured constituency consultations are undertaken in the Nordic-Baltic constituency, which regularly consults and solicits input, views, and comments from respective capitals, shaping common positions on strategic issues through dedicated high-level committees such as the Nordic-Baltic Monetary and Financial Committee (and its alternate); this ensures that high-ranking officials regularly communicate. On the day-to-day work of the executive board, the Nordic-Baltic constituency also confers, not in Washington, but in their own region. The country holding the chair will circulate to the other capitals a draft instruction soliciting comments on key items coming before the board. The chair also prepares a report on a semiannual basis, following the spring and annual meetings, where the most important discussions held by the board in the previous six months are summarized and the positions taken by the Nordic-Baltic chair detailed. Notably, since the spring of 2004, these reports have been published on the Web sites of the ministries and central banks of the constituencies. In the Nordic-Baltic constituency, the fact that regular consultations are undertaken *in the region* as opposed to in Washington is worth remarking because this enhances the potential for engagement, accountability, and capacity of finance ministries within each member country. This effect is further deepened by the reporting and transparency of the group's recording of its positions and actions. This intensive form of group consultation ensures a representation of all the group's concerns.

Table 14.1
Models for enhancing responsiveness of the G20

	Use existing structures	Who represents the group?
Regional	Regional organizations (UN regional organizations or regional development banks)	Fixed or rotating around countries of a region or sub region
Constituencies (not necessarily regional)	Formal IMF-style constituencies with fixed representative	Fixed, alternating, or rotating
Ad Hoc	Networks	Flexible

The *capacity for information-gathering and advocacy* is important for a group of countries to be effective. An example from the IMF is the G7, which has operated par excellence in this regard; so have the EURIMF, the G11 (developing countries' directors), the G24, and the Asia–Pacific group.

These latter informal groups highlight the scope for enhancing G20 responsiveness without necessarily increasing its representativeness (see table 14.1). By building on informal networks and groupings, non-G20 members could enhance their voice within and outside the grouping.[2] Would enhancing the G20's responsiveness be enough?

Does the G20 Need to Be More Inclusive in Its Representation?

Like the G7, the G8, and the finance ministers of the G20, the G20 has no formal rules of membership, no formal authority to make rules, and no formal processes for decision-making or resolving disputes.[3] This gives the G20 freedom for agenda-setting, coordinating policies, and distributing tasks across existing institutions and for building consensus around norms and knowledge. The G20 has also operated as a review mechanism, examining the performance of members and of international organizations in delivering commitments made in the G20 forum.

The G20's effectiveness has sprung from its complementarity with formal institutions. It operates as a network, signaling the intent of powerful countries to cooperate, providing a stage for them to commit to cooperate, and crafting jointly agreed (where they could be) priorities for cooperation. At the risk of laboring the point, the G20 has not been an institution that can make authoritative rules and implement or enforce them. The task of formalizing rules and implementing agreements made by G20 leaders falls to international organizations endowed with formal rules of membership, decision-making, and a formal authority to implement. For these reasons, formal representation is less significant in the G20 than in formal organizations.

What does this mean for the arguments for making the G20 more representative? I would highlight two arguments for expanding the G20: to give it legitimacy and to enhance its responsiveness.

Legitimacy is one rationale given for disbanding or transforming the G20. Put simply, international decisions with binding effect should not be made without any input or consultation from those they will affect. But does the G20 make binding decisions? I would argue that for the most part it does not. The G20 signals the willingness of economically powerful countries to cooperate and, on some issues, to comply with preexisting commitments (such as their WTO commitments). Where they come to new agreements, these are remitted to the relevant formal international organization for a decision. It is therefore the legitimacy of those organizations that we must examine.

As an aside, the decision of the G20 to create the Financial Stability Board (FSB) is an exception to the argument I have just made. Furthermore, following the logic of my own argument, the structure of the FSB and its companion organizations (the Bank for International Settlements and Basel Committee) falls well short of legitimacy requirements. They are involved in setting rules that will affect all countries, yet they do not yet have universal membership.

A second argument for expanding the G20 is to ensure responsiveness. The argument here is that good G20 decisions require adequate information and feedback about the effects of international cooperation on a wide range of countries. For this reason, the G20 process should ensure that a wide range of countries are consulted about each major issue being considered by the G20.

How might the G20's agenda-setting be better informed and more responsive to the impact of cooperation on the 175 or so countries that are not part of the G20? Three important aspects of responsiveness are: consultation, precise and timely information, and provision to make timely inputs. The problem with using existing formal institutions—such as the United Nations—to enhance responsiveness is that they are structured to ensure legitimacy for making decisions that affect all members. The procedures that ensure legitimacy work against timely inputs into agenda-setting. For this reason, there is a strong case for less formal kinds of collective representation.

The first meeting of the G20 leaders set a new agenda with priorities for action and the beginnings of detailed instructions for international organizations. This agenda-setting could not have been done in the IMF, the United Nations, the World Bank, the Bank for International Settlements, or the World Trade Organization. First, each of these organizations has formal authority delegated to it by governments on the condition that the power only be used in elaborately constructed decision-making processes and structures—which protect sovereignty but make these institutions difficult to use, to change, or to adapt, at high speed. Second, existing institutions could not range across each other's mandates; no one of the existing institutions can act as a conductor to the orchestra of organizations to ensure that they work in harmony. It is into these roles that the G20 stepped after the crisis and for which responsiveness is more important than representativeness.

Notes

1. As described by the then-Finance Minister of Canada and G20 Inaugural Chairperson Paul Martin. See www.g8.utoronto.ca/finance/fm992509.htm and interview with Paul Martin at www.cbc.ca/news/canada/story/2010/06/23/f-g20-paulmartin-interview.html.

2. See the eight cases of such networks elaborated in Martinez-Diaz and Woods (2009).

3. For these reasons, Leonardo Martinez Diaz and I describe it as a network: see "The G20—The Perils and Opportunities of Network Governance for Developing Countries," at www.globaleconomicgovernance.org.

References

Al Jazeera, "G20 Agrees on Financial Action Plan," Al Jazeera English, November 15, 2008, http://www.aljazeera.com/news/americas/2008/11/20081115172654553103.html (accessed October 21, 2012).

Blustein, P., 2002, The Chastening: Inside the Crisis That Rocked the Global Financial System and Humbled the IMF, New York: Public Affairs.

Chair's Summary, L'Aquila, 2009, *Documents of the G8 Summit 2009*, available at www.g8italia2009.it/static/G8_Allegato/Chair_Summary%2c1.pdf (accessed October 21, 2012).

"Cosmetic Surgery? The Role of Emerging Markets," *The Economist*, October 3, 2009, available at www.economist.com/node/14558474 (accessed October 21, 2012).

Dewatripont, M., X. Freixas, and R. Portes, 2011, *Macroeconomic Stability and Financial Regulation: Key Issues for the G20,* London: The Centre for Economic Policy Research.

Garrett, G., 2010, "G2 in G20: China, the United States and the World after the Global Financial Crisis," *Global Policy*, 1:29–39.

Helleiner, E. and S. Pagliari, 2009, "Towards a New Bretton Woods? The First G20 Leaders Summit and the Regulation of Global Finance," *New Political Economy*, 14(2):275–287.

IMF, 2012, "IMF Executive Board Reviews Progress Toward Implementation of the 2010 Quota and Governance Reform," Press Release No. 12/309, September 11, 2012, http://www.imf.org/external/np/sec/pr/2012/pr12309.htm, (accessed October 21, 2012).

The Jakarta Post, Suratin, A. "Indonesia and the G20," Jakarta Post, April 3, 2009, http://www.thejakartapost.com/news/2012/06/19/indonesia-and-g20.html (accessed October 21, 2012).

Martinez-Diaz, L., 2009, "The G20 After Eight Years: How Effective a Vehicle for Developing-Country Influence?" in *Networks of Influence: Developing Countries in Networked Global Order*, edited by L. Martinez-Diaz and N. Woods, 39–62. Oxford: Oxford University Press.

Martinez-Diaz, L. and N. Woods, eds., 2009, *Networks of Influence: Developing Countries in Networked Global Order*, Oxford: Oxford University Press.

Payne, A., 2010, "How Many Gs are There in 'Global Governance' after the Crisis? The Perspectives of the 'Marginal Majority' of the World's States," *International Affairs*, 86(3):729–740.

Rubio-Marquez, V., 2009, "The G20: A Practitioner's Perspective," in *Networks of Influence: Developing Countries in Networked Global Order*, edited by L. Martinez-Diaz and N. Woods, 19–38. Oxford: Oxford University Press.

Sarkozy, N., 2010, "Plans for France's G20 Summit in 2011," *G20 Magazine: the Seoul Summit*, November.

Shorr, D. and T. Wright, 2010, "Forum: The G20 and Global Governance: An Exchange," *Survival: Global Politics and Strategy*, 52(2):181–198.

Woods, N., 2010, "Global Governance after the Financial Crisis: A New Multilateralism or the Last Gasp of the Great Powers?" *Global Policy*, 1(1):51–63.

Woods, N. and D. Lombardi, 2006, "Uneven Patterns of Governance: How Developing Countries are Represented in the IMF," *Review of International Political Economy*, 13(3):480.

15

Transforming Global Governance? Structural Deficits and Recent Developments in Security and Finance*

DAVID HELD AND KEVIN YOUNG

Introduction

Different aspects of global governance often have common properties. The interrelationships between finance and security, for example, run deep. Security can be regarded as one of the quintessential public goods that are essential to human welfare. It constitutes a field of action in and of itself—the business of promoting security is a discrete policy area—but it also enables many other fields of action because without a modicum of security the structure of the polity changes completely. Likewise, the system of financial flows and the management of credit in general can also be likened to a kind of essential resource required for full participation in contemporary society. Modern capitalist economies are largely constituted on the basis of credit creation, and thus although financial markets and institutions can be analyzed as a discrete field of action, they also enable much of what we call modern economic life. As such, on one level, both of these policy domains represent collectively shared domains that tie diverse populations, interests, and concerns together into a global community of fate, the very basis of contemporary globalization. Like many infrastructural

---

*This chapter builds on and adapts earlier ideas from Held and Young (2011).

resources that bind our fates together, the provision of security and finance are often only noticeable to us when they break down. And when relatively stable equilibria are disrupted in these domains, the distribution of costs and benefits often becomes highly politicized. Mounting governance challenges in both of these domains, as several contributions to this volume have pointed out, have indeed served to politicize these areas and have encouraged a rethinking of how existing governance arrangements might be improved.

One of the most profound similarities between the domains of security and finance is in the inadequacies of their respective global governance arrangements. The extensive influence of both of these domains over human welfare contrasts to their inadequate governance at the global level—a disparity or governance "deficit" that looms large given the increasing extensity and intensity of global risks. Scholarly critiques of these inadequacies often share a common analytic ethos. Whether analyzing broad governance issues or specific conjunctural events, the emphasis of critique is often on the specific actions taken and not taken surrounding global risks, the (non)provision of global public goods, and the (mis)-management of global bads. In this guise, existing critiques of governance in these domains tend to focus on the *content* of policy decisions—for example, on the predominance of unilateralism in security and neoliberal deregulation in the financial domain. One could argue, for example, that failings in the security environment and financial regulation are consequences of U.S. unilateralism in its various avatars. Alternatively one could point to the powerful vested economic interests in the provision of security and the regulation of finance and the ways in which they enable policy biases that distort the content of governance strategies. Both general global governance problems—such as the inability to provide human security in its more robust sense and the inability to contain and manage global financial contagion, or more specific problems—such as the sluggishness of humanitarian intervention or the inability to regulate hedge funds, are often seen in this way.

In contrast, we argue that the global governance deficiencies in these domains run deeper than any particular content or policy bias. To do so, we focus on the limits of governance capacities, arguing that existing institutional formations are increasingly not fit for purpose when it comes to addressing the evolving nature of global risks. We recognize that multilateral cooperation on any issue is difficult. Yet we argue that the capacity to govern our collective fate has been undermined by the very dynamics of the system of global governance itself. The problem of governance capacity is thus a structural one, and thus as the configuration of geopolitical power changes and political-economic ideology evolves, the inadequacy of global governance arrangements may well remain.

This chapter examines the interrelationships between the provision of human security and the regulation of finance from a global governance perspective. We argue that the "governance deficits" of these domains— that is, the disparity between actual steering, coordination, and control mechanisms at the global level and the extent of the risk needing to be addressed—are larger than is often assumed. By way of analogy, the situation can be likened to the difference between a cyclical deficit and a structural deficit in public finance. A cyclical deficit occurs when a state's revenue is not able to cover its expenditure, usually because of a ("cyclical") slowdown in the economy. In contrast, a structural deficit occurs when the economy is at its full potential; it represents a persistent deficit position, in that irrespective of whether the economy will improve or not, that deficit remains. By way of analogy, the "structural" global governance deficits in the domains of security and finance will remain even if the content of particular decisions and regimes may change in the future. For example, if the neoliberal content of international financial regulatory cooperation changes, this may bring improvements, but it is unlikely to address the deeper, "structural" governance deficits that remain—such as the ability to generate governance capacity to properly address problems of systemic risk. Similarly, if multilateral cooperation is enhanced in a less unilaterally driven international security environment, this may bring improvements to this domain of governance as well, but it won't change the fundamental problems with the system—the "structural" governance deficits.

Our argument proceeds as follows: First we outline some of the basic properties of contemporary global governance, briefly describing some central problems therein. We argue that in the policy domains of finance and of security there exist remarkable similarities both in the way in which these domains underscore human interdependence under conditions of globalization, and in the ways in which the governance of these domains remain inadequate to manage contemporary global risks. We then outline the manifestations of the capacity problem in the governance of finance and security, respectively. The chapter concludes with a brief discussion of the argument outlined in previous sections, and tentatively sets out pathways beyond the current deficits in global governance.

Global Governance and the Paradox of Our Times

It is now increasingly acknowledged that complex global processes, from the financial to the ecological, connect the fate of communities to each other across the world. Global interconnectedness means that emerging risks or policy failures generated in one part of the world can travel quickly around the globe to affect those who had no hand in their generation. Yet the problem-solving capacity of the existing system of global institutions is in many areas not effective, accountable, or fast enough to resolve current global dilemmas. What has been called the paradox of our times refers to the fact that the collective issues with which we must grapple are of growing extensity and intensity, and yet the means for addressing these are weak and incomplete (Held 2006). Global public goods seem to be chronically undersupplied, and global bads build up and continue to threaten livelihoods. Though there are a variety of reasons for the persistence of these problems, at the root the problem is a political–institutional one, a problem of *governance*. Problem-solving capacities at the global and regional level are weak because of a number of structural difficulties that compound the problems of generating and implementing urgent policies. These difficulties are rooted in the postwar settlement and the subsequent development of the multilateral order itself.[1] Thus, properly understood, many current global governance problems have arisen not simply because global cooperation is difficult per se, but because the results of previous global cooperation have actually made it that much harder.

Such problems of governance have a variety of manifestations, but the most pressing one involves significant limits to institutional capacity. Although the globalization of persistent risks means that a growing number of issues spans the domestic and the international domains, the character and scope of institutions are insufficient to deal with the systemic nature of these risks. Institutional fragmentation and competition between states can lead to such policy issues being addressed in an ad hoc, dissonant manner. Even when global dimensions of problems are acknowledged, there is often no clear division of labor among the myriad of international institutions that seek to address them: Their functions often overlap, their mandates conflict, and their objectives often become blurred. In this regard, existing multilateral institutions are seldom afforded the institutional resources to tackle what are effectively global-level policy issues.

These deficiencies are clearly seen within the domains of finance and security. Both domains have a core element that is fundamental to the conditions of modern human welfare. In the case of finance, it is the international organization of a particular social construction central to economic development, the management of credit. In the case of security, it is the access to basic means of physical well-being, most commonly understood as the protection from arbitrary violence. Yet despite the importance of each of these core elements to the well-being of most humans on the planet, the governance of each of these policy domains at the global level remains plagued by governance problems. The global governance of finance and of security remain, to different degrees, subject to problems related to governance capacity: Institutional fragmentation undermines collective action, and institutional inertia means that new paradigmatic approaches to governance are struggling to be actualized under existing governance arrangements.[2]

The Global Governance of Finance

The recent financial crisis demonstrates an important feature of our contemporary world. The interconnectedness afforded by globalization, for all its benefits, also disperses global risks on a rapid scale. The globalization of financial markets has integrated the global economy in unprecedented ways, and yet the rules and institutions that monitor and regulate financial market activity have not kept pace. There are many factors at play in the recent global financial crisis—the near universal incapacity to ameliorate systemic risk, excessive confidence in the efficient market hypothesis, and the powerful private authority of private sector actors to increase the riskiness of their institutions—to name but a few. These contributing forces are highly complex and are outside the scope of this chapter to discuss. It is unquestionable that key national public institutions in the Anglo-American world failed in important ways. Yet another important feature of the recent financial crisis is the failure at the global level of the existing institutions that monitor, contain, and manage global financial risks and their contagion. Existing institutions that govern the way in which financial markets are managed around the world were weak and largely unprepared for the events of autumn 2008, much less able to prevent such a calamity. The global financial crisis has made it clear that the problem-solving capacity of the global system is in many areas not effective, accountable, or rapid enough to resolve mounting global policy challenges.

The lack of governance capacity in global financial governance is somewhat paradoxical. There is no shortage of institutions that get financial policymakers at the table together. Although high-level, multilateral forums exist, such as the IMF and the G20 (Woods chapter 14, this volume), many financial governance institutions are fundamentally "transnational" in character; they reflect cooperative efforts not among heads of state but rather among executive bodies such as national finance ministries, central banking authorities, and national financial regulatory authorities (Baker 2009). Despite the existence of many institutions that facilitate the communication of national financial authorities with one another, taken together the existing set of institutions represents an arrangement that is, for most intents and purposes, relatively weak and fragmented. One institution exists for the management of stock exchanges (the International Organization of Securities Commissioners), one for accounting (the International Accounting Standards Board), one for money laundering (the Financial Action Task Force), one for insurance (the International Association of Insurance Supervisors), and one for banking regulation (the Basel Committee on Banking Supervision). Some institutions, such as the Bank for International Settlements and the Financial Stability Forum, have existed as overarching institutions that seek to monitor and conduct research on global financial risks and to disseminate ideas. Yet their ability to guide the existing constellation of institutions has been weak at best. As Bhattacharya (2009) notes, this collection of institutions resembles a "tangled web."

The historical evolution of global financial governance can go a long way to explain this institutional fragmentation. Although the protection of other areas of governance such as environmental governance and international security have had their activities ordered through UN auspices, institutions of global financial governance have amounted to much more ad hoc arrangements, arising as informal policy communities reacting to particular collective problems. More well-known institutions such as the International Monetary Fund (IMF) had their beginnings firmly entrenched in the UN system, but other institutions just as vital to the governance of international finance have not. For example, the Basel Committee on Banking Supervision was established in 1974 in direct reaction to the contagion effects of cross-border bank failures. Similarly, the Financial Stability Forum was established in 1999 after widespread concerns over the contagion of financial instability following the East Asian financial crises.

Each of these institutions have housed their secretariats in the Bank for International Settlements, an institution established in 1930 with the initial remit to manage the system of German war reparations. In subsequent decades, it expanded to focus on international financial cooperation among central bankers and to conduct research and to disseminate monetary policy ideas. Other institutions, such as the International Accounting Standards Board, are not even governed by public institutions at all but reflect private-sector self-regulatory initiatives.

To be sure, existing institutions have communicated with each other in important ways, and together these institutions have in some respects made important advances, such as the limitation of financial regulatory competition among states, the provision of emergency liquidity, and the occasional coordination of monetary policies. In the midst of the 2008 financial shock, central banks were able to make use of international coordination structures that had built up successfully in previous decades. For example, immediately after the crash of Lehman Brothers, on October 8, 2008, the central banks of Canada, the United Kingdom, the United States, Sweden, and Switzerland, together with the European Central Bank jointly announced interest rate adjustments to compensate for the liquidity shock then occurring in financial markets. This was followed by interest rate cuts in Asia—in particular in China—and in Australia, and represented a relatively well-coordinated policy response that probably weakened the severity of the recession in important ways.

Yet the capacity of this system to detect and to take action on the buildup of global financial risks has not been borne out. Although the buildup of these risks might be traced back to particularities of the Anglo-American economies, it is notable that the existing institutions of global financial governance did not restrain them but rather amplified the regulatory model from these countries and made them models for the global standard.[3] Furthermore, as Mügge has recently pointed out, at crucial junctures during the financial crisis policy responses followed the logic of "dogmatism" over "pragmatism," as entrenched ideas about financial market regulation limited and conditioned the policy responses during the crisis (Mügge 2011). Even if one puts aside the policy biases of existing governance institutions, none of them, it can be noted, has possessed much power to actually take action on important regulatory issues and instead have executed what has been called "soft law" (Abbott and Snidal 2000) through the production of global standards and codes (Gibbon, Ponte, and Vestergaard 2011; Young 2011). It might be argued of course that the lack of supranational enforcement power results from the refusal to cede regulatory authority to a supranational agency (Kahler and Lake 2008). However, another part of the problem arguably lies with the distinct lack of a centralized institution within the system of global financial governance itself. As we shall see in this chapter, this has begun to change, albeit very modestly, through the transformation of the Financial Stability Forum into the new Financial Stability Board.

Compounding this institutional fragmentation has been the fact that most institutions at the center of global financial governance have adopted an exclusionary model to how institutions are run and how policy decisions are made. Despite the wide membership of the IMF, the character of its voting rules skew decision-making power toward great powers, in particular the United States and Europe (Broz and Hawes 2006; Rapkin and Strand 2006). This model of participation has wider implications than is often assumed, especially given the fact that private interests within the United States have been shown to influence IMF policies through the lobbying of the U.S. Congress, for example (Broz 2008). The organization of the IMF's decision-making structure has meant that developing countries have been disproportionately underrepresented in an institution that affects their economic welfare in profound ways.[4] Other more transnational financial governance institutions have until very recently operated on a different decision-making rule but still excluded the vast majority of the world's population from any representative hand in formal decision-making. For example, the Basel Committee on Banking Supervision referred to earlier in this chapter, the global institution that effectively sets the regulatory standards in banking for the entire world, has maintained a highly exclusive approach to its membership, excluding developing countries from formal participation (Cardim de Carvalho and Kregel 2007). Until 2008, its membership reflected the configuration of international financial power in the 1970s, even while states such as Japan, France, and Germany experienced a relative decline in the position of their largest banks, and countries such as China and Brazil a relative increase. Although some institutions have had a less embarrassing record of participation in governance, such as the Bank for International Settlements,[5] the unequal structure of country representation continued despite UN declarations such as the Monterrey Consensus, which insisted that global financial governance institutions should review their membership to include adequate participation from developing countries.[6] As several authors have pointed out, this skewed representation has had negative consequences in terms of financial governance, such as the increased cost of capital to developing countries (Claessens, Underhill, and Zhang 2008; Griffith-Jones and Persaud 2008).

It is important to point out that the global financial crisis of 2008–2009 has led to important changes within global financial governance. The post-crisis system has not been one of stasis. Yet a clear manifestation of capacity problems in financial governance has been the ad hoc way in which the attempt to manage the crisis actually took place. During the crisis and shortly thereafter, all of the transnational financial governance institutions discussed earlier in this chapter began working on new international standards—some of which, such as in the area of financial accounting, had to be addressed immediately. At the same time, however, the lack of any proper multilateral forum to address the big global governance questions of the day meant that a new institution, barely known and barely relevant before this time, emerged to set the agenda: the G20.

The G20 was actually a relatively ad hoc construction in the first place, constructed in the aftermath of the East Asian financial crisis of 1997–1998 (Germain 2001). As its name suggests, the G20 represents a larger share of countries than the G8, as it includes not only these powers but also developing and emerging countries such as Brazil, China, India, and Mexico. The problem with the G20 taking the steering role for global financial governance was that it lacked the kind of administrative structure needed to execute and enforce its marching orders. Rather than enforcement power or a functional bureaucracy, most of its institutional design was established to facilitate high-profile communiques among politicians directed at the public and financial markets. The broad calls for reform that the G20 produced from September 2008 until October 2010 were taken up by the existing international standard-setting bodies, and not coordinated by a centralized institution with a substantive administrative bureaucracy with which to carry them out. Initial signs of ambition dropped off relatively quickly as public attention to reform waned (see Helleiner and Pagliari 2009). Thus financial regulatory reform, even across the G20, has been highly variegated, with some countries instituting strong reforms, others none at all. While unified approaches to the reform of banking regulation, for example, have been thought about at the global level, different national governments (and the EU) have begun to cherry-pick which of these standards they will implement and which not—undermining the idea of a global minimum floor of regulation in the first place.

This is not to say that some of the reforms that have taken place have not been significant. The IMF received a trebling of resources, as well as a general increase in Special Drawing Rights (Woods 2010). Yet its capacity for either generating or enforcing a more robust financial regulatory system has not changed. Much more than actual governance capacity, existing institutions have witnessed a reform to the countries that participate. In November 2008, the G20 leaders called for the international standard-setting bodies to review their memberships. Several months later (in March) before the London G20 Summit, the G20's call for participatory reform led to extensive reform of global financial governance institutions. The Basel Committee on Banking Supervision expanded, first in March 2009 to include regulators and central bank authorities from Australia, Brazil, China, India, South Korea, Mexico, and Russia, and then a second time in June 2009 to include the entire G20, along with Hong Kong and Singapore. The Committee on Payment and Settlement Systems and the Technical Committee of the International Organization of Securities Commissions has also experienced similar participatory reforms as well (Helleiner and Pagliari 2009:6–8). These changes are not merely cosmetic: They are important reforms. In many ways, they represent a long overdue game of historical "catch up," where reforms that should have taken place many years ago have finally been made.[7]

Despite these significant reforms to country membership, there was no real creation of new institutional capacities. An historic opportunity to reframe global financial governance institutions within the auspices of the UN system was missed (see Wade 2012).[8] Instead, existing governance institutions were re-framed, and the world got incremental, rather than fundamental, governance reform (see Moschella and Tsingou 2013). The Financial Stability *Forum* was renamed the Financial Stability *Board* (FSB), and the new institution also modestly expanded its institutional capacities through a small secretariat, a full-time secretary general, a steering committee, and three standing committees (Germain 2011). This more permanent administrative structure means that the FSB is more robust than its predecessor, but the extensity of its powers is still actually quite limited because it is left to engage in monitoring activities and to make broad recommendations (Helleiner 2010:284).

These changes are not insignificant. Yet the relatively modest nature of reform is particularly striking given the severity of the financial crisis. World output declined by 124 percent relative to the average of the five years before and generated what has been called the first post-war global recession (IMF 2009). Yet not only has world output declined but global economic interconnectedness has meant that the costs of governance failures are widely dispersed. In this regard, consider the recent estimates by the World Bank on the marginal effect of the financial crisis on the poorest people on the planet. It has been estimated that by 2015, 20 million more people in sub-Saharan Africa and 53 million more people globally will be in extreme poverty as a result of the crisis (World Bank 2010); 1.2 million more children under the age of five have been predicted to die between 2009 and 2015 as an indirect result of the crisis, and 35,000 more students will not complete primary education by 2015—a pernicious effect especially pronounced for girls (see International Labor Organization 2009a, 2009b; World Bank 2010). As Supachai Panitchpakdi, the secretary general of the United Nations Conference on Trade and Development (UNCTAD) pointed out shortly after the financial crisis hit, even though few developing countries have been directly exposed to securitized mortgages or failed U.S. financial institutions, the vast majority of them have been significantly affected indirectly through reduced availability of credit, stock market panics, and the slowdown in the real economy (Panitchpakdi 2008).

Perhaps the global diffusion of costs from governance failure is indeed part of the problem: Those who govern don't pay the total costs of their malfeasance. Yet the lackluster record on institutional reform is also reflective of the problem of institutional fragmentation. Recognition of specific problems is often segmented and sent off into specific governance institutions. The technocratic nature in which many global financial governance institutions operate facilitates this, and, under some circumstances, there may be good reason to do so. Yet the opportunity to take a broader step back and examine systemic functioning is missed.

Reforms that have taken place have been nonsystemic in nature: Because the existing systems of financial standards and codes have effectively constituted "soft law" arrangements (Abbott and Snidal 2000), financial governance has still relied on the (often unreliable) collaboration of national governments to implement them, and on financial markets to use these standards and codes as signals of credibility and soundness (Ho 2002; Kerwer 2005). Incremental policy responses to governance weaknesses are channeled through existing institutions, rather than through the generation of new ones that limit the governance weaknesses in the first place or that address their underlying causes.

For all the institutional innovation present within the system of global financial governance, the problem of institutional fragmentation has nevertheless persisted. An example can be found in the way the financial crisis and the institutional reactions to it affected trade finance. Reflecting the extent of global economic interdependence, the financial crisis led to a severe decline in the volume of global trade flows. A great deal of the decline in global trade volume was due to financing problems: When the global financial system seized up, so did global trade financing. Yet instead of helping this situation, the response of some global governance institutions was to (unintentionally) make it worse. In an effort to shore up regulatory standards of banks, the design of the new Basel III Accord put new restrictions on the ability of banks to support flows of credit for trade financing purposes. This problem was recognized—not by the collection of financial regulators that sat on the Basel Committee but by other groups far away in their own institutional silos. It took an extensive lobbying campaign by the International Chamber of Commerce, aided by the World Bank and the World Trade Organization, to secure a change in new global financial regulations that addressed this problem; and it wasn't until 2011 that the new banking regulations were changed to address it. Although it is certainly a good thing that changes were made, this example helps to highlight the costs of institutional fragmentation. A more coherent and effective global policy formation could have foreseen and prevented such unintended consequences right from the start.

Policy errors are of course nothing new. And finance is an area notoriously difficult to effectively regulate. Yet what is striking about global financial governance is the way in which new emergent problems are increasingly recognized but not systematically addressed. In this regard, consider two problems that have been brought into sharp relief since the global financial crisis. The first of these is the now mainstream recognition that effective financial regulation has to take place on a macroprudential basis. There is an increased recognition that financial crisis and financial regulation should be understood through the prism of "macroprudentialism" (Baker 2012). What this means is that rather than seeking to regulate the activities of a single financial institution, the best way to regulate finance is to understand the banking system as a coherent, changing whole. The rise of macroprudentialism represents the recognition of a harder problem in that it is technically more difficult but requires much more coordination among different areas of finance and different national jurisdictions. Regulating a single bank is challenging enough, in particular when the bank is large and engages in complex transactions in many different countries. But regulating the banking system as a whole is even more challenging because it means taking stock of banks' interrelationships to the economy as a whole and seeing the "emergent-level" processes at work in the complex adaptive system that is the financial system (Haldane and May 2011; Baker 2012). The new "macroprudential" challenge befalling financial regulators cannot be tackled exclusively at the national level because of the extreme interconnectivity of financial activity worldwide. Thus the concept naturally puts stress on the global dimension. In this vein, tackling financial regulation in a macroprudential way necessarily requires a certain level of global-level monitoring, regulation, and enforcement that is very challenging under a highly fragmented global financial governance system that features a lack of enforcement capacity.

A second "harder problem" that has been put into much sharper relief since the crisis is the problematic nature of the relationship in world savings and demand—a problem often referred to as "global imbalances." This problem is expressed in the disjointed pattern of current account deficits and surpluses that have built up in the global economy in the last decade and a half. It reflects a disjuncture between the high consumption and demand of countries in Western Europe and in North America and the low level of consumption in East Asia. Such a systemic problem has been widely recognized as "one of the main challenges facing the global economy and world community" (Reuters 2011). As Blanchard and Milesi-Ferretti have argued, "[f]ailure to [address global imbalances] could result in the world economy being stuck 'in midstream,' threatening the sustainability of the world recovery" (Blanchard and Milesi-Ferretti 2009). Since the financial crisis, structural imbalances have been at the forefront of policy debates; many have also made the argument that these imbalances contributed in a significant way to the financial crisis itself because deficit countries were able to fuel their credit booms in large part thanks to high saving surplus flows from East Asia.[9]

Despite this increasingly recognized problem, the capacity to address or even manage the problem of structural imbalances has proved severely wanting. A variety of policymakers from the IMF, the FSB, and leading states have all concluded that these global imbalances are extremely serious and that "[l]eft unresolved, these problems could even sow the seeds of the next crisis."[10] Transnational financial governance institutions such as the Bank for International Settlements and the FSB increasingly generate knowledge about how perverse the problem is: but there is a distinct lack of capacity to deal with the problem itself (Bank for International Settlements 2011). At the G20 meeting in Paris, a much more modest proposal was accepted—specifically that countries would agree to a Mutual Assessment Process (MAP) in which public debt, fiscal deficits, and private debt would constitute a set of warning indicators (IMF 2011). There is no enforcement mechanism available, however. As Stiglitz put it, this "is a multilateral problem within a system in disequilibrium."[11]

It is especially in this last regard that security shares a common problem with finance. Just as there has been an increased intellectual recognition of harder problems in financial governance in our midst, so too in the security domain a shift in our paradigm of security has not been met with a commensurate institutional response.

The Global Governance of Security

If the global financial system integrates a common infrastructure for the management of credit, the international security system ensures an arrangement for the management of conflict and violence. This domain of our shared existence, in contrast to finance, has a more well-known set of institutions and rules that govern it. Reflecting the capacity problem, these institutions have evolved over time, but most of their structure and content reflects security dilemmas identified for a world that no longer exists. From the period following World War II until 1989, the nature of national security was shaped decisively by the contest between the United States and the Soviet Union. The dominance of the United States and the USSR as world powers, and the operation of alliances such as NATO and the Warsaw Pact, constrained decision-making for many states in the post-war years. In the post-Cold War world of the 1990s and the 2000s, the constraints upon state security policy have not been eradicated but reconfigured. Instead of bipolarity, the global system now exhibits more of the characteristics of a multipolar distribution of political–economic power. Within this more complex structure, even though the strategic and foreign policy options confronting an individual state are still shaped by its location in the global power hierarchy, there is a great deal more indeterminacy and volatility in the system.

The problem of governance capacity in security is underscored by the inadequacy of existing institutions orienting themselves toward the new emergent paradigm in security: human security, in its most comprehensive sense. The principle of human security was first introduced by the United Nations Development Program (UNDP) World Development

Report in 1994, but it has been amended and refined since its inception.[12] At its core, it sets out a security agenda concerned with protecting the basic prerequisites of human life. Alkire points out that "it does not cover all necessary, important, and profound aspects of human living. Rather, it identifies and protects a limited vital core of human activities and abilities"; namely, the ability to sustain life within a framework of the rule of law and according to human rights standards (2003:3). This emerging paradigm has served, in principle, to subordinate state sovereignty in relation to human security concerns, whereby the vital interests of human beings are given priority over those of the state itself.

The human security paradigm has significant earlier roots, which illuminate further aspects of its meaning. In the early decades of the postwar period, the geopolitical position of the 1945 victors was protected and nurtured through the UN system itself, which entrenched their power while it claimed to represent all states on an equal basis (Held 1995). Yet within this affirmation of state power, sovereignty, and interests, the seeds were laid for a new meaning of security and for a reframed interstate order. The laws of war were increasingly complemented by the conventions on human rights, which, in principle, recast the meaning of sovereignty itself (Held 2004:part 3). Sovereignty was reshaped and reconceived, no longer as effective power but as rightful authority—that is, authority that upholds fundamental democratic values and human rights standards. The law of war and the human rights regime combined to reform the meaning of power and of violence in the postwar order, delimiting in principle not only the behavior of states during times of war but of all state and nonstate actors. Thus the beginnings were established to rethink the meaning of security. In this context, security no longer means the protection of state interests and of bounded territories in the interest of settled power relations. Rather security comes to mean the protection and nurturing of each and every person's interest in self-determination, human rights, and fundamental freedoms. Accordingly, the history of security since 1945 is the history of the development of new conceptions that sought to unsettle the understanding of security as state security and refocus it on the security of each and every person—on human security.

Despite this important shift in thinking, the capacity of existing global governance arrangements to implement it is limited in the ability to carry out a human security approach. Most armed forces of the world are still developed on a model of nation-states at war with one another, and are based on the organizational principle of geopolitical state interests. Global military spending, fueled by such preconceptions, has been on a sustained upward trend. Total global military expenditure in 2008 is estimated to have totaled $1.464 trillion, representing an increase of 4 percent in real terms compared to 2007 and of 45 percent over the ten-year period 1999–2008 (SIPRI 2009a).[13] To put this in perspective, this is $217 for every person on the planet, thirteen times the total spent on all types of development aid, 700 times the total amount spent on global health programs, and roughly the same as the combined total GDP of every country in Africa. The effects of the global financial crisis—in particular, growing government budget deficits and the economic stimulus packages that are aimed at countering the crisis—seem to have had little effect on military spending, with most countries (including the United States and China) remaining committed to further increases in the years ahead. However, of the sixteen major armed conflicts that were active in fifteen locations around the world in 2008, not one was a major interstate conflict (SPRI 2009a:69). Some evidence suggests that the financial crisis has had little impact on global military spending, with total world expenditure in 2009 estimated to have reached $1.531 trillion, representing an increase of 49 percent since 2000.[14]

Institutional fragmentation persists within the security domain. Militaries remain organized on a national, rather than regional or multilateral basis, with vast duplication, overlap, and waste of resources. In countries such as the United Kingdom and the United States, spending levels are now far in excess of any plausible *defensive* needs. With the exception perhaps of the United States and China, no country is capable of acting independently in major conflicts or of intervening against regimes that threaten global peace and security. There is something quite baroque about existing defense positions and tactics.[15] Against this background, the way we conduct and organize military spending looks increasingly anachronistic—for example, total global spending on multilateral operations such as peacekeeping forces is less than 1 percent of total global military expenditures.[16]

Despite the evident failures of the Bush Doctrine, the capacity problem in global security runs deeper than disregard for effective multilateralism.[17] The very instruments of international security provision are perversely oriented for a world in which we no longer live. Our military capacity and technologies are all geared to fighting wars in terms of combating physical forces in discrete and bounded space and time. At the present time, this model cannot deliver in many areas where security is most needed—and as such there is a need to create military capacity that is based on cooperation and on collaboration of armed forces. This poses not only important questions about the collaboration of, and sharing of, personnel, technology, and intelligence. It also poses serious issues about how to link international security to human security more broadly—through commitments to sustainable development and to social justice. The emphasis has to be not just on fighting wars but on securing the safety of human beings more generally (Kaldor 1998; Beebe and Kaldor 2010). In other words, substantial institutional capacity exists, but it is the wrong kind of capacity.[18]

The state, viewed in Weberian terms, is a consolidated monopoly of legitimate violence (Weber 1964:154). Yet when this monopoly is under pressure, a number of additional problems emerge. These can be observed today in diverse situations, from new wars and clandestine networks that operate in shadow (war) economies, to private military companies that operate in an emerging market for violence (Held and McGrew 2007:56–57). Private actors have become major actors in the security arena. As military operations are often conducted with and/or by private companies, there has been a commercialization and globalization of organized violence. For instance, up to 20,000 private security personnel from sixty different international firms operated in Iraq in 2004 (Held and McGrew 2007:57). On the one hand, the states' ability to legitimize violence is questioned by the international community in many instances (e.g., the contested 2003 invasion of Iraq) and, on the other hand, there is a functional redistribution of the monopoly on legitimate violence—varying by context (Held and McGrew 2007:58). In the case of developed states that maintain a stable regulatory regime, this may in fact mean that a state has a monopoly on the ability to legitimize violence but not to monopolize it. In a fragile state context, the state may, in principle, have the ability to legitimize and monopolize violence, though in practice this is a volatile hold on power that is vulnerable to domestic and external threats.

Those groups that are contracted and provide private security functions differ in nature and form from those competing groups that use violence to challenge the state apparatus; the former, in principle, do not aim to replace the state, whereas the latter contest its control directly. In either case, a unifying theme is the erosion of the states' monopoly on violence. This erosion, as well as the evolving notion of state sovereignty and emergence of the human security paradigm, calls for greater collaboration and control over the forces of violence. The challenging harder problems that develop—from terrorism and piracy to failed states and humanitarian disasters—are beyond the scope of a single nation-state to address; they are transborder, intermestic problems. Yet the division of

protective labor (i.e., security forces) is inadequately focused on addressing the new security challenges and on the protection and maintenance of
individual agency (i.e., upholding human rights and democratic standards).
This further highlights the capacity gap between existing military capacities
and the demands of a changing global security environment.

Conclusion: Evolution and Persistence

This chapter has examined the interrelationships between the provision of
human security and the regulation of finance from a global governance
perspective. We have argued that despite the contextual uniqueness of each
of these governance domains, there lie similar inadequacies in the way that
prevailing governance arrangements operate. Although existing critiques
of governance in these domains tend to focus on the *content* of policy decisions, we have focused on what we have called "structural" governance
deficits. This is not to say, however, that a policy-oriented critique is not
valuable. Indeed, such a tradition is to be welcomed: Critical inquiry into
the actual operation of these two important policy domains and normative
critiques of these processes often represent a step forward.

We have argued that the global governance of security and finance
both suffer from governance deficits that go beyond their immediate policy
content or biases—pointing out what we have referred to as more core or
"structural" governance deficits. In the case of global financial governance,
institutional fragmentation and lack of enforcement capability have been
particularly striking. An even starker capacity problem exists in the case of
global security, where existing institutions are at odds with a world in which
patterns of conflict no longer reflect the old structures of interstate relations. One could argue that the fundamental cause of governance deficits
in each of these realms lies not just in the stubborn nature of sovereignty
but also in the particular ways in which global governance institutions
have been built up since the post-war settlement. To be sure, existing policy
biases have not helped. Neoliberal policy biases in global financial regulation have meant that existing multilateral institutions are weaker than they
probably would have been otherwise. Similarly, it might be said that the
United States' pursuit of unilateralism in security affairs has only weakened
the legitimacy and robustness of existing multilateral institutions.

In both security and finance, there have been important shifts in thinking in recent years that provide important future potential (see Woods,

and Kaldor and Theros, respectfully, in this volume). Yet the record so far suggests that the ability of existing institutional formations to more fully actualize the reforms needed is wanting. Acting on the human security paradigm requires a more fundamental reconfiguration of existing security capacities. In the case of finance, the situation is similar when it comes to the conceptual innovation of macroprudentialism and the recognition of the inherently systemic nature of financial risk in the global economy. Questions inevitably remain in any assessment of global governance as to how relations of power might be changing. The recent transformations since the onset of the worst of the global financial crises have been notable, and provide a way of demonstrating some closure in global governance deficits—though serious problems remain. In regard to the domain of security, it is difficult to find evidence of recent transformation of governance structures, although signs of growing multipolarity are one contender. Whether or not these amount to a set of cosmetic changes and whether or not they may cascade into further changes remains to be seen. More clear is the fact that the politicized reaction to the financial crisis has shown that focused, critical public attention and a renewed commitment to multilateralism in the face of demonstrable failure can lead to important improvements in the operation of global governance institutions. As Woods (this volume) points out, there are manifold problems of representation within the newly emergent role of the G20. There may indeed be ways to reform the governance arrangements of these bodies in terms of representation, but one larger issue left remaining is the problem of institutional capacity.

What lies ahead in terms of transforming the multilateral order in a direction that can start to resolve current dilemmas of global governance? Surely the existing configuration of political power represents many challenges. As Ocampo points out (this volume), it is not only an unequal structure of representation, which pervades global governance but a particularly pernicious policy discourse of "level playing fields," which pit unequal players against each other. However the redesign of global governance might be conceived, it is important to underscore this order as one that has powerful vested interests in the continuation of the existing status quo. Established structures nurture preferences for stasis, in that they encourage actors to make resource-specific investments in the already existing system of power, reinforcing its basic structure. As such, it is important to conceive of any future significant transformation in global governance as one that will necessarily be fraught with contestation. Resistance to even the gradual transformation of public authority will likely be with us for some time, yet the recent intensification of globalization processes have engendered new forms of agency and activism that demonstrate some potential to move progressive agendas forward.[19]

The key to the success of any vision for social transformation is to have that vision being undergirded and defended by a coherent power bloc, a socioeconomic coalition of some kind. Ikenberry's contribution to this volume spells out this dynamic well, especially in terms of the geopolitical importance of leadership in securing global cooperation. In this regard, we might ask: Is there a configuration of political forces currently existing that might be expected to increase in size and political power in the future and that would support further steps toward resolving the paradox of our times highlighted earlier in this chapter? Such a question requires much more considered analysis than we can give here, but some speculation based on current trajectories is warranted. Elements of the alter-globalization movement provide some evidence for mass mobilization potential around addressing fundamentally global-level problems (Pleyers 2010). Technocratic elites from many countries appear to be increasingly "multilateralist" in their orientation toward public policy problems. Political parties from various stripes increasingly reach to multilateral policy solutions as a way to address demands from their electorates to deal with current policy constraints. However, there are two other elements of a future socioeconomic coalition that may be even more important.

Prospects for a progressive multilateralist coalition might depend on the future fragmentation of the business community. As multilateral governance capacity is built, policy making can have the effect of fracturing what would otherwise be a coherent bloc of business opposition. For example, although some are right to point out the resistance of many corporate actors to addressing climate change in any meaningful way, it is also true that there is now considerable business conflict over the issue.[20] Even in global finance, there is more business conflict than most depictions appreciate (Young 2012). The politics of any area are an evolving game, and the position of different actors changes as the game changes. In this way, steps in a given policy direction can have the effect of building allies and opening up lines of possibility that were previously closed.

Although their structural power is very different from what it was in the past, trade unions and especially their international associations might also be a critical part of a coalition in support of transforming existing systems of global governance in a more progressive direction. Although some trade union activity is clearly oriented toward protecting gains made at the national level (many of which have been under considerable stress due to neoliberal retrenchment), we should not forget that the labor movement has often had a strong internationalist orientation. It is hardly a surprise then that trade unions in Europe and North America are among the most enthusiastic voices for meaningful global financial governance reform. More so than any elite fraction of the business community, the labor movement has the capacity to establish the broad social base of support from, and connection to, the people most directly affected by global governance deficits. As such, they have the potential to act as natural guardians over future multilateral capacity-building, in the sense that they have a natural aversion to technocratic and elitist global public policy solutions—something that cannot be said for the other actors mentioned previously. At the same time, it is difficult to see a prominent role for organized labor if it is not linked up in some way with global civil society organizations. The recent global diffusion of the "Occupy Wall Street" phenomenon offers clear evidence that civil society can launch relevant agenda-setting campaigns not only to address inefficacies in financial reform but also to address such issues within a broader frame of social justice.[21]

Can the existing multilateral order be reforged and rebuilt to reflect the changing balance of power in the world and the voices of nonstate actors that have emerged with such force and impact over the last few decades? The crucial tests ahead concern the creation of new, effective, and just global deals on trade rules, financial market regulation, climate change, the renewal of a nuclear nonproliferation treaty, as well as on global investment in a low-carbon future, and in the capabilities to cope with crises. We face a choice between an effective and accountable rule-based multilateral order and the fragmentation of the global order into competing regional blocs pursuing their own sectional interests. Which direction we will collectively take hangs in the balance.

Notes

1. For a full explication of these and other deficiencies within the system of global governance, see Held (2004). Our discussion here builds on Held and Young (2011).

2. A further dimension, that of the unequal distribution of global risks relative to accountability and decision-making, is discussed in Held and Young (2011).

3. For example, strong confidence in banks' own internal risk assessments was a cornerstone of the Federal Reserve in the United States and the Financial Services Authority in the United Kingdom, and this confidence was often translated into the global regulatory standards for banking in the Basel II Capital Accord.

4. See Woods and Lombardi (2006). The IMF has not been a statically organized institution, to be sure; however, reforms to the IMF's voting shares in April 2008—which were regarded as substantial by the standards of the past few decades—have amounted to relatively little.

5. This institution had since 2006 included central bankers from Mexico and China as part of its board of directors, and its more general membership is much wider than most transnational financial governance institutions.

6. On the unfulfilled promise of Monterrey, see Kregel (2006:26–28). On the relationship between participation and accountability in financial governance, see Germain (2004:217–242).

7. Notice as well the arbitrary way in which participatory reform took place. Nearly every country in the world was adversely affected by the global financial crisis, yet the logic of participatory expansion was a function of who is on the G20. Expanding such institutions to include the whole world might undermine their basic function, yet the point still remains that the expansions that did take place were relatively arbitrary.

8. According to Wade's (2012) interpretation of events, the crisis saw considerable efforts within the UN General Assembly to offer high-level coordination, analysis, and recommendations on global financial reform, yet high-level diplomatic efforts by the United States and the United Kingdom sought to undercut these efforts.

9. For a useful review, see Borio and Disyatat (2011). Their argument, a variation on a common theme, is that the excess elasticity of the international financial system failed to restrain the buildup of unsustainable credit and asset price booms.

10. See Strauss-Kahn quoted in IFC Review (2011).

11. See Stiglitz quoted in Thornton (2006:50).

12. The UNDP Human Development Report's initial articulation of human security included two distinct elements: "(1) Safety from chronic threats such as hunger, disease, and repression. (2) Protection from sudden and hurtful disruptions in the patterns of daily life—whether in jobs, in homes, or in communities": that is, freedom from want and freedom from fear (UNDP 1994; Alkire 2003).

13. The United States accounts for the majority of the global increase—representing 58 percent of the global increase over the previous ten years, largely due to the wars in Iraq and Afghanistan. However, the United States is far from the only country to pursue such a determined course of militarization. China and Russia have both nearly tripled their military expenditure, while other regional powers—such as Algeria, Brazil, India, Iran, Israel, South Korea, and Saudi Arabia—have also made substantial contributions to the total increase. Of the five permanent members of the UN Security Council, only France has held its spending relatively steady, with a rise of just 3.5 percent over the last decade.

14. The global financial crisis has not had an effect on military spending by the major powers, though it has for some small economies (SIPRI 2010:9, 177)

15. See, for example, the early critique in Kaldor (1982).

16. According to data for 2008, total global spending on multilateral operations such as peacekeeping forces was just $8.2 billion, or 0.56 percent of total global military expenditures (SIPRI 2009b).

17. On the consequences of U.S. multilateralism, and its dynamic relationship with the decline of U.S. soft power in international affairs, see Cox and Quinn (2008:204–213) and Slaughter and Hale (2008:176–186).

18. Learning has been slow, but now some of the world's most senior military figures have taken up the challenge and are changing the way warfare is being conceived. For example, see the remarks in Sengupta (2009) and Petraeus (2010).

19. See Pleyers (2010) for an extended discussion of such dynamics.

20. Compare Falkner (2007, 2010) and Newell and Paterson (2010).

21. The relatively short-lived nature of this movement also speaks to the relative lack of resources and ability to connect to a broader social base that is endemic of many alter-globalization movements as well.

References

Abbott, K. and D. Snidal, 2000, "Hard and Soft Law in International Governance," *International Organization*, 54(3):421–456.

Alkire, S., 2003, "A Conceptual Framework for Human Security," Working Paper 2, Center for Research on Inequality, Human Security and Ethnicity (CRISE), Oxford University.

Baker, A., 2009, "Deliberative Equality and the Transgovernmental Politics of the Global Financial Architecture," *Global Governance*, 15(2):195–218.

———, 2012, "The New Political Economy of the Macroprudential Ideational Shift," *New Political Economy,* forthcoming (available on iFirst, April 2012).

Bank for International Settlements (BIS), 2011, *81st Annual Report*, Basel: Bank for International Settlements.

Beebe, S. and M. Kaldor, 2010, *The Ultimate Weapon Is No Weapon: Human Security and the New Rules of War and Peace*, New York: Public Affairs.

Bhattacharya, A., 2009, "A Tangled Web," *Finance and Development, 46*(1):40–43.

Blanchard, O. and G. Milesi-Ferretti, 2009, "Global Imbalances: In Midstream," IMF Staff Position Note 09/29, December.

Borio, C. and P. Disyatat, 2011, "Global Imbalances and the Financial Crisis: Link or No Link?" *BIS Working Papers*, No. 346.

Broz, J. L., 2008, "Congressional Voting on Funding the International Financial Institutions," *Review of International Organizations, 3*(4):351–374.

Broz, J. L. and M. B. Hawes, 2006, "Congressional Politics of Financing the International Monetary Fund," *International Organization, 60*(2):367–399.

Cardim de Carvalho, F. J. and J. Kregel, 2007, *Who Rules the Financial System?* Rio de Janiero: IBase.

Claessens, S., G. R. D. Underhill, and X. Zhang, 2008, "The Political Economy of Basel II: The Costs for Poor Countries," *The World Economy, 31*(3):313–344.

Cox, M., 2004, "Empire by Denial? Debating American Power," *Security Dialogue, 35*(2):228–261.

Cox, M. and A. Quinn, 2008, "Hard Times for Soft Power? America and the Atlantic Community," in *Cultural Politics in a Global Age: Uncertainty, Solidarity, and Innovation,* edited by D. Held and H. Moore, 204–213. Oxford: Oneworld.

Falkner, Robert, 2007, *Business Power and Conflict in International Environmental Politics,* Basingstoke: Palgrave Macmillan.

———, 2010, "Business and Global Climate Governance: A Neo-Pluralist Perspective," in *Business and Global Governance,* edited by M. Ougaard and A. Leander, 99–117. London: Routledge.

Germain, R., 2001, "Global Financial Governance and the Problem of Inclusion," *Global Governance, 7*:411–426.

———, 2004, "Globalising Accountability within the International Organization of Credit: Financial Governance and the Public Sphere," *Global Society, 18*(3):217–242.

———, 2011, "The Financial Stability Board," in *Handbook of Transnational Governance,* edited by T. Hale and D. Held, 50–54. Cambridge, UK: Polity.

Gibbon, P., S. Ponte, and J. Vestergaard, eds., 2011, *Governing Through Standards: Origins, Drivers and Limitations,* London: Palgrave.

Griffith-Jones, S. and A. Persaud, 2008, "The Pro-cyclical Impact of Basle II on Emerging Markets and its Political Economy," in *Capital Market Liberalization and Development,* edited by J. Stiglitz and J. A. Ocampo, 262–287. Oxford: Oxford University Press.

Group of Twenty-Four, 2009, "Intergovernmental Group of Twenty-Four on International Monetary Affairs and Development," *Communiqué,* April 24.

Haldane, A. and R. May, 2011, "Systemic Risk in Banking Ecosystems," *Nature, 469*:351–355.

Held, D., 1995. *Democracy and the Global Order,* Cambridge, UK: Polity.

———, 2004, *Global Covenant,* Cambridge, UK: Polity.

———, 2006, "Reframing Global Governance: Apocalypse Soon or Reform!" *New Political Economy, 11*(2):157–176.

———, 2007, "Multilateralism and Global Governance: Accountability and Effectiveness," in *Progressive Foreign Policy,* edited by D. Held and D. Mepham, 191–212. Cambridge, UK: Polity.

Held, D. and A. McGrew, 2007, *Globalization/Anti-Globalization: Beyond the Great Divide,* Cambridge, UK: Polity.

Held, D. and K. Young, 2011, "Crisis in Parallel Worlds: The Governance of Global Risks in Finance, Security, and the Environment," in *The Deepening Crisis: Governance Challenges After Neoliberalism,* edited by C. Calhoun and G. Derluguian, 19–42. New York: New York University Press.

Helleiner, E. 2010, "What Role for the New Financial Stability Board? The Politics of International Standards After the Crisis," *Global Policy, 1*(3):282–290.

Helleiner, E. and S. Pagliari, 2009, "Crisis and the Reform of International Financial Regulation" in *Global Finance in Crisis,* edited by E. Helleiner, S. Pagliari, and H. Zimmermann, 6–8. London: Routledge.

Ho, D., 2002, "Compliance and International Soft Law: Why Do Countries Implement the Basel Accord?," *Journal of International Economic Law, 5*:647–648.

IFC Review, 2011, "IMF's Strauss-Kahn: Global imbalances pre-crisis worries returned," February 11.

IMF, 2009, *World Economic Outlook: Crisis and Recovery,* Washington, D.C.: IMF.

IMF, 2011, "G-20 Moves Forward to Tackle Global Imbalances," IMF Survey online, April 16.

International Labor Organization, 2009a, "The Economic Crisis in Asia: It's about Real People, Real Jobs," *ILO Press Release,* June 26.

International Labor Organization, 2009b, "Migrant Working Girls, Victims of the Global Crisis," *ILO Press Release,* June 10.

Kahler, M. and D. Lake, 2008, "Economic Integration and Global Governance: Why So Little Supranationalism?" in *The Politics of Global Regulation,* edited by W. Mattli and N. Woods, 242–276. Princeton: Princeton University Press.

Kaldor, M., 1982, *Baroque Arsenal,* London: Deutsch.

———, 1998, *New and Old Wars,* Cambridge: Polity Press.

Kerwer, D., 2005, "Rules That Many Use: Standards and Global Regulation," *Governance,* (18):661–632.

Kregel, J., 2006, "From Monterrey to Basel: Who Rules the Banks?" *Social Watch Report 2006: Impossible Architecture,* Uruguay: Instituto Del Tercer Mundo, 26–28.

Moschella, M. and E. Tsingou, eds., 2013. *Explaining Incremental Change in the Aftermath of the Global Financial Crisis,* Colchester, UK: ECPR Press.

Mügge, D., 2011, "From Pragmatism to Dogmatism: European Union Governance, Policy Paradigms, and Financial Meltdown," *New Political Economy, 16*(2): 185–206.

Newell, P. and M. Paterson, 2010, *Climate Capitalism: Global Warming and the Transformation of the Global Economy,* Cambridge, UK: Cambridge University Press.

Panitchpakdi, S., 2008, Speech at the Executive Session of the Trade and Development Board on Financing for Development 45th Executive Session, Geneva, November 13.

Petraeus, D., 2010, "Counterinsurgency Concepts: What We Learned in Iraq," *Global Policy, 1*(1):116–117.

Pleyers, G., 2010, *Alter-Globalization: Becoming Actors in a Global Age,* Cambridge, UK: Polity.

Rapkin, D. and J. Strand, 2006, "Reforming the IMF's Weighted Voting System," *The World Economy, 29*(3):305–324.

Reuters, 2011, "UPDATE 2-Trichet warns of widening global imbalances," June 19.

Sengupta, K., 2009, "'West is Failing Afghanistan' says NATO Commander," *The Independent,* September 1.

Slaughter, A. M. and T. Hale, 2008, "Calling All Patriots: The Cosmopolitan Appeal of Americanism," in *Cultural Politics in a Global Age: Uncertainty, Solidarity, and Innovation*, edited by D. Held and H. Moore, 176–186. Oxford: Oneworld Press.

Stockholm International Peace Research Institute (SIPRI), 2009a, *SIPRI Yearbook*, Stockholm: SIPRI.

————, 2009b, SIPRI Multilateral Peace Operations Database, Stockholm: SIPRI, available at www.sipri.org/databases/pko (accessed April 16, 2012).

————, 2010, *2010 SIPRI Yearbook*. Oxford, UK: Oxford University Press.

Thornton, P., 2006, "Stiglitz Doubts IMF Will Make Headway on Global Imbalances," *The Independent*, September 8.

United Nations Development Program, 1994, *Human Development Report*, New York: Oxford University Press.

Wade, R., 2012, "The G192 Report," *Le Monde Diplomatique (English Edition)*, August 15.

Weber, M., 1964, *The Theory of Social and Economic Organization*, New York: Free Press.

Woods, N., 2010, "Global Governance after the Financial Crisis: A New Multilateralism or the Last Gasp of the Great Powers?," *Global Policy*, 1(1):51–63.

Woods, N. and D. Lombardi, 2006, "Uneven Patterns of Governance: How Developing Countries are Represented in the IMF," *Review of International Political Economy*, 13(3):480–515.

World Bank, 2010, *Global Monitoring Report: The MDGs after the Crisis*, Washington, D.C.: IMF and World Bank.

Young, K., 2011, "The Rise of Regulatory Standards in Banking and Their Limits," in *Governing Through Standards: Origins, Drivers and Limitations*, edited by P. Gibbon, S. Ponte, and J. Vestergaard, 25–48. London: Palgrave.

CONTRIBUTORS' NOTES

Joseph E. Aldy is an assistant professor of public policy at Harvard University's John F. Kennedy School of Government, a nonresident fellow at Resources for the Future, and a faculty research fellow at the National Bureau of Economic Research. In the first two years of the Obama administration, he served as the special assistant to the president for energy and environment, reporting through both the National Economic Council and the Office of Energy and Climate Change. Prior to this he has served as codirector of the Harvard Project on International Climate Agreements, codirector of the International Energy Workshop, and treasurer for the Association of Environmental and Resource Economists, and was a staff member of the Council of Economic Advisers. He has edited a number of books, with Robert Stavins, on global environmental governance, the most recent being *Post-Kyoto International Climate Policy: Implementing Architectures for Agreement*.

Sophie Body-Gendrot, PhD in political science (Sciences-Po, Paris), is emeritus professor and the former director of the Center of Urban Studies at the University Paris—Sorbonne. She is an associate researcher at CNRS (Centre National de la Recherche Scientifique) and the past president of the Society of European Criminology. She is an expert adviser on safety and public space for the program Urban Age at the London School of Economics and is a consultant for the European commission on criminological and urban issues. She is a Chevalier of the Legion of Honour. Her interdisciplinary and cross-national research about risk management in cities connects urban violence, ethnic and racial discrimination, and socioeconomic inequalities with broader societal dysfunctions and public policies. Her most recent work in English is *Globalization, Fear, and Insecurity* (Palgrave 2012); *Violence in Europe* (Springer 2007); *The Social Control of Cities?* (Blackwell 2000); and *The Urban Moment* (Sage 2000).

Kemal Dervis is vice president and director of the Global Economy and Development program at the Brookings Institution. He is the former executive head of the United Nations Development Programme, and former chair of the United Nations Development Group. In 2001–2002, Dervis was the minister of economic affairs and of the treasury for Turkey, and member of the Turkish parliament until 2005. Prior to his tenure in government, Dervis worked for twenty-two years at the World Bank, holding positions as vice president for the Middle East and North Africa and vice president for poverty reduction and economic management. Dervis is well known for his academic work on global economics, emerging markets, development, and international institutions. His most recent book, which he coedited, is *Asia and Policymaking for the Global Economy*. He currently coteaches a class on global economic governance at Columbia University.

Misha Glenny is an investigative journalist. He is best known for his coverage of Central and Eastern European issues for the BBC World Service and *The Guardian*, during the 1990s, and for his expertise in global criminal networks and cybercrimes. His most recent book, *DarkMarket: Cyberthieves, Cybercops, and You*, presents his most current research in the field of cybercrime. He is also well known for his extensive research on the globalization of criminal networks, as showcased in his book *McMafia: A Journey Through the Global Criminal Underworld*, which was released in 2008. In 1993, Glenny received a Sony Award for his coverage of Yugoslavia. He has also published a number of books on the fall of Yugoslavia and on political instability in the Balkans, including *The Balkans: Nationalism, War, and the Great Powers, 1804–2012*.

David Held is a master of University College, Durham, and professor of politics and international relations at Durham University. Among his most recent publications are *Cosmopolitanism: Ideals and Realities* (2010);

Globalisation/Anti-Globalisation (2007); *Models of Democracy* (2006); *Global Covenant* (2004); *Global Transformations: Politics, Economics, and Culture* (1999); and *Democracy and the Global Order: From the Modern State to Cosmopolitan Governance* (1995). His main research interests include the study of globalization, changing forms of democracy, and the prospects of regional and global governance. He is a director of Polity Press, which he cofounded in 1984, and general editor of *Global Policy*.

G. John Ikenberry is the Albert G. Milbank Professor of Politics and International Affairs at Princeton University in the department of politics and the Woodrow Wilson School of Public and International Affairs. He is also codirector of Princeton's Center for International Security Studies. In 2013–2014, Ikenberry will be the seventy-second Eastman Visiting Professor at Balliol College, Oxford, a post held previously by Felix Frankfurter, George Kennan, and John Gaddis. Professor Ikenberry is the author of six books, including *Liberal Leviathan: The Origins, Crisis, and Transformation of the American System* (Princeton, 2011). His book, *After Victory: Institutions, Strategic Restraint, and the Rebuilding of Order after Major Wars* (Princeton 2001), won the 2002 Schroeder-Jervis Award presented by the American Political Science Association for the best book in international history and politics. Professor Ikenberry is the codirector of the Princeton Project on National Security, and he is the coauthor, along with Anne-Marie Slaughter, of the final report, "Forging a World of Liberty Under Law."

Mary Kaldor is a professor of global governance and director of the Civil Society and Human Security Research Unit at the London School of Economics. She is the author of many books, including *The Ultimate Weapon is No Weapon: Human Security and the Changing Rules of War and Peace, New and Old Wars: Organised Violence in a Global Era*, and *Global Civil Society: An Answer to War*. Professor Kaldor was a founding member of European Nuclear Disarmament (END) and of the Helsinki Citizen's Assembly. She is also convener of the Human Security Study Group, which reported to Javier Solana and now reports to Cathy Ashton.

Kristine Kern is the universitair docent in the Environmental Policy Group, Department of Social Sciences, Wageningen University, the Netherlands; an associate professor at the department of political science, at Åbo Akademi University, Finland; and an affiliated professor in environmental sciences at the Center for Baltic and East European Studies, Södertörn University,

Sweden. She was chosen to be a member of an international expert panel for the evaluation of Norwegian Centers for Energy and Climate Research by the Research Council of Norway, and a similar panel to evaluate the Finnish Climate Research Program by the Academy of Finland. Her books include *Governing a Common Sea: Environmental Policies in the Baltic Sea Region* (2008) and *Zivilgesellschaft und Sozialkapital: Herausforderungen politischer und sozialer Integration* (Civil society and social capital: Challenges of political and social integration) (2004). She has organized many conferences on climate, energy, and environmental issues in Europe.

Karl Ove Moene is a professor in the department of economics and leader of the Centre of Equality, Social Organization, and Performance, at the University of Oslo. He has held positions as a board member in the environment/development area for the Norwegian Research Council, as editor of the *Scandinavian Journal of Economics*, and as a panel member of *Economic Policy*. He earned the Norwegian Research Council's Award for Excellence in the Communication of Science in 2011. He has held visiting scholar positions at Northwestern University, UCLA, and Stanford University. His most recent books include *Selected Works of Michael Wallerstein, Understanding Choice, Explaining Behaviour: Essays in Honour of Ole-Jørgen Skog*, and *Equality Under Pressure: Challenges for the Scandinavian Model of Distribution*. Moene is a regular contributor to the Norwegian newspaper *Dagens Næringsliv*, among others.

Arthur P. J. Mol is the chair of environmental policy in the department of social sciences and professor of environmental policy at Wageningen University, the director of the Wageningen School of Social Sciences, and a professor of environmental policy at the School of Environment and Natural Resources, Renmin University, China. His research, at the intersection of sociology and environmental issues, looks at the interactions between globalization, social theory, governance, and the environment. He is the coeditor of two book series, *Environmental Governance in Asia* (2002–) and *Nachhaltigkeit und Innovation/Sustainability & Innovations* (2004–). He is the joint editor of the *Journal of Environmental Politics* and a board member of the Research Committee on Environment and Society of the International Sociological Association. He was awarded the Frederik H. Buttel Award by the International Sociological Association and the award for distinguished scholarship by the American Sociological Association, environment and technology section, in 2010.

José Antonio Ocampo is a professor and director of the economic and political development concentration in the School of International and Public Affairs, fellow of the Committee on Global Thought, and copresident of the Initiative for Policy Dialogue at Columbia University. He has occupied numerous positions at the United Nations and in his native Colombia, including UN under-secretary-general for economic and social affairs, executive secretary of the UN Economic Commission for Latin America and the Caribbean (ECLAC), and minister of finance of Colombia. His most recent books include *The Economic Development of Latin America since Independence*, with Luis Bértola (2012); the *Oxford Handbook of Latin American Economics*, edited with Jaime Ros (2011); and *Time for a Visible Hand: Lessons from the 2008 World Financial Crisis*, edited with Stephany Griffith-Jones and Joseph E. Stiglitz (2010).

Leif Pagrotsky is a member of parliament for Sweden, representing the Swedish Social Democratic Party, and vice president of Sveriges Riksbank, which is the Central Bank of Sweden. He was a minister of industry and trade and minister of education, research, and culture in the Swedish government. Before joining the cabinet, Pagrotsky held positions at the Sveriges Riskbank, the Swedish Ministry of Finance, the OECD, the prime minister's office, of which he was briefly director, and the European Investment Bank. He is well known for his keen interest and involvement in global trade and governance issues.

Saskia Sassen is the Robert S. Lynd Professor of Sociology and cochair of the Committee on Global Thought, Columbia University. Her recent books are *Territory, Authority, Rights: From Medieval to Global Assemblages* (Princeton University Press 2008), *A Sociology of Globalization* (W. W. Norton 2007), and the fourth fully updated edition of *Cities in a World Economy* (Sage 2012). Among her older books is *The Global City* (Princeton University Press 1991/2001). Her books have been translated into more than twenty languages. She is a member of the Council on Foreign Relations and a member of the National Academy of Sciences Panel on Cities. She is the recipient of diverse awards and mentions. These range from multiple doctor *honoris causa* to named lectures to being selected as one of the 100 Top Global Thinkers of 2011 by *Foreign Policy* magazine. She has written for *The Guardian*, the *New York Times*, *Le Monde*, and Newsweek International, and she contributes regularly to www.OpenDemocracy.net.

George Soros is chair of Soros Fund Management LLC and the founder of the Open Society Institute. Upon graduating from the London School of Economics, he accumulated a large fortune through an international investment fund he founded and managed. He has since established a network of philanthropic organizations active in more than seventy nations. These organizations are dedicated to promoting the values of democracy and of an open society. Soros has authored twelve books, including most recently *Financial Turmoil in the U.S. and Europe*. His articles and essays on politics, society, and economics regularly appear in major newspapers and magazines around the world.

Robert N. Stavins is the Albert Pratt Professor of Business and Government, director of the Harvard Environmental Economics Program and the Harvard Project on Climate Agreements, chairman of doctoral programs, and cochair of the Harvard Business School–Harvard Kennedy School joint degree programs at Harvard University's John F. Kennedy School of Government. He is also a university fellow for Resources for the Future, a research associate at the National Bureau of Economic Research, coeditor of the *Review of Environmental Economics and Policy*, and a member of the board of directors of Resources for the Future and the Scientific Advisory Board of Fondazione Eni Enrico Mattei. He has authored more than a hundred articles, and has authored or edited nine books on environmental economics and policy, including *Post-Kyoto International Climate Policy: Implementing Architectures for Agreement* (2010) with Joseph Aldy.

Joseph E. Stiglitz is a University Professor and cochair of the Committee on Global Thought at Columbia University, the winner of the 2001 Nobel Memorial Prize in Economics, and a lead author of the 1995 IPCC report, which shared the 2007 Nobel Peace Prize. He was chairman of the U.S. Council of Economic Advisors under President Clinton and was chief economist and senior vice president of the World Bank from 1997 to 2000. Stiglitz received the John Bates Clark Medal, awarded biennially to the American economist under 40 who has made the most significant contribution to the subject. He was a Fulbright Scholar at Cambridge University, held the Drummond Professorship at All Souls College Oxford, and has also taught at M.I.T, Yale, Stanford, and Princeton. He is the author most recently of *The Price of Inequality: How Today's Divided Society Endangers Our Future*.

Tony Travers is a visiting professor of government and the director of LSE London, a research center, at the London School of Economics and Political Science. He is an advisor to the House of Commons Children, Schools, and Families Select Committee and the Communities and Local Government Select Committee, a board member of the Centre for Cities, and an honorary member of the Chartered Institute of Public Finance & Accountancy. He has served as senior associate of the Kings Fund, as well as on the Arts Council's Touring Panel, the Audit Commission, and the Urban Task Force Working Group on Finance. His books on local and regional government and public reform include *The Politics of London: Governing the Ungovernable City* (2004), *Education and Housing: How does the Centre Pull the Purse Strings?* (2000), and *Failure in British Government: The Politics of the Poll Tax* (1995).

Ngaire Woods is the director of the Global Economic Governance Programme, the inaugural dean of the Blavatnik School of Government, and professor of economic governance at the University of Oxford. She founded the Global Economic Governance Programme and helped lead the creation of the Blavatnik School. She is recognized as a leading researcher on global economic governance, the challenges of globalization, and the role of international institutions. Her recent books include *Networks of Influence? Developing Countries in a Networked Global Order* (2009), *The Politics of Global Regulation* (with Walter Mattli, 2009), and *The Globalizers: The IMF, the World Bank and their Borrowers* (2006). She has served as an advisor to the IMF Board, the UNDP's Human Development Report, and the Commonwealth Heads of Government, and is the World Economic Forum GAC chair, as well as serving as a member of the IMF European Regional Advisory Group.

Kevin Young is an assistant professor in the department of political science at the University of Massachusetts–Amherst. Previously, he was a post-doctoral fellow at the Niehaus Center for Globalization and Governance at Princeton University, and a fellow in Global Politics at the London School of Economics and Political Science (where he also obtained his PhD in 2010). His research focuses on interest groups in financial governance, and his research appears in *Review of International Political Economy* and *Public Administration*.

INDEX

cyber crime, 152–153
cyclical governance deficit, 357
Czech Republic: as bridgeheads for
Russian criminal syndicates, 148; sex
worker trafficking, 149

Darfur, strategy of targeting civilians, 121
DCRI (Directorate of Domestic
Intelligence) France, 267–268
DDR (disarmament, demobilization,
and reintegration), 130
dead weight loss, 190n15
debt, macroeconomic stability and, 36
decentralized threats to security, 94
Declaration of the Conference on the
Environment and Development, 326
defense spending: global increase of
military spending, 369–370, 376n13;
sense of security and, 92
deficits: global democratic deficit,
309–312; governance, 357;
macroeconomic stability and, 36
deforestation, carbon emissions and, 184
Democracy in America, 48
Democratic Republic of Congo, civilian
casualties, 120
deregulation: automatic stabilizers,
44n4; basis for, 20; role of
globalization in, 3; and weakening
social protections, 44n3
Dervis, Kemal, 75–79, 382
deterrence, 100
developing countries: developing-
country–friendly international
system, 328; need for equitable
participation in global governance,
332–333; social protection for, 78–79
development: global cooperation
for, 316; role of G20 in, 347; of
societies, 315
"development aid" concept, 318, 323
diffuse threats: to international peace
and security, 94; to United States,
97–98

Directorate of Domestic Intelligence
(DCRI) (France), 267–268
disarmament, demobilization, and
reintegration (DDR), 130
distribution zones, drug trade, 147–148
distributive concerns, emissions
mitigation, 179–180
divided cities, 281
dividend tax paradox, 44n10
domestic security, connection to global
security, 92–93
double dividend model, burden sharing,
192–194
double redistribution, Scandinavia,
68–69
drone air strikes, 122
drug trade: Afghanistan, 147,
150–151; Colombia, 147–148;
medical marijuana industry, 151;
zones of consumption, 147; zones
of distribution, 147; zones of
production, 147
duellum, 119
Duggan, Mark, 264
dynamic efficiency, 59
DynCorp LLC, 124

Earth Summit (Rio agreement) 1992,
159, 182, 326–327
East Asia bilateral partnerships, 108
Economic and Social Council
(ECOSOC), 319, 335–338
economic and social governance:
accountability, 335–338; basing
governance system on representative
institutions, 333–334; challenge
of coherence, 335; challenges
in, 332–338; global cooperation
for development, nature, scope,
and limits of, 320–324; global
cooperation for development,
objectives of, 314–320; global
governance structures, 329–332;
importance of regional institutions

in, 332; marginalization of United
Nations from global economic
decision-making, 333; need for
equitable participation of developing
countries in global governance, 332–
333; overview, 313–314; surveillance
mechanisms, 337; world economic
asymmetries, 322–328
economic globalization, role in pressure
on cities, 249
economic recession, 153
economic security: catalytic role of
social protection for government,
40–42; coping with instability,
37–38; improving efficiency of social
protection, 40; macroeconomic
stability, 35–36; misalignment
between private incentives and social
returns, 41; regulatory policies, 36;
severance pay, 37
ECOSOC (Economic and Social
Council), 319, 335–338
education, Sweden, 81–82
efficiency: competition and efficiency
concept, 75–79; dynamic, 59; effect
of coordinated wage compression
on, 59–60; insufficiency of improved
energy efficiency, 58–59; static, 59
emerging economies: carbon tax treaty,
220–221; coalitions of, 329; effect of
emission leakage on, 208; inclusion
of in G20, 344–347
emission permits, 167, 175, 178–179
emission-reduction-credit system
(CDM), 221–223
emission reductions: adaptation
assistance, 218–219; "free rider"
problem, 8; geoengineering and,
219; research and development for,
218; sector-level agreements for,
217–218
emissions. See GHG emissions
employers, as supporter of equality
(Scandinavia), 55–56

empowerment: cities' capacity for,
271–272; of nonstate transnational
actors, 102; of weak groups with
welfare spending, 63–64
energy: insufficiency of improved
efficiency, 172–173; urbanizing
global governance, 235–236, 244
enforcement mechanisms:
environmental protection agreement,
159–160; global governance, 11–12.
See also international agreements
environmental protection: Copenhagen
Accord, 158; enforcement
mechanisms for, 159–160; equitable
burden sharing, 171–175; "free
rider" problem, 8, 157–159; Kyoto
Protocol, 158, 175, 207–210, 241;
obstacles to achieving enforceable
agreement, 159; Rio agreement 1992,
159, 182, 326–327. See also burden
sharing, environmental protection;
climate governance; sustainable
development, global social justice for
equal emission permits per capita,
175–177
equality: gender, role in human
security, 131; gender, Scandinavia,
50; pretax, 63–64. See also
Scandinavian equality
equality–generosity pattern, welfare
spending in Scandinavian countries,
61–62
equality magnifying effect, Scandinavia,
62–63
equality multiplier, 65
"equal wages for equal work" principle,
60
equitable burden sharing, environmental
protection, 171–175
EU. See European Union
EU ETS (European Union's Emission
Trading Scheme), 221
euro: challenges to, 11; reforms to
sustain, 311–312

United Nations High Commissioner for
Refugees (UNHCR), 120–121
United Nations Special Session on
Disarmament (1982), 277
United States: ability to use military
force unilaterally, 3; anti-inflation
policies, 78; building protective
infrastructure, 106; cotton subsidies,
10; defense spending, 4–5; effect
of rise of Asia on security, 98–99;
equality multiplier, 65; fragility of
financial system, 5; "liberal order
building", 96, 104–106; policing
strategies, 269–271; polluter pays
principle, 9; post-Cold War position,
4; private security contractors in
Iraq, 124; rebuilding alliances,
108–109; reforming global security
institutions, 109–110; renewing
hegemonic authority, 110–112;
reviving cooperative security,
106–108; role in global increase
of military spending, 376n13;
Scandinavian equality versus U.S.
model, 68; shifting sources of
violence and insecurity, 99–104;
suicide bombings, 122; threat
environment, 97–98; use of global
institutions to maintain power, 9–10;
war in Afghanistan, 5; weakening of
social protections, 25
Universal Declaration of Human Rights,
103, 318
Universal Postal Union (UPU), 340n2
Urbact program, 271
urban climate governance: Climate
Change Act of 2008 (United
Kingdom), 292; greenhouse gas
emissions in cities, 288; hierarchical
climate governance, 290–293;
horizontal climate governance,
298–300; Intergovernmental Panel
on Climate Change, 290; Local Area

Agreements, 292; Organization
for Economic Cooperation and
Development, 289; overview,
288–289; research on, 289; vertical
climate governance, 293–297
urbanizing global governance:
asymmetric wars, 236; challenges
to, 243–244; "Cities for Climate
Protection" global initiative, 242;
city level governance, advantages
of, 233–234; climate governance,
234–236; horizontal governance,
234; Local Government Climate
Roadmap, 241–242; research and,
286; urban capacities for ensuring
order, 269–273; urban sustainability,
247–248, 250–251; urban violence,
237; wider applications of city
governance, 282–283. See also cities;
cities, violence in
urban violence, 237. See also cities,
violence in
Uruguay Round agreement (1994), 186
U.S. Mayors Climate Protection
Agreement, 294
utilitarian social welfare, 29

value-added tax (VAT), 168–169
Van Gogh, Theo, 261
VAT (value-added tax), 168–169
vertical climate governance, 234;
"benchmark for excellence"
mechanism, European Commission,
296–297; C40 Large Cities Climate
Leadership Group, 294–295; Climate
Alliance, 294; Climate Change
Action Plan (2007), London, 294;
Climate Change Strategy (2007),
Tokyo, 294; Clinton Climate
Initiative, 294; Covenant of Mayors,
296; Covenant of Mayors Office, 297;
funding, 296; "A Greener, Greater
New York" campaign (2007),